CASSELL
COMPLETE
PUZZLER'S
LISTS

CASSELL

COMPLETE PUZZLER'S LISTS

The ultimate crossword companion

JOAN BURMAN

CASSELL

The author wishes
to thank Kevin Jones

Cassell
Wellington House, 125 Strand
London WC2R 0BB

387 Park Avenue South
New York, NY 10016–8810

First published 1993

Reprinted 1995

British Library Cataloguing-in-Publication Data
A catalogue entry for this book is
available from the British Library

Library of Congress Cataloging-in-Publication Data
applied for

ISBN 0–304–34642 X

Typeset by Colset Private Limited, Singapore
Printed and bound in Great Britain by
Mackays of Chatham PLC, Chatham, Kent

CONTENTS

Introduction   vii

The lists   1

General index   433

Thematic index   463

INTRODUCTION

This book has been written for two reasons: to help (a) crossword compilers with clues, and (b) crossword solvers with answers. In most of the lists, the words are sorted by both numerical and alphabetical order. For example: a clue reads 'Thomas —, author of *Under the Greenwood Tree* (5)'. You therefore look in the 5-letter section of **Writers**, which list is also indexed in the General Index under the heading **Authors**; or under the 21-letter section of **Book titles**.

The author wishes to stress that the reader will usually find the General Index easier to consult than the Thematic Index, as the General Index is in strict alphabetical order. The Thematic Index, on the other hand, indicates what lists this book contains under their broader categories.

Abbreviations

1

a   acre; area
A   ampere
b   born; bowled
c   caught; cent; circa (about)
C   Celsius, Centigrade; Conservative
d   daughter; denarii (pence); denarius (penny); died
E   east; easterly; eastern
f   feminine; forte; franc
F   Fahrenheit; fellow
g   gram
h   hour
I   island
j   jet (aircraft); judge
k   kilo; knit
K   Kelvin; Köchel enumeration (of Mozart's works)
l   litre
L   Latin; learner; left (stage direction)
m   male; married; masculine; metre; mile; mille (thousand); million
M   mark (German coin); mega-(million times); member; meridies (noon); Monsieur; motorway
n   neuter; noun
N   newton; nitrogen; north; northerly; northern
O   Ohio
p   page; pence; penny; piano; purl
q   query; question
Q   queen
r   rupee
R   regina (queen); rex (king); right (stage direction); river; royal
s   second; shilling; singular; son
S   Saint; south; southerly; southern
v   verb; verse; versus (against); vide (see)
V   volt
W   watt; west; westerly; western

2

A1   First class in Lloyd's Register
A.A.   Alcoholics Anonymous; anti-aircraft; Automobile Association

A.B.	able-bodied seaman
A.C.	alternating current
a/c	account
A.D.	Anno Domini (in the year of our Lord)
A.F.	Admiral of the Fleet
A.G.	Adjutant-General
A.I.	artificial insemination
AK	Alaska
AL	Alabama
a.m.	ante meridiem (before noon)
A.P.	Associated Press
AR	Arkansas
A.S.	Anglo-Saxon
At.	Atomic
Au.	Ångström unit; astronomical unit
av.	average
A.V.	Authorized version
AZ	Arizona
B.A.	Bachelor of Arts; British Academy; British Airways; Buenos Aires
B.B.	Boys' Brigade
B.C.	Before Christ; British Columbia
B.D.	Bachelor of Divinity
b.e.	bill of exchange
b.l	bill of lading
B.M.	British Museum
b.p.	boiling point
Bp	bishop
B.P.	British Pharmacopoeia
B.R.	British Rail
Bt.	baronet
B.T.	British Telecom
CA	California
C.A.	chartered accountant
C.B.	citizen's band; Companion of the Order of the Bath; confined to barracks
cc	cubic centimetre
C.C.	chamber of commerce; county council; county councillor; cricket club
C.D.	civil defence; compact disc; corps diplomatique
C.E.	Christian Era; Church of England; civil engineer
cf.	confer (compare)

C.F.	Chaplain to the Forces
Ch.	chapter
C.H.	Companion of Honour
C.I.	Channel Islands; Lady of Imperial Order of the Crown of India
C.J.	Chief Justice
cl	class; clause
C.L.	Companion of Literature
cm	centimetre
CO	Colorado
c/o	care of
Co.	company; county
C.O.	Colonial Office; commanding officer; conscientious objector
C.P.	Communist Party
Cr.	credit; creditor
CT	Connecticut
C.T.	Civic Trust
cu.	cubic
C.U.	Cambridge University
c.v.	curriculum vitae
D.A.	District Attorney
dB	decibel
D.C.	de capo (from the beginning); detective constable; direct current; District of Colombia
D.D.	direct debit; doctor of divinity
DE	Delaware
D.F.	Defender of the Faith
D.G.	Dei gratia (by the grace of God); Deo gratias (thanks be to God)
D.I.	Detective Inspector
D.L.	Deputy Lieutenant
DM	Deutschmark
D.M.	Doctor of Medicine
do.	ditto (the same)
D.P.	displaced person
dr	drachm
Dr.	debtor; doctor; drive
D.V.	Deo volente (God willing)
ea.	each
E.C.	East Central (London district); European Community; Electricity Council

Ed.	editor
E.D.	Efficiency Decoration
E.E.	electrical engineer; errors excepted
e.g.	exempli gratia (for example)
Ep.	Epistle
EP	electroplated; extended play
eq.	equal
E.R.	Eduardus Rex (King Edward); Elizabetha Regina (Queen Elizabeth)
ex.	example
F.A.	Football Association
F.C.	football club
F.D.	Fidei Defensor (Defender of the Faith)
ff	fortissimo
F.H.	fire hydrant
FL	Florida
fl.	floruit (flourished)
F.M.	field marshal; frequency modulation
fo.	folio
F.O.	Foreign Office
f.p.	freezing point
Fr.	French
ft	feet; foot
GA	Georgia
G.B.	Great Britain
G.C.	George Cross
G.I.	government issue (a soldier in the U.S. army)
gm	gram
G.M.	George Medal; Grand Master
G.P.	general practitioner
gr.	grain; grammar; gross
Gr.	Greek
G.R.	Georgius Rex (King George)
gs.	guineas
Gt.	great
H.C.	House of Commons
H.E.	high explosive; His Eminence; His/Her Excellency
hf.	half
H.F.	high frequency
H.H.	His/Her Highness
HI	Hawaii
H.M.	headmaster; headmistress; His/Her Majesty

H.O.	Home Office
hp	high pressure; horsepower
H.P.	hire purchase
H.Q.	headquarters
hr	hour
H.R.	holiday route; House of Representatives
ht	height
H.T.	high tension
H.V.	health visitor; high velocity; high voltage
Hz.	hertz
IA	Iowa
I.A.	Institute of Actuaries
I.D.	Idaho
id.	idem (the same)
I.D.	identification
i.e.	id est (that is)
IL	Illinois
IN	Indiana
in.	inch
I.Q.	intelligence quotient
I.R.	Inland Revenue
Is.	island
J.C.	Jesus Christ; Julius Caesar
J.P.	justice of the peace
Jr.	junior
kc	kilocycle
K.C.	King's Counsel; Knight Commander
kg	kilogram
K.G.	Knight of the Order of the Garter
km	kilometre
K.O.	knockout
K.P.	Knight of the Order of St Patrick
KS	Kansas
Kt	Knight
K.T.	Knight of the Order of the Thistle
kV	kilovolt
kW	kilowatt
KY	Kentucky
LA	Louisiana
L.A.	local authority; Los Angeles
lb	libra (pound)
l.c.	lower case (small letters)

L.C.	Lord Chancellor
Ld.	lord
l.f.	low frequency
l.h.	left hand
L.J.	Lord Justice
L.M.	Licentiate in Midwifery
L.P.	long-playing; low pressure
L.S.	locus sigilli (place of the seal)
Lt	lieutenant
L.T.	low tension
L.W.	long-wave
MA	Massachusetts
M.A.	Master of Arts
M.B.	Bachelor of Medicine
M.C.	Master of Ceremonies; Military Cross
MD	Maryland
M.D.	Managing Director; Medicinae Doctor (Doctor of Medicine)
ME	Maine; myalgic encephalitis
M.E.	Middle English
mf	mezzoforte
m.f.	medium frequency
mg	milligram
MI	Michigan
M.I.	military intelligence; mounted infantry
mm	millimetre
MM.	Messieurs
M.M.	Military Medal
MN	Minnesota
M.N.	Merchant Navy
MO	Missouri
M.O.	medical officer
m.p.	melting point
M.P.	Member of Parliament; Metropolitan Police; Military Police
M.R.	Master of the Rolls
MS	manuscript; Mississippi; multiple sclerosis
M.S.	Master in Surgery
Mt	Mount
MT	Montana
N.A.	North America; not applicable
N.B.	nota bene (note well)
NC	North Carolina

n.d.	no date (of books)
ND	North Dakota
NE	Nebraska
N.E.	north-east; north-eastern
N.F.	National Front
NH	New Hampshire
N.I.	National Insurance; Northern Ireland
NM	New Mexico
No.	number
n.p.	new pence
N.P.	new paragraph; notary public
N.R.	Northern Region
N.T.	National Trust; New Testament
NV	Nevada
N.W.	north-west; north-western
NY	New York
N.Z.	New Zealand
ob.	obiit (died)
O.B.	outside broadcast
O.C.	officer commanding
O.E.	Old Etonian
OH	Ohio
OK	Oklahoma
O.M.	Order of Merit
o.p.	out of print
Op.	opus (work)
O.P.	Order of Preachers (Dominicans)
OR	Oregon
O.S.	ordinary seaman; Ordnance Survey; outsize
O.T.	occupational therapy; Old Testament
O.U.	Open University; Oxford University
oz	ounce
p.a.	per annum
PA	Pennsylvania
P.A.	personal assistant; press association
p.c.	per cent; postcard
P.C.	parish council; personal computer; police constable; privy councillor
pd.	paid
p.d.	potential difference
P.E.	physical education
P.G.	parental guidance; paying guest; postgraduate

pl.	place; plural
P.M.	Polar Medal; Postmaster; post meridiem; post-mortem; Prime Minister; Provost Marshal
P.O.	petty officer; pilot officer; post office; postal order
pp.	pages; pianissimo
p.p.	per procurationem (by proxy)
P.Q.	Parliamentary Question; Province of Quebec
PR	Puerto Rico
P.R.	proportional representation; public relations
Ps.	Psalm
P.S.	postscript; private secretary
pt.	part; pint; point
Pt.	Port
P.T.	physical training
Q.B.	Queen's Bench
Q.C.	Queen's Counsel
Q.M.	quartermaster
qr	quarter; quire
Q.S.	Quarter Sessions
qt	quart
q.v.	quod vide (which see)
R.A.	rear admiral; Research Association; Royal Academy; Royal Artillery
R.C.	Red Cross; Roman Catholic
Rd	road
R.D.	refer to drawer; rural dean
R.E.	religious education; Royal Engineers
r.h.	relative humidity
R.H.	right hand
RI	Rhode Island
R.I.	religious instruction; Royal Institution
R.K.	religious knowledge
R.M.	resident magistrate; Royal Mail; Royal Marines
R.N.	Royal Navy
ro.	recto (on the right-hand page)
R.P.	Reformed Presbyterian; received pronunciation; Regius professor
R.S.	Royal Society
R.U.	Rugby Union
R.V.	Revised Version
s.a.	sex appeal
S.A.	Salvation Army; South Africa; South America; South Australia

sc.	scilicet (that is)
s.c.	small capitals
SC	South Carolina
SD	South Dakota
S.E.	south-east; south-eastern
S.F.	science fiction
s.g.	specific gravity
S.G.	Scots Guards; Solicitor General
S.J.	Society of Jesus (Jesuits)
S.M.	sergeant-major
sq.	sequens (the following); square
Sr.	senior
s.s.	same size
S.S.	steamship
St	Saint; stone; street; stumped
s.v.	sub verbo (under the entry)
S.W.	south-west; south-western
T.A.	Territorial Army
t.b.	torpedo boat
T.B.	tubercle bacillus (tuberculosis)
T.D.	Territorial Decoration
T.F.	Territorial Force
T.H.	Trinity House
T.M.	trade mark; transcendental meditation
TN	Tennessee
tr.	transpose
T.T.	teetotal; tuberculin tested
T.U.	trade union
TV	television
TX	Texas
u.c.	upper case (capital letters)
U.K.	United Kingdom
UN	United Nations
U.P.	United Press
U.S.	United States
UT	Utah
VA	Virginia
V.C.	Vice-Chancellor; Victoria Cross
V.D.	venereal disease
V.E.	Victory in Europe
v.g.	very good
V.J.	Victory over Japan

V.L.	Vice-Lieutenant (of a county)
V.M.	Virgin Mary
vo.	verso (on the left-hand page)
V.O.	Victorian Order
V.P.	Vice-President
V.R.	Victoria Regina (Queen Victoria); Volunteer Reserve
V.S.	veterinary surgeon; vital statistics
VT	Vermont
WA	Washington (State)
W.C.	water closet; West Central (London District)
WI	Wisconsin
W.I.	West Indies; Women's Institute
wk	week
Wm.	William
W.O.	warrant officer
W.P.	word processor
W.S.	Writer to the Signet
WV	West Virginia
WY	Wyoming
XL	extra large
yd	yard

3

A.A.A.	Amateur Athletics Association; Automobile Association of America
A.A.G.	Assistant Adjutant-General
A.B.A.	Amateur Boxing Association
A.B.C.	alphabet
ABM	anti-ballistic missile
Abp	archbishop
abr.	abridged
abs.	absolute
A.C.A.	Associate of the Institute of Chartered Accountants
A.C.F.	Army Cadet Force
A.C.T.	Advisory Council on Technology
A.D.C.	aide-de-camp; Amateur Dramatic Club
adj.	adjective
Adj.	adjutant
Adm.	admiral
adv.	adverb
A.E.A.	Atomic Energy Authority
A.E.U.	Amalgamated Engineering Union

A.F.A.	Amateur Football Association
A.F.C.	Air Force Cross
A.F.L.	American Federation of Labor
A.F.M.	Air Force Medal
A.G.M.	annual general meeting
AGR	advanced gas-cooled reactor
A.I.A.	Associate of the Institute of Actuaries
A.I.B.	Associate of the Institute of Bankers
A.I.D.	Agency for International Development; artificial insemination (by) donor
A.L.A.	Associate of the Library Association
A.L.S.	Associate of the Linnean Society
alt.	altitude
amp.	ampere
A.M.U.	atomic mass unit
anc.	ancient
ANC	African National Congress
A.O.B.	any other business
A.O.C.	air officer commanding; Army Ordnance Corps
A.O.D.	Army Ordnance Depot
A.O.F.	Ancient Order of Foresters
A.P.M.	Assistant Provost Marshal
Apr	April
A.P.R.	annual percentage rate
A.P.T.	advanced passenger train
A.R.A.	Associate of the Royal Academy
A.R.C.	Agricultural Research Council
A.R.P.	Air Raid Precautions
arr.	arrival; arrive(s)
A.S.A.	Advertising Standards Authority; Amateur Swimming Association
A.S.H.	Action on Smoking and Health
A.T.C.	Air Traffic Control; Air Training Corps
A.T.S.	Auxiliary Territorial Service
Aug	August
aux.	auxiliary
Ave	avenue
B.A.A.	British Airports Authority; British Astronomical Association
B.A.C.	British Aircraft Corporation
B.A.F.	British Athletic Federation
B.B.C.	British Broadcasting Corporation
B.C.L.	Bachelor of Civil Law
B.D.A.	British Dental Association

Bde.	brigade
B.D.S.	Bachelor of Dental Surgery
B.Ed.	Bachelor of Education
B.E.M.	British Empire Medal
B.G.C.	British Gas Corporation
b.h.p.	brake horsepower
B.I.M.	British Institute of Management
B.M.A.	British Medical Association
B.M.C.	British Medical Council; British Motor Corporation
B.M.J.	British Medical Journal
B.O.C.	British Oxygen Company
bor.	borough
B.O.T.	Board of Trade
bro.	brother
B.R.S.	British Road Services
B.Sc.	Bachelor of Science
B.S.C.	British Steel Corporation
B.S.I.	British Standards Institution
B.S.T.	British Standard Time: British Summer Time
B.T.A.	British Tourist Authority
B.Th.	Bachelor of Theology
Btu	British thermal unit
B.V.A.	British Veterinary Association
B.V.M.	Blessed Virgin Mary
B.W.B.	British Waterways Board
C.A.A.	Civil Aviation Authority
C.A.D.	computer-aided design
cal.	calorie
C.A.M.	computer-aided manufacture
cap.	capital
CAP	Common Agricultural Policy
C.B.E.	Commander of the Order of the British Empire
C.B.I.	Confederation of British Industry
C.D.C.	Commonwealth Development Corporation
Cdr.	commander
C.D.S.	Campaign for Democratic Socialism; Chief of Defence Staff
C.E.I.	Council of Engineering Institutions
C.E.T.	Central European Time
C.F.E.	college of further education
C.G.M.	Conspicuous Gallantry Medal
C.G.S.	Chief of General Staff
C.I.A.	Central Intelligence Agency
C.I.D.	Criminal Investigation Department

C.I.E.	Companion of the Order of the Indian Empire
c.i.f.	cost, insurance and freight
C.I.I.	Chartered Insurance Institute
C.I.O.	Congress of Industrial Organizations
C.I.S.	Chartered Institute of Secretaries; Commonwealth of Independent States
C.L.B.	Church Lads' Brigade
C.M.G.	Companion of the Order of St Michael and St George
C.M.S.	Church Missionary Society
C.N.D.	Campaign for Nuclear Disarmament
C.O.D.	cash on delivery
C.O.I.	Central Office of Information
Col.	colonel; column
Con.	Conservative
cos	cosine
C.P.C.	Communist Party of China
C.P.R.	Canadian Pacific Railway
C.R.O.	cathode ray oscilloscope; Criminal Records Office
C.S.C.	Commonwealth Scientific Committee; Conspicuous Service Cross
C.S.E.	Certificate of Secondary Education
C.S.I.	Companion of the Order of the Star of India
C.S.M.	company sergeant major
C.T.C.	Cyclists' Touring Club
C.V.O.	Commander of the (Royal) Victorian Order
cwt.	hundredweight
D.A.G.	Deputy Adjutant-General
D.B.E.	Dame Commander of the Order of the British Empire
D.C.B.	Dame Commander of the Order of the Bath
D.C.L.	Doctor of Civil Law
D.C.M.	Distinguished Conduct Medal
D.D.S.	Doctor of Dental Surgery
DDT	dichlorodiphenyltrichloroethane
Dec	December
deg.	degree
D.E.S.	Department of Education and Science
D.F.C.	Distinguished Flying Cross
D.F.E.	Department for Education
D.F.M.	Distinguished Flying Medal
D.I.A.	Design and Industries Association
dil.	dilute
dip.	diploma
div.	dividend

D.I.Y.	do-it-yourself
D.L.O.	Dead Letter Office
D.N.A.	deoxyribonucleic acid
D.N.B.	Dictionary of National Biography
D.O.A.	dead on arrival
D.O.B.	date of birth
D.O.E.	Department of the Environment
D.O.I.	Department of Industry
D.o.T.	Department of Transport
doz	dozen
D.P.P.	Director of Public Prosecutions
D.Sc.	Doctor of Science
D.S.C.	Distinguished Service Cross
D.S.M.	Distinguished Service Medal
D.S.O.	Companion of the Distinguished Service Order
D.S.S.	Department of Social Security
D.Th.	Doctor of Theology
D.T.I.	Department of Trade and Industry
D.V.A.	Dunkirk Veterans' Association
dwt	pennyweight
E.C.G.	ectrocardiogram; electrocardiograph
E.C.S.	European Communication Satellite
E.C.T.	electroconvulsive therapy
E.E.C.	European Economic Community (Common Market)
E.M.A.	European Monetary Agreement
emf	electromotive force
E.M.S.	European Monetary System
e.m.u.	electromagnetic unit
enc.	enclosed; enclosure
E.N.E.	east-north-east
E.N.T.	Ear Nose and Throat
E.O.C.	Equal Opportunities Commission
E.R.A.	Electrical Research Association; engine room artificer
E.S.E.	east-south-east
Esq.	Esquire
etc.	et cetera
F.A.A.	Fleet Air Arm
F.A.O.	Food and Agriculture Organization
f.a.s	free alongside ship
F.B.A.	Fellow of the British Academy
F.B.I.	Federal Bureau of Investigation
F.B.S.	Fellow of the Botanical Society
F.C.A.	Fellow of the Institute of Chartered Accountants

F.C.O.	Foreign and Commonwealth Office
Feb	February
Fed.	federal; federation
fem.	feminine
F.G.S.	Fellow of the Geological Society
F.I.A.	Fellow of the Institute of Actuaries
fig.	figure
F.I.S.	family income supplement
F.L.A.	Fellow of the Library Association
F.M.C.	Federal Maritime Commission
f.o.b.	free on board
F.O.C.	free of charge
F.P.A.	Family Planning Association
F.P.S.	Fellow of the Pharmaceutical Society
Fri	Friday
F.R.S.	Fellow of the Royal Society
F.S.A.	Fellow of the Society of Antiquaries
fur	furlong
fwd.	forward
F.Z.S.	Fellow of the Zoological Society
gal	gallon
G.B.E.	Knight/Dame Grand Cross of the Order of the British Empire
G.B.H.	grievous bodily harm
G.C.A.	Ground Control Approach
G.C.B.	Knight/Dame Grand Cross of the Order of the Bath
G.C.E.	General Certificate of Education
G.C.F.	greatest common factor
G.C.M.	greatest common measure
G.D.P.	gross domestic product
G.D.R.	German Democratic Republic
Gen.	general
G.H.Q.	general headquarters
Gib	Gibraltar
G.L.C.	Greater London Council
G.M.C.	General Medical Council
G.M.T.	Greenwich Mean Time
G.N.P.	gross national product
G.O.C.	general officer commanding
G.O.M.	Grand Old Man
G.O.P.	Grand Old Party (U.S. Republican Party)
G.P.O.	General Post Office
G.S.O.	general staff officer
G.T.C.	Girls' Training Corps

Gym	gymnasium
H.C.F.	highest common factor
Heb.	Hebrew
H.G.V.	heavy goods vehicle
H.I.H.	His/Her Imperial Highness
H.I.M.	His/Her Imperial Majesty
HIV	human immunodeficiency virus
H.L.I.	Highland Light Infantry
H.M.I.	His/Her Majesty's Inspector
H.M.S.	His/Her Majesty's Service; His/Her Majesty's Ship
H.N.C.	Higher National Certificate
H.N.D.	Higher National Diploma
Hon.	Honorary; Honourable
H.R.H.	His/Her Royal Highness
hrs	hours
H.S.H.	His/Her Serene Highness
h.w.m.	high-water mark
I.B.A.	Independent Broadcasting Authority
I.C.I.	Imperial Chemical Industries
I.C.J.	International Court of Justice
I.C.T.	International Computers and Tabulators
I.D.A.	International Development Association
I.E.A.	International Energy Agency
I.F.C.	International Finance Corporation
ign.	ignotus (unknown)
i.h.p.	indicated horsepower
I.H.S.	Iesus Hominum Salvator (Jesus, Saviour of Men)
I.L.O.	International Labour Organization
I.M.F.	International Monetary Fund
inc.	incorporated
I.O.F.	Independent Order of Foresters
I.O.M.	Isle of Man
I.O.W.	Isle of Wight
I.P.A.	International Phonetic Alphabet
I.R.A.	Irish Republican Army
I.R.C.	International Red Cross
I.S.O.	Imperial Service Order
I.T.A.	Independent Television Authority
ITV	Independent Television
I.W.A.	Inland Waterways Association
Jan	January
Jas.	James

Jos.	Joseph
Jun.	junior
K.B.E.	Knight Commander of the Order of the British Empire
K.C.B.	Knight Commander of the Order of the Bath
K.G.B.	Komitet Gosudarstvennoi Bezopasnosti (Committee of State Security)
K.K.K.	Ku Klux Klan
K.L.I.	King's Light Infantry
Lab.	Labour
L.A.C.	London Athletic Club
Lat.	latitude
l.b.w.	leg before wicket
L.C.C.	London County Council
L.C.D.	liquid crystal display; lowest common denominator
L.C.J.	Lord Chief Justice
l.c.m.	lowest common multiple
L.D.S.	Licentiate in Dental Surgery
L.E.A.	Local Education Authority
Lib.	Liberal
LL.B.	Legum Baccalaureus (Bachelor of Laws)
LL.D.	Legum Doctor (Doctor of Laws)
loq.	loquitur (speaks)
L.P.G.	liquefied petroleum gas
L.P.O.	London Philharmonic Orchestra
L.P.S.	Lord Privy Seal
l.s.d.	Librae, solidi, denarii (pounds, shillings, pence)
L.S.D.	lysergic acid diethyamide
L.S.E.	London School of Economics
L.S.O.	London Symphony Orchestra
L.T.A.	Lawn Tennis Association
Ltd	Limited
l.w.m.	low-water mark
Maj.	major
Mar	March
max.	maximum
M.B.E.	Member of the Order of the British Empire
M.C.C.	Marylebone Cricket Club
M.E.P.	Member of the European Parliament
Met.	meteorological; meteorology
M.F.H.	Master of Foxhounds
min.	mineralogy; minimum
M.L.R.	minimum lending rate

Mme.	Madame
M.O.D.	Ministry of Defence
M.O.H.	medical officer of health
Mon	Monday; month
M.O.T.	Ministry of Transport
m.p.g.	miles per gallon
m.p.h.	miles per hour
M.R.C.	Medical Research Council
M.Sc.	Master of Science
MSS	manuscripts
M.T.B.	motor torpedo boat
M.V.O.	Member of the Royal Victorian Order
N.C.B.	National Coal Board
N.C.O.	non-commissioned officer
N.C.P.	National Car Parks
N.C.T.	National Childbirth Trust
N.C.V.	no commercial value
N.E.C.	National Executive Committee; National Exhibition Centre
neg.	negative
N.F.U.	National Farmers' Union
N.G.A.	National Graphical Association
n.h.p.	nominal horsepower
N.H.S.	National Health Service
N.N.E.	north-north-east
N.N.W.	north-north-west
nos.	numbers
Nov	November
N.P.C.	National Parks Commission; National Ports Council
N.P.G.	National Portrait Gallery
N.R.A.	National Rifle Association
N.S.B.	National Savings Bank
N.S.W.	New South Wales
N.U.J.	National Union of Journalists
N.U.M.	National Union of Mineworkers
N.U.R.	National Union of Railwaymen
N.U.S.	National Union of Seamen; National Union of Students
N.U.T.	National Union of Teachers
O.A.P.	old-age pensioner
O.B.E.	Officer of the Order of the British Empire
obs.	observed; obsolete
Oct	October
O.E.D.	Oxford English Dictionary

O.F.M.	Order of Friars Minor (Franciscans)
O.N.C.	Ordinary National Certificate
O.N.D.	Ordinary National Diploma
o.n.o.	or near offer
Ont.	Ontario
ops.	operations
O.S.A.	Order of St Augustine
O.S.B.	Order of St Benedict
O.S.F.	Order of St Francis
O.T.C.	Officers' Training Corps
Pan.	Panama
P & O	Peninsular and Oriental (Steam Navigation Company)
par.	paragraph; parallel; parish
P.C.C.	Parochial Church Council; Press Complaints Commission
Ph.D.	Doctor of Philosophy
P.L.A.	Port of London Authority
Plc	Public Limited Company
P.L.O.	Palestine Liberation Organization
P.M.G.	Postmaster General
pop.	population
P.O.W.	prisoner of war
P.P.E.	Philosophy, Politics and Economics
P.P.S.	parliamentary private secretary
P.R.A.	President of the Royal Academy
pro	professional
P.R.O.	Public Records Office; public relations officer
P.T.A.	Parent–Teacher Association
Pte.	private
P.T.O.	please turn over
PVC	polyvinyl chloride
P.W.D.	Public Works Department
R.A.C.	Royal Armoured Corps; Royal Automobile Club
R.A.E.	Royal Aircraft Establishment
R.A.F.	Royal Air Force
R.A.M.	random-access memory; Royal Academy of Music
R.B.A.	Royal Society of British Artists
R.B.S.	Royal Society of British Sculptors
R.C.A.	Royal College of Art
R.C.M.	Royal College of Music
R.C.N.	Royal College of Nursing
R.C.P.	Royal College of Physicians
R.C.S.	Royal College of Surgeons

ref.	reference
Rep.	representative; republic; republican
Rev.	Reverend
R.H.A.	Royal Horse Artillery
R.H.S.	Royal Horticultural Society; Royal Humane Society
R.I.P.	requiescat in pace (may he/she rest in peace)
R.M.A.	Royal Military Academy
R.M.C.	Royal Military College
R.O.M.	read only memory
rpm	revolutions per minute
R.S.A.	Royal Society of Arts
R.S.C.	Royal Shakespeare Company
R.S.M.	regimental sergeant-major
R.U.C.	Royal Ulster Constabulary
R.Y.S.	Royal Yacht Squadron
s.a.e.	stamped addressed envelope
S.A.S.	Special Air Service
Sat	Saturday
S.C.C.	Sea Cadet Corps
S.C.M.	state certified midwife; Student Christian Movement
S.D.P.	Social Democratic Party
Sec.	second; secretary
Sen.	senior
S.E.N.	state enrolled nurse
seq.	sequens (the following)
S.E.T.	Selective Employment Tax
Sgt.	sergeant
sin	sine
S.L.R.	single-lens reflex
S.N.P.	Scottish National Party
Soc.	society
Sop.	soprano
S.O.S.	distress signal
S.P.G.	Society for the Propagation of the Gospel
S.R.N.	state registered nurse
S.S.C.	Solicitor to the Supreme Court
S.S.E.	south-south-east
S.S.F.	Society of St Francis
S.S.W.	south-south-west
S.T.D.	subscriber trunk dialling
Stg.	sterling
s.t.p.	standard temperature and pressure
str.	stroke

Sun	Sunday
tan	tangent
T.N.T.	trinitrotoluene
T.U.C.	Trades Union Congress
T.W.A.	Thames Water Authority
T.Y.C.	Thames Yacht Club
typ.	typography
U.D.A.	Ulster Defence Association
U.D.I.	unilateral declaration of independence
uhf	ultra-high frequency
uht	ultra-high temperature
ult.	ultimo (last month)
U.N.O.	United Nations Organization
U.S.A.	United States of America
V & A	Victoria and Albert Museum
V.A.D.	Voluntary Aid Detachment
V.A.T.	value added tax
V.D.U.	visual display unit
Ven.	Venerable
Vet.	veterinary surgeon
vhf	very high frequency
V.I.P.	very important person
viz.	videlicet (namely)
vlf	very low frequency
vol.	volume
Vol.	volunteer
V.S.O.	Voluntary Service Overseas
W.C.C.	World Council of Churches
Wed.	Wednesday
W.M.S.	Wesleyan Missionary Society
W.N.W.	west-north-west
W.P.C.	woman police constable
w.p.m.	words per minute
W.S.W.	west-south-west
W.W.F.	World Wildlife Fund
Y.H.A.	Youth Hostels Association

4

A.B.T.A.	Association of British Travel Agents
A.C.A.S.	Advisory Conciliation and Arbitration Service
A.C.I.S.	Associate of the Chartered Institute of Secretaries
actg.	acting
advt.	advertisement

A.I.C.E.	Associate of the Institution of Civil Engineers
AIDS	acquired immune deficiency syndrome
anon.	anonymous
A.P.E.X.	advance purchase excursion; Association of Professional, Executive, Clerical and Computer Staff
A.R.A.M.	Associate of the Royal Academy of Music
A.R.C.M.	Associate of the Royal College of Music
A.R.C.O.	Associate of the Royal College of Organists
A.R.C.S.	Associate of the Royal College of Science
a.s.a.p.	as soon as possible
asst.	assistant
attn.	attention
at. wt.	atomic weight
A.U.E.W.	Amalgamated Union of Engineering Workers
A.W.O.L.	absent without leave
B.A.O.R.	British Army of the Rhine
Bart.	baronet
B.Com.	Bachelor of Commerce
B.Eng.	Bachelor of Engineering
B.Mus.	Bachelor of Music
B.P.A.S.	British Pregnancy Advisory Service
B.R.C.S.	British Red Cross Society
Brit.	British
bros.	brothers
B.Th.U.	British Thermal Unit
Cant.	canticles
Capt.	captain
Card.	cardinal
C.A.R.D.	Campaign Against Racial Discrimination
Cdre.	commodore
C.E.G.B.	Central Electricity Generating Board
C.Eng.	Chartered Engineer
cent.	centigrade
cert.	certificate; certified; certify
C.E.T.S.	Church of England Temperance Society
Chas.	Charles
C-in-C	commander-in-chief
Cllr.	councillor
C.N.A.A.	Council for National Academic Awards
C of E	Church of England
C of S	Church of Scotland
coll.	college
Conn.	Connecticut

cont.	continued
Corp.	corporal; corporation
cosh	hyperbolic cosine
D.C.M.G.	Dame Commander of the Order of St Michael and St George
D.C.V.O.	Dame Commander of the Royal Victorian Order
dept.	department
D.Lit.	Doctor of Literature
D.Mus.	Doctor of Music
E & O.E.	errors and omissions excepted
Ebor.	Eboracum (of York)
E.C.S.C.	European Coal and Steel Community
E.F.T.A.	European Free Trade Association
elec.	electrical; electricity
E.N.S.A.	Entertainments National Service Association
Epis.	episcopal
E.P.N.S.	electroplated nickel silver
F.A.N.Y.	First Aid Nursing Yeomanry
F.C.I.S.	Fellow of the Chartered Institute of Secretaries
F.I.F.A.	International Association Football Federation
F.R.A.M.	Fellow of the Royal Academy of Music
F.R.A.S.	Fellow of the Royal Astronomical Society
F.R.C.M.	Fellow of the Royal College of Music
F.R.C.O.	Fellow of the Royal College of Organists
F.R.C.P.	Fellow of the Royal College of Physicians
F.R.C.S.	Fellow of the Royal College of Surgeons
F.R.G.S.	Fellow of the Royal Geographical Society
F.R.I.C.	Fellow of the Royal Institute of Chemistry
F.R.P.S.	Fellow of the Royal Photographic Society
F.R.S.A.	Fellow of the Royal Society of Arts
F.R.S.L.	Fellow of the Royal Society of Literature
G.A.T.T.	General Agreement on Tariffs and Trade
G.C.H.Q.	Government Communications Headquarters
G.C.I.E.	Knight Grand Commander of the Indian Empire
G.C.M.G.	Knight/Dame Grand Cross of the Order of St Michael and St George
G.C.S.E.	General Certificate of Secondary Education
G.C.S.I.	Knight Grand Commander of the Star of India
geog.	geography
geom.	geometry
gram.	grammar
H.M.S.O.	His/Her Majesty's Stationery Office
hons.	honours

I.A.A.F.	International Amateur Athletic Federation
I.A.B.A.	International Amateur Boxing Association
I.A.T.A.	International Air Transport Association
incl.	included; including; inclusive
inst.	instant (this month); institute; institution
I of M	Isle of Man
I of W	Isle of Wight
ital.	italic
K.C.I.E.	Knight Commander of the Order of the Indian Empire
K.C.M.G.	Knight Commander of the Order of St Michael and St George
K.C.S.I.	Knight Commander of the Star of India
K.C.V.O.	Knight Commander of the (Royal) Victorian Order
L.R.A.M.	Licentiate of the Royal Academy of Music
L.R.C.M.	Licentiate of the Royal College of Music
L.R.C.P.	Licentiate of the Royal College of Physicians
L.R.C.S.	Licentiate of the Royal College of Surgeons
masc.	masculine
M.A.S.H.	mobile army surgical hospital
Mass.	Massachusetts
Matt.	Matthew
mech.	mechanical; mechanics; mechanism
memo.	memorandum
M.I.C.E.	Member of the Institution of Civil Engineers
Mich.	Michigan
M.I.E.E.	Member of the Institution of Electrical Engineers
M.I.M.E.	Member of the Institution of Mechanical Engineers
Minn.	Minnesota
Miss.	Mississippi
Mlle	Mademoiselle
Mont.	Montana
M.R.C.P.	Member of the Royal College of Physicians
M.R.C.S.	Member of the Royal College of Surgeons
Mus.B.	Musicae Baccalaureus (Bachelor of Music)
Mus.D.	Musicae Doctor (Doctor of Music)
myth.	mythological; mythology
N.A.T.O.	North Atlantic Treaty Organization
N.Dak.	North Dakota
Norm.	Norman
N.U.B.E.	National Union of Bank Employees
N.U.P.E.	National Union of Public Employees
O.C.T.U.	Officer Cadets Training Unit
O.E.C.D.	Organization for Economic Co-operation and Development

O.H.M.S.	On His/Her Majesty's Service
Okla.	Oklahoma
O.P.E.C.	Organization of Petroleum Exporting Countries
Oreg.	Oregon
O.U.D.S.	Oxford University Dramatic Society
P.A.Y.E.	pay as you earn
P.D.S.A.	People's Dispensary for Sick Animals
P.R.A.M.	programmable random access memory
pref.	preference
pres.	present
Prof.	professor
P.R.O.M.	programmable read-only memory
prox.	proximo (next month)
R.A.D.A	Royal Academy of Dramatic Art
R.A.M.C.	Royal Army Medical Corps
R.A.O.B.	Royal Antediluvian Order of Buffaloes
R.A.O.C.	Royal Army Ordnance Corps
R.A.S.C.	Royal Army Service Corps
recd.	received
regt.	regiment
R.E.M.E.	Royal Electrical and Mechanical Engineers
R.I.B.A.	Royal Institute of British Architects
R.I.C.S.	Royal Institution of Chartered Surveyors
R.N.I.B.	Royal National Institute for the Blind
R.N.L.I.	Royal National Lifeboat Institution
R.S.P.B.	Royal Society for the Protection of Birds
R.S.V.P.	répondez s'il vous plaît (please reply)
S.A.L.T.	Strategic Arms Limitation Talks
S.A.T.B.	soprano alto tenor bass
S.A.Y.E.	save as you earn
Sept	September
sinh	hyperbolic cosine
S.P.C.K.	Society for Promoting Christian Knowledge
sp.gr.	specific gravity
Supt.	superintendent
Surg.	surgeon
tanh	hyperbolic tangent
Tenn.	Tennessee
T.G.W.U.	Transport and General Workers' Union
Thos.	Thomas
Toc H	Talbot House
T.O.P.S.	Training Opportunities Scheme
U.C.C.A.	Universities Central Council on Admissions

U.E.F.A.	Union of European Football Associations
U.P.O.W.	Union of Post Office Workers
W.A.A.C.	Women's Army Auxiliary Corps
W.A.A.F.	Women's Auxiliary Air Force
W.Cdr.	wing commander
W.R.A.C.	Women's Royal Army Corps
W.R.A.F.	Women's Royal Air Force
W.R.N.S.	Women's Royal Naval Service
W.R.V.S.	Women's Royal Voluntary Service
Y.M.C.A.	Young Men's Christian Association
Y.W.C.A.	Young Women's Christian Association
zool.	zoology

5

ad lib.	ad libitum (as much as desired)
Apocr.	Apocrypha
A.R.C.Sc.	Associate of the Royal College of Science
A.R.I.B.A.	Associate of the Royal Institute of British Architects
A.R.I.C.S.	Associate of the Royal Institution of Chartered Surveyors
A.S.L.E.F.	Associated Society of Locomotive Engineers and Firemen
assoc.	associate; association
B.A.F.T.A.	British Academy of Film and Television Arts
Barts	St Bartholomew's Hospital
B.Litt.	Bachelor of Letters
B.Phil.	Bachelor of Philosophy
CAMRA	Campaign for Real Ale
C and G	City and Guilds
CENTO	Central Treaty Organization
C.O.H.S.E.	Confederation of Health Service Employees
Corpn.	corporation
D.Litt.	Doctor of Literature
D.Phil.	Doctor of Philosophy
E.P.R.O.M.	erasable programmable read-only memory
equiv.	equivalent
E.R.N.I.E.	Electronic Random Number Indicator Equipment
et seq.	et sequens (and what follows)
F.R.I.B.A.	Fellow of the Royal Institute of British Architects
F.R.I.C.S.	Fellow of the Royal Institution of Chartered Surveyors
incog.	incognito
Lieut.	lieutenant
Litt.D.	Doctor of Letters
L.R.C.V.S.	Licentiate of the Royal College of Veterinary Surgeons

Lt.Col.	lieutenant colonel
Lt.Com.	lieutenant commander
Lt.Gen.	lieutenant general
Lt.Gov.	lieutenant governor
Mlles	Mesdemoiselles
M.Phil.	Master of Philosophy
M.R.C.V.S.	Member of the Royal College of Veterinary Surgeons
N.A.A.F.I.	Navy, Army and Air Force Institutes
N.A.L.G.O.	National Association of Local Government Officers
N.S.P.C.C.	National Society for the Prevention of Cruelty to Children
N.U.G.M.U.	National Union of General and Municipal Workers
Oxfam	Oxford Committee for Famine Relief
R and D	research and development
Ro.S.P.A.	Royal Society for the Prevention of Accidents
R.S.P.C.A.	Royal Society for the Prevention of Cruelty to Animals
Rt.Hon.	Right Honourable
Rt.Rev.	Right Reverend
S.E.A.T.O.	South-East Asia Treaty Organization
S.H.A.P.E.	Supreme Headquarters Allied Powers in Europe
S.O.G.A.T.	Society of Graphical and Allied Trades
suppl.	supplement
Thurs.	Thursday
treas.	treasurer
Xtian	Christian

6

A.Dip.Ed.	Advanced Diploma in Education
approx.	approximately
attrib.	attribute
Cantab.	of Cambridge
Dunelm.	of Durham
I.Chem.E.	Institute of Chemical Engineers
I.Mech.E.	Institution of Mechanical Engineers
Lit.Hum.	literae humaniores (study of classics)
Maj-Gen.	major-general
matric.	matriculation
Messrs.	Messieurs
per pro.	per procurationem (by proxy)
prelim.	preliminary
pro tem.	pro tempore (for the time being)

UNESCO	United Nations Educational, Scientific and Cultural Organisation
UNICEF	United Nations International Children's Emergency Fund

7

A.I.Mech.E.	Associate of the Institution of Mechanical Engineers
Cantuar.	of Canterbury
M.Inst.C.E.	Member of the Institution of Civil Engineers

8

Interpol	International Criminal Police Commission
Lieut.Col.	lieutenant colonel
Lieut.Gen.	lieutenant general
Lieut.Gov.	lieutenant governor

African peoples

3	4	5	5
Ewe	Hima	Chopi	Swazi
Fon	Hutu	Dinka	Tonga
Ibo	Lala	Dogon	Tussi
Ijo	Lozi	Galla	Tutsi
Iru	Mali	Ganda	Venda
Suk	Meru	Gissi	Xhosa
Tiv	Nama	Grebo	
Vai	Nupe	Hausa	6
Yao	Nyan	Iraqu	Angoni
	Riff	Kamba	Bakota
4	Teso	Lulua	Balega
Agni	Yako	Lunda	Basuto
Baga	Zulu	Masai	Bateke
Bena		Mende	Bayaka
Bete	5	Mossi	Berber
Bini	Afars	Nandi	Chagga
Bisa	Anuak	Ngoni	Fulani
Bubi	Bamum	Nguni	Herero
Fang	Bantu	Nguru	Ibibio
Fula	Bassa	Pygmy	Kikuyu
Guro	Baule	Rundi	Kpwesi
Haya	Bemba	Shona	Lumbwa
Hehe	Chewa	Sotho	Luvale

6	7	7	8
Murozi	Ashanti	Mashona	Matabele
Ngwato	Baganda	Namaqua	Tallensi
Nilote	Bakweii	Samburu	
Rolong	Bambara	Shillak	9
Sambas	Bangala	Songhai	Hottentot
Senufo	Bapende	Turkana	Kgalagedi
Somali	Barotse	Watutsi	
Sukuma	Barundi		10
Thonga	Basonge	8	Bathlaping
Tiokwa	Batonka	Bergdama	Karamojong
Tsonga	Batutsi	Bushongo	
Tswana	Bunduka	Kipsigis	11
Tuareg	Bushmen	Mamprusi	Bangarwanda
Veddah	Dagomba	Mandingo	
Warega	Griquas		12
Yoruba			Lunda-Bajokwe

Agriculture

3	3	4	4
awn	pig	bull	holt
bin	pip	byre	hops
cob	ram	calf	hull
cod	ret	cart	husk
cow	rye	clay	kine
cub	sow	corn	lamb
dig	ted	cote	lime
ear	teg	crop	loam
ewe	tup	culm	lyme
feu	vat	curb	malm
hay		drey	mare
hep	4	dung	marl
hip	akee	farm	meal
hoe	aril	foal	milk
hog	bale	gait	neat
kid	barn	gape	neep
kip	beam	harl	nide
lea	beef	haum	oast
moo	bent	herd	oats
mow	bran	hind	odal

4	5	5	6
peat	chaff	shuck	farmer
pest	churn	spelt	fodder
pony	couch	spuds	forage
rake	croft	stall	furrow
rape	crone	stock	gaucho
rime	crops	straw	gluten
root	dairy	swill	grains
roup	ditch	tilth	grange
rust	drill	tuber	harrow
ryot	drove	veldt	heifer
sand	durra	wagon	hogget
scab	ergot	wheat	hogsty
seed	farcy	withe	hopper
sere	fruit	withy	inspan
shaw	fungi	worms	linhay
silo	gavel	yield	manger
skep	glume		manure
skip	grain	6	mealie
slob	grass	angora	merino
soil	graze	animal	millet
soya	guano	arable	mowing
span	haugh	arista	nubbin
teff	haulm	barley	pampas
toft	hedge	beeves	piglet
tope	hilum	binder	pigsty
udal	hoove	bottle	plough
vale	horse	butter	podzol
weed	humus	cattle	polder
wold	kulak	cereal	porker
yean	llano	clover	potato
zebu	maize	colter	punner
	mould	corral	raggee
5	mower	cowman	raking
aphid	mummy	cratch	realty
baler	ovine	cutter	reaper
beans	plant	digger	roller
borax	ranch	disbud	sheave
bosky	rumen	dobbin	silage
bothy	sheaf	drover	socage
calve	sheep	fallow	sowing
carse	shoat	farina	stable

6

steppe
swathe
trough
turnip
warble
weevil
winnow

7

acidity
aerator
alfalfa
anthrax
battery
binding
boscage
budding
bullock
buttery
cabbage
calving
combine
compost
coulter
cowherd
cowshed
demesne
digging
dipping
docking
drought
droving
farming
fee tail
foaling
foot rot
forcing
fox trap
granger
grazing
harvest

7

hay cart
hay rick
hedging
herding
hop pole
implant
infield
lambing
laniary
lucerne
marlite
milk can
milking
multure
murrain
nursery
paddock
pannage
pasture
piggery
pinetum
pinfold
popcorn
poultry
prairie
praties
predial
pruning
rancher
reaping
rearing
rhizome
rundale
rustler
stacker
station
stubble
subsoil
swinery
thwaite
tillage

7

tilling
tractor
trammel
trekker
trotter
udaller
vaquero
wagoner
windrow
yardman

8

agronomy
branding
breeding
clipping
cropping
ditching
drainage
elevator
ensilage
farmyard
forestry
gleaning
grafting
hayfield
haymaker
haystack
haywagon
hopfield
kohlrabi
landgirl
loosebox
milkcart
pedigree
pig swill
plougher
rootcrop
rotation
shearing
sheep dip

8

vineyard
watering
wireworm

9

allotment
cornfield
dairy farm
dairymaid
fertility
free range
fungicide
gathering
grassland
harrowing
harvester
haymaking
hop picker
husbandry
implement
incubator
livestock
pasturage
penthouse
phosphate
pig trough
ploughing
rice field
screening
separator
shorthorn
sugar beet
sugar cane
swineherd
thrashing
threshing

10

agronomist
battery hen
cattle cake

10	10	11	11
cultivator	transplant	cultivation	water trough
fertiliser	weed killer	factory farm	weed control
fertilizer	wheatfield	fertilising	
harvesting		fertilizing	12
husbandman	11	germination	agricultural
irrigation	agriculture	insecticide	feeding stock
mould board	cake crusher	motor plough	fermentation
plantation	chaff cutter	pastureland	horticulture
rounding up	chicken farm	poultry farm	insemination
self binder	crude plough	reclamation	market garden
		stocktaking	smallholding

Air Force ranks, British and US

3	7	9	11
AC1	Aviator	Drum-Major	Master Pilot
AC2	Captain (US)	Navigator	Second Pilot
LAC	Colonel (US)		
	General (US)	10	12
4	Private (US)	Air Marshal	Air Commodore
WAAF		Apprentice	Group Captain
WRAF	8	Balloonist	Major General
	Armourer	Bombardier	(US)
5	Corporal	(US)	Pilot Officer
Major (US)	Mechanic	Nose Gunner	
Pilot	Observer	Rear Gunner	13
	Sergeant	Tail Gunner	Flying Officer
6			Sergeant Major
Airman	9	11	(US)
Fitter	Air Gunner	Aircraftman	Staff Sergeant
Rigger	Bomb Aimer	Belly Gunner	(US)
			Wing
			Commander

14	14	15
Air Vice Marshal	Squadron Leader	First Lieutenant
Flight Engineer	Warrant Officer	(US)
Flight Mechanic		Master Navigator
Flight Sergeant	15	Master Signaller
Master Engineer	Air Chief Marshal	
Master Sergeant (US)	Chief Technician	

16	18	25
Flight Lieutenant	Leading Aircraftman	Marshal of the Royal
Junior Technician		Air Force
Second Lieutenant (US)	19	
	Aircraftman 1st Class	27
17	Aircraftman 2nd Class	Master Air Electronic
Senior Aircraftman	Master Air Loadmaster	Operator

Alloys

4	7	8	11
alni	alcomax	vicalloy	supermalloy
beta	alumnel	zircaloy	supermendur
	amalgam		
5	chromel	9	12
alpha	columan	duralumin	ferrosilicon
brass	Elinvar	hastelloy	German silver
Invar	inconel	permalloy	silver solder
mazac	kanthal	Perminvar	
Monel	mumetal	type metal	13
steel	nimonic		ferrochromium
		10	ferrotungsten
6	8	constantan	ferrovanadium
alnico	cast iron	misch metal	
Babbit	dowmetal	Muntz metal	14
bronze	gunmetal	Rose's metal	Admiralty metal
cunico	hipernik	superalloy	Britannia metal
cunife	kirksite	Wood's metal	ferromanganese
feroba	manganin		phosphor bronze
pewter	nichrome	11	stainless steel
solder		cupronickel	
		electrotype	

Alphabets

Greek alphabet

alpha	epsilon
beta	zeta
gamma	eta
delta	theta

Greek alphabet

iota	rho
kappa	sigma
lambda	tau
mu	upsilon
nu	phi
xi	chi
omicron	psi
pi	omega

Hebrew alphabet

aleph	mem
beth	nun
gimel	samekh
daleth	ayin
he	pe
vav	sadi
zayin	koph
cheth	resh
teth	shin
yod	sin
kaph	tav
lamed	

American Indian nations and peoples

3	4	5	6
Fox	Yuma	Lipan	Abnaki
Oto	Zuni	Miami	Apache
Ute		Moqui	Atsina
	5	Nahua	Aymara
4	Aztec	Omaha	Aztecs
Cree	Blood	Osage	Biloxi
Crow	Caddo	Sioux	Caribs
Hopi	Campa	Slave	Cayuga
Hupa	Creek	Teton	Cocopa
Iowa	Haida	Wappo	Dakota
Maya	Huron	Yaqui	Dogrib
Moki	Incas	Yuchi	Kichai
Pima	Kansa	Yunca	Mandan
Sauk	Kaska	Yurok	Micmac
Tupi	Kiowa		Mixtec

6	7	8	9
Mohave	Arikara	Comanche	Menominee
Mohawk	Beothuk	Delaware	Penobscot
Navaho	Catawba	Flathead	Tahagmiut
Navajo	Chilcal	Illinois	Tillamook
Nootka	Chinook	Iroquois	Tsimshian
Ojibwa	Choktaw	Kickapoo	Tuscarora
Oneida	Hidatsa	Kootenay	Winnebago
Ostisk	Ingalik	Kwakiuti	
Ottawa	Kutchin	Menomini	10
Paiute	Mapuche	Muskogee	Algonquian
Pawnee	Mohegan	Nez Percé	Araucanian
Pequot	Mohican	Okanogan	Assiniboin
Pericu	Natchez	Onondaga	Athabascan
Piegan	Ojibway	Powhatan	Bella Coola
Pueblo	Orejone	Quichuan	Kaviagmiut
Quakaw	Quechua	Seminole	Leni-Lenape
Quapaw	Shawnee	Shoshoni	Minnetaree
Salish	Shuswap	Shushwap	Montagnais
Santee	Stonies	Tutchone	Potawatomi
Sarcee	Tlingit		Shoshonean
Seneca	Tonkawa	9	
Tanana	Wichita	Algonkian	11
Toltec	Wyandot	Algonquin	Root Diggers
Warrau		Apalachee	Susquehanna
Yakima	8	Ashochimi	
	Aguaruna	Blackfoot	12
7	Algonkin	Chickasaw	Narragansett
Abenaki	Cherokee	Chipewyan	Pasamaquoddy
Arapaho	Cheyenne	Chippeway	
Araucan	Chippewa	Karankawa	

American States

4	Nickname	Capital
Iowa	Hawkeye State	Des Moines
Ohio	Buckeye State	Columbus
Utah	Beehive State	Salt Lake City

5	Nickname	Capital
Idaho	Gem of the Mountains; Gem State	Boise City
Maine	Pine Tree State	Augusta
Texas	Lone Star State	Austin

6		
Alaska	Land of the Midnight Sun; The Last Frontier	Juneau
Hawaii	Aloha State	Honolulu
Kansas	Jayhawk State; Sunflower State	Topeka
Nevada	Sagebrush State; Battle Born State; Silver State	Carson City
Oregon	Beaver State	Salem

7		
Alabama	Heart of Dixie; Cotton State; Yellowhammer State	Montgomery
Arizona	Grand Canyon State; Apache State	Phoenix
Florida	Peninsula State; Sunshine State	Tallahassee
Georgia	Empire State of the South; Peach State	Atlanta
Indiana	Hoosier State	Indianapolis
Montana	Treasure State	Helena
New York	Empire State	Albany
Vermont	Green Mountain State	Montpelier
Wyoming	Equality State	Cheyenne

8		
Arkansas	Land of Opportunity; Wonder State; Bear State	Little Rock
Colorado	Centennial State	Denver
Delaware	First State; Diamond State	Dover
Illinois	Prairie State	Springfield
Kentucky	Bluegrass State	Frankfort
Maryland	Free State; Old Line State	Annapolis
Michigan	Wolverine State	Lansing
Missouri	Show Me State	Jefferson City
Nebraska	Beef State; Tree Planter's State; Cornhusker State	Lincoln
Oklahoma	Sooner State	Oklahoma City
Virginia	Cavalier State; The Old Dominion	Richmond

9	Nickname	Capital
Louisiana	Creole State; Sugar State; Pelican State; Bayou State	Baton Rouge
Minnesota	Gopher State; North Star State	St Paul
New Jersey	Garden State	Trenton
New Mexico	Sunshine State; Land of Enchantment	Santa Fe
Tennessee	Volunteer State	Nashville
Wisconsin	Badger State	Madison

10		
California	Golden State	Sacramento
Washington	Chinook State; Evergreen State	Olympia

11		
Connecticut	Constitution State; Nutmeg State	Hartford
Mississippi	Magnolia State	Jackson
North Dakota	Flickertail State; Sioux State	Bismarck
Rhode Island	Little Rhody	Providence
South Dakota	Sunshine State; Coyote State	Pierre

12		
New Hampshire	Granite State	Concord
Pennsylvania	Keystone State	Harrisburg
West Virginia	Panhandle State; Mountain State	Charleston

13		
Massachusetts	Old Colony State; Bay State	Boston
North Carolina	Old North State; Tar Heel State	Raleigh
South Carolina	Palmetto State	Columbia

Americanisms

British	American
action replay	instant replay
adrenaline	epinephrine
aerodrome	airdrome
aerofoil	airfoil
aeroplane	airplane
anaesthetics	anesthesiology
anaesthetist	anesthesiologist
Armistice Day	Veterans Day

British	American
aubergine	eggplant
autumn	fall
back boiler	water back
beetroot	red beet
bill	check
biscuit	cookie
black pudding	blood sausage
blowlamp	blowtorch
blue-eyed boy	fair-haired boy
bonnet	hood
boot	trunk
bowler	derby
braces	suspenders
Breathalyzer	drunkometer
breeze block	cinder block
candy floss	cotton candy
caravan	trailer
catapult	slingshot
catch pit	catch basin
cornflour	cornstarch
cos	romaine
courgette	zucchini
crochet	quarter note
current account	checking account
cut-throat	straight razor
delivery van	panel truck
demisemiquaver	thirty-second note
dinner jacket	tuxedo
dosshouse	flophouse
downpipe	downspout
draughts	checkers
drawing pin	thumbtack
dual carriageway	divided highway
dumb waiter	lazy Susan
dummy	comforter
dustbin	garbage can; trash can
dustcart	garbage truck
duster	dust cloth
estate car	station wagon
fanlight	transom
flat	apartment

British	American
flex	cord
fly-past	flyover
four-stroke	four-cycle
French windows	French doors
Friesian	Holstein
funeral parlour	funeral home
funny bone	crazy bone
gramophone	phonograph
grey mullet	mullet
hair slide	barrette
hemlock	poison hemlock
holdall	carryall
jelly	jello
jump leads	jumper cables
kennel	doghouse
ladybird	ladybug
left-luggage office	checkroom
level crossing	grade crossing
lift	elevator
loose cover	slipover
lorry	truck
luggage van	baggage car
maize	corn
merry-go-round	carousel
mileometer	odometer
minim	half-note
mudguard	fender
music hall	vaudeville
nappy	diaper
nosebag	feedbag
notice board	bulletin board
open day	open house
ordinary shares	common stock
patience	solitaire
pavement	sidewalk
pedestrian crossing	crosswalk
petrol	gasoline
Plough	Big Dipper
pram	baby carriage
preference shares	preferred stock
quaver	eighth note

British	American
ragworm	clamworm
rear light	tail light; tail lamp
red mullet	goatfish
repertory company	stock company
reversing light	back-up light
right-angled triangle	right triangle
ring road	beltway
roof rack	carrier
roundabout	traffic circle
rubber	eraser
rucksack	backpack
season ticket	commutation ticket
semibreve	whole note
semiquaver	sixteenth note
shop	store
shopwalker	floorwalker
shorthand typist	stenographer
silencer	muffler
skirting board	baseboard; mopboard
sleeve	jacket
socket	outlet
stockbroker belt	exurbia
suspender belt	garter belt
swede	rutabaga
sweets	candy
tap	faucet
tea towel	dishtowel
Terylene	Dacron
tie	necktie
tiepin	stick pin
tram	streetcar; trolley car
treacle	molasses
truncheon	night stick
turn up	cuff
Underground	subway
underseal	undercoat
Ursa Minor	Little Dipper
valve	vacuum tube
Virginia creeper	Boston ivy
waistcoat	vest
windmill	pinwheel

British	American
windscreen	windshield
windscreen wiper	windshield wiper
wing	fender
wintergreen	shinleaf

Animals

2	4	4	5
ai	anoa	mule	coati
ox	axis	musk	coypu
	bear	napu	crone
3	boar	oryx	cuddy
ape	buck	oxen	dingo
ass	bull	paca	drill
bat	calf	pard	eland
cat	cavy	pika	filly
cob	colt	pony	fitch
cow	cony	puma	genet
cub	coon	roan	goral
cur	deer	runt	hinny
dam	eyra	rusa	horse
doe	fawn	saki	hound
dog	foal	seal	hyena
dzo	gaur	sika	hyrax
elk	goat	stag	indri
ewe	hack	thar	izard
fox	hare	titi	kiang
gnu	hart	vole	koala
hog	hind	wolf	lemur
kid	ibex	zebu	liger
nag	jade		llama
pad	joey	5	loris
pig	kudu	addax	moose
ram	lamb	ariel	morse
rat	lion	bison	mouse
roe	lynx	bongo	nagor
sow	mare	brock	okapi
teg	mink	burro	oribi
tod	moke	camel	otary
tup	mole	civet	otter

5	6	6	7
ounce	badger	macaco	brocket
panda	beaver	mammal	buffalo
pekan	bharal	marmot	bullock
pongo	bobcat	marten	caracal
potto	bronco	monkey	caribou
puppy	brumby	musk ox	chamois
rasse	cattle	musmon	cheetah
ratel	cayuse	nilgai	clumber
sable	chital	ocelot	colobus
saiga	coaita	onager	courser
sasin	cougar	porker	dasyure
sheep	coyote	quagga	dolphin
shoat	cuscus	rabbit	echidna
shrew	desman	racoon	foumart
skunk	dik-dik	red fox	gazelle
sloth	dobbin	reebok	giraffe
sorel	donkey	rhesus	glutton
spitz	dugong	rodent	gorilla
steed	ermine	sambur	guanaco
steer	fennec	sea cow	hackney
stirk	ferret	serval	jackass
stoat	galago	sifaka	jumbuck
swine	gerbil	suslik	klipdas
tapir	gibbon	talbot	lambkin
tatou	gopher	tarpan	lemming
tiger	grison	teledu	leopard
tigon	guenon	tenrec	leveret
vixen	heifer	vervet	linsang
waler	hogget	vicuna	macaque
whale	howler	walrus	mammoth
whelp	impala	wapiti	manatee
zebra	inyala	weasel	markhor
zibet	jackal	wether	meerkat
zoril	jaguar	wisent	mongrel
	jennet	wombat	muntjak
	jerboa		muskrat
6	kalong	7	mustang
alpaca	kelpie	ant bear	narwhal
aoudad	kitten	aurochs	noctule
argali	koodoo	bighorn	opossum
aye-aye	langur	blesbok	palfrey

7	8	9	10
panther	fruit bat	binturong	angora goat
peccary	grysbock	blackbuck	babiroussa
polecat	hedgehog	blue whale	Barbary ape
potoroo	Irish elk	cart horse	cacomistle
pricket	kangaroo	chickadee	camelopard
primato	kinkajou	chiropter	catarrhine
raccoon	mandrill	dromedary	chevrotain
roebuck	mangabey	flying fox	chimpanzee
roe deer	marmoset	glyptodon	chinchilla
rorqual	mastodon	groundhog	cottontail
sapajou	mongoose	guinea pig	fallow deer
sapling	moufflon	hamadryad	fieldmouse
sassaby	musk deer	ichneumon	giant panda
sea bear	musquash	lagomorph	hartebeest
sea lion	pangolin	marsupial	hippogriff
siamang	porpoise	monotreme	hippogryph
sumpter	reedbuck	mouse deer	jaguarondi
sun bear	reindeer	orang-utan	jaguarundi
tamarin	ruminant	pachyderm	Kodiak bear
tarsier	sea otter	pademelon	pichiciago
tigress	sei whale	percheron	pine marten
unicorn	serotine	petaurist	prairie dog
wallaby	squirrel	phalanger	rhinoceros
warthog	staggard	polar bear	river horse
wildcat	stallion	porcupine	rock badger
	steenbok	prongbuck	rock rabbit
8	steinbok	pronghorn	shrew mouse
aardvark	suricate	race horse	sperm whale
aardwolf	talapoin	royal stag	timber wolf
anteater	tamandua	shearling	vampire bat
antelope	viscacha	silver fox	white whale
babirusa	wallaroo	sloth bear	wildebeest
behemoth	water rat	springbok	
bontebok	wild boar	steinbock	11
bush-baby	yeanling	thylacine	chiropteran
bushbuck	yearling	tree shrew	douroucouli
cachalot		waterbuck	flying lemur
capybara	9	water vole	grizzly bear
chipmunk	armadillo	white bear	harbour seal
dormouse	bandicoot	wolverine	honey badger
elephant	babirussa	woodchuck	jumping deer

11	12	14
kangaroo rat	hippopotamus	capuchin monkey
killer whale	klipspringer	clouded leopard
orang-outang	mountain goat	flying squirrel
pipistrelle	mountain lion	ground squirrel
prairie wolf	rhesus monkey	squirrel monkey
rat kangaroo	spider monkey	Tasmanian devil
red squirrel	water buffalo	
sea elephant		15
snow leopard	13	flying phalanger
	American tiger	mountain panther
12	anthropoid ape	proboscis monkey
catamountain	Père David deer	
elephant seal	sable antelope	
harvest mouse	Tasmanian wolf	

Animals and their gender

Animal	Male	Female
antelope	buck	doe
ass	jackass	jennyass
badger	boar	sow
bear	boar	sow
bobcat	tom	lioness
buffalo	bull	cow
camel	bull	cow
caribou	stag	doe
cat	tom	queen
cattle	bull	cow
chicken	cock	hen
cougar	tom	lioness
coyote	dog	bitch
deer	stag	doe
dog	dog	bitch
donkey	jackass	jennyass
eland	bull	cow
elephant	bull	cow
ferret	jack	jill
fox	fox	vixen
giraffe	bull	cow
goat	billygoat	nannygoat

Animal	Male	Female
hare	buck	doe
hartebeest	bull	cow
horse	stallion	mare
impala	ram	ewe
kangaroo	buck	doe
leopard	leopard	leopardess
lion	lion	lioness
moose	bull	cow
ox	bullock	cow
pig	boar	sow
rabbit	buck	doe
rhinoceros	bull	cow
seal	bull	cow
sheep	ram	ewe
tiger	tiger	tigress
walrus	bull	cow
weasel	boar	cow
whale	bull	cow
wolf	dog	bitch
zebra	stallion	mare

Animals and their young

Animal	Young	Animal	Young
antelope	cub	elk	calf
badger	cub	fox	cub
bear	cub	giraffe	calf
beaver	kitten	goat	kid
bobcat	kitten	hare	leveret
buffalo	calf	hartebeest	calf
camel	calf	horse	foal
caribou	fawn	kangaroo	joey
cat	kitten	leopard	cub
cattle	calf	lion	cub
cougar	kitten	monkey	infant
coyote	puppy	ox	stot
deer	fawn	pig	piglet
dog	puppy	rhinoceros	calf
eland	calf	seal	calf
elephant	calf	sheep	lamb

Animal	Young	Animal	Young
tiger	cub	whale	calf
walrus	cub	wolf	cub
weasel	kit	zebra	foal

Applied arts people

3
Low, Sir David (cartoonist)

4
Capp, Alfred Caplin (cartoonist)
Dior, Christian (fashion designer)
Erté (Romain de Tirtoff) (fashion designer)
Ward, Sir Leslie (caricaturist)

5
Atget, Eugene (photographer)
Brown (Capability), Lancelot B. (landscape gardener)
Giles, Carl Ronald (cartoonist)
Klint, Kaare (furniture designer)
Leach, Bernard (potter)
Leech, John (caricaturist)
Nadar, Gaspard Felix Tournachon (photographer/caricaturist)
Phyfe, Duncan (cabinet-maker/furniture designer)
Quant, Mary (fashion designer)
Vicky (Victor Weisz) (cartoonist)

6
Beaton, Cecil (photographer)
Bewick, Thoms (wood engraver)
Boulle, André Charles (cabinet-maker)
Bailey, David (photographer)
Brandt, Bill (photographer)
Cardin, Pierre (fashion designer)
Chanel, Coco (fashion designer)
Scarfe, Gerald (cartoonist)
Searle, Ronald William (cartoonist)

7
Astbury, John (potter)
Cameron, Julia Margaret (photographer)
Daumier, Honoré (caricaturist)
Fabergé, Peter Carl (goldsmith/jeweller)
Gillray, James (caricaturist)
Lalique, René (jeweller/glassmaker)
Le Nôtre, André (landscape gardener)
Palissy, Bernard (potter)
Snowdon, Anthony Armstrong-Jones, Earl of (photographer)
Tenniel, Sir John (cartoonist)

8
Cressent, Charles (cabinet-maker)
Robinson, William Heath (cartoonist)
Sheraton, Thomas (furniture designer)
Wedgwood, Josiah (potter)
Woollett, William (engraver)

9
Courrèges, André (fashion designer)
Muybridge, Eadweard (photographer)
Stieglitz, Alfred (photographer)

10
Cruikshank, George (caricaturist)
Rowlandson, Thomas (caricaturist)
Senefelder, Aloys (engraver)

11
Chippendale, Thomas (cabinet-maker)
Hepplewhite, George (cabinet-maker/furniture designer)

12
Saint-Laurent, Yves (fashion designer)
Schiaparelli, Elsa (fashion designer)

14
Cartier-Bresson, Henri (photographer)

Archbishops of Canterbury

3

Oda

4

Lang, Cosmo Gordon
Laud, William
Pole, Reginald
Rich, Edmund
Tait, Archibald Campbell
Wake, William

5

Abbot, George
Blund, John
Carey, George
Deane, Henry
Grant, Richard
Islip, Simon
Juxon, William
Kempe, John
Moore, John

6

Anselm
Becket, Thomas
Benson, Edward White
Cobham, Thomas
Coggan, Frederick Donald
De Gray, John
Fisher, Geoffrey Francis
Howley, William
Hutton, Matthew
Justus
Lyfing
Mepham, Simon
Morton, John
Nevill, Ralph
Offord, John
Parker, Matthew

6

Pecham, John
Potter, John
Ramsey, Arthur Michael
Runcie, Robert Alexander Kennedy
Secker, Thomas
Sumner, John Bird
Sutton, Charles Manners
Temple, Frederick
Walden, Roger
Walter, Hubert
Warham, William

7

Aelfric
Arundel, Thomas
Baldwin
Burnell, Robert
Cranmer, Thomas
Dunstan
Eadsige
Grindal, Edmund
Herring, Thomas
Langham, Simon
Langton, Stephen
Longley, Charles Thomas
Nothelm
Sheldon, Gilbert
Stigand
Sudbury, Simon
Tatwine
Tenison, Thomas
Wulfred

8

Aelfheah
Aelfsige
Bancroft, Richard
Ceolnoth

8
Chichele, Henry
Davidson, Randall Thomas
D'Escures, Ralph
Honorius
Lanfranc
Mellitus
Plegmund
Reginald
Reynolds, Walter
Sancroft, William
Stafford, John
Whitgift, John
Wulfhelm

9
Aethelgar
Aethelred
Augustine
Breguwine
Courtenay, William
Deusdedit
Feologild
Kilwardby, Robert
Stratford, John
Theodorus
Tillotson, John

10
Aethelhelm
Aethelnoth
Beorhthelm
Bourcchier, Thomas
Cornwallis, Frederick

10
Cuthbeorht
Jaenbeorht
Laurentius
Whittlesey, William
Winchelsey, Robert

11
Aethelheard
Beorhtweald
Bradwardine, Thomas
Fitzjocelin, Reginald

12
Sigeric Serio

13
Theobald of Bec

14
Richard of Dover

15
Boniface of Savoy
Walter of Evesham

16
Adam of Chillenden
Robert of Jumièges
William of Corbeil

19
John of Sittingbourne

Architects

4
Adam, Robert
Kahn, Louis Isadore
Kent, William

4
Loos, Adolph
Nash, John
Shaw, Norman

4
Wood, John of Bath
Wren, Sir Christopher

5
Aalto, Alvar
Barry, Sir Charles
Campi, Giulio
Dance, George
Gaudi, Antonio
Gibbs, James
Horta, Victor
Jones, Inigo
Le Vau, Louis
Nervi, Pier Luigi
Pugin, Augustus
Scott, Sir George Gilbert
Soane, Sir John
Wyatt, James

6
Archer, Thomas
Breuer, Marcel Lajos
Casson, Sir Hugh
Lasdun, Sir Denys
Lescot, Pierre
Paxton, Sir Joseph
Spence, Sir Basil
Voysey, Charles Francis Annesley
Wright, Frank Lloyd

7
Alberti, Leon Battista
Behrens, Peter
Bernini, Gianlorenzo
Delorme, Philibert
Fontana, Domenico
Gropius, Walter
Guarini, Guarino
Herrera, Francisco de, The
  Younger
Herrera, Juan de

7
Holland, Henry
Lutyens, Sir Edwin Landseer
Maderno, Carlo
Mansart, François
Mansart, Jules
Neumann, Balthasar

8
Campbell, Colen
Chambers, Sir William
Niemeyer, Oscar
Palladio, Andrea
Saarinen, Eero
Soufflot, Jacques Germain
Stirling, Sir James
Sullivan, Louis Henry
Vanbrugh, Sir John

9
Borromini, Francesco
Cockerell, Charles Robert
Hawksmoor, Nicholas

10
Burlington, Richard Boyle, Earl of
Richardson, Henry Hobson
Waterhouse, Alfred

11
Abercrombie, Sir Patrick
Butterfield, William
Le Corbusier (Charles Edouard
  Jeanneret)

12
Brunelleschi, Filippo
Michelangelo (Michelangelo
  Buonarroti)

13
Williams-Ellis, Sir Clough

14	16
Mies van der Rohe, Ludwig	Fischer von Erlach, Johann Bernhard

15	23
Hardouin-Mansart, Jules	Michelozzo di Bartolommeo

Army ranks and appellations

5	7	8	9
Cadet	Captain	Fencible	Man-at-Arms
Fifer	Colonel	Fusilier	Musketeer
Jäger	Cossack	guerilla	Paymaster
Major	Dragoon	Havildar	Pipe-Major
Miner	Drummer	Janizary	Signaller
Piper	General	Marksman	Subaltern
Scout	hoplite	Messmate	tactician
Sepoy	Marshal	Partisan	Town-Major
Spahi	Officer	Rifleman	Trumpeter
Tommy	Orderly	sentinel	Volunteer
Uhlan	Pioneer	Sergeant	
	Private	Spearman	10
6	recruit	turncoat	Aide-de-Camp
Batman	Redcoat		Bandmaster
Bomber	Reserve	9	Bombardier
Bugler	Saddler	Beefeater	Campaigner
Cornet	Soldier	Brigadier	Carabineer
Driver	Trooper	Centurion	Cavalryman
Ensign	veteran	combatant	Commandant
Gunner	warrior	Commander	Cuirassier
Gurkha		Conductor	Drummer Boy
Hetman	8	conscript	Footguards
Hussar	Adjutant	Drum-Major	Halberdier
Jaeger	Armourer	field rank	Instructor
Lancer	Bandsman	Fife-Major	Lansquenet
Ranger	Cavalier	Grenadier	Lieutenant
ranker	Commando	Guardsman	Lifeguards
Sapper	Corporal	guerrilla	Paratroops
Zouave	deserter	Home Guard	Roughrider
		irregular	strategist
		Janissary	

11	12	14
Artillerist	Royal Signals	Medical Officer
Auxiliaries	Staff Officer	Military Police
Bashi-Bazouk	Storm-Trooper	Orderly Officer
Bersaglieri	Territorials	Provost Marshal
condottiere		Royal Artillery
crossbowman	13	Royal Engineers
Gendarmerie	Army Commander	Royal Tank Corps
Horse Guards	Brevet Colonel	Signals Officer
Infantryman	Dispatch Rider	Standard Bearer
mosstrooper	Drill Sergeant	Warrant Officer
Parachutist	First Sergeant	
Paratrooper	Generalissimo	15
shock troops	Lance Corporal	Adjutant General
storm troops	Lance Sergeant	First Lieutenant
	Lifeguardsman	Gentleman-at-Arms
12	Light Infantry	Household Troops
Armour-Bearer	Machine-Gunner	Lance Bombardier
Artilleryman	Marine officer	Mounted Infantry
Ensign-Bearer	prisoner of war	
Field Marshal	Quartermaster	16
Field Officer	Sergeant Major	Second Lieutenant
Horse Soldier	Staff Sergeant	
Major General		17
Master Gunner	14	Lieutenant Colonel
Officer Cadet	Colonel-in-Chief	Lieutenant General
P.T. Instructor	Colour Sergeant	21
Royal Marines	Liaison Officer	Quartermaster Sergeant

Art terms

2	3	4	4
Op	Pop	chic	halo
	sit	Dada	herm
3		daub	icon
fec	4	draw	ikon
hue	base	etch	limn
inc	body	flat	line
key	bust	form	nude
oil	cast	gild	pose

4	5	6	7
size	scene	ormolu	collage
swag	sculp	ox gall	contour
term	secco	pastel	Dadaism
tone	sepia	patina	daubing
wash	shade	pencil	diagram
	study	plaque	diptych
5	stump	Pop Art	drawing
batik	style	purism	etching
bloom	tondo	reflex	faience
blush	torso	relief	Fauvism
board	trace	rhythm	felt tip
brush	virtu	Rococo	gliding
burin		school	glazing
cameo	6	sculpt	gouache
chalk	action	shadow	graphic
couch	artist	sitter	impasto
draft	ashcan	sketch	lacquer
easel	bistre	statue	linocut
fecit	canvas	stucco	lunette
frame	colour	studio	modello
genre	crayon	stylus	montage
gesso	Cubism	uncial	mordant
glaze	depict	verism	outline
glory	design		painter
gloss	emblem	7	palette
hatch	emboss	academy	picture
inert	enamel	acrylic	pigment
japan	fresco	archaic	plaster
model	Gothic	Art Deco	plastic
mount	ground	atelier	profile
mural	Kitcat	aureole	realism
naive	kitsch	Baroque	remodel
Op Art	limner	Bauhaus	replica
paint	mastic	biscuit	reredos
Pietà	medium	bitumen	scumble
prime	mobile	cabinet	sfumato
print	mosaic	camaieu	shading
putto	niello	cartoon	sketchy
rebus	nimbus	carving	stabile
salon	object	classic	stencil

7	8	9	9
stipple	majolica	Byzantine	Vorticism
support	maquette	capriccio	woodblock
surface	monotype	cartouche	zylograph
tableau	mounting	cloisonné	
tempera	negative	colourist	10
tessera	oil paint	damascene	accidental
texture	ornament	distemper	anaglyphic
tracery	painting	embossing	anaglyptic
T square	panorama	encaustic	Art Nouveau
varnish	pastiche	engraving	assemblage
woodcut	plein air	geometric	atmosphere
	portrait	grisaille	automatism
8	predella	grotesque	avant-garde
abstract	repoussé	highlight	background
academic	Romantic	indelible	biomorphic
air-brush	seascape	Indian ink	body colour
allegory	Seicento	landscape	caricature
anaglyph	staffage	mahlstick	cire-perdue
appliqué	symmetry	Mannerism	cornucopia
aquatint	tachisme	marquetry	craquelure
armature	tapestry	maulstick	embossment
arriccio	tectonic	mezzotint	embroidery
artistic	tesserae	miniature	fitch brush
Barbizon	throwing	modelling	Florentine
caryatid	Trecento	oil colour	foreground
charcoal	triglyph	oleograph	full length
drypoint	triptych	phototype	India paper
emulsion	Venetian	polyptych	lithograph
engraver	vignette	primitive	monochrome
figurine		sculpture	morbidezza
fixative	9	scumbling	naturalism
freehand	alla prima	serigraph	night piece
frottage	anti-cerne	statuette	paint brush
futurism	aquarelle	still life	pencilling
gargoyle	arabesque	stippling	pentimento
graffiti	asymmetry	strapwork	photograph
grouping	autograph	Symbolism	Raphaelism
half tone	ball point	Symbolist	Raphaelite
hatching	bas relief	tailpiece	Romanesque
intaglio	blockbook	tattooing	serigraphy
intonaco	brushwork	Tenebrism	silhouette

10
silk screen
Surrealism
terracotta
turpentine
xylography

11
alto-relievo
aquatinting
Biedermeier
calligraphy
carolingian
chiaroscuro
chinoiserie
Cinquecento
colour print
composition
connoisseur
draughtsman
eclecticism
electrotype
foreshorten
French chalk
illusionism

11
imprimatura
life drawing
lithography
masterpiece
oil painting
pavement art
perspective
photography
picturesque
Pointillism
portraiture
Renaissance
restoration
trompe l'oeil
watercolour

12
acrylic paint
anamorphosis
illumination
illustration
palette knife
Quattrocento

12
scraperboard
stained glass
tracing paper

13
architectonic
black and white
daguerreotype
decorative art
Expressionism
Impressionism
Postmodernism
Pre-Raphaelite
primary colour

14
action painting
chromatography
Constructivism
pavement artist

17
conversation piece
Post-Impressionism

Arthurian legend

3
Kay

6
Arthur
Avalon
Gawain
Merlin
Vivien

7
Camelot
Galahad
Mordred

8
Lancelot
Perceval

9
Excalibur
Guinevere
Holy Grail

11
Morgan Le Fay

13
Lady of the Lake

Astronomers Royal

4
Airy, Sir George Biddell
Pond, John
Ryle, Sir Martin

5
Bliss, Nathaniel
Dyson, Sir Frank Watson
Jones, Sir Harold Spencer
Smith, Professor Sir Francis
  Graham

6
Halley, Edmund

7
Bradley, James
Woolley, Sir Richard

8
Christie, Sir William H.M.

9
Flamsteed, John
Maskelyne, Nevil

10
Wolfendale, Arnold

Astronomy

(A = asteroid; C = constellation; Co = comet; MS = meteor shower; P = planet;
S = satellite; St = star)

2
Io (S)

3
Ara (C)
Leo (C)
orb
Ram (C)
Sun (St)

4
Apus (C)
Belt
Bull (C)
Crab (C)
Crux (C)
Eros (P)
Grus (C)
halo

4
Hebe (P)
Juno (P)
Leda (S)
Lion (C)
Luna (S)
Lynx (C)
Lyra (C)
Mars (P)
Moon (S)
node
nova
Pavo (C)
Puck (S)
Rhea (S)
Ross (St)
star
Vega (St)
Wolf (St)

5
Ariel (S)
Aries (C)
Atlas (S)
Biela (Co)
Carme (S)
Ceres (A)
Cetus (C)
comet
Cygni (St)
Deneb (St)
Dione (S)
Draco (C)
Earth (P)
Elara (S)
Hydra (C)
Indus (C)
Janus (S)
Lepus (C)

5
Libra (C)
lunar
Lupus (C)
Mensa (C)
Metis (S)
Mimas (S)
Musca (C)
Norma (C)
orbit
Orion (C)
Pluto (P)
Rigel (St)
solar
space
Spica (St)
stars
Thebe (S)
Titan (S)

5

Twins (C)
Venus (P)
Vesta (A)
Virgo (C)

6

Adhara (St)
Altair (St)
Ananke (S)
Antlia (C)
Apollo
Aquila (C)
Archer (C)
astral
Auriga (C)
aurora
Bianca (S)
Caelum (C)
Cancer (C)
Castor (St)
Charon (S)
Corvus (C)
Crater (C)
Cygnus (C)
Davida (A)
Deimos (S)
Dorado (C)
Europa (S)
Fishes (C)
Fornax (C)
galaxy
Gemini (C)
Halley (CO)
Helene (S)
Hydrus (C)
Juliet (S)
Kruger (St)
Luyten (St)
Lyrids (MS)
meteor
Nereid (S)

6

Oberon (S)
Pallas (A)
Phobos (S)
Phoebe (S)
Pictor (C)
Pisces (C)
planet
Plough (C)
Pollux (St)
Portia (S)
Saturn (P)
Scales (C)
Sinope (S)
Sirius (St)
sphere
Taurus (C)
Tethys (S)
Triton (S)
Tucana (C)
Uranus (P)
Ursids (MS)
Volans (C)
Zodiac

7

Antares (St)
Belinda (S)
Calypso (S)
Canopus (St)
Capella (St)
Cepheus (C)
cluster
Columba (C)
Cygnids (MS)
eclipse
equator
equinox
Himalia (S)
Jupiter (P)
Lacerta (C)
Lalande (St)

7

Lapetus (S)
Leonids (MS)
Mercury (P)
Miranda (S)
Neptune (P)
new moon
Ophelia (S)
Pandora (S)
Pegasus (C)
Perseus (C)
Phoenix (C)
Polaris (St)
Procyon (St)
Regulus (St)
Sagitta (C)
Scorpio (C)
Serpens (C)
Sextans (C)
Sputnik
stellar
Tau Ceti (St)
Taurids (MS)
Telesto (S)
Titania (S)
Umbriel (S)

8

Archernar (St)
Adrastea (S)
Amalthea (S)
Aquarius (C)
Arcturus (St)
asteroid
Callisto (S)
Cepheids (MS)
Circinus (C)
Cordelia (S)
Cressida (S)
Equuleus (C)
Eridanus (C)
full moon

8

Ganymede (S)
Geminids (MS)
Hercules (C)
Hyperion (S)
Leo Minor (C)
Loadstar
Lodestar
Lysithea (S)
Milky Way
Orionids (MS)
Pasiphae (S)
Perseids (MS)
Rosalind (S)
Sculptor (C)
solstice
spectrum
starless
universe

9

Aldebaran (St)
Andromeda (C)
astrology
astronomy
celestial
Centaurus (C)
Chameleon (C)
Delphinus (C)
Desdemona (S)
Enceladus (S)
Fomalhaut (St)
Great Bear (C)
Monoceros (C)
North Star
Ophiuchus (C)
planetary
Reticulum (C)
satellite
star gazer
starlight
supernova

9
telescope
Ursa Major (C)
Ursa Minor (C)
Vulpecula (C)

10
astrologer
astronomer
atmosphere
Australids (MS)
Betelgeuse (St)
Canis Major (C)
Canis Minor (C)
Cassiopeia (C)
Charioteer (C)
Copernican
cosmic rays
Epimetheus (S)
Little Bear (C)
lunar cycle
lunar month
microscope
outer space
Prometheus (S)

10
star gazing
Triangulum (C)

11
Capricornus (C)
Epsilon Indi (St)
Evening Star
falling star
Hunter Orion (C)
last quarter
minor planet
Morning Star
observatory
planetarium
Quadrantids (MS)
Sagittarius (C)
solar system
Telescopium (C)
terrestrial
Water Bearer (C)

12
Barnard's Star (St)
Capricornids (MS)
first quarter

12
Kapteyn's Star (St)
lunar eclipse
Microscopium (C)
shooting star
solar eclipse
spectroscope

13
Alpha Centauri (St)
Canes Venatici (C)
Coma Berenices (C)
constellation
Southern Cross (C)
Southern Crown (C)

14
Aurora Borealis
Camelopardalis (C)
Epsilon Eridani (St)
summer solstice
winter solstice

15
Corona Australis (C)
Piscis Austrinus (C)

Australian states and territories

8	**Capital cities**
Tasmania	Hobart
Victoria	Melbourne
10	
Queensland	Brisbane
13	
New South Wales	Sydney

14 South Australia	**Capital cities** Adelaide

16
Western Australia   Perth

Territories
17
Northern Territory   Darwin

26
Australian Capital Territory Canberra

Dependencies
12
Cocos Islands

13
Norfolk Island

14
Keeling Islands

15
Christmas Island
Coral Sea Islands

23
Heard and McDonald Islands

25
Ashmore and Cartier Islands

28
Australian Antarctic Territory

Aviation and space travel

3	3	3	4
ace	fin	jet	bank
air	fly	leg	bump
bay	gap	rev	buzz
car	gas	yaw	crew

4	5	7	7
dive	glide	aircrew	ripcord
dope	pilot	airdrop	rolling
flap	pitch	airflow	shuttle
fuel	plane	airfoil	Sputnik
hull	prang	airlane	take-off
kite	pylon	airlift	taxiing
knot	stall	airline	twin jet
land	strut	airport	wingtip
lane	stunt	air-raid	
lift	valve	airship	8
loop		aviator	aerofoil
Mach	6	ballast	aeronaut
nose	aerial	balloon	aerostat
prop	air bus	biplane	air brake
roll	air car	bale out	airborne
slip	Airman	bomb bay	aircraft
trim	airway	capsule	airfield
veer	beacon	ceiling	Air Force
wash	bomber	charter	airframe
wind	camber	chassis	airliner
wing	canard	chopper	airplane
zoom	cruise	clipper	air route
	cut out	cockpit	airscrew
5	flight	compass	airspace
aloft	floats	contact	airspeed
apron	flying	co-pilot	airstrip
bends	gasbag	cowling	airwoman
cabin	glider	descent	altitude
cargo	hangar	fighter	approach
chock	intake	gliding	autogiro
chord	launch	inflate	aviation
cleat	module	jump-jet	ballonet
climb	nose up	landing	bomb-rack
craft	piston	lift-off	Concorde
crash	ram.,et	Mae West	corridor
crate	refuel	nacelle	cruising
ditch	rudder	nose-cap	elevator
drift		on board	envelope
flaps	7	pancake	flat spin
flier	aileron	payload	fuel pipe
float	air-base	re-entry	fuselage

8

grounded
heliport
in flight
intercom
jet pilot
jet plane
joystick
jumbo jet
nose-cone
nose-dive
pitching
radiator
seaplane
sideslip
spaceman
squadron
stopover
tail skid
terminal
throttle
triplane
turbojet
twin-tail
volplane
warplane
wind cone
windsock
wing flap
Zeppelin

9

aerodrome
aeroplane
air intake
air pocket
airworthy
altimeter
amphibian
astrodome
astronaut
autopilot

9

backplate
cabin crew
cosmonaut
countdown
crash-land
crow's foot
delta-wing
dirigible
empennage
fuel gauge
gyropilot
gyroplane
gyroscope
jet bomber
launch pad
launching
longerons
low-flying
monocoque
monoplane
navigator
overshoot
parachute
power dive
propeller
sailplane
satellite
semirigid
spacecrew
spaceship
spacesuit
space walk
test pilot
touch down
turboprop
twin-screw
wind gauge

10

aerobatics
aero-engine

10

aeronautic
aerostatic
air balloon
air control
air defence
air hostess
air service
air steward
air support
air traffic
anemometer
astrohatch
balloonist
cantilever
cargo plane
dive bomber
flight deck
flight path
flight plan
flying boat
fuel intake
gas balloon
ground crew
helicopter
hovercraft
hydroplane
jet fighter
landing run
Mach number
outer space
oxygen mask
pilot plane
robot plane
slipstream
solo flight
spacecraft
space probe
splashdown
stabiliser
stabilizer
stewardess

10

supersonic
test flight
V-formation

11

aeronautics
aerostatics
air terminal
combat plane
ejector seat
fire balloon
ground speed
heat barrier
heavy bomber
kite balloon
mooring-mast
parachutist
retractable
retro-rocket
soft landing
space centre
space flight
space rocket
space travel
stunt flying
weather-vane

12

aerodynamics
airfreighter
belly landing
control tower
crash landing
ejection seat
fighter pilot
flying saucer
freight plane
gliding angle
jet-propelled
landing light
landing speed

12	12	13	14
launching pad	space station	ground control	Flying Bedstead
maiden flight	space vehicle	in-line engines	heavier-than-air
manned rocket	trailing edge	radiolocation	lighter-than-air
night fighter		shock absorber	looping the loop
pilot balloon	13	stratocruiser	passenger plane
pressure suit,	airworthiness		
radar scanner	control column	14	15
radial engine	cruising speed	escape velocity	aircraft-carrier
sound barrier	decompression	flight recorder	semiretractable
space capsule	forced landing		

Ballet terms

3	5	7	8
pas	sauté	allonge	cagneaux
	serré	arrondi	danseuse
4		attaque	demi-plié
demi	6	balance	derrière
jeté	aplomb	danseur	glissade
plié	à terre	deboîté	pas brisé
posé	attack	emboîté	pistolet
saut	baisse	étendre	renverse
tutu	ballon	fouetté	serpette
volé	cambre	jarreté	spotting
	chaine	leotard	stulchik
5	change	maillot	tonnelet
arque	chassé	marquer	
barre	croisé	pas seul	9
battu	detire	poisson	arabesque
beats	écarté	ramasse	ballabile
brisé	effacé	sissone	ballerina
coupé	elancé	soutenu	ballerino
decor	entrée	taquete	battement
elevé	épaule		cou de pied
fondu	étendu	8	developpe
ligne	étoile	assemble	elevation
passé	failli	attitude	entrechat
piqué	monter	ballonne	enveloppé
pivot	penché	ballotte	equilibre
porté	pointe	batterie	hortensia
rosin	relevé	cabriole	juponnage

9	10	11	13
limbering	battements	contretemps	choreographer
marcheuse	epaulement	pas de basque	corps de ballet
pas de chat	pas ballone		sur les pointes
pas de deux	soubresaut	12	
pirouette	taqueterie	choreography	14
raccourci		enchaînement	closed position
revoltade		gargouillade	divertissement
variation			prima ballerina

Battles and sieges

3	4	5	5
Hue	Novi	Burma	Liège
Lys (The)	Onao	Cadiz	Ligny
Tet	Orel	Cairo	Lissa
Ulm	Riga	Carpi	Luzon
	St Lô	Cesme	Maida
4	Toba	Crécy	Malta
Acre	Truk	Crete	Marne (The)
Aden	Zeim	Dak To	Maxen
Agra		Delhi	Mudki
Alma (The)	5	Douro	Namur
Aong	Accra	Dover	Nikko
Bega	Alamo (The)	Downs (The)	Ostia
Cuba	Aland	Elena	Paris
Gaza	Ambur	El Teb	Patay
Gelt (The)	Anzio	Engen	Pered
Guam	Arcot	Eylau	Podol
Ivry	Arnee	Genoa	Poona
Jena	Arrah	Goits	Ramla
Kars	Arras	Hanau	Redan (The
Kiev	A Shau	Herat	Great)
Kulm	Auray	Imola	Reims
Laon	Bahur	Kagul	Rhine
Leck (The)	Banda	Kalpi	Rouen
Lens	Basra	Karee	Sedan
Lodz	Berea	Kolin	Selby
Metz	Betwa (The)	Kotah	Seoul
Nile (The)	Boyne (The)	La Paz	Sluys
Nive	Bulge (The)	Leyte	Somme (The)

5	6	6	6
Spurs	Boyaca	Lützen	Rocroi
Texel (The)	Busaco	Macalo	Rolica
Tours	Calais	Madras	Rumani
Valmy	Callao	Madrid	Sacile
Varna	Camden	Maidan	Sadowa
Vasaq	Campen	Majuba	Saigon
Wavre	Cannae	Málaga	Ste Foy
Worth	Chizai	Malaya	Saints (The)
Ypres	Concon	Manila	Sangro
Zenta	Danzig	Manuta	Shiloh
Znaim	Dargai	Mardis	Sicily
	Delium	Medola	Sinope
6	Dessau	Minden	Tetuan
Aachen	Dieppe	Morawa	Tobruk
Abukir	Dunbar	Moscow	Torgau
Actium	Dundee	Mukden	Toulon
Alford	Erbach	Mytton	Towton
Alhama	Gazala	Nachod	Tsinan
Amiens	Gebora	Najara	Tudela
Ancona	Gerona	Narvik	Ushant
Arbela	Gisors	Naseby	Varese
Arcola	Hallue	Norway	Varmas
Argaon	Harlaw	Novara	Venice
Arklow	Havana	Olmütz	Verdun
Armada (The)	Hexham	Oporto	Vienna
Arnhem	Hochst	Orthez	Vyborg
Arques	Inchon	Ostend	Wagram
Artois	Ingavi	Oswego	Waizan
Asiago	Ingogo	Patila	Warsaw
Aspern	Isonzo (The)	Peking	Werben
Atbara (The)	Jersey	Plei Me	Wiazma
Azores	Jhansi	Plevna	Zalaka
Bardia	Khelat	Poland	Zurich
Barnet	Kokein	Prague	
Basing	Komorn	Puente	7
Baylen	Kronia	Quebec	Aboukir
Beauge	Landau	Rabaul	Abraham, Plains
Bender	Le Mans	Raszyn	of
Bergen	Lérida	Rheims	Abu Klea
Beylan	Lonato	Rhodes	Alamein
Bilbao	Lutter	Rivoli	Albuera

7	7	7	7
Algiers	Dunkeld	Lepanto	St Kitts
Alkmaar	Dunkirk	Leuthen	St Lucia
Almansa	Eckmuhl	Lindley	Salerno
Amakusa	El Caney	Locninh	San Juan
Antwerp	Elk Horn	Loftcha	Sealion, Operation
Ascalon	Essling	Lucknow	Segewar
Ashdown	Falkirk	Magenta	Senekal
Athenry	Ferrara	Malakov	Sharqat
Baghdad	Fleurus	Malnate	Sinuiju
Balkans	Flodden	Marengo	Skalitz
Bapaume	Fornovo	Margate	Surinam
Barossa	Franlin	Matapan, Cape	Svistov
Bassano	Fulford	Memphis	Tanjore
Batavia	Fushimi	Messina	Taranto
Bautzen	Galicia	Methven	Te-Li-Ssu
Belmont	Goraria	Minorca	Tournai
Benburb	Gorlice	Mogilev	Tunisia
Biberac	Granada	Mortara	Turbigo
Bourbon	Graspan	Moskowa	Ukraine
Brescia	Grenada	Nam Dong	Vimeiro
Breslau	Gwalior	Nanking	Vinaroz
Brienne	Haarlem	Nations (The)	Vitoria
Bull Run	Haslach	Neuwied	Warburg
Cadsand	Hill 875	Newbury	Wepener
Calafat	Hill 881	Niagara	Wimpeen
Caracha	Isaszcq	Nivelle	Winkovo
Cassano	Iwo Jima	Okinawa	
Cassino	Jamaica	Opequan	8
Châlons	Java Sea	Orleans	Aberdeen
Chetate	Jutland	Palermo	Alicante
Clissau	Kapolna	Plassey	Almenara
Colenso	Kharkov	Plovdiv	Antietam
Colombo	Khe Sanh	Polotsk	Assundun
Cordova	Kilsyth	Preston	Atlantic
Coronel	Kinloss	Pultava	Auldearn
Corunna	Komatsu	Pultusk	Ayacucho
Craonne	Krasnoi	Rio Seco	Azimghur
Cravant	La Hogue	Rumania	Bastille (The)
Crefeld	L'Ecluse	Sabugal	Bastogne
Crotoye	Leghorn	Sagunto	Beaumont
Dresden	Leipzig	St Denis	Beda Fomm

8	8	8	9
Belgrade	Gunzburg	Portland	Abensberg
Bellevue	Hastings	Pyramids (The)	Agincourt
Berezina	Herrings (The)	Pyrenees	Aiguillon
Blenheim	Hong Kong	Richmond	Alcantara
Blueberg	Inkerman	Rossbach	Alresford
Borodino	Jémappes	Roveredo	Altendorf
Bosworth	Kandahar	Saalfeld	Amstetten
Boulogne	Katzbach	St Albans	Angostura
Brooklyn	Khartoum	Ste Croix	Aquidaban
Buzenval	Kumanovo	St Pierre	Auerstadt
Calcutta	Langport	St Privat	Balaclava
Caldiero	Langside	St Thomas	Ballymore
Carabobo	La Puebla	Saratoga	Barcelona
Carlisle	Le Câteau	Shanghai	Benevento
Carrical	Leitskau	Silistra	Bergfried
Carthage	Liaoyang	Smolensk	Bhurtpore
Castella	Liegnitz	Sorauren	Black Rock
Cawnpore	Lobositz	Spion Kop	Bluff Cove
Cheriton	Lys River	Stirling	Bois-le-Duc
Chévilly	Mafeking	St Mihiel	Borghetto
Clontarf	Marathon	Stockach	Brentford
Cocherel	Maubeuge	Stratton	Bucharest
Colombey	Medellin	Suvla Bay	Cape Henry
Coral Sea	Medenine	Talavera	Caporetto
Culloden	Messines	Tayeizan	Castillon
Custozza	Metaurus	Temesvar	Chacabuco
Czarnovo	Montreal	Toulouse	Chaeronea
Damascus	Mortmant	Trinidad	Champagne
Dominica	Moskirch	Tsingtao	Charasiab
Drogheda	Mouscron	Valletta	Coulmiers
Edgehill	Musa Bagh	Valutino	Crosskeys
Espinosa	Navarino	Veleneze	Dennewitz
Ethandun	Niquitas	Velletri	Dettingen
Fair Oaks	Normandy	Verneuil	Ebro River
Flanders	Omdurman	Villiers	Edersberg
Flushing	Onessant	Volturno	Edgeworth
Fontenoy	Ostrowno	Waterloo	El Alamein
Formigny	Overlord,	Wiesloch	Elchingen
Freiburg	Operation	Würzburg	Empingham
Gaulauli	Pea Ridge	Yorktown	Five Forks
Gitschin	Poitiers	Zorndorf	Friedland

9	9	9	10
Frontiers (The)	Oudenarde	Yalu River	Guadeloupe
Gallipoli	Pelischat	Zeebrugge	Habbaniyah
Gibraltar	Perpignan		Hastenbeck
Gladsmuir	Pharsalus	10	Heligoland
Glen Fruin	Primolano	Adrianople	Heliopolis
Guinegate	Princeton	Ahmadnagar	Hollabrunn
Gumbinnen	Ramillies	Aladja Dagh	Inverlochy
Heilsberg	Roseburgh	Alexandria	Königgratz
Hochkirch	St Charles	Ancrum Moor	Kornspruit
Hochstadt	St Quentin	Artois-Loos	Kunersdorf
Hyderabad	Salamanca	Aspromonte	Kut-el-Amara
Kara Burur	San Lazaro	Austerlitz	Lake George
Kassassin	Santander	Ball's Bluff	La Rochelle
Kimberley	Saragossa	Beachy Head	La Rothière
Kissingen	Schwechat	Beausejour	Loudon Hill
Kizil-Tepe	Sedgemoor	Bennington	Louisbourg
Ladysmith	Sheerness	Blore Heath	Luleburgaz
Lansdowne	Sherstone	Brandywine	Lundy's Lane
Le Bourget	Singapore	Calatafimi	Maastricht
Leningrad	Solferino	Camperdown	Maharajpur
Lexington	Spicheren	Campo Santo	Malplaquet
Leyte Gulf	Stadtlohn	Carthagena	Mareth Line
Lowenberg	Stormberg	Cedar Creek	Mariendahl
Magdeburg	Stralsund	Charleston	Martinique
Malegnano	Tarragona	Chevy Chase	Michelberg
Mansfield	Tchernaya	Chippenham	Middleburg
Maria Zell	Tolentino	Copenhagen	Montebello
Millesimo	Tou Morong	Dalmanutha	Montenotte
Mohrungen	Tourcoing	Dogger Bank	Montevideo
Montereau	Trafalgar	Dunganhill	Montfaucon
Morazzone	Trautenau	Englefield	Montmirail
Nagy-Sarlo	Vaalkranz	Futteypore	Mount Tabor
Nashville	Varaville	Gaines' Mill	Naroch Lake
Navarrete	Vauchamps	Garigliano	Neerwinden
Negapatam	Vicksburg	Germantown	New Orleans
New Guinea	Vimy Ridge	Gettysburg	Nordlingen
New Market	Vionville	Goose Green	Ostrolenka
Nijufghur	Wakefield	Gorodeczno	Paardeberg
Ocean Pond	Wandiwash	Gothic Line	Palestrina
Oltenitza	Worcester	Grant's Hill	Pandu Naddi
Otterburn		Gravelotte	Pen Selwood

10	10	11	11
Perryville	Tippermuir	Coldharbour	Montmorenci
Petersburg	Utsonomiya	Diamond Hill	Noisseville
Piave River	Val-és-Dunes	Dolni-Dubnik	Northampton
Pont Valain	Wartemberg	Driefontein	Pearl Harbor
Port Arthur	Wattignies	Durrenstein	Philiphaugh
Port Hudson	Wilderness (The)	Elands River	Pieter's Hill
Porto Bello	Winchester	Ferrybridge	Pondicherry
Porto Praya		Fisher's Hill	Prestonpans
Quatre Bras	11	Fort St David	Quiberon Bay
River Plate	Alam el Halfa	Gibbel Rutts	Rajahmundry
Ruhr Pocket	Alessandria	Gorni-Dubnik	Reddersberg
Rumersheim	An Lao Valley	Gross-Beeren	Rheinfelden
Sanna's Post	Bannockburn	Guadalajara	Rorke's Drift
Seine Mouth	Belleau Wood	Guadalcanal	Rotto Freddo
Sevastopol	Bismarck Sea	Halidon Hill	Rowton Heath
Seven Pines	Bladensburg	Hohenlinden	Saldanha Bay
Shrewsbury	Blanquefort	Hondschoote	San Giovanni
Sidi Rezegh	Breitenfeld	Ile de France	Sidi Barrani
Stalingrad	Buenos Aires	Isandhlwana	Tarawa-Makin
Stillwater	Bunker's Hill	Langensalza	Teuttlingen
Stolhoffen	Carbiesdale	Lostwithiel	Thermopylae
Stone River	Carenage Bay	Malvern Hill	Ticonderoga
Talana Hill	Castiglione	Marston Moor	Trincomalee
Tannenberg	Champaubert	Masulipatam	Vinegar Hill
Tashkessen	Chapultepec	Mersa Matruh	Waltersdorf
Tel-el-Kebir	Chattanooga	Mill Springs	Weissenburg
Tewkesbury	Chickamauga	Modder River	White Russia
Tinchebrai	Chilianwala	Monte Lezino	

12	12	12
Adwalton Moor	Fort Donelson	Pinkie Cleugh
Algeciras Bay	Hampton Roads	Port Republic
Arcis-sur-Aube	Harper's Ferry	Prairie Grove
Atherton Moor	Hedgeley Moor	Rich Mountain
Banda Islands	Homildon Hill	Roncesvalles
Bergen-op-Zoom	Kirch-Denkern	Roundway Down
Bloemfontein	Konigswartha	San Sebastian
Braddock Down	Kursk Salient	Secunderbagh
Chickahominy	Midway Island	Southwold Bay
Elandslaagte	Münchengratz	Spotsylvania
Flodden Field	Murfreesboro	Sungari River

12
Tet Offensive (The)
Villa Viciosa
Wilson's Creek

13
Baduli-Ki-Serai
Belle-Ile-en-Mer
Bosworth Field
Cape St Vincent
Castelnaudary
Cedar Mountain
Chandernagore
Cuidad Rodrigo
Fort Frontenac
Inverkeithing
Kasserine Pass
Killiecrankie
Little Big Horn
Magersfontein
Masurian Lakes
Molinos del Rey
Neville's Cross
Northallerton
Passchendaele
Peleliu-Angaur
Philippine Sea
Roanoke Island
South Mountain
Sudley Springs
White Oak Swamp
Youghioghenny
Zusmarshausen

14
Berwick-on-Tweed
Bristoe Station

14
Cape Finisterre
Chalgrove Field
Château-Thierry
Constantinople
Cropredy Bridge
Fredericksburg
Kovel-Stanislav
La Belle Famille
Loosecoat Field
Mariana Islands
Mortimer's Cross
Peach Tree Creek
Pusan Perimeter
Rouvray-St-Denis
Santiago de Cuba
Savage's Station
Secessionville
Solomon Islands
Stamford Bridge
Stirling Bridge
Vittorio Veneto

15
Aleutian Islands
Appomattox River
Battle of Britain
Beaune-la-Rolande
Beaver's Dam Creek
Frankfurt-on-Oder
Gross-Jägersdorf
Heligoland Bight
Maloyaroslavets
Missionary Ridge
Plains of Abraham
Seven Days' Battle
Spanish Galleons

16
Bataan-Corregidor
Bronkhorst Spruit
Cambrai-St Quentin
Chancellorsville
Fort William Henry
Kinnesaw Mountain
Monongahela River
Queenston Heights
Salum-Halfaya Pass

17
Burlington Heights
Dodecanese Islands
Gustav-Cassino Line
Kwajalein-Eniwetok
La Fère Champenoise
Pittsburgh Landing
Poland-East Prussia
Van Tuong Peninsula

18
Meuse-Argonne Forest

19
Chu Pong-Ia Drang
  River
Glorious First of June

20
Shannon and
  Chesapeake
Thirty-Eighth Parallel

21
Rhine and the Ruhr
  Pocket

Biblical characters

3	5	6	7
Abe	Caleb	Esther	Obadiah
Asa	David	Gideon	Pharaoh
Eli	Devil (The)	Haggai	Raphael
Eve	Enoch	Isaiah	Rebecca
God	Herod	Israel	Rebekah
Ham	Hiram	Jairus	Shallum
Job	Hosea	Joseph	Solomon
Lot	Isaac	Joshua	Stephen
	Jacob	Martha	Zebulon
4	James	Miriam	
Abel	Jesse	Naboth	8
Adam	Jesus	Nathan	Barabbas
Ahab	Jonah	Philip	Barnabas
Amos	Judah	Pilate	Benjamin
Baal	Judas	Rachel	Caiaphas
Boaz	Laban	Reuben	Herodias
Cain	Linus	Salome	Hezekiah
Esau	Lydia	Samson	Jeremiah
Joab	Micah	Samuel	Jeroboam
John	Moses	Simeon	Jonathan
Jude	Nahum	Thomas	Matthias
Leah	Naomi		Mordecai
Levi	Peter	7	Nehemiah
Luke	Sarah	Abraham	Philemon
Magi (The)	Satan	Absalom	
Mark	Silas	Delilah	9
Mary	Simon	Ephraim	Abimelech
Moab	Titus	Ezekiel	Bathsheba
Noah	Uriah	Gabriel	Nathaniel
Paul		Goliath	Nicodemus
Ruth	6	Ishmael	Zachariah
Saul	Andrew	Jehovah	Zacharias
Seth	Christ	Jezebel	
Shem	Daniel	Lazarus	10
	Darius	Lucifer	Belshazzar
5	Dorcas	Malachi	Methuselah
Aaron	Elijah	Matthew	
Annas	Elisha	Michael	

11	13	14
Bartholomew	Judas Iscariot	John the Baptist
Jehoshaphat	Mary Magdalene	Nebuchadnezzar
	Pontius Pilate	

Biology, botany and zoology

3	4	4	5
bud	corm	urea	genus
ear	cyst	vein	gland
egg	food	wilt	gonad
eye	foot	wing	graft
fin	gall	wood	heart
gel	gene	yolk	hilum
gum	germ		humus
gut	gill	**5**	hymen
jaw	haem	aorta	ileum
lip	hair	aster	imago
ova	hand	auxin	larva
pod	head	berry	latex
rib	hoof	birth	liver
rod	host	blood	lymph
sap	iris	bract	molar
sex	leaf	brain	mouth
	lens	calyx	mucus
4	life	chyle	nasal
anal	limb	chyme	nerve
anus	lung	cline	order
apex	milk	clone	organ
axon	neck	colon	ovary
bark	node	cycad	ovule
bile	ovum	cycle	penis
bird	pith	death	petal
body	pome	digit	plant
bone	pore	drupe	resin
bulb	root	druse	scale
burr	salt	fauna	semen
cell	seed	femur	sense
claw	skin	fibre	sepal
cone	stem	flora	shell
cork	tail	fruit	shoot

5	6	6	7
sinus	coccyx	pelvis	bladder
skull	cocoon	phloem	cambium
smell	coelom	phylum	capsule
sperm	cornea	pistil	cardiac
spine	cortex	plasma	carotid
spore	dermis	pollen	chalaza
stoma	embryo	radius	chorion
sweat	enzyme	rectum	cochlea
taste	facial	retina	conifer
testa	fibril	sacrum	corolla
thigh	fibula	spinal	cranium
tibia	floral	spleen	creeper
touch	flower	stamen	cristae
trunk	foetus	stigma	culture
tuber	forest	stolon	cuticle
urine	gamete	sucker	cutting
vagus	growth	tannin	diploid
virus	gullet	tendon	dormant
whorl	hybrid	thorax	ecdysis
wrist	hyphae	tissue	ecology
xylem	joints	tongue	epigeal
	labial	turgor	gastric
6	labium	ureter	genital
achene	labrum	uterus	gizzard
aerobe	lamina	vagina	glottis
albino	larynx	vessel	habitat
amnion	leaves	vision	haploid
animal	lignin	zygote	hearing
annual	mammal		hormone
anther	mantle	7	humerus
artery	marrow	abdomen	incisor
atrium	mucous	adenine	insulin
biceps	muscle	adrenal	jejunum
biotic	mutant	albumen	keratin
botany	nastic	anatomy	lacteal
branch	nectar	annulus	medulla
caecum	neuron	antenna	meiosis
canine	palate	antigen	mitosis
carpel	pappus	atavism	nectary
caudal	pecten	auricle	nostril
chitin	pelvic	biology	nucleus

7	8	8	9
organic	bile duct	papillae	digestion
oviduct	bisexual	parasite	dura mater
petiole	blastula	pectoral	endocrine
pharynx	brachial	perianth	epidermis
pigment	carapace	pericarp	excretion
pinnate	carotene	perineum	forebrain
plastid	cellular	placenta	germinate
plumule	cerebral	plankton	gestation
protein	cerebrum	pregnant	gynaecium
radicle	chordate	ribosome	herbivore
rhizoid	clavicle	root hair	hindbrain
rhizome	cleavage	ruminant	histology
species	coenzyme	scleroid	hypocotyl
spindle	cytology	seedling	ingestion
sternum	dendrite	skeleton	intestine
stomach	duodenum	taxonomy	life cycle
synapse	ectoderm	tegument	middle ear
tetanus	endoderm	tentacle	migration
thallus	feedback	thalamus	mutagenic
thyroid	follicle	tympanum	nerve cell
trachea	ganglion	vascular	notochord
triceps	genetics	vertebra	nucleolus
trophic	genitals	virology	olfactory
tropism	genotype	zoospore	operculum
urethra	germ cell		optic lobe
vacuole	hypogeal	9	organelle
viscera	inner ear	adrenalin	pacemaker
vitamin	lamellae	allantois	perennial
zoology	lenticel	anabolism	pericycle
	life span	appendage	phagocyte
8	ligament	arteriole	phenotype
alkaloid	maxillae	capillary	phylogeny
allogamy	membrane	carnivore	pituitary
alveolus	meristem	cartilage	proboscis
anaerobe	midbrain	chromatin	pulmonary
antibody	moulting	chrysalis	recessive
appendix	muscular	commensal	reticulum
auditory	mutation	corpuscle	sclerotic
autogamy	mycelium	cotyledon	sebaceous
bacteria	nerve net	cytoplasm	secretion
biennial	pancreas	diaphragm	secretory

9	10	10	11
selection	coleoptile	population	orientation
sporangia	copulation	protoplasm	pollination
sterility	dehiscence	subspecies	respiration
succulent	entomology	succession	
symbiosis	epiglottis	vegetation	12
umbilical	epithelium	vertebrate	bacteriology
unisexual	fibrinogen		biochemistry
ventricle	generation	11	central canal
xerophyte	geotropism	antheridium	fermentation
	glomerulus	antibiotics	invertebrate
10	grey matter	archegonium	microbiology
alimentary	hereditary	carnivorous	nerve impulse
androecium	incubation	chlorophyll	red blood cell
antheridia	integument	environment	reproduction
anticlinical	metabolism	gall bladder	
archegonia	monoecious	genetic code	13
biological	morphology	germination	fallopian tube
catabolism	nerve fibre	hibernation	fertilisation
cerebellum	pathogenic	muscle fibre	fertilization
		nucleic acid	marine biology

Birds

3	4	4	4
auk	barb	kaka	shag
cob	chat	kite	skua
emu	cock	kiwi	smew
hen	coot	knot	sora
jay	crow	koel	swan
kea	dodo	lark	teal
moa	dove	loon	tern
owl	duck	lory	tody
pen	erne	mina	wavy
poe	eyas	myna	wren
roc	fowl	pern	
tit	guan	rail	5
tui	gull	rhea	agami
	hawk	rook	booby
	hern	ruff	capon
	ibis	runt	chick

5	5	6	7
crake	wader	mopoke	bunting
crane	whaup	oriole	bustard
diver		osprey	buzzard
drake	**6**	parrot	cariama
eagle	avocet	peahen	catbird
egret	bantam	peewit	cheeper
eider	barbet	petrel	chicken
finch	brolga	pigeon	coaltit
galah	bulbul	plover	corella
goose	canary	pouter	courlan
grebe	chough	puffin	courser
heron	chukar	pullet	creeper
hobby	condor	redcap	dorking
junco	corbie	roller	dovekie
lowan	coucal	rotche	dunnock
macaw	cuckoo	scoter	fantail
mavis	curlew	sea-mew	fern owl
merle	cushat	shrike	fig bird
mynah	cygnet	siskin	gadwall
noddy	darter	sultan	gorcock
ouzel	dipper	takahe	goshawk
owlet	drongo	tercel	gosling
pewit	dunlin	thrush	grackle
pipit	eaglet	tomtit	greylag
poult	falcon	toucan	halcyon
quail	fulmar	trogon	harrier
raven	gander	turaco	hen hawk
reeve	gannet	turbit	hoatzin
robin	gentoo	turkey	impeyan
saker	godwit	turtle	jackass
saury	grouse	whidah	jackdaw
scaup	hoopoe	whydah	jacobin
scray	jabiru	wigeon	kestrel
serin	jacana	willet	lapwing
snipe	jaeger	yaffle	leghorn
solan	kakapo		lich-owl
stilt	lanner	**7**	mallard
stork	linnet	babbler	manakin
swift	magpie	barn owl	marabou
twite	martin	bittern	martlet
	merlin	bluetit	migrant
	missel		

7	7	8	8
minivet	wagtail	garganey	shelduck
moorhen	warbler	great tit	shoebill
mudlark	waxbill	grosbeak	snowy owl
oilbird	waxwing	guacharo	songbird
ortolan	widgeon	hawfinch	songlark
oscines	wood owl	hazel hen	songster
ostrich	wrybill	hemipode	starling
peacock	wryneck	hernshaw	tawny owl
peafowl		hornbill	thrasher
pelican	8	killdeer	thresher
penguin	accentor	kingbird	throstle
phoenix	aigrette	landrail	titmouse
pintado	amadavat	lanneret	tragopan
pochard	araponga	laverock	umbrette
poultry	avadavat	lorikeet	waterhen
quetzal	bateleur	lovebird	wheatear
redpoll	bee-eater	lyrebird	whimbrel
redwing	bellbird	marsh tit	whinchat
rooster	blackcap	megapode	whistler
rosella	bluebird	moorcock	whipbird
ruddock	boatbill	moorfowl	white-eye
sawbill	bobolink	moorgame	wildfowl
sea-cock	bob white	mute swan	woodchat
seafowl	caracara	nestling	woodcock
seagull	cardinal	nightjar	woodlark
seriema	cockatoo	notornis	
sirgang	cockerel	nuthatch	9
skimmer	curassow	ovenbird	albatross
skylark	dabchick	oxpecker	blackbird
sparrow	didapper	parakeet	black swan
squacco	dinornis	pheasant	bowerbird
staniel	dotterel	popinjay	brambling
sunbird	duckling	pygmy owl	broadbill
swallow	eagle owl	redshank	bullfinch
tanager	fish-hawk	redstart	chaffinch
tinamou	flamingo	ringdove	chickling
titlark	gamebird	ringtail	cockatiel
titling	gamecock	rock-dove	cormorant
touraco	gang-gang	screamer	corncrake
vulture	garefowl	sea eagle	crossbill

9	9	10	11
currawong	shoveller	sacred ibis	stilt petrel
fieldfare	snakebird	saddleback	stone curlew
firecrest	snow goose	sage-grouse	stone plover
francolin	spoonbill	sanderling	storm petrel
friarbird	stock dove	sand-grouse	treecreeper
frogmouth	stonechat	screech owl	wall creeper
gallinule	storm bird	shearwater	whitethroat
goldcrest	thickhead	sheathbill	woodcreeper
goldeneye	thornbill	song thrush	wren babbler
goldfinch	trumpeter	stone hatch	
grass wren	turnstone	sun bittern	12
guillemot	waterfowl	tailorbird	burrowing owl
guinea hen		tropic bird	capercaillie
gyrfalcon	10	turtledove	collared dove
heathcock	Arctic tern	weaverbird	cuckoo-shrike
Jenny wren	brent goose	woodpecker	dabbling duck
kittiwake	budgerigar	woodpigeon	fairy penguin
little owl	chiffchaff	zebra finch	flowerpecker
mallemuck	crested tit		greylag goose
merganser	demoiselle	11	hedge sparrow
nighthawk	diving duck	black grouse	honeycreeper
ossifrage	flycatcher	brush turkey	house sparrow
pardalote	grassfinch	butcher-bird	lanner falcon
parrakeet	greenfinch	button quail	mandarin duck
partridge	greenshank	Canada goose	marsh harrier
peregrine	guineafowl	carrion crow	mistle thrush
phalarope	hammerhead	diamond-bird	mourning dove
ptarmigan	harpy eagle	frigate-bird	perching duck
razorbill	hen harrier	gnatcatcher	standard wing
redbreast	honeyeater	golden eagle	stormy petrel
red grouse	hooded crow	herring gull	umbrella bird
riflebird	jungle fowl	hummingbird	whippoorwill
ring ouzel	kingfisher	lammergeier	yellowhammer
sandpiper	kookaburra	laughing owl	
scrub-bird	mallee fowl	mockingbird	13
scrub fowl	mutton-bird	Muscovy duck	adjutant stork
scrub wren	night heron	nightingale	American eagle
sea parrot	nutcracker	reedwarbler	barnacle goose
shearbill	pratincole	snow-bunting	carrier pigeon
sheldrake	ring plover	sparrowhawk	crocodile bird

13	13	15
fairy bluebird	whooping crane	Impeyan pheasant
harlequin duck	willow warbler	laughing jackass
hawaiian goose	yellow wagtail	passenger pigeon
long-tailed tit		peregrine falcon
oystercatcher	14	Philippine eagle
passerine bird	bird of paradise	
secretary bird	golden pheasant	17
whistling duck	stilt sandpiper	great crested grebe

Birthstones

January	garnet
February	amethyst
March	bloodstone/aquamarine
April	diamond
May	emerald
June	pearl
July	ruby
August	sardonyx/peridot
September	sapphire
October	opal
November	topaz
December	turquoise

Boats and ships

3	4	4	5
Ark	buss	ship	float
cog	dhow	snow	funny
gig	dory	yawl	kayak
hoy	grab		ketch
tub	hulk	5	liner
tug	junk	balsa	praam
	pram	barge	prahu
4	proa	canoe	razee
Argo	punt	coble	shell
bark	raft	craft	skiff
boat	saic	E-boat	sloop
brig	scow	ferry	smack

5

tramp
U-boat
umiak
whiff
xebec
yacht

6

argosy
banker
barque
bawley
bireme
caique
carvel
cutter
dinghy
dogger
dugout
galley
galiot
hooker
hopper
launch
lorcha
lugger
packet
pirate
randan
sampan
sealer
settee
slaver
tanker
tartan
tender
trader
vessel
whaler
wherry

7

bumboat
caravel
carrack
clipper
coaster
collier
coracle
corsair
cruiser
currach
dredger
drifter
dromond
felucca
flyboat
frigate
galleon
galliot
gondola
gunboat
iceboat
lighter
monitor
pinnace
piragua
polacca
polacre
pontoon
rowboat
sculler
shallop
steamer
towboat
trawler
trireme
tugboat
warship

8

bilander
car ferry

8

cockboat
corvette
dahabiya
fireship
flagship
gallivat
ice-yacht
ironclad
lifeboat
longboat
longship
mailboat
man-of-war
sailboat
schooner
showboat
steam-tug
trimaran
waterbus

9

bucentaur
canal boat
cargo boat
catamaran
destroyer
ferryboat
freighter
houseboat
hydrofoil
jolly-boat
lightship
minelayer
motorboat
oil tanker
outrigger
powerboat
privateer
river boat
rotor ship
sand yacht

9

slave ship
speedboat
steamboat
steamship
storeship
submarine
troopship

10

banana boat
battleship
brigantine
Hovercraft
hydroplane
icebreaker
motor yacht
narrow boat
ocean liner
packet boat
paddle boat
patrol boat
picket boat
pirate ship
quadrireme
rescue boat
river craft
rowing boat
supply ship
tea clipper
train ferry
Viking ship
watercraft
windjammer

11

barquentine
capital ship
chasse-marée
cockleshell
dreadnought
fishing boat

11	12	12	13
hopper barge	cabin cruiser	sailing barge	trading vessel
minesweeper	ferry steamer	sailing craft	transport ship
motor launch	fishing smack	sculling boat	
motor vessel	hospital ship	stern-wheeler	14
naval vessel	landing craft		Channel steamer
quinquereme	light cruiser	13	coasting vessel
sailing boat	merchant ship	battle cruiser	floating palace
sailing ship	motor trawler	paddle-steamer	ocean greyhound
slave-trader	pleasure boat	passenger boat	
three-master	police launch	passenger ship	15
torpedo boat			aircraft-carrier

Book titles

3

Kim (Rudyard Kipling)
She (Sir Henry Rider Haggard)

4

Dr No (Ian Fleming)
Emma (Jane Austen)
Gigi (Colette)
Nana (Emile Zola)
N or M? (Agatha Christie)
Ruth (Mrs Gaskell)

5

Chéri (Colette)
Jalna (Mazo de la Roche)
Kipps (H.G. Wells)
Scoop (Evelyn Waugh)
Sybil (Benjamin Disraeli)

6

Amelia (Henry Fielding)
Ben Hur (Lew Wallace)
Fiesta (Ernest Hemingway)
Ghosts (Henrik Ibsen)
Lolita (Vladimir Nabokov)
Rob Roy (Sir Walter Scott)

6

Trilby (George du Maurier)
Utopia (Sir Thomas More)

7

Babbitt (Sinclair Lewis)
Camilla (Fanny Burney)
Candide (Voltaire)
Catch 22 (Joseph Heller)
Cecilia (Fanny Burney)
Curtain (Agatha Christie)
Don Juan (Lord Byron)
Dracula (Bram Stoker)
Evelina (Fanny Burney)
Ivanhoe (Sir Walter Scott)
Lord Jim (Joseph Conrad)
Marazan (Nevil Shute)
Nemesis (Agatha Christie)
Rebecca (Daphne du Maurier)
Shirley (Charlotte Brontë)
Tancred (Benjamin Disraeli)
Ulysses (James Joyce)

8

Adam Bede (George Eliot)
Catriona (R.L. Stevenson)

8

Cranford (Mrs Gaskell)
Germinal (Emile Zola)
Jane Eyre (Charlotte Brontë)
Lucky Jim (Kingsley Amis)
Montrose (John Buchan)
Pale Fire (Vladimir Nabokov)
Pastoral (Nevil Shute)
Peter Pan (J.M. Barrie)
Tom Jones (Henry Fielding)
Tom Thumb (Henry Fielding)
Villette (Charlotte Brontë)
Waverley (Sir Walter Scott)

9

Aaron's Rod (D.H. Lawrence)
Agnes Grey (Anne Brontë)
Coningsby (Benjamin Disraeli)
Cup of Gold (John Steinbeck)
Good Wives (Louisa M. Alcott)
I Claudius (Robert Graves)
Kidnapped (R.L. Stevenson)
Men at Arms (Evelyn Waugh)
Moonraker (Ian Fleming)
Pendennis (W.M. Thackeray)
The Clocks (Agatha Christie)
The Egoist (George Meredith)
The Heroes (Charles Kingsley)
The Hobbit (J.R.R. Tolkien)
The Hollow (Agatha Christie)
Third Girl (Agatha Christie)
Whiteoaks (Mazo de la Roche)
Woodstock (Sir Walter Scott)

10

Animal Farm (George Orwell)
Don Quixote (Cervantes)
East of Eden (John Steinbeck)
Goldfinger (Ian Fleming)
His Last Bow (Sir Arthur Conan
   Doyle)
Howards End (E.M. Forster)
Hungry Hill (Daphne du Maurier)

10

In Chancery (John Galsworthy)
Jamaica Inn (Daphne du Maurier)
Kenilworth (Sir Walter Scott)
Lorna Doone (R.D. Blackmore)
Mary Barton (Mrs Gaskell)
Most Secret (Nevil Shute)
On The Beach (Nevil Shute)
Persuasion (Jane Austen)
Sad Cypress (Agatha Christie)
The Big Four (Agatha Christie)
The Citadel (A.J. Cronin)
Vanity Fair (W.M. Thackeray)
Westward Ho! (Charles Kingsley)

11

Black Beauty (Anna Sewell)
Cakes and Ale
   (W. Somerset Maugham)
Dumb Witness (Agatha Christie)
Gone to Earth (Mary Webb)
Grand Canary (A.J. Cronin)
Greenmantle (John Buchan)
Little Women (Louisa M. Alcott)
Lost Horizon (James Hilton)
Middlemarch (George Eliot)
Shannon's Way (A.J. Cronin)
Silas Marner (George Eliot)
The Big Sleep (Raymond Chandler)
The Cruel Sea (Nicholas Monsarrat)
The Newcomes (W.M. Thackeray)
Towards Zero (Agatha Christie)
War and Peace (Leo Tolstoy)
Women in Love (D.H. Lawrence)

12

Anna Karenina (Leo Tolstoy)
Brighton Rock (Graham Greene)
Casino Royale (Ian Fleming)
Crooked House (Agatha Christie)
Endless Night (Agatha Christie)
Frankenstein (Mary Shelley)

12

Guy Mannering (Sir Walter Scott)
Morte D'Arthur (Sir Thomas Malory)
Murder Is Easy (Agatha Christie)
Of Mice and Men (John Steinbeck)
Precious Bane (Mary Webb)
Rhoda Fleming (George Meredith)
Round the Bend (Nevil Shute)

12

The Alchemist (Benjamin Jonson)
The Dogs of War (Frederick Forsyth)
The Go-Between (L.P. Hartley)
The Judas Tree (A.J. Cronin)
The Moonstone (Wilkie Collins)
The Pale Horse (Agatha Christie)
The Parasites (Daphne du Maurier)
The Scapegoat (Daphne du Maurier)

13

A Modern Comedy (John Galsworthy)
Brave New World (Aldous Huxley)
Crusader's Tomb (A.J. Cronin)
Daniel Deronda (George Eliot)
Dead Man's Folly (Agatha Christie)
Doctor Zhivago (Boris Pasternak)
Finch's Fortune (Mazo de la Roche)
Finnegan's Wake (James Joyce)
Joseph Andrews (Henry Fielding)
Just-So Stories (Rudyard Kipling)
Les Misérables (Victor Hugo)
Live and Let Die (Ian Fleming)
Mansfield Park (Jane Austen)
North and South (Mrs Gaskell)
Return to Jalna (Mazo de la Roche)
Smiley's People (John le Carré)
Sons and Lovers (D.H. Lawrence)
Stephen Morris (Nevil Shute)
Tarka the Otter (Henry Williamson)
The ABC Murders (Agatha Christie)
The Odessa File (Frederick Forsyth)
The Razor's Edge (W. Somerset Maugham)
To a God Unkown (John Steinbeck)
Zuleika Dobson (Sir Max Beerbohm)

14

A Man of Property (John Galsworthy)
A Room with a View (E.M. Forster)
A Town Like Alice (Nevil Shute)
An Old Captivity (Nevil Shute)
Death on the Nile (Agatha Christie)

14

Decline and Fall (Evelyn Waugh)
Five Little Pigs (Agatha Christie)
Goodbye, Mr Chips (James Hilton)
Hallowe'en Party (Agatha Christie)
Jude the Obscure (Thomas Hardy)
Masterman Ready (Frederick Marryat)
Morning at Jalna (Mazo de la Roche)
My Cousin Rachel (Daphne du Maurier)
Our Man in Havana (Graham Greene)
Robinson Crusoe (Daniel Defoe)
Sleeping Murder (Agatha Christie)
The Forsyte Saga (John Galsworthy)
The Great Gatsby (F. Scott Fitzgerald)
The Long Goodbye (Raymond Chandler)
The Secret Agent (Joseph Conrad)
The Time Machine (H.G. Wells)
The Water Babies (Charles Kingsley)
The White Monkey (John Galsworthy)
Treasure Island (R.L. Stevenson)
Tristram Shandy (Laurence Sterne)

15

A Farewell to Arms (Ernest Hemingway)
A Passage to India (E.M. Forster)
After The Funeral (Agatha Christie)
At Bertram's Hotel (Agatha Christie)
Cards on the Table (Agatha Christie)
Evil under the Sun (Agatha Christie)
Frenchman's Creek (Daphne du Maurier)
Gone with the Wind (Margaret Mitchell)
Lord Edgware Dies (Agatha Christie)
Mrs McGinty's Dead (Agatha Christie)
Murder in the Mews (Agatha Christie)
Northanger Abbey (Jane Austen)
Partners in Crime (Agatha Christie)
Peril at End House (Agatha Christie)
Portrait of a Lady (Henry James)
Requiem for a Wren (Nevil Shute)
Taken at the Flood (Agatha Christie)
The Chequer Board (Nevil Shute)
The Faerie Queene (Edmund Spenser)

15

The Glass Blowers (Daphne du Maurier)
The Hound of Death (Agatha Christie)
The Invisible Man (H.G. Wells)
The Moving Finger (Agatha Christie)
The Secret Garden (Frances Hodgson Burnett)
The Trumpet Major (Thomas Hardy)
The Valley of Fear (Sir Arthur Conan Doyle)
The Woman in White (Wilkie Collins)
Three-Act Tragedy (Agatha Christie)
Three Men in a Boat (Jerome K. Jerome)

16

A Clockwork Orange (Anthony Burgess)
A Pocket Full of Rye (Agatha Christie)
Centenary at Jalna (Mazo de la Roche)
Death in the Clouds (Agatha Christie)
Gulliver's Travels (Jonathan Swift)
Mr Midshipman Easy (Frederick Marryat)
Sparkling Cyanide (Agatha Christie)
Tender is the Night (F. Scott Fitzgerald)
The Grapes of Wrath (John Steinbeck)
The Master of Jalna (Mazo de la Roche)
The Northern Light (A.J. Cronin)
Wakefield's Course (Mazo de la Roche)
Whiteoak Heritage (Mazo de la Roche)
Wuthering Heights (Emily Brontë)

17

A Caribbean Mystery (Agatha Christie)
Alice in Wonderland (Lewis Carroll)
Dr Jekyll and Mr Hyde (R.L. Stevenson)
King Solomon's Mines (Sir Henry Rider Haggard)
Ordeal by Innocence (Agatha Christie)
Poirot's Early Cases (Agatha Christie)
Pride and Prejudice (Jane Austen)
The Compleat Angler (Isaak Walton)
The Lord of the Rings (J.R.R. Tolkien)
The Mill on the Floss (George Eliot)
The War of the Worlds (H.G. Wells)
They Came to Baghdad (Agatha Christie)
Wives and Daughters (D.H. Lawrence)

18

A Murder is Announced (Agatha Christie)
Anna of the Five Towns (Arnold Bennett)
Cat among the Pigeons (Agatha Christie)
Death Comes as the End (Agatha Christie)
Destination Unknown (Agatha Christie)
Hickory Dickory Dock (Agatha Christie)
Nineteen Eighty-Four (George Orwell)
One Two Buckle My Shoe (Agatha Christie)
Poirot Investigates (Agatha Christie)
The Building of Jalna (Mazo de la Roche)
The Canterbury Tales (Geoffrey Chaucer)
The Deserted Village (Oliver Goldsmith)
The Moon and Sixpence (W. Somerset Maugham)
The Old Man and the Sea (Ernest Hemingway)
The Prisoner of Zenda (Anthony Hope)
The Railway Children (E. Nesbitt)
The Secret Adversary (Agatha Christie)
The Thirty-Nine Steps (John Buchan)
The Three Musketeers (Alexandre Dumas)

19

Brideshead Revisited (Evelyn Waugh)
For Whom the Bell Tolls (Ernest Hemingway)
Murder in Mesopotamia (Agatha Christie)
Sense and Sensibility (Jane Austen)
The Body in the Library (Agatha Christie)
The History of Mr Polly (H.G. Wells)
The House on the Strand (Daphne du Maurier)
The Keys of the Kingdom (A.J. Cronin)
The Murder on the Links (Agatha Christie)
The Pilgrim's Progress (John Bunyan)
The Power and the Glory (Graham Greene)
The Riddle of the Sands (Erskine Childers)
The Secret of Chimneys (Agatha Christie)
The Sittaford Mystery (Agatha Christie)
The Thirteen Problems (Agatha Christie)
The Vicar of Wakefield (Oliver Goldsmith)
The Whiteoak Brothers (Mazo de la Roche)
The Wind in the Willows (Kenneth Grahame)
They Do It with Mirrors (Agatha Christie)
Tom Brown's Schooldays (Thomas Hughes)

20

And Then There Were None (Agatha Christie)
Appointment with Death (Agatha Christie)
Lady Chatterley's Lover (D.H. Lawrence)
Little Lord Fauntleroy (Frances Hodgson Burnett)
Officers and Gentlemen (Evelyn Waugh)
Passenger to Frankfurt (Agatha Christie)
Principia Mathematica (Sir Isaac Newton)
Strangers and Brothers (C.P. Snow)
Tenant of Wildfell Hall (Anne Brontë)
The Bride of Lammermoor (Sir Walter Scott)
The Devil's Alternative (Frederick Forsyth)
The Flight of the Falcon (Daphne du Maurier)
The Grand Babylon Hotel (Arnold Bennett)
The Heart of Midlothian (Sir Walter Scott)
The Labours of Hercules (Agatha Christie)
The Listerdale Mystery (Agatha Christie)
The Man in the Brown Suit (Agatha Christie)
The Seven Dials Mystery (Agatha Christie)
Variable Winds at Jalna (Mazo de la Roche)
Why Didn't They Ask Evans? (Agatha Christie)

21

Adventures of Two Worlds (A.J. Cronin)
Miss Marple's Final Cases (Agatha Christie)
Tess of the D'urbervilles (Thomas Hardy)
The Beautiful and Damned (F. Scott Fitzgerald)
Under the Greenwood Tree (Thomas Hardy)

22

Far from the Madding Crowd (Thomas Hardy)
Parker Pyne Investigates (Agatha Christie)
The Mayor of Casterbridge (Thomas Hardy)
The Murder at the Vicarage (Agatha Christie)
The Picture of Dorian Gray (Oscar Wilde)
The Shape of Things to Come (H.G. Wells)
The Swiss Family Robinson (J.D. Wyss)
Through the Looking Glass (Lewis Carroll)
Tinker, Tailor, Soldier, Spy (John le Carré)
Trustee from the Toolroom (Nevil Shute)
Unconditional Surrender (Evelyn Waugh)
Where Angels Fear to Tread (E.M. Forster)

23

By the Pricking of My Thumbs (Agatha Christie)
Hercule Poirot's Christmas (Agatha Christie)
The History of Henry Esmond (W.M. Thackeray)
The Murder of Roger Ackroyd (Agatha Christie)

24

Murder on the Orient Express (Agatha Christie)
The Adventures of Tom Sawyer (Mark Twain)
The Life of Charlotte Brontë (Mrs Gaskell)
The Prime of Miss Jean Brodie (Muriel Spark)

25

The Innocence of Father Brown (G.K. Chesterton)
The Return of Sherlock Holmes (Sir Arthur Conan Doyle)

26

Around the World in Eighty Days (Jules Verne)
The Memoirs of Sherlock Holmes (Sir Arthur Conan Doyle)

27

The Case Book of Sherlock Holmes (Sir Arthur Conan Doyle)
The Mysterious Affair at Styles (Agatha Christie)

29

The Mirror Crack'd from Side to Side (Agatha Christie)

30

The Adventures of Huckleberry Finn (Mark Twain)

32

Twenty Thousand Leagues under the Sea (Jules Verne)

33

The Adventure of the Christmas Pudding (Agatha Christie)

Books of the Bible

Old Testament

Genesis	II Chronicles	Daniel
Exodus	Ezra	Hosea
Leviticus	Nehemiah	Joel
Numbers	Esther	Amos
Deuteronomy	Job	Obadiah
Joshua	Psalms	Jonah
Judges	Proverbs	Micah
Ruth	Ecclesiastes	Nahum
I Samuel	The Song of Solomon	Habakkuk
II Samuel	Isaiah	Zephaniah
I Kings	Jeremiah	Haggai
II Kings	Lamentations	Zechariah
I Chronicles	Ezekiel	Malachi

New Testament

Matthew	I Timothy
Mark	II Timothy
Luke	Titus
John	Philemon
The Acts of the Apostles	Hebrews
Romans	James
I Corinthians	I Peter
II Corinthians	II Peter
Galatians	I John
Ephesians	II John
Philippians	III John
Colossians	Jude
I Thessalonians	Revelation
II Thessalonians	

Apocrypha

I Esdras	Baruch, with Epistle of Jeremiah
II Esdras	Song of the Three Children
Tobit	Susanna
Judith	Bel and the Dragon
The Rest of Esther	Prayer of Manasses
Wisdom	I Maccabees
Ecclesiasticus	II Maccabees

Boys' names

2	3	4	4
Al	Mat	Alva	Ewan
Cy	Max	Amos	Ezra
Ed	Mel	Andy	Fred
	Nat	Axel	Gary
3	Ned	Bart	Gene
Abe	Nye	Beau	Glen
Alf	Pat	Bert	Glyn
Ben	Pip	Bill	Greg
Bob	Rab	Bing	Gwyn
Dai	Ray	Boyd	Hank
Dan	Reg	Brad	Hans
Del	Rex	Bram	Herb
Des	Rob	Bret	Hugh
Don	Rod	Carl	Hugo
Eli	Ron	Cary	Iago
Ern	Roy	Chad	Iain
Gil	Sam	Chas	Ifor
Gus	Seb	Clem	Igor
Guy	Sid	Dale	Ivan
Hal	Stu	Dana	Ivor
Huw	Syd	Dave	Jack
Ian	Ted	Davy	Jake
Ike	Tim	Dean	Jeff
Jay	Tom	Dick	Jess
Jed	Vic	Dion	Jock
Jem	Vin	Dirk	Joel
Jim	Wal	Doug	Joey
Job	Zak	Drew	John
Joe		Duke	Josh
Jon	4	Earl	Juan
Ken	Abel	Eddy	Judd
Kit	Adam	Eden	Jude
Lee	Alan	Emil	Kane
Len	Alec	Eric	Karl
Leo	Aled	Erle	Keir
Les	Alex	Esau	Kent
Lew	Algy	Euan	King
Lou	Alun	Evan	Kirk

4	4	5	5
Kris	Saul	Anson	Colin
Kurt	Sean	Anton	Conan
Leon	Seth	Archy	Cosmo
Levi	Shem	Artie	Craig
Liam	Stan	Athol	Cyril
Luke	Stew	Barry	Cyrus
Lyle	Theo	Basil	Damon
Marc	Toby	Benjy	Danny
Mark	Todd	Benny	Darcy
Matt	Tony	Berny	Daryl
Merv	Trev	Berty	David
Mick	Vere	Billy	Denis
Mike	Walt	Bjorn	Denys
Milo	Ward	Blair	Derek
Mort	Wilf	Blake	Deryk
Muir	Will	Blase	Dicky
Neil	Yves	Bobby	Digby
Nick	Zack	Bonar	Donny
Noah	Zane	Boris	Duane
Noel		Brent	Dylan
Norm	5	Brett	Eamon
Olaf	Aaron	Brian	Earle
Olav	Abner	Brice	Eddie
Omar	Abram	Bruce	Edgar
Otho	Adolf	Bruno	Edwin
Otis	Aidan	Bryan	Edwyn
Otto	Alain	Bryce	Elias
Owen	Alban	Byron	Eliot
Paul	Albin	Caius	Ellis
Pete	Alden	Caleb	Elmer
Phil	Aldis	Calum	Elton
Rafe	Aldus	Carol	Elvis
Rene	Alfie	Cecil	Emile
Rhys	Algie	Chris	Emlyn
Rick	Allan	Chuck	Emrys
Rolf	Alvar	Clark	Enoch
Rory	Alvis	Claud	Ernie
Ross	Alwyn	Cliff	Errol
Rudi	Amyas	Clint	Ewart
Russ	André	Clive	Felix
Ryan	Angus	Clyde	Floyd

5	5	5	5
Frank	Judah	Oscar	Timmy
Franz	Judas	Pablo	Titus
Fritz	Jules	Paddy	Tommy
Garry	Karel	Paolo	Uriah
Garth	Karol	Pedro	Vince
Gavin	Keith	Perce	Vitus
Geoff	Kenny	Percy	Waldo
Gerry	Kevin	Perry	Wally
Giles	Lance	Peter	Wayne
Glenn	Larry	Piers	Willy
Grant	Lauri	Quinn	Woody
Gregg	Leigh	Ralph	
Hardy	Leroy	Ramon	6
Harry	Lewis	Randy	Adolph
Haydn	Lloyd	Raoul	Adrian
Heath	Lorne	Ricki	Aeneas
Henri	Louie	Ricky	Albert
Henry	Louis	Rikki	Aldous
Hiram	Lucas	Roald	Aldred
Humph	Luigi	Robin	Alexis
Hyman	Madoc	Roddy	Andrew
Hymie	Manny	Roger	Angelo
Hywel	Marco	Rollo	Anselm
Inigo	Mario	Rolly	Antony
Irvin	Marty	Rolph	Archer
Irwin	Micah	Rufus	Archie
Isaac	Micky	Sacha	Armand
Izaak	Miles	Sammy	Arnaud
Jabez	Monty	Sandy	Arnold
Jacky	Moray	Scott	Arthur
Jacob	Moses	Selby	Ashley
James	Myles	Serge	Aubrey
Jamie	Neddy	Shane	August
Jared	Neill	Shaun	Austin
Jason	Nevil	Shawn	Aylmer
Jemmy	Niall	Silas	Barney
Jerry	Nicky	Simon	Barrie
Jesse	Nigel	Steve	Benito
Jesus	Nikki	Teddy	Bernie
Jimmy	Norry	Terri	Bertie
Jonah	Ollie	Terry	Billie
	Orson		

6	6	6	6
Blaine	Elijah	Hilton	Magnus
Blaise	Elliot	Hobart	Marcel
Bobbie	Ernest	Holman	Marcus
Caesar	Esmond	Horace	Marius
Callum	Eugene	Howard	Martin
Calvin	Evelyn	Howell	Martyn
Carlos	Fabian	Hubert	Marvin
Caspar	Fergus	Hughie	Marvyn
Cedric	Finlay	Irvine	Melvin
Claude	Franco	Irving	Melvyn
Conrad	Fraser	Isaiah	Merlin
Curtis	Frazer	Israel	Mervin
Dafydd	Freddy	Jackie	Mervyn
Damian	Gareth	Jarrod	Mickey
Damien	Garnet	Jarvis	Morris
Daniel	Gasper	Jasper	Mostyn
Darrel	George	Jeremy	Murray
Darren	Gerald	Jerome	Nathan
Darryl	Gerard	Jethro	Neddie
Declan	Gideon	Johnny	Nelson
Dennis	Godwin	Jolyon	Ninian
Denzil	Gordon	Jordan	Norman
Dermot	Graeme	Joseph	Norrie
Deryck	Graham	Joshua	Norris
Dexter	Gregor	Josiah	Norton
Dickie	Gunter	Josias	Nowell
Donald	Gussie	Julian	Oliver
Dorian	Gustaf	Julius	Osbert
Dougal	Gustav	Justin	Osmond
Dudley	Gwylim	Kenton	Osmund
Duggie	Hamish	Kieran	Oswald
Duncan	Hamlet	Laurie	Pascal
Dustin	Hamlyn	Lawrie	Pascoe
Dwayne	Harley	Leslie	Pelham
Dwight	Harold	Lester	Philip
Eamonn	Harvey	Lionel	Pierre
Edmond	Hayden	Lucian	Prince
Edmund	Haydon	Lucien	Rafael
Eduard	Hector	Lucius	Ramsay
Edward	Hedley	Ludwig	Ramsey
Egbert	Herman	Luther	Randal
Eldred	Hilary	Lyndon	Rayner

6	6	7	7
Raynor	Warren	Dominic	Lachlan
Reggie	Wesley	Donovan	Lambert
Reuben	Wilbur	Douglas	Lazarus
Richie	Willie	Edouard	Leonard
Robbie	Willis	Elliott	Leopold
Robert	Wilmer	Emanuel	Lindsay
Rodger	Yehudi	Ephraim	Linford
Rodney		Eustace	Ludovic
Roland	7	Everard	Malachi
Ronald	Abraham	Ezekiel	Malcolm
Ronnie	Absalom	Fitzroy	Manfred
Rowley	Ainsley	Florian	Matthew
Rudolf	Ainslie	Francis	Maurice
Rupert	Alfonso	Frankie	Maxwell
St John	Ambrose	Freddie	Michael
Samson	Andreas	Fredric	Montagu
Samuel	Aneirin	Gabriel	Murdoch
Sefton	Aneurin	Gaylord	Neville
Selwyn	Anthony	Georgie	Nicolas
Sergei	Antonio	Gerrard	Obadiah
Sergio	Artemas	Gervais	Orlando
Shamus	Baldwin	Gervase	Osborne
Shelly	Barnaby	Gilbert	Patrick
Sidney	Barnard	Godfrey	Phillip
Simeon	Bernard	Grahame	Phineas
Steven	Bertram	Gregory	Quentin
Stevie	Bradley	Gunther	Quintin
Stuart	Brendan	Gustave	Randall
Sydney	Cameron	Hadrian	Raphael
Teddie	Charles	Hartley	Raymond
Thomas	Charley	Herbert	Raymund
Tobias	Charlie	Hermann	Redvers
Travis	Chester	Hillary	Reynard
Trevor	Clayton	Horatio	Ricardo
Tyrone	Clement	Humbert	Richard
Vaughn	Clinton	Isidore	Rodolph
Vernon	Crispin	Jacques	Rodrigo
Victor	Cyprian	Jeffery	Rowland
Vivian	Darrell	Jeffrey	Royston
Vivien	Denholm	Jocelyn	Rudolph
Wallis	Derrick	Johnnie	Russell
Walter	Desmond	Kenneth	Sergius

7	8	8	9
Seymore	Benedict	Melville	Dionysius
Sheldon	Benjamin	Meredith	Ethelbert
Sigmund	Bertrand	Montague	Ferdinand
Solomon	Beverley	Mordecai	Francesco
Spencer	Boniface	Mortimer	Francisco
Stanley	Campbell	Nehemiah	Gerontius
Stephen	Clarence	Nicholas	Granville
Stewart	Claudius	Octavius	Grenville
Swithin	Clifford	Perceval	Jefferson
Terence	Courtney	Percival	Llewellyn
Timothy	Crispian	Philemon	Marcellus
Torquil	Diarmuid	Randolph	Marmaduke
Travers	Dominick	Reginald	Nathaniel
Tristan	Ebenezer	Roderick	Nicodemus
Ulysses	Emmanuel	Salvador	Peregrine
Vaughan	Ethelred	Septimus	Sebastian
Vincent	Farquhar	Sheridan	Siegfried
Wallace	Fernando	Silvanus	Sigismund
Warwick	Fletcher	Sinclair	Silvester
Wilfred	Franklin	Stafford	Stanislas
Wilfrid	Frederic	Stirling	Sylvester
William	Garfield	Sylvanus	Valentine
Winston	Geoffrey	Terrence	Zacharias
Woodrow	Gustavus	Thaddeus	Zechariah
Wyndham	Harrison	Theobald	
Wynford	Hercules	Theodore	10
Zachary	Hereward	Tristram	Barrington
Zebedee	Hezekiah	Vladimir	Caractacus
	Humphrey	Winthrop	Carmichael
8	Ignatius		Hildebrand
Adolphus	Jeremiah	9	Maximilian
Alasdair	Johannes	Alexander	Montgomery
Alastair	Jonathan	Alphonsus	Stanislaus
Algernon	Kingsley	Archibald	Washington
Alistair	Lancelot	Athelstan	Willoughby
Aloysius	Laurence	Augustine	
Alphonse	Lawrence	Balthasar	11
Alphonso	Leighton	Broderick	Bartholomew
Augustus	Llewelyn	Christian	Christopher
Barnabas	Marshall	Cornelius	Constantine
Benedick	Matthias	Courtenay	Sacheverell

Boys' schools and colleges

4	7	8	10
Eton	Bloxham	Sedbergh	Summerhill
Leys (The)	Clifton	Whitgift	Wellington
	Dulwich		Winchester
5	Felsted	**9**	
Dover	Lancing	Blundells	**11**
Epsom	Loretto	Bradfield	Berkhamsted
King's	Malvern	Bryanston	Framlingham
Rugby	Mercers	Cranbrook	Giggleswick
Stowe	Oratory	Cranleigh	Gordonstoun
Trent	Rossall	Dean Close	Marlborough
	St Paul's	Liverpool	Westminster
6	Taunton	Sherborne	
Durham	Warwick	Tonbridge	**12**
Eltham		Uppingham	Charterhouse
Exeter	**8**	Wakefield	City of London
Fettes	Abingdon		Monkton Combe
Harrow	Ardingly	**10**	
Oakham	Beaumont	Ampleforth	**14**
Oundle	Blue Coat	Birkenhead	Hurstpierpoint
Radley	Brighton	Bromsgrove	Wellingborough
Repton	Denstone	Cheltenham	
St Bees	Downside	Eastbourne	**15**
	Highgate	Haileybury	Christ's Hospital
7	Mill Hill	Royal Naval	Imperial Service
Bedales	St Albans	Shrewsbury	Merchant Taylors'
Bedford	St Olaves	Stonyhurst	

Building and architecture

3	3	4	4
bar	key	ambo	bead
bay	mew	apse	bell
cap	pub	arch	bema
die	spa	area	boss
hip	sty	band	byre
hut		bank	café
inn		barn	cage

4	4	5	5
cell	pale	annex	hovel
club	pane	arris	igloo
cowl	pave	attic	inlay
crib	pier	block	Ionic
cyma	pile	booth	jetty
dado	plan	bower	joint
dais	post	brace	joist
dike	quay	brest	kiosk
dome	rail	brick	latch
door	ramp	build	ledge
exit	rink	built	lobby
fane	roof	cabin	lodge
flag	room	coign	manse
flat	ruin	compo	newel
flue	sash	court	niche
foil	seat	crown	order
fret	shed	crypt	oriel
gaol	shop	dairy	paned
gate	sill	depot	panel
hall	sink	domed	patio
jail	site	Doric	plank
jamb	slat	drain	plaza
keep	stay	eaves	putty
kiln	step	entry	quoin
kirk	stoa	erect	rails
lath	stud	fence	ranch
lift	tile	flats	range
lock	tomb	floor	Roman
loft	trap	folly	scape
mart	vane	forum	sewer
maze	wall	gable	shaft
mews	wing	glass	shelf
mill	wood	glaze	shell
mint	yard	glyph	slate
moat		grate	slatt
mole	5	grout	socle
nave	abbey	gully	spire
nook	abode	harem	stack
oast	aisle	helix	stage
ogee	alley	hotel	stair
oven	ambry	house	stake

5	6	6	6
stall	casino	gutter	plinth
stand	castle	hangar	portal
steps	cellar	hearth	priory
stile	cement	hostel	prison
stone	chalet	impost	pulpit
store	chapel	inwall	quarry
stove	chevet	Ionian	rabbet
strut	church	ladder	rafter
study	cinema	larder	recess
suite	closet	lean-to	Rococo
talon	coffer	linhay	rubble
thorp	column	lintel	rustic
tiled	coping	locker	saloon
tower	corbel	lockup	school
truss	corona	loggia	scroll
Tudor	coving	log hut	sedile
vault	cupola	louvre	shanty
verge	debris	lyceum	smithy
villa	dentil	mantel	soffit
wharf	design	market	spence
works	donjon	merlon	square
	drains	mihrab	stable
6	dugout	morgue	stairs
abacus	estate	mortar	stores
access	façade	mosaic	stucco
adytum	fascia	mosque	studio
alcove	fillet	museum	subway
annexe	finial	mutule	tavern
arbour	flèche	Norman	temple
arcade	fresco	office	thatch
ashlar	friary	outlet	thorpe
asylum	frieze	pagoda	tiling
atrium	garage	palace	timber
aviary	garret	paling	trench
bakery	gazebo	pantry	trough
batten	girder	parget	turret
belfry	glazed	parvis	veneer
bourse	Gothic	paving	vestry
bricks	grange	pharos	vihara
broach	grille	piazza	volute
canopy	grotto	pillar	wattle

6	7	7	7
wicket	echinus	pentice	tracery
window	edifice	plaster	tracing
	embassy	portico	transom
7	entasis	postern	trellis
academy	eustyle	pyramid	trumeau
air duct	factory	railing	varnish
air flue	fixture	rebuild	vaulted
ancones	fleuron	rectory	veranda
annulet	fluting	re-edify	viaduct
archway	foundry	reeding	village
Baroque	gadroon	regency	voluted
bastion	galilee	rejoint	
brewery	gallery	repairs	**8**
builder	gateway	reredos	abutment
cabinet	granary	rockery	acanthus
canteen	grating	roofing	air drain
capital	grounds	rosette	airtight
cavetto	hip roof	rostrum	apophyge
ceiling	hospice	rotunda	approach
chamber	joinery	roundel	arboured
chancel	lantern	sanctum	astragal
chantry	lattice	sawmill	atheneum
château	laundry	seawall	atlantes
chevron	library	section	baluster
chimney	lunette	shelter	banister
citadel	mansard	shelves	bartizan
college	mansion	shingle	basilica
compost	masonry	shutter	building
conduit	mill dam	slating	bungalow
convent	minaret	Spanish	buttress
cornice	minster	stadium	caryatid
cottage	mullion	staging	casement
crocket	munnion	station	causeway
cubicle	narthex	steeple	cenotaph
culvert	nursery	surgery	centring
deanery	obelisk	systyle	cincture
demesne	oratory	tambour	cloister
distyle	paddock	tegular	Coliseum
doorway	pantile	terrace	concrete
dovecot	parapet	tessera	contract
dungeon	parvise	theatre	corridor
	passage	tie beam	crescent

8	8	8	9
cresting	kingpost	transept	cloisters
cupboard	lathwork	triglyph	clubhouse
deadwall	lichgate	tympanum	coalhouse
decorate	lychgate	underpin	colonnade
detached	magazine	verandah	colosseum
dipteral	memorial	vicarage	composite
door case	millpond	vignette	construct
doornail	monolith	wainscot	consulate
doorpost	monument	woodwork	cooperage
doorstep	mortuary		copestone
dovecote	moulding	9	courtyard
dowel pin	openwork	acropolis	crossbeam
drainage	outhouse	aerodrome	decastyle
dwelling	overhang	alignment	dripstone
elevator	palisade	almshouse	doorstone
emporium	panelled	apartment	dormitory
entrance	pantheon	apex stone	earthbank
entresol	pavement	arabesque	elevation
epistyle	pavilion	arch brick	escalator
erection	pedestal	architect	esplanade
espalier	pediment	archivolt	excavator
estimate	pentroof	archstone	farmhouse
excavate	pilaster	aerostyle	firebrick
extrados	pinnacle	ashlaring	fireplace
fanlight	platform	athenaeum	flagstone
fireclay	plumbing	bakehouse	framework
flooring	pointing	bay window	front door
fortress	rocaille	belltower	grotesque
freehold	rockwork	belvedere	guildhall
fretwork	scaffold	boathouse	gymnasium
frontage	skirting	bow window	headstone
gargoyle	skylight	brick clay	hermitage
grouting	solarium	brick dust	hexastyle
handrail	spandrel	brick-kiln	homestead
hoistway	spandril	Byzantine	hypocaust
hospital	stuccoed	campanile	hypostyle
hostelry	sunproof	cartouche	infirmary
intrados	tectonic	cathedral	inglenook
jalousie	tenement	centering	ironworks
Jacobean	tollgate	claystone	jettyhead
keystone	town hall	cloakroom	kerbstone

9	10	10	11
leasehold	antechapel	plate glass	hearthstone
lift shaft	architrave	post office	latticework
linenfold	backstairs	presbytery	louvre board
mausoleum	ballflower	proscenium	mantelpiece
mezzanine	balustrade	pycnostyle	mantelshelf
monastery	battlement	quadrangle	observatory
mouldings	bell turret	repointing	office block
octastyle	brick-built	repository	oriel window
Palladian	cantilever	Romanesque	outbuilding
parquetry	chimneypot	rose window	picture rail
parsonage	cinquefoil	round tower	plasterwork
parthenon	clock tower	sanatorium	postern gate
partition	coach-house	settlement	public house
party wall	conversion	skyscraper	reconstruct
penthouse	Corinthian	structural	renaissance
peristyle	covered way	tetrastyle	residential
promenade	crown glass	Tudor style	scaffolding
quicklime	dampcourse	university	sub-contract
rainproof	dispensary	varnishing	summerhouse
refectory	distillery	ventilator	tiled hearth
rendering	ditriglyph	water-tower	trelliswork
reservoir	drawbridge	wicket gate	Tuscan order
residence	Dutch tiles	window sash	ventilation
sallyport	excavation		wainscoting
staircase	facia panel	**11**	war memorial
stonework	foundation	antechamber	water supply
structure	glasshouse	castellated	weathercock
stylobate	grandstand	cementation	window frame
swinecote	greenhouse	compartment	window glass
synagogue	Ionic order	coping stone	window ledge
tenements	Ionic style	cornerstone	wrought iron
threshold	laboratory	dovetailing	
town house	Lady chapel	entablature	**12**
triforium	lancet arch	fan vaulting	amphitheatre
turnstile	lighthouse	fingerplate	building site
vestibule	maisonette	florid style	chimney shaft
warehouse	manor house	foundations	chimneystack
wastepipe	market town	frieze panel	cockle stairs
water tank	Norman arch	glass mosaic	conservatory
windproof	overmantel	ground floor	construction
wire gauze	plastering	harelip arch	constructure

12	12	13	14
country house	town planning	entrance lobby	filling station
covered court	tracing cloth	Grecian temple	mezzanine floor
dormer window	tracing linen	lattice window	Portland cement
draught-proof	tracing paper	master builder	reconstruction
entrance hall	unventilated	Norman doorway	Venetian window
floor timbers	valance board	Portland stone	whispering dome
folding doors	Venetian door	skirting board	
half-timbered	wainscotting	specification	15
Ionian column	weatherproof	sub-contractor	air conditioning
louvre window		transom window	damp-proof
parquet floor	13	triumphal arch	course
power station	architectural	vaulting shaft	electric heating
Purbeck stone	chimney corner	Venetian blind	foundation stone
purpose-built	compass window		hydraulic cement
spiral stairs	coursing joint	14	pleasure gardens
sub-structure	dwelling house	Catherine wheel	pleasure grounds
three-ply wood	dwelling place	central heating	spiral staircase

Business, trade and commerce

2	3	4	4
A1	tax	deal	glut
SA	tip	dear	GmbH
		debt	gold
3	4	deed	good
bid	agio	dole	hire
buy	back	dues	idle
cut	bail	dump	kite
fee	bank	duty	lend
Inc.	bear	earn	levy
job	bill	easy	lien
lot	bond	even	loan
Ltd	boom	fine	loss
net	bull	firm	mart
owe	call	free	mint
par	cash	fund	nett
pay	cess	gain	note
PLC	chip	gild	owed
rig	coin	gilt	pool
sum	cost	giro	post

4	5	5	6
punt	cover	telex	credit
rate	crash	tight	crisis
rent	cycle	token	dealer
ring	debit	trade	deal-in
risk	draft	trend	debtor
sale	entry	trust	defray
sell	ex div	usury	demand
sink	float	value	docket
sold	folio	wages	drawer
stag	funds	worth	equity
tare	goods	yield	estate
term	gross		excise
turn	hedge	6	expend
vend	house	accept	export
wage	index	accrue	factor
	issue	advice	figure
5	lease	agency	fiscal
agent	limit	amount	freeze
asset	money	assets	growth
audit	notes	assign	hammer
award	offer	at cost	holder
batch	order	banker	honour
bears	owing	barter	import
bid-up	panic	bearer	income
block	paper	borrow	in debt
board	payee	bought	insure
bonds	pound	bounce	jobber
bonus	price	bounty	job lot
brand	proxy	branch	labour
bribe	quota	broker	ledger
buyer	quote	budget	lender
buy-in	rally	burden	liable
buy-up	rates	buying	Lloyd's
bylaw	remit	buy-out	lock-up
cargo	repay	byelaw	margin
cheap	share	bylaws	market
check	shark	change	mark-up
chips	short	charge	mature
clear	slump	cheque	merger
clerk	stock	client	minute
costs	taxes	coupon	notice

6	6	7	7
office	stocks	cashier	invoice
oncost	strike	ceiling	jobbing
one-off	supply	certify	leasing
option	surety	charter	lending
outbid	surtax	company	limited
outlay	tariff	consols	lottery
outlet	taxman	convert	lump sum
output	teller	customs	manager
parity	tender	cut-rate	minutes
pay day	ticket	damages	nest egg
paying	tithes	dealing	net gain
pay-off	trader	declare	no funds
pay-out	tycoon	default	on offer
pledge	unload	deficit	on order
plunge	unpaid	deflate	package
policy	usurer	deposit	partner
profit	vendor	draw out	payable
public	volume	economy	pay cash
punter	wealth	embargo	payment
quorum	wind up	endorse	pay rise
racket		engross	payroll
rating	7	entrust	pay slip
rebate	account	ex bonus	pension
recoup	actuary	expense	per cent
redeem	advance	exploit	pre-empt
refund	annuity	exports	premium
remedy	arrears	factory	prepaid
rental	auction	failure	pricing
report	auditor	fall due	product
retail	average	finance	profits
return	backing	flutter	promote
salary	bad debt	freight	pro rata
sample	balance	funding	pyramid
saving	banking	haulage	realize
sell in	bargain	hedging	receipt
sell up	bidding	imports	reissue
set off	bonanza	imprest	renewal
shares	bullion	inflate	reserve
silver	buy back	in funds	returns
spiral	byelaws	insured	revenue
staple	capital	interim	rigging

7	8	8	8
royalty	bank giro	exporter	recovery
salvage	bank loan	feedback	reinvest
selling	banknote	finances	reserves
sell out	bank rate	goodwill	retailer
service	bankrupt	gratuity	retainer
sold out	basic pay	hallmark	scarcity
solvent	below par	hard cash	schedule
spin-off	blue chip	hard sell	security
squeeze	borrower	importer	shipment
stipend	business	increase	sinecure
storage	buying-in	indebted	solvency
subsidy	carriage	industry	spending
surplus	cashbook	interest	sterling
swindle	cash sale	in the red	supertax
takings	clearing	investor	swindler
tax free	commerce	lame duck	takeover
tonnage	computer	manifest	tax dodge
trade-in	consumer	mark down	taxpayer
trading	contract	markings	trade gap
traffic	creditor	maturing	transfer
trustee	currency	maturity	treasury
utility	customer	merchant	turnover
vending	cut price	monetary	undercut
venture	dealings	monopoly	wage rate
war bond	defrayed	mortgage	warranty
war loan	delivery	net price	windfall
warrant	director	on strike	write-off
wound-up	disburse	operator	
write-up	discount	ordinary	9
	dividend	overtime	ad valorem
8	earnings	passbook	aggregate
above par	embezzle	pin money	allotment
accounts	employee	poundage	allowance
act of God	employer	price cut	appraisal
after tax	emporium	price war	appraiser
appraise	equities	proceeds	assurance
assignee	estimate	producer	averaging
assigner	evaluate	property	bank stock
auditing	exchange	purchase	book value
bank bill	ex gratia	receipts	borrowing
bankbook	expenses	receiver	break even

9

brokerage
by-product
carry-over
certified
chartered
clearance
commodity
cost price
death duty
debenture
debit note
deduction
defaulter
deflation
depletion
depositor
directors
dishonour
easy money
easy terms
economics
economise
economize
emolument
exchequer
executive
extortion
face value
fair price
fair trade
financial
financier
firm offer
firm price
flotation
franchise
free trade
fully paid
gilt edged
going rate
guarantee

9

guarantor
hard money
import tax
in arrears
incentive
income tax
indemnity
indenture
inflation
insolvent
insurance
inventory
leasehold
liability
liquidate
list price
logistics
mail order
marketing
middleman
mortgagee
mortgagor
negotiate
net income
order book
outgoings
overdraft
overdrawn
overheads
packaging
paymaster
pecuniary
personnel
petty cash
portfolio
preferred
price list
price rise
prime cost
principle
profiteer
promotion

9

purchaser
quotation
ratepayer
ready cash
recession
redundant
reimburse
repayable
repayment
resources
restraint
reversion
royalties
secretary
sell short
shift work
shortfall
short time
sold short
speculate
stamp duty
statement
stock list
stockpile
subscribe
subsidise
subsidize
surcharge
syndicate
tax return
trade fair
trademark
trade name
tradesman
treasurer
undersell
unit trust
utilities
valuation
wage claim
warehouse

9

wealth tax
wholesale
winding-up
work force
work sheet
work study

10

acceptance
accountant
accounting
accumulate
adjustment
advice note
appreciate
assessment
assignment
attachment
auctioneer
automation
bank credit
bank return
bankruptcy
bearer bond
bill of sale
bondholder
bonus issue
bonus share
bookkeeper
bulk-buying
calculator
capitalise
capitalize
capitalism
capitalist
chain store
chequebook
closed shop
closing bid
collateral
commercial

10

commission
compensate
consortium
contraband
conversion
credit card
credit note
credit slip
cumulative
depreciate
depression
direct cost
encumbered
engrossing
evaluation
excise duty
ex dividend
fax machine
first offer
fiscal year
fixed costs
fixed price
fixed trust
floor price
forwarding
free market
funded debt
gross value
ground rent
honorarium
import duty
income bond
industrial
insolvency
instalment
investment
joint stock
liquidator
living wage
management
marked down

10

mass market
mercantile
money order
monopolise
monopolize
negotiable
nonpayment
note of hand
obligation
open cheque
open credit
open market
open policy
opening bid
option rate
overcharge
paper money
pawnbroker
percentage
plough back
pre-emption
preference
prepayment
price index
price level
production
profitable
profits tax
prospector
prospectus
prosperity
prosperous
provide for
purchasing
pure profit
quarter day
ready money
real estate
real income
recompense
redeemable

10

redemption
redundancy
remittance
remunerate
rock bottom
sales force
second-hand
securities
selling-out
settlement
share index
sole agency
speculator
statistics
stockpiles
subscriber
tax evasion
trade price
trade union
typewriter
underwrite
unemployed
wage freeze
wall street
wholesaler
working day
work-to-rule

11

accountancy
account book
acquittance
advance note
advertising
arbitration
asking price
auction sale
bank account
bank balance
bank holiday
bank of issue

11

beneficiary
big business
billionaire
bill of entry
black market
blank cheque
bonded goods
bonus scheme
bookkeeping
budget price
businessman
capital gain
cash account
central bank
certificate
circulation
commitments
commodities
common stock
competition
competitive
comptometer
consignment
consumption
co-operative
corporation
counterfeit
customs duty
days of grace
defence bond
deposit rate
deposit slip
devaluation
discounting
dishonoured
distributor
double entry
down payment
economic law
endorsement
expenditure

11	11	12	12
fixed assets	realization	branch office	joint account
fixed charge	reserve bank	bridging loan	keep accounts
fixed income	revaluation	buyer's market	life interest
fluctuation	safe deposit	capital gains	liquid assets
foreclosure	sales ledger	capital goods	manufacturer
free on board	savings bank	capital stock	marginal cost
freight note	shareholder	carrying-over	mass-produced
gross income	single entry	cash and carry	maturity date
high finance	sinking fund	chemical bank	merchant bank
indemnified	small trader	clearing bank	money changer
ingredients	speculation	closing price	national bank
job analysis	stockbroker	common market	national debt
joint return	stock market	compensation	nominal value
legal tender	stockpiling	contract note	Pay-As-You-Earn
liquidation	stocktaking	cost of living	pay in advance
loan capital	subsistence	credit rating	paying-in slip
manufacture	supermarket	current price	policy holder
market price	take-home-pay	defence bonds	present worth
mass-produce	takeover bid	denomination	price ceiling
merchandise	transaction	depreciation	price control
millionaire	underwriter	differential	productivity
minimum wage	with profits	direct labour	profiteering
money-lender		disbursement	profit margin
negotiation	**12**	discount rate	profit taking
net interest	above the line	distribution	public sector
net receipts	account payee	Dutch auction	rate of growth
outstanding	amalgamation	earned income	raw materials
package deal	appreciation	economy drive	redeployment
partnership	assembly line	embezzlement	remuneration
pay on demand	balance sheet	entrepreneur	remunerative
photocopier	banker's draft	exchange rate	reserve price
point-of-sale	banker's order	first refusal	rising prices
postal order	bargain price	fixed capital	running costs
poverty line	below the line	frozen assets	sale or return
premium bond	bill of lading	going concern	sales manager
price freeze	board meeting	hard currency	salesmanship
property tax	board of trade	hire purchase	severance pay
purchase tax	bonded stores	inter-company	share capital
queer street	bought ledger	interest rate	shareholders
raw material		invoice clerk	sliding scale
realisation		irredeemable	statistician

12
stock-in-trade
tax avoidance
tax collector
tax exemption
terms-of-trade
trade balance
trading stamp
transfer deed
treasury bill
treasury bond
treasury note
trial balance
underwriting
welfare state

13
appropriation
articled clerk
bank statement
bullion market
clearing house
consumer goods
credit control
credit squeeze

13
crossed cheque
current assets
dividend yield
Dow-Jones index
exchequer bill
gross receipts
incomes policy
interim report
Lombard Street
not negotiable
ordinary share
participating
private sector
profitability
profit sharing
public company
rateable value
sales forecast
specification
stock exchange
taxable income
trade discount
value-added tax
wheeler-dealer
word processor

14
advance freight
apprenticeship
balance of trade
bill of exchange
bureau de change
capitalisation
capitalization
consumer credit
corporation tax
current account
current balance
debenture stock
decimalisation
decimalization
deposit account
economic growth
finance company
fringe benefits
full employment
general manager
holding company
infrastructure
letter of credit
limited company

14
Lloyd's Register
loan conversion
market research
monthly account
mortgage broker
option dealings
ordinary shares
oversubscribed
preferred stock
promissory note
purchase ledger
quality control
random sampling
rate of exchange
rate of interest
receiving order
short-term gains
social security
superannuation
surrender value
trading account
unearned income
working capital

15
bonded warehouse
building society
commission agent
consignment note
dividend warrant
ex gratia payment
foreign exchange
interim dividend
investment trust
nationalisation

15
nationalization
non-contributory
preference stock
preferred shares
public ownership
public relations
purchasing power
rationalisation
rationalization
redemption yield

15
reducing balance
sleeping partner

16
company secretary
personnel manager

20
profit and loss account

Calendars

Chinese

Xiao Han (January)
Da Han (January/February)
Li Chun (February)
Yu Shui (February/March)
Jing Zhe (March)
Chun Fen (March/April)
Qing Ming (April)
Gu Yu (April/May)
Li Xia (May)
Xiao Man (May/June)
Mang Zhong (June)
Xia Zhi (June/July)
Xiao Shu (July)
Da Shu (July/August)
Li Qui (August)
Chu Shu (August/September)
Bai Lu (September)
Qui Fen (September/October)
Han Lu (October)
Shuang Jiang (October/November)
Li Dong (November)
Xiao Xe (November/December)
Da Xue (December)
Dong Zhi (December/January)

French Revolutionary

Vendémiaire (vintage) (September/October)
Brumaire (fog) (October/November)
Frimaire (sleet) (November/December)
Nivôse (snow) (December/January)
Pluviôse (rain) (January/February)
Ventôse (wind) (February/March)
Germinal (seed) (March/April)
Floreal (blossom) (April/May)
Prairial (pasture) (May/June)
Messidor (harvest) (June/July)
Fervidor (heat) (July/August)
Fructidor (fruit) (August/September)

Gregorian

January	July
February	August
March	September
April	October
May	November
June	December

Hebrew

Shevat (January/February)
Adar (February/March)
Nisan (March/April)
Iyar (April/May)
Sivan (May/June)
Tammuz (June/July)
Av (July/August)
Elul (August/September)
Tishri (September/October)
Heshvan (October/November)
Kislev (November/December)
Tevet (December/January)

Islamic

(The Gregorian equivalents of the Islamic months vary from year to year)
Muharram
Safar
Rab I
Rab II
Jumada I
Jumada II
Rajab
Sha'ban
Ramadan
Shawwal
Dhual-Qu'Dah
Dhual-Hijjah

Cats

3
Rex
Van

4
Manx

5
cream
Korat
moggy
Smoke
tabby

6
Angora
Birman
Havana
Sphynx
tortie

7
Burmese
Persian
Ragdoll
red self
Siamese

7
spotted
Turkish

8
Devon Rex
longhair
red tabby

9
blue cream
Maine Coon

10
Abyssinian
brown tabby
Chinchilla
Cornish Rex

11
Blue Burmese
British Blue
Colourpoint
Russian Blue
silver tabby

12
Brown Burmese

13
chestnut brown
Red Abyssinian
Tortoiseshell

14
long-haired blue
tortie and white

15
red-point Siamese

16
blue-point Siamese
seal-point Siamese

17
lilac-point Siamese
tabby-point Siamese

18
tortie-point Siamese

21
chocolate-point Siamese

Cattle

3
Gir

5
Devon
Kerry
Kyloe
Luing

6
Dexter
Jersey
Sussex

7
beefalo
Brangus

8
Ayrshire
Friesian
Galloway
Guernsey
Hereford
Highland
Limousin

9
Charolais
Shorthorn
Simmental

10
Brown Swiss
Lincoln Red

10	11	13
Murray Grey	Jamaica Hope	Aberdeen Angus
Welsh Black	Marchigiana	Droughtmaster
		Texas Longhorn

Cereals

3	5	6	9
rye	emmer	groats	buckwheat
	grain	mealie	seed grain
4	grist	millet	sweet corn
bran	maize	quinoa	
corn	paddy		10
dura	panic	7	barleycorn
malt	spelt	cassava	barley meal
meal	wheat	corncob	guinea corn
oats		sorghum	Indian corn
rice	6	tapioca	
	barley		11
5	casava	8	pearl barley
doura	dhurra	semolina	pearl millet
durra	farina	wild rice	
			12
			Indian millet
			winter barley

Cheeses

4	6	7	8
blue	Cantal	Ricotta	Pecorino
Brie	Danish	Stilton	Taleggio
curd	Fourme		
Edam	Romano	8	9
feta		Ayrshire	Camembert
	7	Beaufort	Emmenthal
5	Boursin	Bel Paese	Leicester
cream	Cheddar	Cheshire	Limburger
Derby	cottage	Emmental	Lymeswold
Gouda	Gruyère	Parmesan	Port Salut
Leigh			

9
Roquefort
Sage Derby

10
Caerphilly
Danish Blue

10
Dolcelatte
Gloucester
Gorgonzola
Lancashire
Mozzarella
Red Windsor

11
Petit-Suisse
Pont l'Evêque
Wensleydale

12
Red Leicester

16
Double
  Gloucester

Chemical elements

3
tin (Sn)

4
gold (Au)
iron (Fe)
lead (Pb)
neon (Ne)
zinc (Zn)

5
argon (Ar)
boron (B)
radon (Rn)
xenon (Xe)

6
barium (Ba)
carbon (C)
cerium (Ce)
cobalt (Co)
copper (Cu)

6
curium (Cm)
erbium (Er)
helium (He)
indium (In)
iodine (I)
nickel (Ni)
osmium (Os)
oxygen (O)
radium (Ra)
silver (Ag)
sodium (Na)

7
arsenic (As)
bismuth (Bi)
bromine (Br)
cadmium (Cd)
caesium (Cs)
calcium (Ca)
fermium (Fm)
gallium (Ga)

7
hafnium (Hf)
holmium (Ho)
iridium (Ir)
krypton (Kr)
lithium (Li)
mercury (Hg)
niobium (Nb)
rhenium (Re)
rhodium (Rh)
silicon (Si)
sulphur (S)
terbium (Tb)
thorium (Th)
thulium (Tm)
uranium (U)
wolfram (W)
yttrium (Y)

8
actinium (Ac)
antimony (Sb)

8
astatine (At)
chlorine (Cl)
chromium (Cr)
europium (Eu)
fluorine (F)
francium (Fr)
hydrogen (H)
lutetium (Lu)
nitrogen (N)
nobelium (No)
platinum (Pt)
polonium (Po)
rubidium (Rb)
samarium (Sm)
scandium (Sc)
selenium (Se)
tantalum (Ta)
thallium (Te)
titanium (Ti)
tungsten (W)
vanadium (V)

9
aluminium (Al)
americium (Am)
berkelium (Bk)
beryllium (Be)
columbium (Cb)
germanium (Ge)
lanthanum (La)

9
magnesium (Mg)
manganese (Mn)
neodymium (Nd)
neptunium (Np)
palladium (Pd)
plutonium (Pu)
potassium (K)

9
ruthenium (Ru)
strontium (Sr)
tellurium (Te)
ytterbium (Yb)
zirconium (Zr)

10
dysprosium (Dy)
gadolinium (Gd)
lawrencium (Lr)
molybdenum (Mo)
phosphorus (P)
promethium (Pm)
technetium (Tc)

11
californium (Cf)
einsteinium (Es)
mendelevium (Md)
unnilhexium (Unh)

12
praseodymium (Pr)
protactinium (Pa)
unnilpentium (Unp)
unnilquadium (Unq)
unnilseptium (Uns)

Chemistry and metallurgy

3
azo
fat
gas
ion
ore

4
acid
acyl
alum
aryl
atom
base
bond
clay
meta
mica
mole
neon
rust
salt

5
alkyl
alloy
amide
amine
amino
anode

5
borax
brass
chalk
ester
ether
group
imine
ionic
metal
nylon
oxide
ozone
redox
resin
steel
sugar
vinyl

6
acetal
acidic
alkali
alkane
alkene
atomic
biuret
borate
bronze
buffer

6
butane
carbon
cation
chrome
dry ice
enzyme
ethane
ferric
isomer
ketone
liquid
litmus
methyl
octane
oxygen
period
phenol
phenyl
radium
reduce
ribose
silica
sinter
starch

7
acetate
acetone
acidity

7
aerosol
alchemy
alcohol
alumina
amalgam
ammonia
analyse
aniline
anodise
anodize
antacid
bonding
bromate
bromide
bromine
calcium
chemist
chloric
cyanate
cyanide
diamond
dioxide
element
entropy
ferment
ferrate
ferrous
gelatin
glucose

7

halogen
hydrate
iridium
isotope
lithium
methane
neutral
neutron
nitrate
nitride
nitrite
organic
osmosis
osmotic
oxidant
oxidise
oxidize
pentane
peptide
pig-iron
plastic
polymer
propane
protein
quinine
reagent
silicon
soluble
solvent
sulphur
terpene
titrate
toluene
valence
valency
vitamin
vitriol

8

actinide
actinium

8

aldehyde
alkaline
ammonium
analysis
antimony
aromatic
asbestos
bakelite
bessemer
carbonic
carbonyl
cast iron
catalyst
charcoal
chemical
chlorate
chloride
chlorine
chromate
chromite
chromium
covalent
dissolve
electron
emission
enthalpy
fluoride
fluorine
glycerol
graphite
hydrated
hydrogen
hydroxyl
magnesia
methanol
molecule
nicotine
nitrogen
noble gas
non-metal
particle

8

peroxide
reactant
reaction
refining
rock salt
saturate
silicate
solution
sulphate
sulphide
sulphite
test tube

9

acetylene
acylation
alchemist
alcoholic
aliphatic
aluminium
amino acid
apparatus
carbonate
carbonium
catalysis
cellulose
chemistry
corrosion
galvanise
galvanize
haematite
histamine
hydration
hydroxide
indicator
inorganic
insoluble
isomerism
lanthanum
limestone
limewater

9

magnesium
molecular
nitration
oxidation
petroleum
phosphate
phosphide
polyester
polythene
polyvinyl
potassium
quicklime
reduction
saltpetre
sulphuric
synthetic
tellurium
titration

10

acetic acid
amphoteric
analytical
bond energy
chemically
chloroform
double bond
electronic
enantiomer
laboratory
lactic acid
lanthanide
metallurgy
natural gas
neutralise
neutralize
nitric acid
phosphorus
rare earths
transition

11	11	12	13
acetylation	precipitate	condensation	precipitation
bicarbonate	prussic acid	covalent bond	radioactivity
cholesterol	quicksilver	distillation	sulphuric acid
crystallise	radioactive	electrolysis	
crystallize	ribonucleic	fermentation	14
dehydration	sublimation	halogenation	carbon monoxide
endothermic	wrought iron	hydrochloric	oxidising agent
equilibrium		hydrogen bond	oxidizing agent
free radical	12	permanganate	polysaccharide
hydrocarbon	alkali metals		
laughing gas	atomic number	13	15
litmus paper	atomic weight	Bessemer steel	Bessemer process
napthalene	blast furnace	carbon dioxide	electrochemical
non-metallic	carbohydrate	chain reaction	molecular weight
phosphorous	carbonic acid	lattice energy	
polystyrene	chlorination	periodic table	

Clergy

4	6	8	10
dean	bishop	cardinal	archbishop
pope	curate	chaplain	archdeacon
	deacon	minister	prebendary
5	parson		
canon	pastor	9	
elder	priest	deaconess	
vicar	rector		

Clothes and materials

3	3	3	4
aba	fur	obi	abba
alb	hat	PVC	band
bag	hem	rag	belt
bib	kid	rep	boot
boa	lap	sox	brim
bra	lei	tie	calf
cap	mac	wig	cape
fez	net	zip	clog

4	4	5	5
coat	slip	frill	shako
cony	slop	frock	shawl
cope	sock	gauze	shift
cord	spat	get-up	shirt
cowl	spur	glove	sisal
cuff	stud	habit	skirt
down	suit	heels	smock
drag	toga	jabot	snood
felt	togs	jeans	spats
garb	torc	jupon	stays
gear	tutu	khaki	stock
gown	vamp	lapel	stola
haik	veil	Levis	stole
hemp	vest	linen	straw
hide	wool	lisle	stuff
hood	wrap	lurex	suede
hose		middy	tails
kepi	5	mitre	tammy
kilt	abaya	mitts	teddy
lace	amice	moiré	tiara
lamé	apron	mufti	topee
lawn	baize	ninon	toque
mask	benjy	nylon	train
maxi	beret	Orlon	trews
mesh	boots	pants	tulle
midi	braid	parka	tunic
mini	busby	piqué	tweed
mink	chaps	plaid	twill
mitt	cloak	pleat	visor
muff	clogs	plume	vizor
mule	cloth	plush	V neck
pelt	crepe	print	voile
pump	crown	pumps	weeds
robe	denim	purse	
ruff	derby	rayon	6
sack	dhoti	ruche	angola
sari	dress	sable	angora
sash	drill	sabot	anorak
shoe	ephod	satin	barret
silk	fichu	scarf	basque
skin	floss	serge	beanie

6	6	6	6
beaver	diaper	muslin	top-hat
berber	dirndl	napery	topper
biggin	dolman	nylons	torque
bikini	domino	ocelot	toupee
biretz	duster	osprey	tricot
blazer	earcap	outfit	trilby
blouse	edging	panama	trunks
boater	ermine	peplum	t-shirt
bodice	fabric	pleats	tucker
bolero	fedora	pompon	turban
bonnet	flares	poncho	tuxedo
bootee	fleece	poplin	tweeds
boucle	fox fur	puttee	ulster
bowler	fringe	rabbit	undies
bow tie	gaiter	raglan	uplift
boxers	garter	red fox	velure
braces	girdle	reefer	velvet
breton	guimpe	ribbon	waders
briefs	gusset	rig-out	whites
brogan	halter	rochet	wimple
brogue	hankie	rubber	woolly
buckle	helmet	ruffle	
buskin	insole	sandal	7
bustle	jacket	sarong	acrylic
button	jerkin	sateen	apparel
calico	jersey	sequin	armband
canvas	jumper	serape	art silk
capote	kaftan	sheath	bandeau
catgut	kimono	shimmy	bandore
chintz	kirtle	shorts	baroque
choker	lappet	shroud	basinet
cloche	lining	slacks	beretta
coatee	livery	sleeve	biretta
collar	loafer	smalls	blanket
corset	mantle	sunhat	blue fox
cotton	mantua	tabard	bottine
cravat	marmot	tartan	box cape
crepon	magyar	tights	box coat
Dacron	mitten	tinsel	brocade
damask	mobcap	tippet	brogans
diadem	mohair	tissue	buckram

7	7	7	8
bunting	flat cap	raw silk	all-in-one
burnous	flat hat	regalia	appliqué
calotte	flounce	rompers	asbestos
cambric	fur coat	rubbers	balmoral
capuche	gaiters	sacking	bandanna
cassock	garment	satinet	barathea
casuals	gingham	silk hat	bath robe
chamois	g-string	singlet	batswing
chemise	guipure	ski boot	bearskin
chiffon	gum-boot	slip-ons	bed-linen
chip hat	gum shoe	slipper	bed socks
chlamys	gym shoe	spencer	biggonet
chopine	gymslip	sporran	bloomers
chrisom	handbag	stetson	boat neck
civvies	hatband	suiting	bobbinet
clobber	hessian	sunsuit	body belt
clothes	homburg	sweater	body coat
cockade	hosiery	taffeta	bone lace
coronet	kashmir	tank top	box-cloth
corsage	layette	tea-gown	breeches
cossack	leather	textile	buckskin
costume	leotard	ticking	burberry
cowhide	loafers	top-boot	burnoose
coxcomb	Mae West	topcoat	calfskin
culotte	mantlet	tricorn	camisole
cut-away	muffler	tunicle	cape line
doeskin	nankeen	turn-ups	cardigan
doublet	necktie	twinset	cashmere
drawers	netting	uniform	celanese
drip-dry	nightie	veiling	chaperon
duchess	oilskin	velours	chausses
ear muff	organza	viscose	chenille
epaulet	overall	Viyella	cloth cap
Eton cap	paisley	webbing	collaret
falsies	panties	wedgies	corduroy
fashion	parasol	wellies	corselet
felt hat	pigskin	wetsuit	cretonne
felting	pillbox	wing tie	culottes
filibeg	pyjamas	woollen	dandy hat
fishnet	raiment	worsted	diamante
flannel	rawhide	wrapper	dress tie
		y-fronts	

8	8	8	9
drilling	moccasin	sunshade	camel-hair
duchesse	musquash	surplice	cartwheel
dunce cap	neckband	swimsuit	cassimere
dust-coat	necklace	tail-coat	chantilly
dutch cap	negligee	tapestry	coat dress
ear muffs	nightcap	tarboosh	coat shirt
ensemble	nylon mac	Terylene	cocked hat
Fair Isle	oilcloth	Thai silk	comforter
flannels	opera hat	trainers	coolie hat
flimsies	organdie	trencher	courtelle
footwear	overalls	trimming	cowboy hat
frilling	overcoat	trousers	crinoline
frippery	overshoe	two-piece	Cuban heel
furbelow	philibeg	umbrella	dog collar
galoshes	pinafore	vestment	dress-coat
gauntlet	platinum	wardrobe	dress suit
glad rags	playsuit	wax-cloth	duffle bag
goatskin	plimsoll	whipcord	dungarees
gold lamé	polo neck	wild mink	epaulette
gossamer	pullover	wild silk	flannelet
guernsey	pure silk	woollens	flip-flops
gumboots	raincoat	woollies	forage-cap
gym shoes	sand-shoe		frock-coat
half-hose	shantung	**9**	full dress
half slip	sheeting	alice band	full skirt
headband	shirting	alpine hat	fur collar
head-gear	shoelace	ankle boot	fur fabric
hipsters	shot silk	astrakhan	gabardine
homespun	ski boots	baby linen	garibaldi
jack-boot	ski pants	balaclava	gauntlets
jodhpurs	skullcap	ball dress	georgette
jump-suit	slipover	bandoleer	glengarry
kerchief	slippers	bandolier	great-coat
knickers	smocking	beachwear	grosgrain
knitwear	sneakers	bed jacket	hair-cloth
lambskin	snowshoe	billicock	headdress
leggings	sombrero	billycock	headpiece
lingerie	squirrel	blue jeans	head scarf
mantelet	stocking	bowler hat	helmet cap
mantilla	straw-hat	brassière	high heels
material	sundress	bush shirt	hoop skirt
			horsehair

9	9	10	10
house coat	sack dress	angelus cap	fascinator
inverness	safety-pin	angora wool	feather boa
jack-boots	sailcloth	ankle socks	flying suit
jockey cap	sailor cap	baby bonnet	fustanella
juliet cap	sailor-hat	balbriggan	gold thread
kid gloves	sanbenito	ballet shoe	grass cloth
knee socks	satinette	basic dress	grass skirt
lambswool	school cap	bathing cap	halterneck
loincloth	scoop neck	beaverteen	hop sacking
long dress	separates	bellboy cap	horsecloth
long skirt	sheepskin	blouse coat	Irish linen
long socks	shower cap	broadcloth	jersey silk
mini-skirt	silk serge	bobbin lace	jersey wool
millinery	silver fox	bobby socks	jigger coat
moccasins	sloppy joe	boiler suit	khaki drill
moiré silk	snakeskin	bush jacket	lounge suit
night-gown	snowshoes	buttonhole	lumberjack
night-wear	spun rayon	canvas shoe	mackintosh
off-the-peg	stockinet	cape collar	mess jacket
outer wear	stockings	chatelaine	middy skirt
overdress	strapless	chemisette	mock velvet
overshirt	suede coat	chinchilla	mousseline
overshoes	sunbonnet	coolie coat	needlecord
overskirt	swansdown	court dress	night-dress
panama hat	sweat band	court shoes	night-shirt
pantalets	sword-belt	coverchief	opera cloak
panty hose	tarpaulin	crepe soles	overblouse
patchwork	tent dress	cricket cap	Oxford bags
peaked cap	thigh boot	cummerbund	pantaloons
petersham	towelling	dance dress	party dress
petticoat	tracksuit	dinner suit	picture hat
pixie hood	trilby hat	diving suit	pinstripes
plimsolls	trousseau	drainpipes	pith helmet
plus fours	underwear	dress shirt	plastic mac
point lace	velveteen	dress shoes	poke bonnet
polyester	vestments	duffel coat	port-pie hat
press stud	waistband	embroidery	print dress
quaker hat	waistcoat	espadrille	sailor suit
redingote	wedge heel	Eton collar	seersucker
round neck	witch's hat	Eton jacket	service cap
sackcloth	wristband	fancy dress	shirtwaist

10

shoe buckle
shoestring
slingbacks
sports coat
sportswear
string vest
suspenders
sweatshirt
three-piece
thrown silk
trench coat
turtle neck
underpants
underskirt
waterproof
winceyette
windjammer
Windsor tie
wing-collar
wrap-around

11

Aran sweater
baby flannel
ballet shoes
bathing-suit
battle-dress
bedford cord
bellbottoms
bib and brace
black patent
bomber cloth
brushed wool
can-can dress
candy-stripe
canvas shoes
cap and bells
cavalier hat
cheesecloth
clodhoppers
cloth-of-gold

11

cowboy boots
crash helmet
dancing clog
deerstalker
dinner dress
dirndl skirt
Dolly Varden
dreadnought
du-pont rayon
espadrilles
evening gown
evening slip
farthingale
flannelette
flared skirt
football cap
formal dress
hand-me-downs
Harris tweed
herringbone
Honiton lace
hostess gown
Irish poplin
Kendal green
leather coat
leatherette
leopardskin
morning coat
morning suit
mortarboard
neckerchief
Norfolk suit
overgarment
panty girdle
Persian lamb
ready-to-wear
riding habit
rubber apron
running shoe
Russian boot
scotch plaid

11

shoe leather
shoulder bag
slumberwear
stiff collar
stockinette
string glove
suede jacket
swagger coat
tam o'shanter
tennis dress
tennis skirt
trouser suit
Tyrolean hat
undergirdle
underthings
watered silk
wedding gown
wedding veil
wellingtons
widow's weeds
windbreaker
windcheater
yachting cap

12

baseball boot
bathing dress
battle jacket
billycock hat
body stocking
bolting cloth
brushed rayon
business suit
cavalry twill
chastity belt
chemise dress
chemise frock
chesterfield
college scarf
cotton velvet
crêpe-de-chine

12

dinner-jacket
divided skirt
donkey jacket
dress clothes
dressing-gown
Easter bonnet
evening dress
evening shoes
evening skirt
football boot
handkerchief
Indian cotton
knee-breeches
leather skirt
lounging robe
lumber-jacket
mandarin coat
monkey-jacket
morning dress
plain clothes
pleated skirt
Quaker bonnet
roll-on girdle
service dress
shetland wool
shirtwaister
sleeping suit
slipper satin
sports jacket
tailored suit
ten-gallon hat
underclothes
undergarment
wedding dress
welsh flannel

13

bellboy jacket
Bermuda shorts
cashmere shawl
Chantilly lace

13

chinchilla fur
combing jacket
cotton flannel
cotton worsted
crushed velvet
football scarf

13

football shirt
Hawaiian skirt
leather jacket
mother hubbard
Norfolk jacket
patent leather

13

pinafore dress
platform soles
Russia leather
Sam Browne belt
smoking jacket

13

sports clothes
suspender belt
swaddling band
teddy-bear coat
underclothing

14

afternoon dress
artificial silk
bathing-costume
chamois leather
dressing jacket
Egyptian cotton
Egyptian sandal
evening sweater
Fair Isle jumper
knickerbockers

14

riding breeches
Shetland jumper
shooting jacket

15

cardigan sweater
Fair Isle sweater
ostrich feathers
parachute fabric
tropical suiting

16

broderie anglaise
candlewick fabric
going-away costume
swaddling clothes

17

confirmation dress
foundation garment
swallow-tailed coat

Clouds

6

cirrus
nimbus

11

altocumulus
altostratus

12

cumulonimbus
nimbostratus

7

cumulus
stratus

12

cirrocumulus
cirrostratus

13

stratocumulus

Coins and currency

2

as
at
xu

3

ban
bit

3

bob
cob
dam
ecu
far
kip
lat

3

lek
leu
lev
mil
mna
ore
pie

3

pul
pya
ree
rei
sen
sho
sol

3	4	5	6
sou	rand	medio	bawbee
won	real	mohar	bezart
yen	rial	mohur	bupiah
	riel	mongo	condor
4	ryal	naira	copang
anna	tael	ngwee	copeck
baht	taka	noble	copper
beka	unik	obang	dalasi
biga	yuan	paisa	decime
birr		paolo	dirham
buck	**5**	pence	doblon
cash	agora	pengo	dollar
cedi	angel	penni	escudo
cent	asper	penny	filler
chon	belga	plack	florin
daum	betso	pound	forint
dime	broad	qursy	fourte
doit	butut	riyal	gourde
dong	colon	rupee	guinea
fils	conto	sceat	gulden
inti	copec	scudi	heller
jeon	crown	scudo	kopeck
joey	daric	semis	koruna
kobo	dinar	soldo	kwacha
kran	ducat	stica	lepton
kyat	eagle	styca	likuta
lira	eyrir	sucre	makuta
mail	franc	sycee	markka
mark	groat	thebe	monkey
merk	grosz	tical	nickel
mite	krona	toman	pagode
obol	krone	uncia	peseta
para	kroon	unite	pesewa
peag	kurus	zaïre	poisha
peso	leone	zloty	qintar
pice	liard		rouble
pony	libra	**6**	sceatt
pula	litas	amania	sequin
puls	livre	aureus	shekel
pyas	locho	balboa	stangs
quid	louis	baubee	stater

6

stiver
talari
talent
tanner
tester
teston
thaler
tomaun
tugrik
zechin

7

afghani
angelot
austral
bolivar
carolus
centava
centavo
centime
centimo
cordoba
cruzado
denarii
drachma
guarani
guilder

7

halalas
jacobus
lempira
milreis
moidore
ngusang
pfennig
piastre
pistole
quarter
quetzal
sextans
stooter
tambala
testoon
unicorn

8

ambrosin
cruzeiro
denarius
didrachm
doubloon
ducatoon
farthing
florence
groschen

8

johannes
kreutzer
louis d'or
maravedi
millieme
napoleon
new pence
new penny
picayune
quetzale
sesterce
shilling
sixpence
stotinki

9

boliviano
centesimo
cuartillo
didrachma
dupondius
gold broad
gold noble
gold penny
half-crown
halfpenny
pistareen

9

pound coin
rix-dollar
rose-noble
schilling
sestertia
sestertii
sovereign
spur royal
yellow boy

10

easterling
first brass
gold stater
half-guinea
quadrussis
sestertium
sestertius
silverling
stour-royal
tripondius
venezolano

11

Deutschmark
karbovanets
silver penny
spade guinea

12

Deutsche Mark
mill sixpence
one-pound coin
one-pound note
silver stater
ten-pound note
tetradrachma
tribute penny

13

five-pound note
franc malgache
half sovereign
ten-pence piece
threepenny bit
twopenny piece
two-pound piece

14

fifty-pound note
five pence piece
Hong Kong dollar

15

threepenny piece
twenty-pound note

16

twenty pence piece

Collective names and group terms

apes (shrewdness)
asses (herd; pace)
baboons (troop)
badgers (cete)
bears (sloth)
bees (erst; swarm)
birds (flock)
bishops (bench)
bison (herd)
bitterns (sedge)
boars (sounder)
buffaloes (herd)
caterpillars (army)
cattle (drove; herd)
choughs (chattering)
colts (rag)
coots (covert)
cranes (herd)
crows (murder)
deer (herd)
dogs (kennel)
doves (flight)
ducks (paddling)
elephants (herd)
elk (gang)
ferrets (business)
fish (shoal)
flies (swarm)
foxes (skulk)
geese (gaggle; skein)
giraffes (herd)
goats (herd; tribe)
goldfinches (charm)
grouse (covey; pack)
gulls (colony)
hares (down; husk)
hens (brood)
herons (sedge; siege)
horses (harras; stable; stud)

hounds (mute; pack)
hunters (blast)
kangaroos (troop)
kittens (kindle; litter)
lapwings (desert)
larks (exaltation)
leopards (leap; lepe)
lions (pride; sawt; souse; troop)
locusts (swarm)
magpies (tittering)
mallards (sord; sute)
mares (stud)
martens (richesse)
mice (nest)
moles (labour)
monkeys (troop)
mules (barren; span)
nightingales (watch)
owls (parliament; stare)
oxen (herd; yoke)
partridges (covey)
peacocks (muster)
pigeons (flight; flock)
pigs (herd; litter)
plovers (wing)
porpoises (school)
pups (litter)
rabbits (bury; nest)
racehorses (string)
rhinoceros (crash)
rooks (building; clamour)
sheep (flock)
snipe (wisp)
starlings (murmuration)
swine (doylt; sounder)
teal (spring)
trout (hover)
turkeys (rafter)
wasps (nest)

whales (school)
whiting (pod)
widgeon (company; knob)
wildfowl (plump; sord; sute)

witches (coven)
wolves (pack; rout)
woodcocks (fall)
woodpeckers (descent)

Colours, dyes and paints

3	5	5	6
dun	amber	peach	lac dye
hue	ashen	pearl	litmus
jet	azure	prune	madder
red	basic	rouge	maroon
tan	beige	ruddy	motley
	black	sable	orange
4	blond	sandy	oyster
anil	brown	snowy	pastel
blue	camel	sooty	pearly
buff	capri	taupe	purple
ecru	cocoa	tawny	raisin
fast	coral	white	rubric
fawn	cream		russet
gilt	delft	**6**	sallow
gold	ebony	auburn	salmon
grey	flame	bistre	sanded
hoar	flesh	blonde	shrimp
jade	grain	bluish	sienna
kohl	green	bronze	silver
lake	hazel	cerise	sorrel
navy	henna	cherry	spotty
pale	hoary	chrome	titian
pink	ivory	citron	vermil
plum	khaki	claret	violet
puce	lemon	cobalt	yellow
roan	light	copper	
rose	lilac	damask	**7**
ruby	livid	enamel	apricot
rust	maize	flaxen	aureate
sage	mauve	garnet	biscuit
sand	ochre	ginger	caramel
	olive	golden	carmine
	paint	indigo	carroty
		jasper	

7	7	8	9
catechu	tea rose	oak stain	Delft blue
crimson	tile red	ochreous	double dye
cyanine	verdant	off-white	draconine
darkish	whitish	pea green	duck green
emerald	xanthic	pistache	Dutch pink
filbert		poppy red	dusty pink
filemot	**8**	primrose	dyer's weed
flavine	absinthe	purplish	dye-stuffs
fuchsia	alizarin	rose-hued	euchloric
fulvous	amaranth	rubrical	flesh pink
greyish	amethyst	sanguine	green-blue
grizzle	baby blue	sapphire	harlequin
heather	baby pink	saxe blue	indian red
ingrain	burgundy	sea green	jade green
jacinth	capucine	shagreen	kalsomine
magenta	cardinal	speckled	lamp-black
mordant	carotene	spectrum	leaf green
mottled	chestnut	streaked	lily-white
mustard	cinnabar	titanium	moonstone
nacarat	cinnamon	viridian	moss green
nankeen	croceate	xanthine	Nile green
natural	croceous	xanthium	oil colour
neutral	cyclamen		oxidation
old gold	disperse	**9**	parchment
old rose	eau de nil	alizarine	pearl grey
piebald	eggshell	aubergine	prasinous
pigment	glaucous	azure blue	raspberry
pinkish	greenish	azure tint	royal blue
reddish	grizzled	blue-green	safflower
red lead	gun metal	brilliant	sage green
ruby red	hyacinth	cadet blue	sallowish
saffron	iron grey	cadet grey	santaline
scarlet	jet black	carnation	sapan wood
sea blue	lavender	carnelian	saxon blue
silvery	litharge	champagne	snow-white
sky blue	mahogany	chocolate	steel blue
solvent	mazarine	cochineal	tangerine
spotted	mole grey	colour box	tomato red
streaky	mulberry	columbine	Turkey red
striped	navy blue	coralline	turquoise
sulphur	nut brown	developer	verdigris

9
vermilion
virescent
white lead
yellowish

10
apple green
aquamarine
auriferous
body colour
bois-de-rose
braziletto
burnt umber
cobalt blue
double-dyed
ensign blue
erubescent
flavescent
florentine
French navy
heliotrope
indigo blue
indigotine
marina blue
mosaic gold
olive green

10
Oxford blue
petrol blue
powder blue
salmon pink
strawberry
terracotta

11
aerial tints
ash-coloured
bottle green
burnt almond
burnt orange
burnt sienna
cardinal red
cinnamon red
crimson lake
flame colour
flesh colour
fluorescent
forest green
hunter's pink
lemon yellow
neutral tint
peacock blue
ultramarine

11
Venetian red
walnut brown
yellow ochre

12
airforce blue
canary yellow
castilian red
Egyptian blue
electric blue
emerald green
feuillemorte
golden yellow
hunter's green
hyacinth blue
Lincoln green
midnight blue
pillar-box red
Prussian blue
rose-coloured
sapphire blue
Tyrian purple
verdant green
wedgwood blue

13
Cambridge blue
chestnut brown
flame-coloured
flesh-coloured
mother of pearl
multicoloured
pepper and salt
primary colour
tortoiseshell
rainbow-tinted
turquoise blue

14
Brunswick black
Brunswick green
heather mixture
periwinkle blue
turquoise green

15
Caledonian
  brown
chartreuse green
secondary colour

16
chartreuse yellow

Composers

3
Bax, Sir Arnold
Sor, Fernando

4
Adam, Adolphe
Arne, Thomas
Bach, Carl Philipp Emanuel
Bach, Johann Christian
Bach, Johann Sebastian

4
Berg, Alban
Blow, John
Bull, John
Bush, Alan Dudley
Byrd, William
Cage, John
Ives, Charles
Lalo, Edouard
Nono, Luigi

4

Orff, Carl
Wolf, Hugo

5

Alkan, Charles
Auber, Daniel
Auric, Georges
Berio, Luciano
Bizet, Georges
Bliss, Sir Arthur
Bloch, Ernest
Boyce, William
Brian, Havergal
Bruch, Max
D'Indy, Vincent
Dufay, Guillaume
Dukas, Paul
Dupré, Marcel
Elgar, Sir Edward
Falla, Manuel de
Fauré, Gabriel
Field, John
Friml, Rudolph
Glass, Philip
Gluck, Christoph Willibald
Grieg, Edvard
Haydn, (Franz) Joseph
Henze, Hans Werner
Holst, Gustav
Ibert, Jacques
Lehar, Franz
Liszt, Franz
Locke, Matthew
Lully, Jean Baptiste
Parry, Sir Hubert
Ravel, Maurice
Reger, Max
Satie, Erik
Smyth, Dame Ethel
Sousa, John Philip
Spohr, Louis

5

Verdi, Giuseppe
Weber, Carl Maria von
Weill, Kurt
Widor, Charles Marie

6

Arnold, Malcolm
Barber, Samuel
Bartok, Bela
Berlin, Irving
Bishop, Sir Henry
Boulez, Pierre
Brahms, Johannes
Bridge, Frank
Burney, Charles
Busoni, Ferruccio
Carter, Elliott
Casals, Pablo
Chopin, Frederic
Clarke, Jeremiah
Cowell, Henry
Davies, Sir Peter Maxwell
Delius, Frederick
Dibdin, Charles
Duparc, Henri
Dvořák, Antonin
Enesco, Georges
Flotow, Friedrich von
Franck, César Auguste
Gounod, Charles
Grétry, André
Halévy, Jacques
Handel, George Frederick
Harris, Roy
Hummel, Johann Nepomuk
Joplin, Scott
Kodály, Zoltán
Krenek, Ernst
Lassus, Roland de
Ligeti, Gyorgy
Mahler, Gustav

6

Morley, Thomas
Mozart, Wolfgang Amadeus
Porter, Cole
Previn, André
Rameau, Jean Philippe
Rubbra, Edmund
Schütz, Heinrich
Tallis, Thomas
Varese, Edgard
Wagner, Richard
Walton, Sir William

7

Albéniz, Isaac
Allegri, Gregorio
Antheil, George
Babbitt, Milton
Bellini, Vincenzo
Bennett, Richard Rodney
Berlioz, Hector
Borodin, Aleksandr
  Porfirevich
Britten, Benjamin
Caccini, Giulio
Campion, Thomas
Cavalli, Francesco
Copland, Aaron
Corelli, Arcangelo
Debussy, Claude
Delibes, Leo
Dowland, John
Farnaby, Giles
Galuppi, Baldassare
Gibbons, Orlando
Górecki, Henryk
Ireland, John
Janácek, Leos
Joachim, Joseph
Lambert, Constant
Litolff, Henry
Martinu, Bohuslav
Menotti, Gian Carlo

7

Milhaud, Darius
Nicolai, Otto
Nielsen, Carl
Okeghem, Jean d'
Poulenc, Francis
Puccini, Giacomo
Purcell, Henry
Rodrigo, Joaquín
Rossini, Gioacchino
Roussel, Albert
Ruggles, Carl
Salieri, Antonio
Schuman, William
Smetana, Bedrich
Stainer, Sir John
Stamitz, Johann
Strauss, Johann
Strauss, Richard
Tavener, John
Thomson, Virgil
Tippett, Sir Michael
Vivaldi, Antonio
Warlock, Peter
Webern, Anton
Weelkes, Thomas
Wellesz, Egon
Xenakis, Yannis

8

Albinoni, Tomaso
Berkeley, Sir Lennox
Bruckner, (Josef) Anton
Chabrier, Emmanuel
Chausson, Ernest
Cimarosa, Domenico
Clementi, Muzio
Couperin, François
Dohnányi, Erno
Gershwin, George
Gesualdo, Carlo
Glazunov, Aleksandr
  Konstantinovich

8

Goossens, Sir Eugene
Grainger, Percy
Granados, Enrique
Honegger, Arthur
Maconchy, Elizabeth
Marenzio, Luca
Mascagni, Pietro
Massenet, Jules
Messager, André
Messiaen, Olivier
Musgrave, Thea
Paganini, Niccolò
Respighi, Ottorino
Schubert, Franz
Schumann, Robert
Scriabin, Aleksandr
Sessions, Roger
Sibelius, Jean
Stanford, Sir Charles
Sullivan, Sir Arthur
Taverner, John
Telemann, Georg Philipp
Victoria, Tomas Luis de

9

Addinsell, Richard
Balakirev, Mily Alekseevich
Beethoven, Ludwig van
Bernstein, Leonard
Buxtehude, Dietrich
Cherubini, Luigi
Donizetti, Gaetano
Dunstable, John
Hindemith, Paul
Hoddinott, Alun
Malipiero, Gian Francesco
Meyerbeer, Giacomo
Offenbach, Jacques
Pachelbel, Johann
Pergolesi, Giovanni
Prokofiev, Sergei

9

Scarlatti, Alessandro
Scarlatti, Domenico

10

Birtwistle, Harrison
Boccherini, Luigi
Monteverdi, Claudio
Mussorgski, Modest Petrovich
Paderewski, Ignacy
Palestrina, Giovanni da
Penderecki, Krzysztof
Praetorius, Michael
Rawsthorne, Alan
Rubinstein, Anton
Saint-Saëns, Camille
Schoenberg, Arnold
Skalkottas, Nikos
Stravinsky, Igor
Villa-Lobos, Heitor

11

Charpentier, Gustave
Humperdinck, Engelbert
Leoncavallo, Ruggiero
Lloyd Webber, Sir Andrew
Lutoslawski, Witold
Mendelssohn, Felix
Rachmaninov, Sergei
Stockhausen, Karlheinz
Szymanowski, Karol
Tchaikovsky, Peter Ilich
Wolf-ferrari, Ermanno

12

Dallapiccola, Luigi
Khachaturian, Aram Ilich
Shostakovich, Dmitri

13

Rouget de Lisle, Claude

14	15
Josquin Des Prez	Vaughan Williams, Ralph
Rimsky-Korsakov, Nikolai	
	17
15	Strauss the Younger, Johann
Coleridge-Taylor, Samuel	
Jacques-Dalcroze, Emile	

Computer language

1	5	7	10
C	ALGOL	MACLISP	transputer
K	basic	network	vacuum tube
	chill	program	
3	clear	prestel	11
ADA	COBOL	scanner	spreadsheet
AED	COMAL		work station
APL	CORAL	8	
AWK	forth	databank	12
bit	KAPSE	database	minicomputer
CPL	MOHLL	hard disk	user-friendly
CSL	mossa	keying-in	
IAL	mouse	resistor	13
LEX		software	bulletin board
POL	6	terminal	microcomputer
POP	analog	videotex	relay switches
RAM	edison		semiconductor
ROM	hacker	9	
RPG	jovial	character	14
VDT	memory	conductor	electronic mail
VDU	modula	FRANZLISP	microprocessor
	pascal	hard-wired	
4	PROLOG	laser disk	15
BCPL	screen	mainframe	digital computer
byte	simula	mircrochip	
chip	SNOBOL	smalltalk	16
data			voice recognition
disk	7	10	
FRED	archive	binary code	22
ikon	babbage	electronic	artificial
lisp	circuit	floppy disk	intelligence
logo	fortran	transistor	
REXX			
YACC			

Conductors

4	6	8
Böhm, Karl	Rattle, Simon	Ansermet, Ernest
Orff, Carl	Walter, Bruno	Goossens, Sir Eugene
Wood, Sir Henry		Messager, André

7

Beecham, Sir Thomas

5

Boult, Sir Adrian
Bülow, Hans Guido
 von
Davis, Sir Colin
Halle, Sir Charles
Munch, Charles
Solti, Sir Georg

6

Bishop, Sir Henry
 Rowley
Boulez, Pierre
Casals, Pablo
Cortot, Alfred
Groves, Sir Charles
Jochum, Eugen
Maazel, Lorin
Mahler, Gustav
Previn, André

7

Beecham, Sir Thomas
Berlioz, Hector
Giulini, Carlo Maria
Karajan, Herbert von
Kubelik, Rafael
Lambert, Constant
Monteux, Pierre
Nicolai, Otto
 Ehrenfried
Nielsen, Carl
Nikisch, Arthur
Ormandy, Eugene
Richter, Hans
Salieri, Antonio
Sargent, Sir Malcolm
Strauss, Richard
Thomson, Virgil

9

Ashkenazy, Vladimir
Barenboim, Daniel
Bernstein, Leonard
Boulanger, Nadia
Klemperer, Otto
Mackerras, Sir Charles
Stokowski, Leopald
Toscanini, Arturo

10

Barbirolli, Sir John
Mengelberg, William
Saint-Saëns, Camille

11

Furtwängler, Wilhelm
Rachmaninov, Sergei

17

Strauss the Younger,
 Johann

Cookery terms

3	4	4	5
fry	bone	peel	baste
	chop	pipe	blend
4	coat	rare	broil
bake	hang	stew	brown
bard	hash	stir	carve
beat	lard	toss	chill
boil	pare	trim	cream

5	5	6	8
daube	steam	simmer	marinate
drain	stuff	strain	pot roast
dress	sweat		
flute	truss	7	9
glaze		al dente	fricassee
grill	6	clarify	
knead	blanch	garnish	10
pluck	braise	parboil	blanquette
poach	fillet	stir-fry	chaudfroid
prove	flambé	supreme	cordon bleu
purée	fold in		
roast	fondue	8	11
rub-in	gratin	barbecue	belle hélène
sauté	grease	chasseur	bourguignon
scald	infuse	devilled	hollandaise
score	reduce	escalope	
slice		macerate	13
		marinade	deep fat frying

Counties — England

(* = former counties)	**Administrative centres**
4	
Avon	Bristol
Kent	Maidstone
5	
Devon	Exeter
Essex	Chelmsford
Salop	Shrewsbury
6	
Dorset	Dorchester
Durham	Durham
Surrey	Kingston-upon-Thames
*Sussex	Lewes
7	
Cumbria	Carlisle
Norfolk	Norwich

7	**Administrative centres**
*Rutland	Oakham
Suffolk	Ipswich

8	
Cheshire	Chester
Cornwall	Truro
Somerset	Taunton

9	
Berkshire	Reading
Cleveland	Middlesbrough
Hampshire	Winchester
Wiltshire	Trowbridge
*Yorkshire	York

10	
*Cumberland	Carlisle
Derbyshire	Matlock
East Sussex	Lewes
Humberside	Beverley
Lancashire	Preston
Merseyside	Liverpool
Shropshire	Shrewsbury
West Sussex	Chichester

11	
Isle of Wight	Newport
Oxfordshire	Oxford
Tyne and Wear	Newcastle upon Tyne
*Westmorland	Kendal

12	
Bedfordshire	Bedford
Lincolnshire	Lincoln
Warwickshire	Warwick
West Midlands	Birmingham

13	
*Herefordshire	Hereford
Hertfordshire	Hertford
Staffordshire	Stafford
West Yorkshire	Wakefield

14	**Administrative centres**
Cambridgeshire	Cambridge
Leicestershire	Leicester
Northumberland	Morpeth
North Yorkshire	Northallerton
South Yorkshire	Barnsley
*Worcestershire	Worcester

15	
Buckinghamshire	Aylesbury
Gloucestershire	Gloucester
*Huntingdonshire	Huntingdon
Nottinghamshire	Nottingham

16	
Northamptonshire	Northampton

17	
Greater Manchester	Manchester

20	
Hereford and Worcester	Worcester

Counties — Northern Ireland

4	**County towns**
Down	Downpatrick

6	
Antrim	Belfast
Armagh	Armagh
Tyrone	Omagh

9	
Fermanagh	Enniskillen

11	
Londonderry	Londonderry

Counties — Republic of Ireland

4	5	7	8
Cork	Meath	Donegal	Limerick
Mayo	Sligo	Kildare	Longford
Leix		Leitrim	Monaghan
	6	Wexford	
5	Carlow	Wicklow	**9**
Cavan	Dublin		Roscommon
Clare	Galway	**8**	Tipperary
Kerry	Offaly	Kilkenny	Waterford
Louth		Laoighis (= Leix)	Westmeath

Provinces

6	7	8
Ulster	Munster	Connacht
		Leinster

Counties and regions — Scotland

(*former counties — most may have shire added to their names)

3	**Administrative centres**
Ayr	Ayr

4	
*Bute	Rothesay
Fife	Glenrothes

5	
*Angus	Forfar
*Banff	Banff
*Moray	Elgin
*Nairn	Nairn
*Perth	Perth

6	
*Argyll	Lochgilphead
*Lanark	Hamilton
Orkney	Kirkwall

7	**Administrative centres**
*Berwick	Duns
Borders	Newton St Boswells
Central	Stirling
*Kinross	Kinross
Lothian	Edinburgh
*Peebles	Peebles
*Renfrew	Paisley
*Selkirk	Selkirk
Tayside	Dundee
*Wigtown	Stranraer
Zetland	Lerwick

8	
*Aberdeen	Aberdeen
*Dumfries	Dumfries
Grampian	Aberdeen
Highland	Inverness
*Roxburgh	Newton St Boswells
Shetland	Lerwick
Stirling	Stirling

9	
*Caithness	Wick
*Dumbarton	Dumbarton
*Inverness	Inverness

10	
*Kincardine	Stonehaven
*Midlothian	Edinburgh
*Sutherland	Golspie

11	
*Clackmannan	Alloa
*East Lothian	Haddington
Strathclyde	Glasgow
*West Lothian	Linlithgow

12	
Western Isles	Stornoway

13	**Administrative centres**
*Kirkcudbright	Kirkcudbright

15	
*Ross and Cromarty	Dingwall

19	
Dumfries and Galloway	Dumfries

Counties — Wales

(* = former counties)

5	**Administrative centres**
Clwyd	Mold
Dyfed	Carmarthen
Gwent	Cwmbran
Powys	Llandrindod Wells

7	
Gwynedd	Caernarfon

8	
*Anglesey	Llangefni

9	
*Glamorgan	Cardiff
*Merioneth	Dolgellau

10	
*Flintshire	Mold

11	
*Breconshire	Brecon
*Radnorshire	Llandrindod Wells

12	
*Denbighshire	Ruthin
Mid Glamorgan	Cardiff

13	**Administrative centres**
*Cardiganshire	Aberystwyth
*Monmouthshire	Newport
*Pembrokeshire	Haverfordwest
West Glamorgan	Swansea

14	
South Glamorgan	Cardiff

15	
*Caernarvonshire	Caernarvon
*Carmarthenshire	Carmarthen
*Montgomeryshire	Welshpool

Countries of the world

	Capital
4	
Chad	N'Djamena
Cuba	Havana
Fiji	Suva
Iran	Tehran
Iraq	Baghdad
Laos	Vientiane
Mali	Bamako
Oman	Muscat
Peru	Lima
Togo	Lomé
5	
Benin	Porto-Novo
Burma	Rangoon
Chile	Santiago
China	Peking
Congo	Brazzaville
Egypt	Cairo
Gabon	Libreville
Ghana	Accra
Haiti	Port-au-Prince
India	New Delhi
Italy	Rome

5	**Capital**
Japan	Tokyo
Kenya	Nairobi
Libya	Tripoli
Malta	Valletta
Nepal	Katmandu
Niger	Niamey
Qatar	Doha
Spain	Madrid
Sudan	Khartoum
Syria	Damascus
Tonga	Nuku'alofa
Yemen	Sana'a
Zaïre	Kinshasa

6	
Angola	Luanda
Belize	Belmopan
Bhutan	Thimphu
Bosnia	Sarajevo
Brazil	Brasília
Brunei	Bandar Seri Begawan
Canada	Ottawa
Cyprus	Nicosia
France	Paris
Gambia (The)	Banjul
Greece	Athens
Guinea	Conakry
Guyana	Georgetown
Israel	Jerusalem
Jordan	Amman
Kuwait	Kuwait City
Latvia	Riga
Malawi	Lilongwe
Mexico	Mexico City
Monaco	Monaco-Ville
Norway	Oslo
Panama	Panama City
Poland	Warsaw
Russia	Moscow
Rwanda	Kigali
Sweden	Stockholm

6	Capital
Taiwan	Taipei
Turkey	Ankara
Tuvalu	Funafuti
Uganda	Kampala
Zambia	Lusaka

7	
Albania	Tirana
Algeria	Algiers
Andorra	Andorra la Vella
Antigua	St John City
Armenia	Yerevan
Austria	Vienna
Bahamas	Nassau
Bahrain	Manama
Belarus	Minsk
Belgium	Brussels
Bolivia	La Paz
Burundi	Bujumbura
Comoros	Moroni
Croatia	Zagreb
Denmark	Copenhagen
Ecuador	Quito
Eritrea	Asmara
Estonia	Tallinn
Finland	Helsinki
Georgia	Tbilisi
Germany	Bonn/Berlin
Grenada	St George's
Hungary	Budapest
Iceland	Reykjavik
Ireland	Dublin
Jamaica	Kingston
Lebanon	Beirut
Lesotho	Maseru
Liberia	Monrovia
Moldova	Chisinau
Morocco	Rabat
Nigeria	Abuja
Romania	Bucharest
St Lucia	Castries

7	**Capital**
Senegal	Dakar
Somalia	Mogadishu
Tunisia	Tunis
Uruguay	Montevideo
Ukraine	Kiev
Vanuatu	Vila
Vietnam	Hanoi

8	
Barbados	Bridgetown
Botswana	Gaborone
Bulgaria	Sofia
Cambodia	Phnom-Penh
Cameroon	Yaoundé
Colombia	Bogotá
Djibouti	Djibouti
Dominica	Roseau
Ethiopia	Addis Ababa
Honduras	Tegucigalpa
Hong Kong	Victoria
Kiribati	Tarawa
Malaysia	Kuala Lumpur
Maldives	Malé
Mongolia	Ulan Bator
Pakistan	Islamabad
Paraguay	Asunción
Portugal	Lisbon
Slovakia	Bratislava
Slovenia	Ljubljana
Sri Lanka	Colombo
Suriname	Paramaribo
Tanzania	Dodoma
Thailand	Bangkok
Zimbabwe	Harare

9	
Argentina	Buenos Aires
Australia	Canberra
Cape Verde	Praia
Costa Rica	San José
Guatemala	Guatemala City

9	**Capital**
Indonesia	Jakarta
Lithuania	Vilnius
Macedonia	Skoplje
Mauritius	Port Louis
Nicaragua	Managua
San Marino	San Marino
Singapore	Singapore City
Swaziland	Mbabane
Venezuela	Caracas

10	
Azerbaijan	Baku
Bangladesh	Dhaka
El Salvador	San Salvador
Ivory Coast	Abidjan/Yamoussoukro
Kazakhstan	Alma-Ata
Kyrgyzstan	Bishkek
Luxembourg	Luxembourg-Ville
Madagascar	Antananarivo
Mauritania	Nouakchott
Mozambique	Maputo
New Zealand	Wellington
North Korea	Pyongyang
Seychelles	Victoria
South Korea	Seoul
Tajikistan	Dushanbe
Uzbekistan	Tashkent
Yugoslavia	Belgrade

11	
Afghanistan	Kabul
Burkina Faso	Ouagadougou
Côte D'Ivoire	Yamoussoukro
Netherlands (The)	Amsterdam
Philippines (The)	Manila
Saudi Arabia	Riyadh
Sierra Leone	Freetown
South Africa	Pretoria
Switzerland	Berne

12	**Capital**
Guinea-Bissau	Bissau
Turkmenistan	Ashkhabad
Western Samoa	Apia

13	
Czech Republic	Prague
Liechtenstein	Vaduz
United Kingdom	London

14	
Papua New Guinea	Port Moresby
Solomon Islands	Honiara

15	
St Kitts and Nevis	Basseterre

16	
Equatorial Guinea	Malabo

17	
Dominican Republic	Santo Domingo
Trinidad and Tobago	Port of Spain

18	
São Tomé and Principe	São Tomé
United Arab Emirates	Abu Dhabi

21	
United States of America	Washington DC

22	
Central African Republic	Bangui

25	
St Vincent and the Grenadines	Kingstown

Dances

3	6	8	10
bop	can-can	habanera	strathspey
dog	cha-cha	hand-jive	striptease
gig	chasse	hornpipe	sword dance
hop	maxina	hula-hula	tarantella
jig	minuet	rigadoon	torch-dance
	morris	saraband	turkey-trot
4	pavane	tap-dance	
bump	shimmy		11
jive	valeta	9	floral dance
jota		arabesque	Lambeth walk
pogo	7	barn dance	morris dance
reel	beguine	bossa nova	palais glide
	bourrée	cha-cha-cha	rock and roll
5	csardas	clog dance	schottische
bebop	fox-trot	cotillion	slow fox-trot
caper	gavotte	ecossaise	square dance
conga	lancers	farandole	square tango
fling	landler	folk dance	varsovienne
galop	madison	horn dance	
gavot	maypole	jitterbug	12
gigue	mazurka	paso doble	breakdancing
limbo	measure	Paul Jones	country dance
mambo	morisco	pirouette	
polka	one-step	polonaise	13
rondo	planxty	poussette	eightsome reel
rumba	two-step	quadrille	Highland fling
samba		quickstep	
shake	8	rock'n'roll	15
stomp	bunny-hug		military two-step
tango	cachucha	10	St Bernard's
twist	cakewalk	Boston reel	waltz
valse	chaconne	Charleston	
waltz	cotillon	furry dance	18
	courante	Gay Gordons	Sir Roger de
6	danseuse	hokey-cokey	Coverley
bolero	fandango	locomotion	
boogie	galliard	saltarello	

Decorations and medals (in descending order)

VC	Victoria Cross
GC	George Cross
KG	Knight of the Most Noble Order of the Garter
KT	Knight of the Most Ancient and Most Noble Order of the Thistle
GCB	Knight Grand Cross of the Most Honourable Order of the Bath
OM	Member of the Order of Merit
GCMG	Knight/Dame Grand Cross of the Most Distinguished Order of St Michael and St George
GCVO	Knight/Dame Grand Cross of the Royal Victorian Order
GBE	Knight/Dame Grand Cross of the Most Excellent Order of the British Empire
CH	Member of the Order of Companions of Honour
KCB	Knight Commander of the Most Honourable Order of the Bath
DCB	Dame Commander of the Most Honourable Order of the Bath
KCMG	Knight Commander of the Most Distinguished Order of St Michael and St George
DCMG	Dame Commander of the Most Distinguished Order of St Michael and St George
KCVO	Knight Commander of the Royal Victorian Order
DCVO	Dame Commander of the Royal Victorian Order
KBE	Knight Commander of the Most Excellent Order of the British Empire
DBE	Dame Commander of the Most Excellent Order of the British Empire
CB	Companion of the Most Honourable Order of the Bath
CMG	Companion of the Most Distinguished Order of St Michael and St George
CVO	Commander of the Royal Victorian Order
CBE	Commander of the Most Excellent Order of the British Empire
DSO	Companion of the Distinguished Service Order
LVO	Lieutenant of the Royal Victorian Order
OBE	Officer of the Most Excellent Order of the British Empire
ISO	Companion of the Imperial Service Order
MVO	Member of the Royal Victorian Order
MBE	Member of the Most Excellent Order of the British Empire
RRC	Member of the Royal Red Cross
DSC	Distinguished Service Cross

MC	Military Cross
DFC	Distinguished Flying Cross
AFC	Air Force Cross
ARRC	Associate of the Royal Red Cross
DCM	Distinguished Conduct Medal
CGM	Conspicuous Gallantry Medal
GM	George Medal
DSM	Distinguished Service Medal
MM	Military Medal
DFM	Distinguished Flying Medal
AFM	Air Force Medal
SGM	Medal for Saving Life at Sea (Sea Gallantry Medal)
CMP	Colonial Police Medal for Gallantry
QGM	Queen's Gallantry Medal
BEM	British Empire Medal

Deserts

4	6	7	10
Gobi	Mojave	Painted	Australian
Thar	Sahara	Simpson	Taklamakan
	Somali	Sonoran	
5	Syrian		**11**
Namib	Turfan	**8**	Death Valley
Negev		Colorado	
Nubia	**7**	Kalahari	**17**
Ordos	Arabian	Kyzyl Kum	Desierto de
Sinai	Atacama		Sechura
Sturt	Kara Kum	**9**	
		Dasht-E-Lut	

Dickens, Charles: books and their characters

Titles of books	Number of letters
(1) A Christmas Carol	15
(2) A Tale of Two Cities	16
(3) Barnaby Rudge	12
(4) Bleak House	10

Titles of books	Number of letters
(5) David Copperfield	16
(6) Dombey and Son	12
(7) Edwin Drood	10
(8) Great Expectations	17
(9) Hard Times	9
(10) Little Dorrit	12
(11) Martin Chuzzlewit	16
(12) Master Humphrey's Clock	20
(13) Nicholas Nickleby	16
(14) Oliver Twist	11
(15) Our Mutual Friend	15
(16) Pickwick Papers	14
(17) Sketches by Boz	13
(18) The Battle of Life	15
(19) The Chimes	9
(20) The Cricket on the Hearth	21
(21) The Haunted Man	13
(22) The Mudfog Papers	15
(23) The Old Curiosity Shop	19

Characters (number = book reference)

2

Jo (4)

3

Bet, Betsy (14)
Gay, Walter (6)
Jip, (Dog) (5)
Joe (16)
Tox, Miss (6)

4

Anne (6)
Baps (6)
Begs, Mrs Ridger (5)
Bray, Madeline/Walter (13)
Dick, Mr (5)
Fips, Mr (11)
Fogg (16)
Gamp, Mrs Sarah (11)
Grip (bird) (3)

4

Hawk, Sir Mulberry (13)
Heep, Uriah (5)
Hugh (3)
Jupe, Cecilia (9)
Knag, Miss (13)
Mary (16)
Mell, Charles (5)
Pell, Solomon (16)
Peps, Dr Parker (6)
Pott, Minerva (16)
Rugg, Anastasia (10)
Tigg, Montague (11)
Wade, Miss (10)
Wegg, Silas (15)

5

Bates, Charley (14)
Brass, Sally/Sampson (23)
Brick, Jefferson (11)

5

Brown, Alice/Mrs (6/17)
Casby, Christopher (10)
Chick, John/Louisa (6)
Clare, Ada (4)
Crupp, Mrs (5)
Daisy, Solomon (3)
Diver, Colonel (11)
Drood, Edwin (7)
Fagin (14)
Flite, Miss (4)
Giles (14)
Gills, Solomon (6)
Gowan, Harry (10)
Guppy, William (4)
Janet (5)
Krook (4)
Lobbs, Maria/'Old' (16)
Lorry, Jarvis (2)
Lupin, Mrs (11)
Miggs, Miss (3)
Mills, Julia (5)
Molly (8)
Mould (11)
Nancy (14)
Noggs, Newman (13)
Perch (6)
Pinch, Ruth/Tom (11)
Price, 'Tilda (13)
Pross, Miss/Solomon (2)
Quale (4)
Quilp, Daniel (23)
Rudge, Barnaby/Mary (3)
Scott, Tom (23)
Sikes, Bill (14)
Slyme, Chevy (11)
Smike (13)
Squod, Phil (4)
Toots, Mr P. (6)
Trent, Frederick/Nellie (23)
Twist, Oliver (14)
Venus, Mr (15)
Wosky, Dr (17)

6

Badger, Dr Bayham/Laura/Malta/
  Matthew/Quebec/Woolwich (4)
Bailey, Benjamin (11)
Bamber, Jack (16)
Bantam, Angelo Cyrus (16)
Barkis (5)
Barley, Clara (8)
Barney (14)
Bedwin, Mrs (14)
Bitzer (9)
Boffin, Henrietta/Nicodemus (15)
Briggs (6/17)
Bumble (14)
Bunsby, Captain (6)
Buzfuz, Sergeant (16)
Carker, Harriet/James/John (6)
Carton, Sydney (2)
Codlin, Thomas (23)
Corney, Mrs (14)
Cuttle, Captain Ned (6)
Darnay, Charles (2)
Dartle, Rosa (5)
Dennis, Ned (3)
Dodson (16)
Dombey, Fanny/Florence/Louisa/
  Paul (6)
Dorrit, Amy/Edward/Fanny/
  Frederick/William (10)
Dowler, Captain (16)
Fat Boy (16)
Feeder (6)
George, Mr (4)
Gordon, Lord George (3)
Graham, Mary (11)
Harmon, John (15)
Harris, Mrs (11)
Hawdon, Captain (4)
Jarley, Mrs (23)
Jingle, Alfred (16)
Lammle, Alfred (15)
Magnus, Peter (16)

6

Marley, Jacob (1)
Marton (23)
Maylie, Mrs/Rose (14)
Merdle, Mr (10)
Milvey, Rev. Frank (15)
Mivins (16)
Moddle, Augustus (11)
Mullet, Professor (11)
Nipper, Susan (6)
Pancks (10)
Perker (16)
Phunky (16)
Pipkin, Nathaniel (16)
Pirrip, Philip (8)
Pocket, Herbert/Matthew/
  Sarah (8)
Pogram, Elijah (11)
Raddle, Mr/Mrs (16)
Rigaud, Monsieur (10)
Sapsea, Thomas (7)
Sawyer, Bob (16)
Sleary, Josephine (9)
'Sloppy' (15)
Strong, Dr (5)
Tapley, Mark (11)
Toodle (6)
Tupman, Tracy (16)
Varden, Dolly/Gabriel (3)
Wardle, Emily/Isabella/Mr/
  Rachel (16)
Weller, Sam (16)
Wilfer, Bella/Lavinia/Reginald (15)
Willet, Joe/John (3)
Winkle, Mr (16)

7

Barbara (23)
Bardell Mrs Martha/Tommy (16)
Bazzard (7)
Blimber, Dr (6)
Blotton (16)
Bobster, Cecilia/Mr (13)

7

Boldwig, Captain (16)
Brooker (13)
Browdie, John (13)
Bullamy (11)
Chester, Edward/Sir John (3)
Chillip, Dr (5)
Chivery, John (10)
Chuffey (11)
Cleaver, Fanny (15)
Crackit, Toby (14)
Creakle (5)
Crewley, Mrs/Rev. Horace/
  Sophy (5)
Dawkins, Jack (14)
Dedlock, Sir Leicester/
  Volumnia (4)
Defarge, Madame (2)
Drummle, Bentley (8)
Edmunds, John (16)
Fleming, Agnes (14)
Gargery, Biddy/Joe/Pip (8)
Garland, Abel/Mr/Mrs (23)
Gazingi, Miss (13)
General, Mrs (10)
Granger, Edith (6)
Gridley (4)
Grimwig (14)
Heyling, George (16)
Jaggers (8)
Jellyby, Caddy/Mrs/Peggy (4)
Jobling, Dr John (11)
Jobling, Tony (4)
Jorkins (5)
Kenwigs, Morleena (13)
Larkins, Mr (5)
Lewsome (11)
Manette, Dr/Lucie (2)
Meagles (10)
Mowcher, Miss (5)
Neckett, Charlotte/Emma/Tom (4)
Nubbles, Christopher (23)
Nupkins, George (16)

7

Pawkins, Major (11)
Pipchin, Mrs (6)
Podsnap, Georgiana/Mr (15)
Sampson, George (15)
Scadder, Zephaniah (11)
Scrooge, Ebenezer (1)
Skewton, Hon. Mrs (6)
Slammer, Dr (16)
Snagsby (4)
Snawley (13)
Snubbin, Sergeant (16)
Sparsit, Mrs (9)
Spenlow, Dora (5)
Squeers, Fanny/Mr Wackford (13)
Stryver, C.J. (2)
Tiny Tim (1)
Todgers, Mrs (11)
Trotter, Job (16)
Trundle (16)
Wackles, Jane/Melissa/Sophie (23)
Wickham, Mrs (6)

8

Blathers (14)
Brownlow, Mr (14)
Claypole, Noah (14)
Cluppins (16)
Cratchit, Belinda/Bob/
  Tiny Tim (1)
Crummles, Ninetta/Vincent (13)
Cruncher, Jeremiah/Jerry (2)
Crushton, Hon. Mr (16)
Finching, Mrs Flora (10)
Fledgeby, Old/Young (15)
Gashford (3)
Havisham, Miss (8)
Hortense (4)
Jarndyce, John (4)
La Creevy, Miss (13)
Lenville (13)
Littimer (5)

8

Losberne (14)
Magwitch, Abel (8)
Micawber, Mr Wilkins (5)
Nickleby, Godfrey/Kate/
  Nicholas (13)
Peggotty, Clara/Daniel/Ham (5)
Pickwick, Mr (16)
Plornish, Thomas (10)
Skiffins, Miss (8)
Skimpole, Arethusa/Harold/Kitty/
  Laura (4)
Sparkler, Edmund (10)
Stiggins (16)
Traddles, Tom (5)
Trotwood, Betsy (5)
Uncle Tom (17)
Westlock, John (11)

9

Belvawney, Miss (13)
Blackpool, Stephen (9)
Charlotte (14)
Cherryble, Charles/Edwin/
  Frank (13)
Chickweed, Conkey (14)
Compeyson (8)
Gradgrind, Louisa/Thomas (9)
Gregsbury (13)
Grewgious (7)
Harthouse, James (9)
Headstone, Bradley (15)
Lightwood, Mortimer (15)
Lillyvick (13)
Mantalini, Mr (13)
Murdstone, Edward/Jane (5)
Pardiggle, Francis/O.A. (4)
Pecksniff, Charity/Mercy/Seth (11)
Riderhood, Pleasant/Roger (15)
Smallweed, Bartholomew/Joshua/
  Judy (4)
Snodgrass, Mr (16)

9

Swiveller, Dick (23)
Tappertit, Simon (3)
Veneering, Anastasia/
  Hamilton (15)
Verisopht, Lord Frederick (13)
Wickfield, Agnes/Mr (5)
Witherden, Mr (23)
Woodcourt, Allan (4)

10

Ayresleigh, Mr (16)
Chuzzlewit, Anthony/Diggory/
  George/Jonas/Martin/Mrs Ned/
  Toby (11)
Flintwinch, Affery/Ephraim/
  Jeremiah (10)
Little Em'ly (5)
Little Nell (23)

10

Rouncewell, Mrs (4)
Sowerberry (14)
Stareleigh, Justice (16)
Steerforth, James (5)
Turveydrop, Prince (4)
Wititterly, Julia (13)

11

Copperfield, Clara/David (5)
Pumblechook (8)
Sweedlepipe, Paul (11)

12

Artful Dodger (14)
Honeythunder (7)
Little Dorrit (10)

Dogs

3	5	6	7
cur	pooch	pye dog	samoyed
pom	puppy	ranger	sheltie
pug	spitz	ratter	shih tzu
pup	whelp	saluki	spaniel
		setter	terrier
4	**6**	talbot	whippet
chow	bandog		wolf dog
peke	beagle	**7**	
tosa	borzoi	basenji	**8**
	briard	bird dog	Airedale
5	canine	bulldog	alsatian
bitch	collie	clumber	chow chow
boxer	eskimo	griffon	coach dog
corgi	gun dog	harrier	elkhound
dhole	kelpie	Maltese	foxhound
dingo	lap dog	mastiff	house dog
hound	pariah	pit bull	keeshond
husky	poodle	pointer	labrador

8
papillon
pekinese
sealyham
sheepdog
springer
turnspit
watchdog

9
chihuahua
dachshund
dalmatian
deerhound
dobermann
great dane
greyhound

9
Kerry Blue
pekingese
red setter
retriever
St Bernard
schnauzer
staghound
wolfhound
yellow dog

10
bloodhound
Clydesdale
fox terrier
otterhound
pomeranian

10
rottweiler
schipperke
weimaraner
Welsh corgi

11
afghan hound
basset hound
bull mastiff
bull terrier
carriage dog
Irish setter
Jack Russell
shepherd dog
Siberian dog
Skye terrier

12
cairn terrier
Gordon setter
Irish terrier
Newfoundland
water spaniel
Welsh terrier

13
affenpinscher
border terrier
Boston terrier
cocker spaniel
Dandie Dinmont
English setter
Scotch terrier
Sussex spaniel

14
German shepherd
Irish wolfhound
Maltese terrier
pit bull terrier

15
Aberdeen terrier
Airedale terrier
American pit bull
golden retriever
Highland terrier
Lakeland terrier

15
Scottish terrier
sealyham terrier
springer spaniel

16
Kerry Blue terrier
Shetland sheepdog
Yorkshire terrier

17
Bedlington terrier
dobermann pinscher
labrador retriever

18
Jack Russell terrier
King Charles spaniel
Old English sheepdog

20
Dandie Dinmont terrier

24
Staffordshire bull
 terrier

Drinks

3	4	6	6
ale	tent	Barsac	stingo
cha	wine	Beaune	Strega
fix		bitter	tisane
gin	5	Bovril	Volnay
nog	anise	brandy	whisky
rum	arack	bubbly	
rye	byrrh	canary	7
tea	cider	cassis	alcohol
	cocoa	claret	aquavit
4	cream	coffee	Bacardi
arak	hyson	Cognac	Baileys
asti	julep	egg-nog	beef-tea
Bass	kvass	elixir	bourbon
beer	lager	gimlet	Campari
bock	Médoc	grappa	catawba
bols	Mosel	Graves	Chablis
char	negus	kirsch	Chandon
cola	pekoe	kummel	Chianti
fino	perry	liquor	cobbler
fizz	plonk	Malaga	cordial
flip	punch	mastic	curaçao
grog	shrub	mescal	dry wine
hock	sirop	muscat	egg-flip
kava	smash	oolong	Falerno
marc	stout	orgeat	liqueur
mead	tafia	Pernod	Madeira
mild	Tizer	porter	Malmsey
milk	toddy	posset	Marsala
Moët	Tokay	poteen	Martini
ouzo	tonic	ptisan	Moselle
port	Vichy	pulque	Orvieto
raki	Vimto	rickey	pale ale
rosé	vodka	Saumur	Perrier
sack	water	Scotch	pink gin
sake		shandy	Pommard
saki	6	sherry	potheen
soda	alegar	spirit	Pouilly
stum	Alsace	squash	ratafia
	arrack		

7	8	9	10
red wine	iron brew	Hermitage	dry Martini
retsina	lemonade	hippocras	ginger beer
schnaps	muscatel	iced water	ginger wine
seltzer	nightcap	Indian tea	horse's neck
sherbet	pekoe tea	lager beer	iced drinks
sidecar	persicot	lambrusco	Jamaica rum
sloe gin	Pilsener	limejuice	lime-squash
spirits	pink lady	Manhattan	malt liquor
tequila	ruby port	metheglin	malt whisky
Vouvray	rum-punch	milk punch	malted milk
whiskey	rum shrub	milkshake	maraschino
	sangaree	mint-julep	Mateus Rosé
8	schnapps	mirabelle	merry widow
absinthe	skim-milk	moonlight	mickey finn
Advocaat	souchong	moonshine	Moselle cup
anisette	sour milk	mulled ale	mulled wine
apéritif	St Julien	oolong tea	Munich beer
apple car	Tia Maria	orangeade	pale sherry
Assam tea	verjuice	orange gin	piña colada
beverage		St Emilion	raisin wine
black tea	9	sauternes	Rhine wines
bock-beer	altar wine	slivovitz	Rhône wines
Bordeaux	angostura	soda-water	rum Collins
Burgundy	apple-jack	soft drink	rye whiskey
calvados	aqua vitae	sundowner	soft drinks
China tea	bitter ale	tarragona	still wines
cider cup	black beer	tawny port	sweet wines
Coca-Cola	brut wines	white lady	Tom Collins
cocktail	Buck's fizz	white port	tonic water
daiquiri	Ceylon tea	white wine	twankay tea
Drambuie	champagne	Wincarnis	Vichy water
Dubonnet	chocolate		white wines
eau de vie	claret cup	10	
espresso	Cointreau	barley wine	11
gin and it	elder wine	Beaujolais	amontillado
gin-sling	Falernian	bitter beer	apple-brandy
green tea	ginger ale	black maria	barley-water
Guinness	ginger pop	bloody mary	beachcomber
high-ball	grenadine	café-au-lait	Benedictine
Horlicks	gunpowder	cappuccino	black velvet
hydromel	Hall's wine	chartreuse	Bristol milk

11	11	12	13
cider-brandy	tomato juice	mulled claret	crème de menthe
Courvoisier	vintage wine	old-fashioned	dandelion wine
cowslip wine		orange-brandy	Darjeeling tea
Earl Grey tea	12	orange-squash	ginger cordial
fallen angel	Champagne cup	Rhenish wines	Liebfraumilch
Irish coffee	cherry brandy	sarsaparilla	liqueur brandy
John Collins	crème de cacao	Scotch whisky	liqueur whisky
lemon-squash	Cyprus sherry	white gin sour	maidens prayer
mountain dew	fine and dandy		mineral waters
orange pekoe	ginger brandy	13	orange bitters
peach brandy	Grand Marnier	aerated waters	pink champagne
pouchong tea	ice-cream soda	aperitif wines	planters punch
souchong tea	India pale ale	apricot-brandy	Pouilly Fuisse
spring water	Irish whiskey	champagne buck	prairie oyster
	Malvern water	Château Lafite	sparkling wine

14	14	15
bamboo cocktail	Moët and Chandon	Martini cocktail
blended whiskey	sparkling wines	Southern Comfort
champagne cider	white wine punch	sparkling waters
champagne punch		
Château Margaux	15	17
French vermouth	green chartreuse	Beaujolais nouveau
	Italian vermouth	

Educational terms

3	G.C.S.E.	5	6
cap	gown	coach	bursar
don	hall	grant	course
ERA	head	house	day boy
fag	hood	lines	degree
LMS	prep	pupil	eights
SAT	swot	scout	fellow
	term	study	incept
4	test	tutor	locker
crib			master
dean	5	6	matron
exam	backs	A-level	O-level
form	class	beadle	

6
reader
rector
school
senate
warden

7
academy
AS-level
boarder
bursary
captain
college
diploma
faculty
head boy
honours
lecture
monitor
nursery
prefect
proctor
project
provost
reading
scholar
seminar
student
teacher
teach-in
tuition

8
academic
backward
dyslexia
examinee
graduate
guidance

8
half term
head girl
headship
homework
key stage
learning
lecturer
mistress
register
research
roll call
seminary
send down
statutes
textbook
tuck-shop
tutorial
vacation

9
art master
art school
classroom
day school
dormitory
great hall
opting-out
playgroup
preceptor
prelector
president
principal
professor
refectory
registrar
scholarly
schoolboy
selection
speech day

10
blackboard
chancellor
common room
day-release
dining hall
eleven plus
exhibition
extra-mural
fellowship
form master
headmaster
illiteracy
imposition
instructor
laboratory
sabbatical
sanatorium
schooldays
schoolgirl
schoolmarm
schoolroom
school year
university

11
examination
games master
head teacher
housemaster
matriculate
mortar-board
music master
polytechnic
scholarship
school hours

12
exhibitioner
headmistress

12
kindergarten
Master of Arts
night classes
public orator
people-teacher
schoolfellow
schoolmaster
Sunday school

13
adult learning
co-educational
comprehension
comprehensive
grammar school
matriculation
mature student
schoolteacher
science master
supply teacher
undergraduate
vice-principal

14
boarding school
language master
Open University
schoolmistress
vice-chancellor

15
grant-maintained
school inspector
secondary
  modern

Elementary particles

2	5	6	8
xi	boson	photon	graviton
	gluon	proton	neutrino
3	meson		positron
eta	omega	7	
phi	quark	fermion	9
psi	sigma	hyperon	neutretto
		neutron	
4	6	tachyon	12
kaon	baryon		antiparticle
muon	hadron	8	beta particle
pion	lambda	deuteron	
	lepton	electron	13
			alpha particle

Engineering

3	4	4	4
amp	bolt	nail	test
cog	burr	oily	tire
erg	cast	pile	tool
fan	cone	pipe	tube
fit	cowl	plan	turn
hob	flaw	rail	tyre
hub	flux	reed	unit
lag	fuel	road	vent
nut	fuse	rope	volt
ohm	gear	rung	weld
oil	glue	rust	wire
ram	hasp	shop	work
rig	kiln	skid	
sag	lens	slag	5
tap	lift	stay	alloy
tie	link	stop	anode
	lock	stud	blast
4	loom	suck	cable
beam	main	sump	clamp
belt	mine	tank	cleat

5	5	6	7
crane	smelt	hinged	adapter
crank	spoke	hooter	air duct
crate	spool	jigger	air pipe
dowel	spout	ladder	air-pump
drill	steam	magnet	air tube
drive	strap	mining	artisan
emery	strut	nipple	autocar
flume	taper	nozzle	battery
flush	tools	oil-can	bearing
force	tooth	output	belting
gauge	train	petrol	booster
joint	valve	pinion	bracket
joist	video	piston	casting
laser	waste	pulley	cathode
level	wedge	repair	chimney
lever	wharf	rigger	cistern
miner	wheel	rocket	conduit
model	wiper	roller	cutting
motor	works	rotary	digital
mould		sawpit	drawing
oakum	6	siding	exhaust
pedal	blower	sluice	factory
pivot	bobbin	smithy	ferrule
plant	boiler	socket	gudgeon
power	bridge	switch	hydrant
press	burner	swivel	lagging
pylon	camber	system	lock-nut
radar	clutch	tackle	machine
radio	couple	tappet	manhole
ratch	cut-out	tender	mill-cog
relay	derail	thrust	monitor
resin	duplex	tie-bar	moulded
rigid	dynamo	tie-rod	moulder
rivet	energy	toggle	nuclear
rusty	engine	torque	oil fuel
screw	fitter	tripod	oil lamp
shaft	flange	tunnel	oil pump
short	funnel	uncoil	pattern
shunt	geyser	vacuum	pig-iron
slack	girder	washer	program
slide	gutter	welded	
		welder	

7

ratchet
reactor
rejoint
riveter
roadway
sawmill
seabank
seawall
shackle
shuttle
sleeper
smelter
spindle
stopper
suction
sump-pit
support
syringe
tension
testing
treadle
trolley
turbine
turning
unscrew
viaduct
voltage
welding

8

air-brake
air valve
annealed
aqueduct
balancer
ball-cock
bevelled
bridging
camshaft
cam wheel
cassette

8

castings
cast-iron
cog-wheel
compound
computer
concrete
coupling
cylinder
Davy lamp
declutch
electric
elevator
engineer
feed-pipe
feed pump
fire-clay
fire-plug
flywheel
fracture
friction
fuse clip
hot blast
ignition
insulate
ironwork
irrigate
laminate
lime-kiln
linchpin
linotype
main line
mechanic
millpond
monotype
moulding
movement
oil store
oil stove
operator
pendulum
platform

8

polarity
pressure
radiator
railroad
recharge
repolish
rheostat
rigidity
ring bolt
rotatory
shearing
smelting
soft iron
strength
tapering
template
terminal
textbook
throttle
tinplate
tractile
traction
tram-road
turbojet
turnpike
windmill
wind-pump
wireless
workshop

9

acoustics
air filter
amplifier
bevel gear
blueprint
brakepipe
brick kiln
chain-belt
chain-pump
clockwork

9

condenser
conductor
cotter pin
craftsman
dead level
diaphragm
disc brake
fire-brick
fishplate
floodgate
fog signal
foot valve
force pump
framework
funicular
galvanise
galvanism
galvanize
gas-engine
gas-fitter
gas-geyser
gas-holder
gasometer
hydraulic
hydrostat
injection
insertion
insulated
insulator
ironsmith
ironworks
jet engine
knife-edge
laminated
lewis bolt
lubricant
lubricate
machinery
machinist
master key
mechanics

9

mechanism
mine shaft
oil engine
oil geyser
perforate
petrol can
piston rod
pneumatic
polariser
polarizer
propeller
prototype
pump break
reflector
regulator
repairing
reservoir
roughcast
sandpaper
slide rule
soldering
spring box
steam pipe
stoke-hole
structure
tin mining
transform
trunk line
tunnel pit
turntable
twin cable
vibration
vulcanise
vulcanize
watermark
water-tank
wire gauze
wire wheel

10

air machine
alarm gauge

10

alternator
automation
bevel wheel
cantilever
Centigrade
discharger
disc wheels
drawbridge
electrical
electronic
emery cloth
emery paper
emery wheel
Fahrenheit
flange rail
footbridge
fuse holder
galvanised
galvanized
gas turbine
glass paper
grid system
guillotine
horsepower
instrument
insulating
insulation
irrigation
laboratory
lamination
locomotive
lubricator
mechanical
nodal point
paper cable
percolator
petrol tank
pneumatics
pulveriser
pulverizer
pump-handle

10

safety-lamp
steam gauge
streamline
structural
swivel hook
temper heat
thermostat
toll bridge
transistor
watertight
water tower
waterwheel
well-boring

11

accelerator
accumulator
anelectrode
bell foundry
block system
cable laying
compression
computation
coupling box
coupling pin
electrician
electricity
electronics
engineering
exhaust-pipe
gas governor
incinerator
iron foundry
low pressure
lubrication
machine-tool
maintenance
mono railway
narrow gauge
oil purifier
oil strainer

11

perforation
pilot engine
reconstruct
revolutions
safety-valve
searchlight
service pipe
skeleton key
socket joint
steam-engine
suction-pipe
suction-pump
swing-bridge
switchboard
synchronism
tappet-valve
transformer
transmitter
underground
water supply
welding heat
workmanship
wrought iron

12

aerodynamics
anti-friction
assembly line
balance wheel
belt fastener
blast furnace
chain reactor
danger signal
diesel engine
differential
disc coupling
disintegrate
driving-shaft
driving-wheel
electric bulb
electric fire

12	12	13	14
electric fuse	ratchet wheel	insulated wire	pneumatic drill
electric iron	rolling press	kinetic energy	reconstruction
electric wire	service cable	magnetic fluid	traction engine
electrolysis	short circuit	pneumatic tyre	
electromotor	specific heat	pressure gauge	15
exhaust valve	spinning mill	printing press	brake horsepower
flexible wire	steam turbine	rack and pinion	Centigrade scale
gas condenser	suction valve	shock absorber	digital computer
gas container	transmission	telegraph line	electric circuit
gas regulator	water turbine	telegraph pole	electric current
high pressure	wheel cutting	telegraph wire	Fahrenheit scale
hydraulic ram		thrust bearing	insulating paper
installation	13	water drainage	irrigation canal
nuclear power	civil engineer		linotype machine
pattern maker	direct current	14	perpetual motion
petrol engine	electric cable	discharge valve	pressure machine
petrol filter	electric light	galvanized iron	smelting furnace
polarisation	electric motor	hydraulic press	specific gravity
polarization	electromagnet	insulated cable	
pressure pump	engine-turning	magnetic needle	

Explorers, pioneers and adventurers

4	5
Byrd, Richard	Drake, Sir Francis
Cook, Captain James	Fuchs, Sir Vivian Ernest
Gama, Vasco da	Oates, Lawrence
Hunt, John, Baron	Parry, Sir William
Park, Mungo	Peary, Robert
Polo, Marco	Scott, Robert Falcon
Ross, Sir James	Speke, John Hanning
Ross, Sir John	Sturt, Charles

5	6
Baker, Sir Samuel	Aldrin, Buzz
Bruce, William Spiers	Baffin, William
Burke, Robert O'Hara	Balboa, Vasco Nuñez de
Cabot, John	Bering, Vitus Jonassen
Cabot, Sebastian	Burton, Sir Richard
Davis, John	Cabral, Pedro Alvarez
	Conway, Sir Martin

6
Cortés, Hernando
El Cano, Sebastián
Forbes, Rosita
Hudson, Henry
Morgan, Sir Henry
Nansen, Fridtjof
Nobile, Umberto
Tasman, Abel Janszoon

7
Blériot, Louis
Cartier, Jacques
Dampier, William
Earhart, Amelia
Fiennes, Sir Ranulph
Fremont, John C.
Gagarin, Yuri Alexeyevich
Gilbert, Sir Humphrey
Hawkins, Sir John
Hillary, Sir Edmund
Johnson, Amy
Markham, Sir Robert
McClure, Sir Robert
Pizarro, Francisco
Raleigh, Sir Walter
Stanley, Sir Henry Morton

8
Amundsen, Roald
Columbus, Christopher
Cousteau, Jacques
Flinders, Matthew
Franklin, Sir John
Magellan, Ferdinand
Vespucci, Amerigo

9
Armstrong, Neil
Champlain, Samuel de
Frobisher, Sir Martin
Lindbergh, Charles
Vancouver, George
Velásquez, Diego

10
Shackleton, Sir Ernest

11
Livingstone, David

12
Bougainville, Louis Antoine de
Leif Eriksson
Nordenskjöld, Nils, Baron

Ferns

4	7	8	11
tree	bracken	polypody	hart's tongue
	osmunda	staghorn	
5			**12**
royal	**8**	**10**	adder's tongue
	club moss	maidenhair	pteridophyte
6	lady fern	spleenwort	
osmund			

Fictional characters

3

Cob, Oliver (*Every Man in His Humour*, Ben Jonson)
Cos (*Cynthia's Revels*, Ben Jonson)
Fox, Br'er (*Uncle Remus*, J.C. Harris)
Gog (*The Tower of London*, W. Harrison Ainsworth)
Hur, Judah Ben (*Ben Hur*, L.Wallace)
Jim, 'Lord' (*Lord Jim*, Joseph Conrad)
Kim (*Kim*, Rudyard Kipling)
Lee, General Robert E. (*Abraham Lincoln*, John Drinkwater)
Owl (*Winnie the Pooh*, A.A. Milne)
Roo (*Winnie the Pooh*, A.A. Milne)
Tom (*The Water Babies*, Charles Kingsley)
Tom, Uncle (*Uncle Tom's Cabin*, Harriet Beecher Stowe)
Yeo, Salvation (*Westward Ho!*, Charles Kingsley)

4

Baba (*Don Juan*, Lord Byron)
Beck, Madame (*Villette*, Charlotte Brontë)
Bede, Adam/Mrs/Seth (*Adam Bede*, George Eliot)
Busy (*Bartholomew Fair*, Ben Jonson)
Cash, Thomas (*Every Man in His Humour*, Ben Jonson)
Cass, Eppie (*Silas Marner*, George Eliot)
Casy, Rev. Jim (*The Grapes of Wrath*, John Steinbeck)
Cave, Mary (*Shirley*, Charlotte Brontë)
Dean, Ellen (*Wuthering Heights*, Emily Brontë)
Dent, Colonel (*Jane Eyre*, Charlotte Brontë)
Eyre, Jane (*Jane Eyre*, Charlotte Brontë)
Gale, John/Mrs (*Shirley*, Charlotte Brontë)
Hall, Margaret/Rev. Cyril (*Shirley*, Charlotte Brontë)
Hogg, Mrs (*Shirley*, Charlotte Brontë)
Home, Paulina (*Villette*, Charlotte Brontë)
Hook, Captain (*Peter Pan*, J.M. Barrie)
Hyde, Mr (*Dr Jekyll and Mr Hyde*, R.L. Stevenson)
Inez, Donna (*Don Juan*, Lord Byron)
Judy (*Wee Willie Winkie*, Rudyard Kipling)
Mole (*The Wind in the Willows*, Kenneth Grahame)
Nana (*Peter Pan*, J.M. Barrie)
Puck (Robin Goodfellow) (*Puck of Pook's Hill*, Rudyard Kipling)
Raby, Aurora (*Don Juan*, Lord Byron)
Rama, Tiger Tiger (*The Jungle Book*, Rudyard Kipling)

4

Reed, Mrs (*Jane Eyre*, Charlotte Brontë)
Ridd, John (*Lorna Doone*, R.D. Blackmore)
Toad, Mr (*The Wind in the Willows*, Kenneth Grahame)
Vane, Lady Isabel (*East Lynne*, Mrs Henry Wood)
Wolf, Br'er (*Uncle Remus*, J.C. Harris)

5

Abbot, Miss (*Jane Eyre*, Charlotte Brontë)
Acres, Bob (*The Rivals*, R.B. Sheridan)
Adams, Parson (*Joseph Andrews*, Henry Fielding)
Akela (*The Jungle Book*, Rudyard Kipling)
Alibi, Tom (*Waverley*, Sir Walter Scott)
Athos (*The Three Musketeers*, Alexandre Dumas)
Baloo (*The Jungle Book*, Rudyard Kipling)
Bluff, Captain (*The Old Bachelor*, William Congreve)
Bones, Captain Billy (*Treasure Island*, R.L. Stevenson)
Booby, Sir Thomas (*Joseph Andrews*, Henry Fielding)
Burns, Helen (*Jane Eyre*, Charlotte Brontë)
Chant, Mercy (*Tess of the D'Urbervilles*, Thomas Hardy)
Darcy, FitzWilliam (*Pride and Prejudice*, Jane Austen)
Deans, Jeanie (*The Heart of Midlothian*, Sir Walter Scott)
Dinah (*Uncle Tom's Cabin*, Harriet Beecher Stowe)
Eager, Rev. Cuthbert (*A Room with a View*, E.M. Forster)
Hands, Israel (*Treasure Island*, R.L. Stevenson)
Hatch, Bennet (*The Black Arrow*, R.L. Stevenson)
Jones, Tom (*Tom Jones*, Henry Fielding)
Kanga (*Winnie the Pooh*, A.A. Milne)
Kipps, Arthur (*Kipps*, H.G. Wells)
Leigh, Amyas (*Westward Ho!*, Charles Kingsley)
March, Amy/Beth/Jo/Meg (*Little Women*, Louisa M. Alcott)
Mercy (*The Pilgrim's Progress*, John Bunyan)
Moore, Mrs. (*A Passage to India*, E.M. Forster)
Moses (*The Vicar of Wakefield*, Oliver Goldsmith)
O'Hara, Kimball (*Kim*, Rudyard Kipling)
O'Hara, Scarlett (*Gone with the Wind*, Margaret Mitchell)
Otter, Mr (*The Wind in the Willows*, Kenneth Grahame)
Paget, Jean (*A Town like Alice*, Nevil Shute)
Polly, Alfred (*The History of Mr Polly*, H.G. Wells)
Poole, Grace (*Jane Eyre*, Charlotte Brontë)
Punch (*Wee Willie Winkie*, Rudyard Kipling)
Remus, Uncle (*Uncle Remus*, J.C. Harris)

5

Ryder, Charles (*Brideshead Revisited*, Evelyn Waugh)
Sambo (*Just So Stories*, Rudyard Kipling)
Sharp, Becky (*Vanity Fair*, W.M. Thackeray)
Slope, Rev. Obadiah (*Barchester Towers*, Anthony Trollope)
Sloth (*The Pilgrim's Progress*, John Bunyan)
Smith, Winston (*1984*, George Orwell)
Snowe, Lucy (*Villette*, Charlotte Brontë)
Topsy (*Uncle Tom's Cabin*, Harriet Beecher Stowe)
Wendy (*Peter Pan*, J.M. Barrie)

6

Aramis (*The Three Musketeers*, Alexandre Dumas)
Bennet, Elizabeth (*Pride and Prejudice*, Jane Austen)
Bessie (*Jane Eyre*, Charlotte Brontë)
Butler, Rhett (*Gone With the Wind*, Margaret Mitchell)
Eeyore (*Winnie the Pooh*, A.A. Milne)
Elaine (*Idylls of the King*, Alfred, Lord Tennyson)
Friday, Man (*Robinson Crusoe*, Daniel Defoe)
Garter, Polly (*Under Milk Wood*, Dylan Thomas)
George (*Three Men in a Boat*, Jerome K. Jerome)
Glover, Catherine (*The Fair Maid of Perth*, Sir Walter Scott)
Hannay, Richard (*The Thirty-Nine Steps*, John Buchan)
Harman, Joe (*A Town like Alice*, Nevil Shute)
Holmes, Sherlock (*The Hound of the Baskervilles*, etc.,
 Sir Arthur Conan Doyle)
Jarvie, Baille Nicol (*Rob Roy*, Walter Scott)
Jeeves (*Thank You, Jeeves*, etc., P.G. Wodehouse)
Jekyll, Henry (*Dr Jekyll and Mr Hyde*, R.L. Stevenson)
Laurie (*Little Women*, Louisa M. Alcott)
Legree, Simon (*Uncle Tom's Cabin*, Harriet Beecher Stowe)
Linton, Edgar (*Wuthering Heights*, Emily Brontë)
Marple, Miss Jane (*The Body in the Library*, etc., Agatha Christie)
Merlin (*Idylls of the King*, Alfred, Lord Tennyson)
Modred, Sir (*Idylls of the King*, Alfred, Lord Tennyson)
Mowgli (*The Jungle Book*, Rudyard Kipling)
Piglet, Henry Pootel (*Winnie the Pooh*, A.A. Milne)
Poirot, Hercule (*The Mysterious Affair at Styles*, etc., Agatha Christie)
Rabbit (*Winnie the Pooh*, A.A. Milne)
Rabbit, Br'er (*Uncle Remus*, J.C. Harris)
Silver, Long John (*Treasure Island*, R.L. Stevenson)
Temple, Miss (*Jane Eyre*, Charlotte Brontë)

6

Thorne, Dr Thomas (*Doctor Thorne*, Anthony Trollope)
Thorpe, Isabella (*Northanger Abbey*, Jane Austen)
Tilney, Henry (*Northanger Abbey*, Jane Austen)
Watson, Dr (*The Hound of the Baskervilles*, etc., Sir Arthur Conan Doyle)
Weston, Mrs (*Emma*, Jane Austen)
Wilkes, Ashley/India (*Gone With the Wind*, Margaret Mitchell)

7

Balfour, David (*Kidnapped*, R.L. Stevenson)
Bingley, Charles (*Pride and Prejudice*, Jane Austen)
Bowling, Tom (*Roderick Random*, Tobias Smollett)
Brandon, Colonel (*Sense and Sensibility*, Jane Austen)
Collins, Rev. William (*Pride and Prejudice*, Jane Austen)
Danvers, Mrs (*Rebecca*, Daphne Du Maurier)
Fairfax, Jane (*Emma*, Jane Austen)
Fairfax, Mrs (*Jane Eyre*, Charlotte Brontë)
Forsyte, Fleur/Irene/Jolyon/Jon/Soames (*The Forsyte Saga*,
  John Galsworthy)
Galahad, Sir (*Idylls of the King*, Alfred, Lord Tennyson)
Geraint, Sir (*Idylls of the King*, Alfred, Lord Tennyson)
Hawkins, Jim (*Treasure Island*, R.L. Stevenson)
Higgins, Professor Henry (*Pygmalion*, George Bernard Shaw)
Jenkins, Rev. Eli (*Under Milk Wood*, Dylan Thomas)
Keeldar, Shirley (*Shirley*, Charlotte Brontë)
Lampton, Joe (*Room at the Top*, John Braine)
Latimer, Darsie (*Redgauntlet*, Sir Walter Scott)
Lawless (*The Black Arrow*, R.L. Stevenson)
Learoyd, Jock (*Soldiers Three*, Rudyard Kipling)
Lumpkin, Tony (*She Stoops to Conquer*, Oliver Goldsmith)
Markham, Gilbert (*The Tenant of Wildfell Hall*, Anne Brontë)
Morland, Catherine (*Northanger Abbey*, Jane Austen)
Porthos (*The Three Musketeers*, Alexandre Dumas)
Red King (*Through the Looking Glass*, Lewis Carroll)
Robsart, Amy (*Kenilworth*, Sir Walter Scott)
Smollet, Captain (*Treasure Island*, R.L. Stevenson)
Wooster, Bertie (*Thank You, Jeeves*, etc., P.G. Wodehouse)

8

Absolute, Sir Anthony (*The Rivals*, R.B. Sheridan)
Backbite, Sir Benjamin (*The School for Scandal*, R.B. Sheridan)
Bagheera (*The Jungle Book*, Rudyard Kipling)
Bedivere, Sir (*The Morte d'Arthur*, Alfred, Lord Tennyson)

8

Casaubon, Rev. Edward (*Middlemarch*, George Eliot)
Crichton (*The Admirable Crichton*, J.M. Barrie)
Dashwood, Henry (*Sense and Sensibility*, Jane Austen)
De Bourgh, Lady Catherine (*Pride and Prejudice*, Jane Austen)
De Winter, Maximilian (*Rebecca*, Daphne Du Maurier)
Earnshaw, Catherine (*Wuthering Heights*, Emily Brontë)
Faithful (*The Pilgrim's Progress*, John Bunyan)
Ffoulkes, Sir Andrew (*The Scarlet Pimpernel*, Baroness Orczy)
Flanders, Moll (*Moll Flanders*, Daniel Defoe)
Gloriana (*The Faerie Queene*, Edmund Spenser)
Gulliver, Lemuel (*Gulliver's Travels*, Jonathan Swift)
Lancelot, Sir (*Idylls of the King*, Alfred, Lord Tennyson)
Languish, Lydia (*The Rivals*, R.B. Sheridan)
Lockwood (*Wuthering Heights*, Emily Brontë)
Malaprop, Mrs (*The Rivals*, R.B. Sheridan)
Mary Jane (*When We Were Very Young*, A.A. Milne)
O'Ferrall, Trilby (*Trilby*, George Du Maurier)
Primrose, Dr Charles (*The Vicar of Wakefield*, Oliver Goldsmith)
Red Queen (*Through the Looking Glass*, Lewis Carroll)
Svengali (*Trilby*, George Du Maurier)
Thatcher, Becky (*The Adventures of Tom Sawyer*, Mark Twain)
Tristram, Sir (*Idylls of the King*, Alfred, Lord Tennyson)
Tulliver, Maggie/Tom (*The Mill on the Floss*, George Eliot)
Water Rat (*The Wind in the Willows*, Kenneth Grahame)
Waverley, Edward (*Waverley*, Sir Walter Scott)
Whiteoak, Family (*The Whiteoak Chronicles*, Mazo De La Roche)
White-Tip (*Tarka the Otter*, Henry Williamson)
Williams, Percival William (*Wee Willie Winkie*, Rudyard Kipling)

9

Alan-A-Dale (*Ivanhoe*, Sir Walter Scott)
Allworthy, Squire (*Tom Jones*, Henry Fielding)
Babberley, Lord Fancourt (*Charley's Aunt*, Brandon Thomas)
Barrymore (*The Hound of the Baskervilles*, Sir Arthur Conan Doyle)
Bracknell, Lady (*The Importance of Being Earnest*, Oscar Wilde)
Christian (*The Pilgrim's Progress*, John Bunyan)
Churchill, Frank (*Emma*, Jane Austen)
D'Artagnan (*The Three Musketeers*, Alexandre Dumas)
Doolittle, Eliza (*Pygmalion*, George Bernard Shaw)
Guinevere (*Idylls of the King*, Alfred, Lord Tennyson)
Leicester, Earl of (*Kenilworth*, Sir Walter Scott)

9

MacGregor, Robin (*Rob Roy*, Sir Walter Scott)
Merrilees, Meg (*Guy Mannering*, Sir Walter Scott)
Pendennis, Arthur (*Pendennis*, W.M.Thackeray)
Quasimodo (*The Hunchback of Notre Dame*, Victor Hugo)
Rochester, Bertha/Edward Fairfax (*Jane Eyre*, Charlotte Brontë)
Tanqueray, Paula (*The Second Mrs Tanqueray*, Sir Arthur Wing Pinero)
Tiger Lily (*Peter Pan*, J.M. Barrie)
Trelawney, Squire (*Treasure Island*, R.L. Stevenson)
Woodhouse, Emma/Isabella (*Emma*, Jane Austen)

10

Belladonna (*Vanity Fair*, W.M. Thackeray)
Crimsworth, William (*The Professor*, Charlotte Brontë)
Greatheart (*The Pilgrim's Progress*, John Bunyan)
Hardcastle, Miss Kate (*She Stoops to Conquer*, Oliver Goldsmith)
Heathcliff (*Wuthering Heights*, Emily Brontë)
Mauleverer, Lord (*Cranford*, Mrs Gaskell)
Quatermain, Allan (*King Solomon's Mines*, Sir Henry Rider Haggard)
Tinker Bell (*Peter Pan*, J.M. Barrie)
Willoughby, John (*Sense and Sensibility*, Jane Austen)
Windermere, Lord Arthur/Margaret (*Lady Windermere's Fan*,
  Oscar Wilde)

11

Montmorency, The Dog (*Three Men in a Boat*, Jerome K. Jerome)
Tamburlaine (*Tamburlaine*, Christopher Marlowe)
White Knight (*Through the Looking Glass*, Lewis Carroll)

12

Brocklehurst (*Jane Eyre*, Charlotte Brontë)
Frankenstein, Victor (*Frankenstein*, Mary Shelley)
Giant Despair (*The Pilgrim's Progress*, John Bunyan)
Humpty-Dumpty (*Through the Looking Glass*, Lewis Carroll)
The Mad Hatter (*Alice in Wonderland*, Lewis Carroll)
The March Hare (*Alice in Wonderland*, Lewis Carroll)

13

The Mock Turtle (*Alice in Wonderland*, Lewis Carroll)
Winnie the Pooh (*Winnie the Pooh*, A.A. Milne)

14

Mephistopheles (*Doctor Faustus*, Christopher Marlowe)
The White Rabbit (*Alice in Wonderland*, Lewis Carroll)

15

Ogmore-Pritchard, Mrs (*Under Milk Wood*, Dylan Thomas)
Valiant for Truth (*The Pilgrim's Progress*, John Bunyan)
Violet Elizabeth (*Just William*, Richmal Crompton)

16

Mr Worldly Wiseman (*The Pilgrim's Progress*, John Bunyan)

Film titles

2	6	8	10
E.T.	Frenzy	Music Man	Blue Velvet
	Gandhi	Oklahoma!	Casablanca
3	Grease	Peter Pan	Cinderella
Hud	Hamlet	Rashomon	City Lights
	Oliver	Rio Bravo	Family Plot
4	Psycho	Star Wars	Going My Way
Dr No		Superman	Goldfinger
Gigi	7	The Birds	L'Avventura
Jaws	Airport	The Sting	Mrs Miniver
M*A*S*H	Amadeus	Tom Jones	My Fair Lady
	Bus Stop		Nine to Five
5	Charade	9	Now Voyager
Annie	Platoon	Chinatown	Rear Window
Bambi	Rain Man	Annie Hall	Spellbound
Ghost	Rebecca	Cavalcade	Stagecoach
Giant	The Robe	Cimmarron	The Misfits
Klute	Tootsie	Cleopatra	Woman in Red
Marty	Vertigo	Dr Zhivago	
Rocky		Funny Face	11
Shane	8	Funny Girl	A Chorus Line
Twins	Cocktail	House Boat	All About Eve
Wings	Fantasia	Moonraker	A Star is Born
	Duck Soup	Octopussy	A View to Kill
6	High Noon	Pinocchio	Call Me Madam
Bat Man	King Kong	Suspicion	Citizen Kane
Ben-Hur	Mon Oncle	Viridiana	Dead of Night

11
High Society
Intolerance
Mary Poppins
Mickey Mouse
Out of Africa
Pretty Woman
The Cruel Sea
The Exorcist
The Graduate
The Magic Bow
The Naked Gun
The Third Man
Thunderball
Torn Curtain

12
A Patch of Blue
Casino Royale
Cool Hand Luke
Duel in the Sun
Ghostbusters
La Règle du Jeu
Rome — Open City
Room at the Top
Seven Samurai
South Pacific
The Godfather

13
101 Dalmatians
Licence to Kill
Some Like It Hot
The Blue Lagoon
The Deer Hunter
The Dirty Dozen
The Jungle Book
The Wizard of Oz
This is the Army
To Be or Not To Be
West Side Story

14
Above and Beyond
Above Suspicion
Adam and Evelyne
A Day at the Races
All The King's Men
Bicycle Thieves
Bonnie and Clyde
Brief Encounter
Broadway Melody
Chariots of Fire
Kramer vs Kramer
Midnight Cowboy
Ordinary People
Sleeping Beauty
Song of the South
The Last Emperor
The Long Weekend
The Lost Weekend

15
Back to the Future
Beverly Hills Cop
Crocodile Dundee
Fatal Attraction
For Your Eyes Only
Gone With The Wind
Lady and the Tramp
Life of Emile Zola
On The Waterfront
Return of the Jedi
River of No Return
Singin' in the Rain
Sunset Boulevard
The Sound of Music
The Tamarind Seed

16
A Clockwork Orange
A Night at the Opera
David Copperfield
Dead Poets Society
La Grande Illusion
Lawrence of Arabia
Night of the Hunter
North by Northwest
Samson and Delilah
Shirley Valentine
The Grapes of Wrath
The Great Ziegfeld
The Maltese Falcon
The Seven Year Itch
The Spy Who Loved Me
Three Men and a Baby

17
A Man for All Seasons
An American in Paris
Forty-Second Street
Mutiny on the Bounty
Terms of Endearment
The Bells of St Mary's
Victor and Victoria

18
Battleship Potemkin
Diamonds are Forever
Forty-Ninth Parallel
From Here to Eternity
Good Morning,
  Vietnam
Never Say Never Again
Saturday Night Fever
The Living Daylights
The Prisoner of Zenda
The Ten
  Commandments
The Towering Inferno

19
Breakfast at Tiffany's
Greatest Show on Earth
How Green Was My Valley
Les Enfants du Paradis
Raiders of the Lost Ark
The French Connection

20
The Empire Strikes Back
The Man Who Knew Too Much
The Poseidon Adventure
Who Framed Roger Rabbit?
You Can't Take It With You

21
Kind Hearts and Coronets

22
Far From the Madding Crowd
Gentlemen Prefer Blondes
How to Marry a Millionaire
The Best Years of Our Lives

23
The Bridge on the River Kwai
The Prince and the Showgirl

25
All Quiet on the Western Front
One Flew Over the Cuckoo's Nest

26
Around the World in Eighty Days
Snow White and the Seven Dwarfs

29
Butch Cassidy and the Sundance
  Kid
Close Encounters of the Third Kind
Indiana Jones and the Last Crusade

30
Indiana Jones and the Temple of
  Doom

31
There's No Business Like Show
  Business

Fish

3	4	4	4
bib	bass	hake	sole
cod	carp	ling	tope
dab	char	opah	tuna
eel	chub	orfe	
gar	coho	parr	5
ide	crab	pike	bleak
ray	dace	rudd	bream
	goby	shad	brill

5

coley
elver
grunt
guppy
loach
perch
porgy
prawn
roach
saury
shark
skate
smelt
smolt
sprat
squid
tench
trout
tunny
whale
whelk

6

barbel
beluga
blenny
bonito
bowfin
burbot
cockle
gunnel
kipper
marlin
minnow
mullet
oyster
plaice
puffer
remora
saithe
salmon

6

shrimp
tarpon
turbot
weever
wrasse

7

alewife
anchovy
batfish
bloater
catfish
cichlid
croaker
dogfish
dolphin
eel-pout
garfish
garpike
gourami
grouper
gudgeon
gurnard
haddock
hagfish
halibut
herring
hogfish
icefish
lamprey
lobster
mudfish
oarfish
octopus
piranha
pollack
pompano
sardine
sawfish
sculpin
sea-bass

7

snapper
sunfish
teleost
tiddler
torpedo
whiting

8

albacore
bluefish
brisling
bullhead
crawfish
crayfish
dragonet
drum-fish
file-fish
flat-fish
flat-head
flounder
frog-fish
goldfish
grayling
John Dory
lung-fish
mackerel
monkfish
moonfish
moray eel
pilchard
pipe-fish
porpoise
sail-fish
sea-horse
sea-perch
sea-robin
skipjack
sting-ray
sturgeon
toad-fish
wolf-fish

9

angel-fish
barracuda
blue shark
cling-fish
conger eel
devil-fish
dover sole
globe-fish
grenadier
jelly-fish
killifish
lemon sole
murray cod
pilot fish
porbeagle
red mullet
red salmon
stargazer
stone-fish
sword-fish
sword-tail
threadfin
whitebait

10

angler-fish
archer-fish
coelacanth
cuttlefish
cyclostome
dragon-fish
flying fish
ghost-shark
parrot fish
pink salmon
ribbon-fish
silverside
sperm whale
tiger shark
whale shark
white shark

11	11	12	13
electric eel	stickleback	fighting-fish	salt-water fish
electric ray	surgeon-fish	rainbow trout	sockeye salmon
moorish idol			

Five senses

5	5	7
sight	taste	hearing
smell	touch	

Food

3	4	4	5
bap	fowl	veal	gravy
bun	game	whey	gruel
cob	ghee	yolk	gumbo
egg	hare		heart
fat	hash	**5**	honey
ham	herb	aspic	icing
ice	junk	bacon	jelly
jam	kale	bagel	joint
Oxo	lamb	bombe	kebab
pie	lard	brawn	liver
roe	loaf	bread	lunch
	loin	brose	manna
4	meat	broth	melba
bean	mint	candy	mince
beef	pâté	chili	pasta
bran	pork	clove	pasty
cake	puff	cream	patty
cate	rice	crepe	pilau
chop	roll	crust	pilaw
chou	roux	curds	pizza
crab	rusk	curry	prune
curd	sago	dough	pulse
duck	snow	dulse	roast
fare	soup	flour	salad
fish	stew	fruit	salmi
flan	suet	fudge	sauce
fool	tart	gigot	scone

5

snack
spice
steak
stock
sugar
sweet
syrup
taffy
tansy
toast
tripe
viand
wafer
yeast

6

almond
batter
biffin
bonbon
borsch
Bovril
brains
brunch
burger
butter
canape
casein
cheese
collop
comfit
cookie
cornet
crumbs
cutlet
dinner
eclair
eggnog
entree
faggot
fillet

6

flitch
gammon
garlic
gateau
ginger
greens
grouse
haggis
hot dog
hotpot
humbug
jujube
junket
kidney
leaven
lights
mornay
mousse
muffin
mutton
noodle
nougat
oxtail
paella
panada
pastry
pepper
pickle
pilaff
polony
potage
potato
quiche
rabbit
ragoût
raisin
rasher
relish
salami
sea-pie
simnel

6

sorbet
sponge
sundae
supper
sweets
tiffin
titbit
toffee
tongue
trifle
viands
waffle
walnut
yogurt

7

baklava
bannock
banquet
bath bun
beef-tea
biltong
biscuit
bouilli
brioche
brisket
calipee
caramel
caviare
chicken
chicory
chowder
chutney
compote
corn-cob
cracker
crouton
crumpet
currant
custard
dariole

7

dessert
fig cake
fritter
game-pie
gelatin
giblets
glucose
goulash
gristle
haricot
jam roll
jam tart
ketchup
lasagne
Marmite
meat pie
mousaka
mustard
oatcake
oatmeal
pancake
paprika
pickles
pikelet
plum jam
plum pie
pottage
poultry
praline
pretzel
pudding
ramekin
rarebit
ravioli
rhubarb
risotto
rissole
rum baba
sausage
saveloy
savoury

7	8	9	9
sea food	frumenty	antipasto	petit four
sherbet	grissini	appetizer	pigeon pie
sirloin	hardbake	arrowroot	potato pie
soufflé	hazelnut	beefsteak	schnitzel
strudel	hotchpot	boiled egg	scotch egg
sucrose	ice cream	breakfast	seasoning
tapioca	iced cake	bubblegum	shellfish
tartlet	julienne	casserole	shortcake
teacake	kedgeree	chipolata	sour cream
treacle	lamb chop	chocolate	spaghetti
truffle	lollipop	condiment	spearmint
venison	luncheon	crackling	sugar-loaf
vinegar	macaroni	cream cake	sweetmeat
	macaroon	croissant	swiss roll
	marzipan	croquette	vol-au-vent
8	meatball	Easter egg	white meat
allspice	meringue	entrecôte	wholemeal
apple pie	mince-pie	entremets	wild honey
baguette	molasses	forcemeat	
béchamel	moussaka	fricassee	10
calipash	mushroom	fried eggs	apple-sauce
chestnut	omelette	fried fish	apricot jam
chop suey	pemmican	fruit-cake	Bath oliver
chow mein	porridge	fruit-tart	bêche-de-mer
coleslaw	preserve	galantine	beefburger
confetti	rice cake	Genoa cake	blancmange
consommé	roly-poly	hamburger	blanquette
couscous	ryebread	honeycomb	bombay duck
cracknel	salt pork	irish stew	brown bread
cream bun	sandwich	lemon curd	buttermilk
dainties	seed-cake	loaf-sugar	cannelloni
date roll	slap-jack	lobscouse	cheesecake
déjeuner	spare rib	lump-sugar	chelsea bun
delicacy	squab-pie	macédoine	comestible
doughnut	steak pie	margarine	confection
dripping	stuffing	marmalade	corned beef
dumpling	tortilla	mincemeat	cornflakes
escalope	turnover	mint-sauce	cottage pie
flapjack	undercut	mutton pie	crispbread
flummery	victuals	nut butter	currant bun
frosting		nutriment	delicacies
fruit pie			

10

frangipane
french loaf
fricandeau
fruit salad
ginger cake
grape sugar
ground rice
hotchpotch
indian corn
jugged hare
lamb cutlet
maple-sugar
marrow-bone
mayonnaise
minced meat
mock-turtle
mutton chop
patisserie
peppermint
poached egg
potted fish
potted meat
puff pastry
raisin loaf
rhubarb pie
rolled oats
saccharine
salmagundi
sauerkraut
shortbread
shortcrust
simnel cake
sponge-cake
stewed meat
sugar-candy
sustenance
sweetbread
tea biscuit
tenderloin
tinned food
vegetables

10

vermicelli
white bread
white sauce

11

baked alaska
banbury cake
barley-sugar
bonne bouche
choux pastry
cream cheese
curry powder
frankfurter
French bread
French toast
gingerbread
golden syrup
griddle cake
hors d'oeuvre
hot cross bun
milk pudding
peppermints
plum pudding
profiterole
raisin bread
refreshment
rice pudding
sago pudding
sausage-roll
short pastry
skirt of beef
stewed fruit
suet pudding
tagliatelle
wedding-cake
welsh rabbit

12

apple fritter
birthday cake
black pudding
burnt almonds
butterscotch
chip potatoes
clotted cream
cornish pasty
corn on the cob
curds and whey
Danish pastry
Dunmow flitch
julienne soup
langue de chat
liver sausage
maid of honour
merry thought
mulligatawny
mushroom soup
peanut butter
pease-pudding
pumpernickel
refreshments
shepherd's pie
sponge finger
sweet and sour
tartare sauce
tripe de roche
Welsh rarebit

13

apple dumpling
béchamel sauce
bouillabaisse
chili con carne
Christmas cake
confectionery
finnan haddock
flitch of bacon

13

German sausage
ginger pudding
prawn cocktail
salad dressing
sauté potatoes
sirloin of beef
sponge pudding
veal and ham pie
vegetable soup

14

apple charlotte
Bologna sausage
charlotte russe
macaroni cheese
mashed potatoes
mock-turtle soup
saddle of mutton
toasted teacake
treacle pudding
Turkish delight
wholemeal bread

15

bubble and squeak
chocolate eclair
Devonshire cream
garlic mushrooms

16

duchesse potatoes
meat and potato pi

18

Knickerbocker
 glory
spaghetti
 bolognese

Football teams

Team	Ground	Nickname
Aberdeen	Pittodrie Stadium	Dons
Airdrieonians	Broomfield Park	Diamonds; Waysiders
Albion Rovers	Cliftonhill	Wee Rovers
Alloa	Recreation Park	Wasps
Arbroath	Gayfield Park	Red Lichties
Arsenal	Highbury	Gunners
Aston Villa	Villa Park	Villans
Ayr United	Somerset Park	Honest Men
Barnsley	Oakwell Ground	Tykes; Reds; Colliers
Berwick Rangers	Shielfield Park	Borderers
Birmingham City	St Andrews	Blues
Blackburn Rovers	Ewood Park	Blue; Whites; Rovers
Blackpool	Bloomfield Road	Seasiders
Bolton Wanderers	Burnden Park	Trotters
Bournemouth	Dean Court	Cherries
Bradford City	Valley Parade	Bantams
Brechin City	Glebe Park	City
Brentford	Griffin Park	Bees
Brighton and Hove Albion	Goldstone Ground	Seagulls
Bristol City	Ashton Gate	Robins
Bristol Rovers	Twerton Park, Bath	Pirates
Burnley	Turf Moor	Clarets
Bury	Gigg Lane	Shakers
Cambridge United	Abbey Stadium	United
Cardiff City	Ninian Park	Bluebirds
Carlisle United	Brunton Park	Cumbrians; Blues
Celtic	Celtic Park	Bhoys
Charlton Athletic	Selhurst Park	Haddicks; Robins; Valiants
Chelsea	Stamford Bridge	Blues
Chester City	Sealand Road	Blues
Chesterfield	Recreation Ground	Blues; Spireites
Clyde	Firhill Park	Bully Wee
Clydebank	Kilbowie Park	Bankies
Colchester United	Layer Road	U's
Coventry City	Highfield Road	Sky Blues
Cowdenbeath	Central Park	Cowden
Crewe Alexandra	Gresty Road	Railwaymen

Team	Ground	Nickname
Crystal Palace	Selhurst Park	Eagles
Darlington	Feethams Ground	Quakers
Derby County	Baseball Ground	Rams
Doncaster Rovers	Belle Vue Ground	Rovers
Dumbarton	Boghead Park	Sons
Dundee	Dens Park	Dark Blues; Dee
Dundee United	Tannadice Park	Terrors
Dunfermline Athletic	East End Park	Pars
East Fife	Bayview Park	Fifers
East Stirlingshire	Firs Park	Shire
Everton	Goodison Park	Toffees
Exeter City	St James Park	Grecians
Falkirk	Brockville Park	Bairns
Forfar Athletic	Station Park	Sky Blues
Fulham	Craven Cottage	Cottagers
Gillingham	Priestfield Stadium	Gills
Grimsby Town	Blundell Park	Mariners
Halifax Town	Shay Ground	Shaymen
Hamilton Academicals	Douglas Park	Accies
Hartlepool United	Victoria Ground	Pool
Heart of Midlothian	Tynecastle Park	Jam Tarts
Hereford United	Edgar Street	United
Hibernian	Easter Road	Hi-bees
Huddersfield Town	Leeds Road	Terriers
Hull City	Boothferry Park	Tigers
Ipswich Town	Portman Road	Blues; Town
Kilmarnock	Rugby Park	Killie
Leeds United	Elland Road	United
Leicester City	Filbert Street	Filberts; Foxes
Leyton Orient	Brisbane Road	O's
Lincoln City	Sincil Bank	Red Imps
Liverpool	Anfield	Reds; Pool
Luton Town	Kenilworth Road	Hatters
Manchester City	Maine Road	Blues
Manchester United	Old Trafford	Red Devils
Mansfield Town	Field Mill Ground	Stags
Meadowbank Thistle	Meadowbank Stadium	Thistle; Wee Jags
Middlesbrough	Ayresome Park	Boro
Millwall	The Den	Lions
Montrose	Links Park	Gable Endies
Morton	Cappielow Park	Ton

Team	Ground	Nickname
Motherwell	Fir Park	Well
Newcastle United	St James Park	Magpies
Northampton Town	County Ground	Cobblers
Norwich City	Carrow Road	Canaries
Nottingham Forest	City Ground	Reds; Forest
Notts County	Meadow Lane	Magpies
Oldham Athletic	Boundary Park	Latics
Oxford United	Manor Ground	U's
Partick Thistle	Firhill Park	Jags
Peterborough United	London Road	Posh
Plymouth Argyle	Home Park	Pilgrims
Portsmouth	Fratton Park	Pompey
Port Vale	Vale Park	Valiants
Preston North End	Deepdale	Lilywhites; North End
Queen of the South	Palmerston Park	Doonhamers; Queens
Queen's Park	Hampden Park	Spiders
Queen's Park Rangers	Loftus Road	Rangers; R's
Raith Rovers	Stark's Park	Rovers
Rangers	Ibrox Stadium	Gers; Blues
Reading	Elm Park	Royals
Rochdale	Spotland	Dale
Rotherham United	Millmoor Ground	Merry Millers
St Johnstone	Muirton Park	Saints
St Mirren	St Mirren Park	Buddies; Paisley Saints
Scarborough	Seamer Road	Boro
Scunthorpe United	Old Show Ground	Iron
Sheffield United	Bramall Lane	Blades
Sheffield Wednesday	Hillsborough	Owls
Shrewsbury Town	Gay Meadow	Shrews; Town
Southampton	Dell	Saints
Southend United	Roots Hall	Shrimpers
Stenhousemuir	Ochilview Park	Warriors
Stirling Albion	Annfield Park	Albion
Stockport County	Edgeley Park	County; Hatters
Stoke City	Victoria Ground	Potters
Stranraer	Stair Park	Blues
Sunderland	Roker Park	Rokerites
Swansea City	Vetch Field	Swans
Swindon Town	County Ground	Robins
Torquay United	Plainmoor Ground	Gulls
Tottenham Hotspur	White Hart Lane	Spurs

Team	Ground	Nickname
Tranmere Rovers	Prenton Park	Rovers
Walsall	Bescot Stadium	Saddlers
Watford	Vicarage Road	Hornets
West Bromwich Albion	Hawthorns	Throstles; Baggies; Albion
West Ham United	Upton Park; Boleyn Ground	Hammers
Wigan Athletic	Springfield Park	Latics
Wimbledon	Selhurst Park	Dons
Wolverhampton Wanderers	Molineux	Wolves
Wrexham	Racecourse Ground	Robins
York City	Bootham Crescent	Minstermen

Fossils, shells, etc.

4
cone

5
amber
conch
mitre
murex
razor
snail
solen
tooth
tulip
whelk

6
chiton
cockle
cowrie
helmet
jingle
limpet
mussel
oyster
quahog

6
triton
turban
volute
winkle

7
abalone
crinoid
ogygian
piddock
scallop
voluted

8
ammonite
argonaut
ceratite
ear shell
echinite
escallop
nautilus
ram's-horn
sea-snail
strombus

9
angel wing
clam shell
comb shell
cone shell
corallite
encrinite
giant clam
harp shell
horn shell
moon shell
nummulite
pink conch
reliquiae
spiny vase
star-shell
stone lily
strombite
trilobite
turnibate

10
blue mussel
coat-of-mail

10
crown conch
eyed cowrie
periwinkle
quahog clam
razor-shell

11
dinotherium
heart cockle
helmet shell
ichthyolite
madreporite
milleporite
money cowrie
music volute
needle shell
needle whelk
onyx slipper
pearl oyster
sting winkle
textile cone
tiger cowrie
trough shell
turtle-shell

12
brocade shell
figured stone
golden cowrie
golden tellin
Japanese cone
lantern shell
Pacific auger
saddle oyster

12
scotch bonnet
slipper shell
spiked limpet
spindle shell
sundial shell
trumpet shell

13
angular volute
cardinal mitre
costate cockle
fighting conch
geography cone
lepidodendron
necklace shell
prickly helmet

13
spiral babylon
sunrise tellin

14
imperial volute
lightning whelk
Panamanian cone
staircase shell
tapestry turban

French phrases

5
à pied (on foot)

6
de luxe (luxurious)
de trop (unwelcome)

7
à gauche (to the left)
à la mode (according to the custom
  or fashion)
à propos (to the point)
de règle (customary)
en masse (all together)
en route (on the way)
oui-dire (hearsay)

8
au revoir (until we meet again)
idée fixe (obsession)
mal de mer (seasickness)

9
bête noire (person or thing
  particularly disliked)
en passant (by the way)
en rapport (in harmony)
entre nous (between ourselves)

10
billet doux (love letter)
dernier cri (latest fashion)
nom de plume (writer's pseudonym)

11
amour propre (self-esteem; vanity)
à votre santé (to your health)
lèse majesté (treason)
nom de guerre (assumed name)
raison d'être (justification for
  existence)
savoir faire (tact)
tour de force (feat of strength or
  skill)

12
coup de soleil (sunstroke)
force majeure (irresistible
  compulsion)
hors de combat (out of condition
  to fight)
ventre à terre (at full speed)

14
double entendre (double meaning)
enfant terrible (child who causes
  embarrassment)

14
noblesse oblige (privilege entails
  responsibility)
preux chevalier (gallant knight)

15
amende honorable (public apology
  and reparation)

Fruit and vegetables

3	5	6	7
cos	cress	greens	genipap
fig	cubeb	kiwano	gherkin
haw	drupe	lentil	haricot
hip	gourd	lichee	kumquat
nut	grape	lychee	lettuce
pea	guava	marrow	morello
yam	lemon	medlar	parsley
	mango	nettle	parsnip
4	melon	orange	pimento
bean	olive	pawpaw	pumpkin
beet	onion	peanut	rhubarb
cole	peach	pepper	satsuma
corn	pecan	pignut	sea-kale
date	prune	potato	shallot
gean	pulse	quince	spinach
kale	savoy	radish	sprouts
kiwi	swede	raisin	
leek		russet	**8**
lime		tomato	bayberry
mast	**6**	turnip	beechnut
okra	almond	walnut	beetroot
pear	banana		betelnut
pepo	carrot		broccoli
plum	cashew	**7**	capsicum
pome	celery	apricot	celeriac
sloe	cherry	avocado	chestnut
taro	citron	bramble	chickpea
ugli	citrus	bullace	cucumber
	cob nut	cabbage	earthnut
5	damson	chicory	eggplant
ackee	endive	coconut	fig apple
apple	garlic	currant	hazelnut
chard	girkin	deal nut	kohlrabi
chive		filbert	

8
mandarin
may apple
mulberry
mushroom
oleaster
pearmain
scallion
soya bean
tamarind
tayberry
zucchini

9
artichoke
asparagus
aubergine
blueberry
brazil-nut
broad bean
courgette
crab apple
cranberry
curly kale
greengage
groundnut
jackfruit
kiwi fruit
love apple
mangetout
musk apple
musk melon
nectarine
persimmon

9
pineapple
pistachio
raspberry
red pepper
star apple
starfruit
sweetcorn
tangerine
tomatillo
Worcester

10
blackberry
clementine
cos lettuce
cow parsnip
Cox's Orange
dried fruit
elderberry
French-bean
gooseberry
grapefruit
kidney bean
King Edward
loganberry
red cabbage
redcurrant
runner bean
strawberry
watercress
water-melon
Welsh onion
wild cherry
winter pear

11
blood orange
cauliflower
coconut palm
French beans
Granny Smith
green pepper
haricot bean
horned melon
horseradish
huckleberry
Jaffa orange
pomegranate
russet apple
scarlet bean
spring onion
sweet potato
winter apple

12
bamboo shoots
bitter almond
blackcurrant
cooking apple
corn on the cob
custard apple
lady's fingers
mangel-wurzel
passion fruit
pistachio nut
savoy cabbage
Spanish onion
spring greens
victoria plum

12
white cabbage
whortleberry
winter cherry

13
honeydew melon
marrowfat peas
morello cherry
scarlet runner
Seville orange
spring cabbage
water chestnut

14
Blenheim Orange
Cape gooseberry
conference pear
mandarin orange
preserved fruit
purple broccoli

15
brussels sprouts
Golden Delicious
vegetable
  marrow

16
Cox's Orange
  Pippin

Fungi

3
cep

5
morel
yeast

6
agaric

7
blewits
truffle

8	9	10	11
basidium	stinkhorn	bread mould	chanterelle
death cap	toadstool	psilocybin	honey fungus
mushroom		rust fungus	
puffball		slime mould	

Furniture, fittings and personal effects

3	4	5	6
bag	till	purse	duster
bar	tray	quill	fender
bed	trug	quilt	fridge
bin	vase	radio	geyser
can		razor	goblet
cot	**5**	shade	hamper
fan	apron	sheet	hearth
hod	basin	shelf	heater
mat	bench	tongs	ice-box
pad	besom	tools	kettle
pen	bidet	torch	ladder
pew	blind	towel	locker
pin	board	trunk	loofah
rug	broom	twine	mangle
urn	chair	watch	mirror
vat	chest		napkin
	china	**6**	needle
4	cigar	air-bed	oilcan
bath	clock	ash-bin	pelmet
bowl	divan	ash-can	pencil
bunk	duvet	awning	pillow
butt	flask	basket	plaque
case	glass	beaker	rocker
cask	globe	bucket	salver
comb	grill	bunker	scales
oven	guard	bureau	screen
rack	label	camera	settee
sack	light	carafe	settle
safe	linen	carpet	sheets
seat	mural	carver	shovel
sofa	paper	casket	shower
tank	piano	cheval	siphon

6	7	7	8
sponge	flannel	whatnot	nail-file
starch	fuse-box	workbox	notebook
string	gas-fire		scissors
syphon	gas-ring	**8**	shoehorn
teapot	goggles	bed quilt	shoelace
tea set	griddle	bedstead	show-case
tea urn	hair-oil	bird-bath	sink unit
tureen	hammock	bird-cage	snuffbox
wallet	handbag	bookcase	soap dish
window	hip bath	bookends	stair-rod
	monocle	cashbook	suitcase
7	ottoman	chattels	sunblind
adaptor	padlock	clay pipe	table mat
aerator	pannier	coat-hook	tea-caddy
ash-tray	pianola	colander	tea-chest
baggage	picture	coverlet	tea-cloth
bath mat	pin-case	crockery	tea-table
bathtub	playpen	cupboard	tweezers
bedding	roaster	curtains	umbrella
beeswax	rush-mat	decanter	wall safe
blanket	satchel	demi-john	wardrobe
blotter	scraper	dog-chain	water tap
bolster	shampoo	doorbell	wax cloth
bunk bed	shelves	doorknob	wireless
cabinet	shoebox	doorstep	
camp bed	steamer	egg-timer	**9**
chalice	stopper	firewood	barometer
chamois	syringe	fly paper	bathtowel
chopper	tallboy	foot-bath	bedspread
cistern	tankard	fuse wire	bookshelf
commode	tea-cosy	handbell	book-stand
compact	tea-tray	hatstand	bric-a-brac
counter	thermos	heirloom	cakestand
curtain	thimble	hip flask	camp chair
cushion	toaster	inkstand	camp-stool
cutlery	tobacco	knapsack	cane-chair
doormat	tool kit	latchkey	card-table
drapery	trolley	linoleum	carpeting
dresser	tumbler	lipstick	casserole
dustbin	valance	matchbox	china bowl
dust-pan		mattress	chinaware

9	9	9	10
cigarette	music book	wall light	foot-warmer
coffee-cup	nail-brush	wash-basin	fourposter
coffee-pot	newspaper	wash-stand	gas-lighter
container	paper-clip	water-butt	gramophone
corkscrew	paper rack	water-tank	grand piano
deck-chair	parchment	wax candle	hair lotion
directory	pepper-pot	wax polish	jardiniere
dishcloth	piggy-bank	window-box	knife-board
dog-basket	plate rack	wine glass	letter-rack
dog-collar	portfolio	work table	loose cover
dog-kennel	port glass		marking ink
dust-sheet	pot pourri	10	music stand
easy chair	powder-box	bedclothes	music stool
eiderdown	punch-bowl	biscuit-tin	musical box
face towel	radiogram	boot polish	napkin ring
fireguard	safety-pin	brown paper	needle-case
fire-irons	serviette	cabbage net	needle-work
fireplace	shoe-brush	candelabra	paper-knife
fish-knife	shower-cap	chandelier	pencil-case
flowerpot	sideboard	chessboard	pepper mill
food-mixer	sidelight	chopsticks	persian rug
footstool	side table	coal bucket	photograph
frying-pan	spin-drier	coal bunker	piano stool
gas-burner	sponge bag	coat hanger	pillowcase
gas-geyser	sprinkler	crumb-brush	pillowslip
gold-plate	stair-rods	curtain rod	pincushion
hairbrush	stamp case	dishwasher	plate-glass
hair tonic	steel wool	dumb-waiter	pocket-book
hall table	stop-watch	escritoire	prayer-book
hand-towel	table lamp	featherbed	riding-whip
haversack	tableware	finger-bowl	rolling-pin
high chair	telephone	fire-basket	salt-cellar
ink bottle	timepiece	fire-escape	scatter rug
inventory	timetable	firescreen	sealing-wax
jewel-case	tinder-box	fish-basket	secretaire
lampshade	tin-opener	fish-carver	soda siphon
lampstand	toothpick	fish-kettle	soda syphon
letter-box	underfelt	floor-cloth	spectacles
light bulb	vanity box	flower-bowl	spirit lamp
master key	wall clock	fly-catcher	stamp album
mouse-trap	wallpaper	fly-swatter	stationery
			step-ladder

10

strip light
tablecloth
table linen
tablespoon
television
time-keeper
time switch
tobacco jar
toilet roll
toothbrush
toothpaste
trug-basket
typewriter
upholstery
warming-pan
wash basket
wassail-cup
watch-chain
window-seat
wine bottle
wine cooler
work basket
wrist-watch

11

account book
address book
airing horse
billiard-cue
bolster-case
boot-scraper
braising-pan
candelabrum
candlestick
centrepiece
cheese board
clothes-hook
clothes-line
clothes pegs
coal scuttle
coffee table

11

counterpane
curtain hook
curtain rail
curtain ring
deep freezer
dining table
fire-lighter
first-aid box
floor polish
floor-dredge
fountain-pen
gaming-table
garden chair
hearth brush
knick-knacks
leather case
linen basket
nut-crackers
ormolu clock
paper-basket
paperweight
picture-rail
pipe-lighter
pocket flask
pocket knife
portmanteau
primus stove
pumice-stone
reading lamp
roll-top desk
safety razor
shopping bag
stair-carpet
tape-measure
tea-canister
thermometer
tissue paper
toilet-cover
tooth-powder
vacuum flask
waffle-irons

11

wash leather
washing line
wassail-bowl
waste-basket
water heater
watering-can
window blind
writing-desk

12

adhesive tape
antimacassar
bedside light
bedside table
bottle-opener
candleholder
carpet beater
chaise longue
chesterfield
clothes-brush
clothes drier
clothes-horse
companion set
electric bulb
electric fire
electric iron
electric lamp
electric oven
field-glasses
flour-dredger
flower-basket
gate-leg table
hot-water tank
ironing board
kitchen table
kneehole desk
looking-glass
paraffin lamp
picnic basket
playing cards
porridge-bowl

12

postage stamp
record-player
refrigerator
rocking chair
rocking horse
standard lamp
table lighter
tallow-candle
tape recorder
thermos flask
toasting fork
tobacco pouch
toilette case
trestle table
visitors' book
upright piano
walking-stick
water pitcher
Welsh dresser
Windsor chair
wine decanter
writing paper
writing table

13

billiard balls
billiard table
blotting paper
carpet sweeper
chopping block
chopping knife
cigarette case
cribbage board
dressing-table
electric clock
electric stove
feather pillow
feeding bottle
filing cabinet
folding screen
medicine glass

13	14	15
newspaper rack	anglepoise lamp	electric blanket
Persian carpet	chest-of-drawers	feather mattress
petrol-lighter	cocktail-shaker	garden furniture
ping-pong table	driving licence	gate-legged table
sewing machine	electric cooker	Japanese lantern
umbrella stand	electric geyser	knitting needles
vacuum cleaner	electric kettle	pestle and mortar
visiting cards	feather bolster	photograph album
wash-hand stand	hot-water bottle	photograph frame
Witney blanket	kitchen dresser	
	meerschaum pipe	
	Venetian blinds	
	washing machine	

Games, sports, hobbies and pastimes

2	3	4	4
go	rod	foil	quiz
	set	fore	race
3	ski	foul	ride
ace	tag	gala	ring
art	tig	game	rink
bat	toy	goal	shot
bet	win	golf	side
bow	won	hunt	skip
box		jack	snap
bye	4	jazz	solo
cue	arts	judo	spar
cup	bait	love	suit
DIY	ball	ludo	swim
fun	bite	meet	team
gym	boat	mime	toss
lap	brag	miss	tote
l.b.w.	club	odds	trap
lob	crib	pace	trot
nap	dice	pawn	turf
oar	dive	play	walk
out	draw	polo	whip
peg	epée	pool	wide
put	faro	punt	

4	5	5	6
yoga	lucky	trump	hunter
yo-yo	match	vault	hurdle
	mount	wager	jockey
5	music	whist	karate
amuse	opera	yacht	kicker
arena	pacer		knight
bails	party	6	kung-fu
bingo	pitch	aikido	lariat
bowls	point	archer	marker
boxer	poker	ballet	mashie
caddy	prize	banker	no-ball
capot	queen	bonsai	not out
cards	quits	bowler	outing
caves	racer	bowman	outrun
chase	rafia	boxing	pacing
cheat	rally	bridge	pac-man
chess	reins	camera	paddle
clubs	relay	casino	pelota
dance	revel	Cluedo	piquet
darts	rider	course	pistol
derby	rifle	crafts	player
deuce	rodeo	crease	poetry
diver	rugby	cup-tie	punter
drama	rummy	dealer	putter
drawn	score	defeat	puzzle
drive	skate	discus	quoits
dummy	skier	diving	racing
extra	slice	domino	racket
fives	slide	driver	raffle
fluke	spade	dyeing	rattle
glaze	spoon	euchre	record
hobby	sport	finish	revoke
joker	stalk	flying	riddle
joust	start	gambit	riding
kendo	stump	gamble	rowing
knave	stunt	gammon	rubber
lasso	swing	go-kart	rugger
links	throw	hazard	runner
lists	track	header	scorer
loser	train	hiking	second
lotto	trial	hockey	see-saw

6	7	7	7
sewing	checker	love all	sliding
shinty	collage	love set	snooker
single	concert	macramé	stadium
skater	contest	mahjong	starter
skiing	cookery	marbles	sub-aqua
soccer	cooking	matador	surfing
soirée	cricket	may pole	tatting
squash	crochet	misdeal	tilting
stroke	croquet	mosaics	tombola
stumps	curling	netball	topiary
tennis	cycling	oarsman	top-spin
tip-cat	cyclist	oarsmen	trained
toss-up	dancing	off-side	trainer
travel	discard	old maid	trapeze
trophy	doubles	origami	vantage
umpire	drawing	outdoor	vaulter
unfair	dribble	outride	walking
victor	driving	pageant	wargame
wicket	eskrima	pastime	weaving
winner	etching	pitcher	weights
yorker	fencing	playing	winning
	fielder	pontoon	wrestle
	fishing	pottery	writing
7	forward	putting	
amateur	fox hunt	rackets	8
angling	gambler	reading	aerobics
archery	glasses	referee	antiques
athlete	glazing	regatta	appliqué
auction	gliding	running	aquatics
average	golf-bag	sailing	baccarat
bathing	gunning	St Leger	baseball
batsman	gymnast	scooter	basketry
batting	hunting	scoring	boat race
bezique	hurling	scratch	boundary
bicycle	innings	sculler	canework
boating	jujitsu	sea-trip	canoeing
bowling	jumping	shuffle	carnival
canasta	keep-fit	singing	catapult
carving	last lap	singles	ceramics
cassino	leaping	skating	champion
century	lottery	ski-jump	charades
charade			

8

cheating
chessmen
climbing
commerce
contract
counters
coursing
cribbage
cup final
dead heat
deck golf
dominoes
draughts
dressage
duelling
exercise
face card
fair play
falconry
fielding
flat race
football
forfeits
fox chase
fretwork
full-back
game laws
gin rummy
goal line
golf ball
golf club
gymkhana
handball
handicap
harriers
high jump
hurdling
jousting
juggling
knitting
lacrosse

8

lapidary
leap frog
long-jump
love game
lucky dip
marathon
Monopoly
motoring
movement
ninepins
Olympiad
Olympics
outsider
painting
patience
ping-pong
pole-jump
printing
proverbs
racquets
rambling
roulette
rounders
sack race
Scrabble
sculling
shooting
sing-song
skipping
skittles
sledding
softball
sparring
speedway
spinning
sporting
stalking
stumping
swimming
tapestry
teamwork

8

toboggan
training
trial run
tricycle
trotting
tug-of-war
tumbling
turf club
umpiring
vaulting
walkover
woodwork
yachting

9

advantage
adventure
amusement
astrology
astronomy
athletics
Aunt Sally
badminton
bagatelle
ball games
bandalore
bicycling
billiards
blackjack
broad-jump
bullfight
camcorder
challenge
checkmate
clock golf
cockfight
conqueror
court card
cricketer
cup winner
decathlon

9

deck games
dirt-track
dog racing
drawn game
dumb-bells
engraving
entertain
fish spear
frivolity
gardening
gate money
genealogy
goal posts
go-karting
golf clubs
grand slam
gymnasium
gymnastic
hopscotch
horseplay
horserace
ice hockey
make merry
marquetry
megaphone
merrimake
merriment
motorboat
Newmarket
night club
novelette
pacemaker
pageantry
palmistry
patchwork
pedalling
philately
plaything
poker dice
pole vault
prize ring
programme

9	10	10	10
promenade	acrobatics	hockey club	team spirit
racehorse	backgammon	humming top	television
reception	ballooning	hunting box	tennis ball
relay race	basketball	hurdle race	tomfoolery
revelment	battledore	ice dancing	tournament
river trip	bear garden	ice skating	travelling
rug-making	bee-keeping	kite flying	trial match
scorecard	beer-making	lace making	tricycling
scrapbook	booby prize	landing net	triple-jump
sculpture	challenger	lawn tennis	unholstery
showplace	chessboard	local derby	victorious
shrimping	collecting	masquerade	volleyball
ski runner	competitor	midget golf	weighing-in
skydiving	conundrums	Monte Carlo	wine-making
skylarker	cricket bat	needlework	word-making
sleighing	deck quoits	opposition	
solitaire	deck tennis	paper chase	11
spectacle	Derby sweep	pentathlon	archaeology
sportsman	dolls' house	pot hunting	bear baiting
springing	embroidery	prize fight	blood sports
sprinting	enamelling	racecourse	bobsledding
square-leg	fancy dress	raceground	bullbaiting
stalemate	fast bowler	recreation	calligraphy
stopwatch	field games	relaxation	chariot race
stroke-oar	fishing net	riding crop	chess player
test match	fishing rod	riding whip	competition
torch race	fisticuffs	rotary club	competitive
touch line	fives court	roundabout	county match
trial game	flat racing	rowing club	cricket ball
trial race	fly fishing	rugby union	croquet ball
trump card	fox hunting	running-out	deck cricket
water jump	goalkeeper	scoreboard	Derby winner
water polo	goalkicker	sea bathing	diving board
whirligig	grandstand	skylarking	dressmaking
whistling	greasy pole	slow bowler	fast bowling
woodcraft	groundbait	somersault	field sports
wrestling	gymnastics	stirrup cup	fishing line
yacht race	handspring	strokesman	folk dancers
yachtsman	hippodrome	surf riding	garden party
	hobby-horse	sweepstake	hang-gliding
	hockey ball	switchback	heavyweight
		tap dancing	

11	11	12	13
hide-and-seek	table tennis	magic lantern	aquatic sports
high jumping	theatre-goer	marathon race	auction bridge
hockey stick	tiddlywinks	marking board	ballad singing
horse racing	tobogganing	mixed doubles	blindman's buff
horse riding	top-spinning	nimble-footed	bubble-blowing
horse trials	vintage cars	obstacle race	cribbage board
hunting horn	water skiing	Olympic Games	cricket ground
lightweight	winning crew	opera glasses	cricket stumps
lithography	winning side	orienteering	croquet mallet
make-believe	winning team	parallel bars	deck billiards
martial arts	world record	parlour games	double-or-quits
masquerader	yacht-racing	pigeon racing	entertainment
merrymaking		pitch and toss	equestrianism
minute watch	**12**	pleasure trip	featherweight
model-making	bantamweight	point-to-point	figure skating
motor racing	bar billiards	pole vaulting	fishing tackle
oarsmanship	beachcombing	prize fighter	happy families
open-air life	billiard ball	prize winning	hare and hound
parachuting	birds-nesting	professional	horizontal bar
photography	bird watching	racing stable	international
picnic party	bobsleighing	rock climbing	jigsaw puzzles
pillow fight	bowling alley	roller-skater	jollification
prize-giving	bullfighting	rope climbing	model railways
prizewinner	butterfly net	shove ha'penny	motor cruising
public stand	caber tossing	shrimping net	musical chairs
river sports	championship	skipping rope	prize fighting
rugby league	club swinging	skittle alley	record breaker
show jumping	cockfighting	starting post	roller skating
shuttlecock	consequences	state lottery	roulette table
sightseeing	cricket match	steeplechase	skate-boarding
skating club	deer stalking	stilt walking	Space Invaders
skating rink	draughtboard	stirrup strap	sportsmanship
skittle pool	field glasses	swimming gala	squash rackets
slot machine	figure skater	table turning	starting-point
slow bowling	flower drying	tennis player	steeplechaser
snowballing	flower making	tennis racket	sword-fighting
soap bubbles	glass blowing	theatre-going	ten-pin bowling
spelling-bee	horsemanship	thoroughbred	train spotting
springboard	hunting horse	tropical fish	weight-lifting
stencilling	huntsmanship	wicket keeper	wicket-keeping
summersault	jigsaw puzzle	winning horse	
		winter sports	

14
- all-in wrestling
- badger-watching
- billiard player
- cake decorating
- children's party
- coin-collecting
- contract bridge
- discus-throwing
- ducks-and-drakes
- flower pressing
- football league
- glass engraving
- hunt-the-slipper
- hunt-the-thimble
- mountaineering
- pigeon fancying
- record-breaking

14
- steeplechasing
- stock-car racing
- Trivial Pursuit
- weight-training

15
- ballroom dancing
- crossword puzzle
- derby sweepstake
- dirt-track racing
- flower arranging
- greyhound racing
- javelin-throwing
- public enclosure
- shell collecting
- stamp collecting
- three-legged race

15
- unsportsmanlike
- youth hostelling

16
- amateur dramatics
- American football
- autograph hunting
- consolation prize
- freestyle skating
- motorcycle racing
- snakes and ladders

18
- clay-pigeon shooting
- freestyle wrestling

19
- association football
- butterfly collecting

Geographical terms

3	4	4	4
ait	bank	ford	mesa
alp	beck	glen	moor
bay	berg	gulf	mull
ben	burn	hill	naze
bog	cape	holm	ness
cay	city	holt	pass
col	comb	inch	peak
cwm	cove	isle	pole
dam	crag	lake	pond
fen	dale	land	port
lea	dell	lane	race
map	dene	loam	reef
sea	dike	loch	rill
tor	dyke	lock	road
voe	dune	marl	rock
	east	mead	spit
	eyot	mere	sudd

4	5	5	6
syke	fjord	state	polder
tarn	fleet	swamp	rapids
town	ghaut	sward	ravine
vale	glade	weald	region
wadi	globe		riding
weir	gorge	6	runlet
west	grove	alpine	runnel
wind	haven	Arctic	seaway
wold	heath	boreal	sierra
wood	hurst	cancer	skerry
wynd	inlet	canton	spinny
zone	islet	canyon	steppe
	karoo	clough	strait
5	kloof	colony	strath
abyss	knoll	colure	stream
alley	kopje	common	street
atlas	llano	county	suburb
atoll	loess	cranny	summit
bayou	lough	crater	tropic
bight	marsh	defile	tundra
brook	mound	desert	upland
canal	mount	dingle	valley
chart	mouth	divide	warren
chasm	north	domain	
chine	oasis	empire	7
cliff	ocean	forest	airport
clime	plain	geyser	austral
coast	point	glacis	bogland
combe	polar	hamlet	channel
creek	poles	inland	commune
crest	reach	island	compass
croft	ridge	isobar	contour
delta	river	jungle	country
donga	sands	karroo	cutting
downs	scarp	lagoon	deltaic
drift	shelf	meadow	drought
duchy	shire	morass	eastern
fault	shoal	nullah	enclave
field	shore	orient	equator
fiord	sound	pampas	estuary
firth	south	parish	exclave

7	8	8	9
glacier	dominion	wild land	waterfall
habitat	downland	woodland	watershed
harbour	easterly		waterside
highway	eastward		westwards
hillock	eminence	9	
hilltop	foreland	Antarctic	10
hummock	frontier	antipodes	county town
iceberg	headland	backwater	equatorial
ice-flow	high road	backwoods	escarpment
insular	highland	cadastral	fluviatile
isthmus	hillside	Capricorn	Frigid Zone
kingdom	interior	catchment	geographer
lowland	landmark	coastline	Gulf Stream
midland	latitude	continent	hemisphere
new town	littoral	coral reef	land-locked
oceanic	lowlands	foothills	market town
plateau	mainland	heathland	no-man's-land
prairie	midlands	highlands	occidental
rivulet	moorland	landslide	palatinate
savanna	mountain	longtitude	peninsular
seaport	neap-tide	marshland	plantation
seaside	northern	monticule	population
straits	occident	north-east	presidency
thicket	oriental	northerly	projection
torrent	province	northward	promontory
tropics	quagmire	north-west	quicksands
village	republic	peninsula	sandy beach
volcano	salt lake	precipice	South Downs
western	savannah	rockbound	spring tide
	seaboard	salt-marsh	table-shore
8	seacoast	sandbanks	tidal creek
alluvial	seashore	shore-line	torrid zone
alluvion	sheading	south-east	water table
alluvium	snow-line	southerly	wilderness
altitude	southern	south-west	
brooklet	sub-polar	streamlet	11
cantonal	township	subalpine	archipelago
cataract	tropical	tableland	bergschrund
crevasse	volcanic	territory	circumpolar
currents	westerly	trade wind	continental
district	westward	tributary	conurbation
		wapentake	

11
coral island
countryside
mountainous
polar circle
polar region
river course
subtropical
territorial
tidal waters
transalpine
transmarine
trout stream
ultramarine
watercourse

12
equatorially
magnetic pole
north-eastern
north-western
principality
protectorate
south-eastern
southernmost
south-western
stratosphere
ultramontane
virgin forest

13
magnetic north
magnetic south
Mediterranean
mother country
neighbourhood
north-easterly

13
north-eastward
north-westerly
north-westward
polar distance
south-easterly
south-eastward
south-westerly
south-westward
Temperate Zone
virgin country
watering place

14
circumnavigate
Tropic of Cancer

15
acclimatisation
acclimatization

15
irrigation canal
magnetic equator
North Frigid
  Zone
South Frigid
  Zone

18
North Temperate
  Zone
South Temperate
  Zone

Geological time divisions

6	**8**	**8**	**9**
Albian	Aalenian	Mesozoic	Arenigian
Aptian	Archaean	Namurian	Barremian
Danian	Bajocian	Pliocene	Bartonian
Emsian	Cambrian	Rhaetian	Bathonian
Eocene	Cenozoic	Rupelian	Callovian
Hadean	Chattian	Scythian	Campanian
Norian	Devonian	Silurian	Coniacian
Visean	Frasnian	Tatarian	Famennian
	Georgian	Tertiary	Gedinnian
7	Givetian	Toarcian	Kungurian
Acadian	Holocene	Triassic	Ludlovian
Anisian	Jurassic	Turonian	Messinian
Archean	Kazanian	Ypresian	Oligocene
Karnian	Ladinian		Oxfordian
Miocene	Langhian		Paleocene
Permian	Lutetian		Paleozoic

9	10	10	12
Sakmarian	Cenomanian	Stephanian	Kimmeridgian
Santonian	Cretaceous	Wenlockian	Llandoverian
Siegenian	Hettangian		Serravallian
Thanetian	Llandelian	**11**	
Tithonian	Ordovician	Burdigalian	**13**
Tortonian	Palaeocene	Hauterivian	Carboniferous
	Palaeozoic	Llanvirnian	Maastrichtian
10	Piacenzian	Pleistocene	Pliensbachian
Aquitanian	Potsdamian	Proterozoic	
Artinskian	Priabonian	Tournaisian	**17**
Ashgillian	Quaternary	Tremadocian	Eifelian/
Berriasian	Sinemurian	Valanginian	Couvinian
Caradocian		Westphalian	

Geometrical figures and curves

3	6	7	9
arc	circle	rhombus	directrix
	conoid	segment	dodecagon
4	octant	tangent	ellipsoid
cone	pencil		hyperbola
cube	radius	**8**	isosceles
line	sector	catenary	loxodrome
loop	sphere	cylinder	pentagram
lune	spiral	diameter	pentangle
oval	spline	envelope	polygonal
ring	square	epicycle	rectangle
zone		geodesic	rhumb line
	7	heptagon	sine curve
5	annulus	involute	trapezium
chord	cycloid	parabola	trapezoid
conic	decagon	pentagon	
locus	ellipse	prismoid	**10**
plane	evolute	quadrant	acute angle
prism	frustum	rhomboid	anchor ring
rhomb	geodesy	roulette	epicycloid
solid	hexagon	spheroid	octahedron
torus	octagon	triangle	paraboloid
wedge	polygon	trochoid	polyhedron
	pyramid		quadrangle

10	11	13
right angle	reflex angle	perpendicular
semicircle	tautochrone	quadrilateral
	tetrahedron	

11		15
heptahedron	12	brachistochrone
hyperboloid	rhombohedron	scalene triangle
hypocycloid	sigmoid curve	
icosahedron		17
Klein bottle	13	icosidodecahedron
Möbius strip	circumference	isosceles triangle
obtuse angle	parallelogram	
pentahedron	parallelotype	19
	pedal triangle	equilateral triangle

Gilbert and Sullivan: operettas and their characters

Title of operetta	Number of letters
(1) H.M.S. Pinafore (The Lass that Loved a Sailor)	11/23
(2) Iolanthe (The Peer and the Peri)	8/17
(3) Patience (Bunthorne's Bride)	8/15
(4) Princess Ida (Castle Adamant)	11/13
(5) Ruddigore (The Witch's Curse)	9/14
(6) The Gondoliers (The King of Barataria)	13/18
(7) The Grand Duke (The Statutory Duet)	12/16
(8) The Mikado (The Town of Titipu)	9/15
(9) The Pirates of Penzance (The Slave of Duty)	20/14
(10) The Sorcerer	11
(11) The Yeomen of The Guard (The Merryman and His Maid)	19/21
(12) Thespis (The Gods Grown Old)	7/15
(13) Trial by Jury	11
(14) Utopia Limited (The Flowers of Progress)	13/20

Characters (number = operetta reference)

4	4	5
Arac (4)	Ko-Ko (8)	Aline (10)
Gama (4)	Luiz (6)	Celia (2)
Hebe (1)	Ruth (5/9)	Cyril (4)
Inez (6)		Edith (9)
Kate (9/11)		Edwin (13)

5

Fleta (2)
Guron (4)
James (9)
Leila (2)
Mabel (9)
Tessa (6)
Zorah (5)

6

Alexis (10)
Apollo (12)
Calynx (14)
Dr Daly (10)
Ghosts (5)
Giulia (6)
Isabel (9)
Melene (14)
Mikado (8)
Notary (10)
Peep-Bo (8)
Phylla (14)
Salata (14)
Samuel (9)
Tarara (14)
Yum-Yum (8)

7

Antonio (6)
Casilda (6)
Florian (4)
Georgio (6)
Katisha (8)
Melissa (4)
Phantis (14)
Phyllis (2)
Pooh-Bah (8)
Scaphio (14)

8

Angelina (13)
Annibale (6)
Fiametta (6)
Frederic (9)
Gianetta (6)
Hilarion (4)
Iolanthe (2)
Nanki-Poo (8)
Patience (3)
Pish-Tush (8)
Strephon (2)
The Judge (13)
Vittoria (6)

9

Bob Becket (1)
Constance (10)
Francesco (6)
Jack Point (11)
Josephine (1)
Pitti-Sing (8)
Scynthius (4)
Tom Tucker (1)

10

Dame Hannah (5)
Hildebrand (4)
Lady Psyche (4)
Mr Goldbury (14)
Mrs Partlet (10)
Rose Maybud (5)
Sacharissa (4)

11

Bill Bobstay (1)
Dick Deadeye (1)
Lady Blanche (4)
Mad Margaret (5)
Princess Ida (4)
The Headsman (11)
The Lady Jane (3)

12

Elsie Maynard (11)
Phoebe Meryll (11)
The Lady Sophy (14)

13

Earl Tolloller (2)
Lady Sangazure (10)
Leonard Meryll (11)
Marco Palmieri (6)
Mr Blushington (14)
Private Willis (2)
Robin Oakapple (5)
The Lady Angela (3)
The Lady Saphir (3)
The Pirate King (9)

14

Colonel Fairfax (11)
Dame Carruthers (11)
Lord Dramaleigh (14)
Ralph Rackstraw (1)
Sergeant Meryll (11)

15

Captain Corcoran (1)
Little Buttercup (1)
Major Murgatroyd (3)
The Princess Zara (14)
Wilfred Shadbolt (11)

16

Colonel Calverley (3)
Giuseppe Palmieri (6)
Old Adam Goodheart (5)
Richard Dauntless (5)
Sergeant of Police (9)

17

Earl of Mountararat (2)
Queen of the Fairies (2)
Reginald Bunthorne (3)
Sergeant of Marines (1)
The Lord Chancellor (2)
The Princess Kalyba (14)
The Princess Nekaya (14)

18

Archibald Grosvenor (3)
Sir Bailey Barre, Q.C., M.P. (14)
The Duke of Plaza-Toro (6)

19

John Wellington Wells (10)
Major-General Stanley (9)

20

Captain Fitzbattleaxe (14)
Don Alhambra Del Bolero (6)
Sir Despard Murgatroyd (5)
Sir Roderic Murgatroyd (5)
Sir Ruthven Murgatroyd (5)

21

King Paramount The First (14)
Mr Bunthorne's Solicitor (3)
The Duchess of Plaza-Toro (6)

22

Sir Richard Cholmondeley (11)

23

Lieut. The Duke of Dunstable (3)
Sir Marmaduke Pointdextre (10)

26

The Rt Hon. Sir Joseph Porter, K.G.B. (1)

27

Captain Sir Edward Corcoran, K.G.B. (14)

Girls' names

2	3	3	3
Di	Deb	Ivy	Mae
Em	Dee	Jan	May
Jo	Dot	Jay	Meg
Vi	Eda	Jen	Mel
	Ena	Joy	Mia
3	Eva	Kay	Nan
Ada	Eve	Kim	Pam
Amy	Fay	Kit	Pat
Ann	Flo	Lee	Peg
Ava	Gay	Lil	Pen
Bea	Ida	Liz	Pia
Bee	Ina	Lou	Pru
Cis	Isa	Lyn	Rae

3	4	4	4
Ria	Edie	Jill	Nell
Ros	Edna	Joan	Nina
Sal	Ella	Jodi	Nita
Sam	Elma	Jody	Nola
Sue	Elsa	Joss	Nora
Una	Else	Judi	Nova
Val	Emma	Judy	Olga
Viv	Emmy	June	Oona
Win	Enid	Kara	Peta
Zoë	Erin	Kate	Phil
	Eryl	Kath	Phyl
4	Esme	Katy	Poll
Abby	Etta	Kaye	Prue
Addy	Etty	Keri	Rena
Aime	Evie	Kyle	Rene
Alex	Faye	Lana	Rhea
Ally	Fifi	Leah	Rina
Alma	Fran	Lela	Rita
Alys	Gabi	Lena	Roma
Anna	Gaby	Lila	Rona
Anne	Gail	Lisa	Rosa
Anya	Gale	Lita	Rose
Avis	Gaye	Liza	Rosy
Babs	Gert	Lois	Roxy
Beat	Gill	Lola	Ruby
Bess	Gina	Lora	Ruth
Beth	Glad	Lori	Sara
Bett	Gwen	Lorn	Sian
Cara	Hebe	Lucy	Suky
Cass	Hedy	Lulu	Susy
Cath	Hope	Lynn	Suzy
Ceri	Ilse	Mair	Tana
Ciss	Inez	Mary	Tara
Clem	Iona	Maud	Tess
Cleo	Iris	Meta	Thea
Cora	Irma	Mimi	Tina
Dana	Isla	Mina	Toni
Daph	Jade	Moll	Trix
Dawn	Jane	Mona	Vera
Doll	Jean	Myra	Vida
Dora	Jess	Nada	Viki

4	5	5	5
Wynn	Betty	Elise	Honor
Zana	Biddy	Ellen	Hulda
Zara	Bobby	Ellie	Hylda
Zena	Bonny	Elsie	Ilona
Zita	Britt	Emily	Irene
Zola	Bunty	Emmie	Ismay
Zora	Candy	Erica	Isold
	Carla	Erika	Jacky
5	Carly	Esmee	Janet
Abbey	Carol	Ethel	Janey
Abbie	Casey	Ettie	Janie
Addie	Cathy	Evita	Janis
Adela	Celia	Faith	Jayne
Adèle	Cerys	Fanny	Jemma
Aggie	Chloë	Faron	Jenna
Agnes	Chris	Fiona	Jenny
Ailsa	Cilla	Fleur	Jessy
Aimee	Cindy	Flora	Jinny
Alana	Cissy	Floss	Jodie
Alexa	Clara	Freda	Josie
Alice	Clare	Gabby	Joyce
Alina	Coral	Gayle	Julia
Aline	Daisy	Gemma	Julie
Allie	Debra	Gerda	Karen
Amber	Delia	Gerty	Karin
Angie	Della	Gilda	Katey
Anita	Diana	Ginny	Kathy
Annie	Diane	Grace	Katie
Anwen	Dilys	Greer	Kelly
April	Dinah	Greta	Kerry
Avril	Dione	Gussy	Kirby
Barbi	Dodie	Hatty	Kitty
Becci	Dolly	Hazel	Kylie
Becky	Donna	Hedda	Laura
Bella	Doria	Heidi	Lauri
Belle	Doris	Helen	Leigh
Berny	Dotty	Helga	Leila
Beryl	Dulce	Henny	Leona
Bessy	Edith	Hetty	Letty
Betsy	Effie	Hilda	Libby
Bette	Elena	Holly	Liesl

5	5	5	5
Lilla	Moyra	Rosie	Verna
Lilly	Myrna	Sadie	Vicki
Linda	Nadia	Sally	Vicky
Lindy	Nance	Sammy	Vikki
Lizzy	Nancy	Sandy	Vilma
Loren	Nanny	Sarah	Vinny
Lorna	Naomi	Shani	Viola
Lorne	Nelly	Shari	Wanda
Lotty	Nerys	Shena	Wendy
Lucia	Nesta	Shirl	Wilma
Lucie	Netta	Shona	Wynne
Lydia	Nicky	Sibyl	Xenia
Lynda	Nikki	Sissy	Zelda
Lynne	Noele	Sonia	Zelma
Mabel	Norah	Sonja	Zorah
Mable	Norma	Sonya	
Madge	Nyree	Sophy	6
Maeve	Olive	Stacy	Alexia
Magda	Olwen	Sukey	Alexis
Mamie	Olwyn	Susan	Alicia
Mandy	Oriel	Susie	Alison
Marge	Owena	Sybil	Althea
Margo	Pansy	Tammy	Alyson
Maria	Patsy	Tania	Amabel
Marie	Patti	Tansy	Amanda
Marta	Patty	Tanya	Amelia
Martu	Paula	Terri	Aminta
Marty	Pearl	Terry	Anabel
Matty	Peggy	Tessa	Andrea
Maude	Penny	Thora	Angela
Mavis	Petra	Tilly	Annika
Meave	Phebe	Tonia	Anthea
Megan	Pippa	Tonya	Arleen
Mercy	Polly	Topsy	Arlene
Merle	Poppy	Tracy	Armina
Milly	Raine	Trudi	Astrid
Mitzi	Renée	Trudy	Audrey
Moira	Rhian	Valda	Auriel
Molly	Rhoda	Vanda	Auriol
Morag	Rhona	Velda	Aurora
Moyna	Robyn	Velma	Averil

6	6	6	6
Barbie	Dagmar	Gabbie	Jemima
Barbra	Daphne	Gaenor	Jennie
Beatty	Davida	Gaynor	Jessie
Benita	Davina	Gertie	Joanna
Bernie	Deanna	Ginger	Joanne
Bertha	Deanne	Gladys	Joline
Bessie	Debbie	Glenda	Judith
Bethan	Denise	Glenis	Juliet
Beulah	Dianne	Glenys	Karina
Bianca	Dionne	Glinys	Keeley
Biddie	Dorcas	Gloria	Kellie
Birgit	Doreen	Glynis	Kerrie
Blanch	Dorice	Goldie	Kirsty
Bobbie	Dorita	Gracie	Lallie
Bonita	Dorrie	Gretel	Laurel
Bonnie	Dottie	Gussie	Lauren
Brenda	Dulcie	Gwenda	Laurie
Bridie	Dympna	Gwynne	Lavina
Brigid	Eartha	Hannah	Leanne
Brigit	Edwina	Hattie	Leilah
Briony	Eileen	Hayley	Lenore
Bryony	Elaine	Helena	Leonie
Canice	Elinor	Helene	Lesley
Carina	Elisha	Hester	Leslie
Carmel	Elissa	Hilary	Lettie
Carmen	Eloise	Honora	Liamme
Carola	Elvira	Honour	Liesel
Carole	Emilia	Imelda	Lilian
Carrie	Esther	Imogen	Lillah
Cassie	Eunice	Ingrid	Lillie
Catrin	Evadne	Isabel	Linnet
Cecile	Evelyn	Iseult	Lizzie
Cecily	Evonne	Isobel	Lolita
Celina	Fannie	Isolda	Lottie
Celine	Farren	Isolde	Louisa
Cherie	Fatima	Jackie	Louise
Cherry	Fedora	Jacqui	Luella
Cheryl	Felice	Janice	Maddie
Cicely	Flavia	Janine	Maggie
Cissie	Franca	Jeanie	Maisie
Claire	Frieda	Jeanne	Marcia
Connie			Marcie

6	6	6	7
Margie	Psyche	Tamsin	Annabel
Margot	Rachel	Teresa	Annette
Marian	Ramona	Thelma	Anouska
Marina	Renata	Tracey	Antonia
Marion	Rhonda	Tricia	Ariadne
Marisa	Robbie	Trisha	Arianna
Marita	Robina	Trixie	Arletta
Marsha	Rosina	Trudie	Arlette
Martha	Rosita	Ursula	Augusta
Marthe	Roslyn	Verena	Aurelia
Martie	Rowena	Verity	Aureola
Mattie	Roxana	Verona	Aureole
Maudie	Roxane	Vickie	Aveline
Maxine	Sabina	Vinnie	Barbara
Melita	Salena	Violet	Beatrix
Melody	Salina	Vivian	Beattie
Meriel	Salome	Vivien	Belinda
Millie	Sandie	Vyvyan	Bernice
Minnie	Sandra	Wallis	Bethany
Miriam	Selena	Winnie	Bettina
Mollie	Selina	Xanthe	Beverly
Monica	Serena	Yasmin	Billy-Jo
Mureen	Sharon	Yvette	Blanche
Muriel	Shauna	Yvonne	Blodwen
Myrtle	Sheena	Zandra	Branwen
Nadine	Sheila	Zillah	Bridget
Nellie	Shelly	Zinnia	Bronwen
Nettie	Sherri		Bronwyn
Nicola	Sherry	7	Camilla
Nicole	Sheryl	Abigail	Camille
Noelle	Silvia	Adelina	Candice
Noreen	Simona	Adeline	Candida
Odette	Simone	Adriana	Carleen
Olivia	Sophia	Ainsley	Carlene
Pamela	Sophie	Ainslie	Carmela
Pammie	Stacey	Alberta	Carolyn
Pattie	Stella	Aledwen	Cecilia
Petula	Stevie	Alfreda	Cecilie
Phoebe	Sylvia	Allison	Celeste
Portia	Sylvie	Aloisia	Charity
Prissy	Tamara	Aloysia	Charley

7	7	7	7
Charlie	Fenella	Kristen	Melodie
Chrissy	Feodora	Kristin	Michèle
Clarice	Florrie	Larissa	Mildred
Clarrie	Flossie	Lavinia	Minerva
Claudia	Frances	Letitia	Mirabel
Clodagh	Francie	Lettice	Miranda
Colette	Frankie	Lettuce	Modesty
Colleen	Georgia	Lillian	Monique
Coralie	Georgie	Lindsay	Myfanwy
Corinna	Gillian	Lindsey	Nanette
Corrine	Ginette	Linette	Natalia
Crystal	Giselle	Lisbeth	Natalie
Cynthia	Gwynedd	Lizanne	Natasha
Daniela	Gwyneth	Lizbeth	Nerissa
Darlene	Harriet	Lizette	Nichola
Davinia	Heather	Loraine	Noelina
Deborah	Hellena	Loretta	Octavia
Deirdre	Heloise	Lorette	Olympia
Delilah	Hillary	Lorinda	Ophelia
Demelza	Honoria	Loveday	Pandora
Desirée	Isadora	Luciana	Paulina
Dolores	Jacinta	Lucilla	Pauline
Dorinda	Jacinth	Lucille	Perdita
Dorothy	Janetta	Lucinda	Petrina
Dorrice	Janette	Lynette	Phyllis
Dymphna	Jasmine	Mabella	Rachael
Eleanor	Jeannie	Mabelle	Rafaela
Elfreda	Jessica	Manuela	Rebecca
Elfrida	Jillian	Margery	Rebekah
Ellenor	Jocelyn	Marilyn	Rhonwen
Ellinor	Johanna	Marissa	Roberta
Elspeth	Jonquil	Marjory	Romaine
Emeline	Josepha	Marlene	Rosalie
Estella	Juanita	Martina	Rosalyn
Estelle	Juliana	Martine	Rosanna
Eugenie	Justina	Matilda	Rosanne
Eulalia	Justine	Maureen	Roseann
Eulalie	Kathryn	Melanie	Rosetta
Evelina	Katrina	Melinda	Roxanna
Eveline	Katrine	Meliora	Roxanne
Felicia	Kirsten	Melissa	Sabrina

7	8	8	8
Saffron	Beatrice	Florinda	Magdalen
Sanchia	Berenice	Francine	Magnolia
Scarlet	Beverley	Fredrica	Marcella
Sharron	Birgitta	Fredrika	Marcelle
Sheilah	Brigitta	Georgina	Margaret
Shelagh	Brigitte	Germaine	Marianne
Shelley	Brunetta	Gertrude	Marietta
Shirley	Carlotta	Gretchen	Mariette
Sibella	Carolina	Griselda	Marigold
Sibilla	Caroline	Gwynneth	Marjorie
Sibylla	Cathleen	Harriett	Melicent
Siobhan	Catriona	Hermione	Melisent
Susanna	Charlene	Hortense	Melloney
Susanne	Charmian	Hyacinth	Mercedes
Suzanna	Chrissie	Iolanthe	Meredith
Suzanne	Clarabel	Isabella	Michaela
Suzette	Clarissa	Isabelle	Michelle
Sybilla	Claudine	Jacobina	Morwenna
Tabitha	Clemency	Jeanette	Murielle
Theresa	Clotilda	Jeannine	Patience
Thérèse	Concepta	Jennifer	Patricia
Tiffany	Cordelia	Joscelin	Paulette
Titania	Cornelia	Joycelyn	Penelope
Trissie	Courtney	Julianne	Phillida
Valerie	Cressida	Julienne	Phillipa
Vanessa	Cytherea	Juliette	Phyllida
Yolanda	Danielle	Kathleen	Primrose
Yolande	Delphine	Kimberly	Prudence
Zenobia	Dionysia	Kristina	Prunella
Zuleika	Dominica	Kristine	Raphaela
	Dorothea	Lauraine	Richenda
8	Drusilla	Lauretta	Rosaleen
Adelaide	Eleanora	Laurette	Rosalind
Adrianne	Emanuela	Lavender	Rosaline
Adrienne	Emmeline	Lorraine	Rosamond
Angelica	Euphemia	Lucienne	Rosamund
Angelina	Eustacia	Lucretia	Roseanne
Angeline	Felicity	Lucrezia	Roseline
Angharad	Florence	Lynnette	Rosemary
Arabella	Floretta	Madelina	Samantha
Araminta	Florette	Madeline	Sapphira

8	9	9	9
Sapphire	Cassandra	Gwendolyn	Thomasina
Scarlett	Catharine	Gwenllian	Thomasine
Sheelagh	Catherine	Harriette	Valentine
Stefanie	Celestina	Henrietta	Véronique
Susannah	Celestine	Henriette	Winnifred
Tamasine	Charlotte	Hildegard	
Theodora	Charmaine	Hortensia	10
Thomasin	Christina	Hyacintha	Antoinette
Timothea	Christine	Jacquelyn	Bernadette
Veronica	Claudette	Jacquetta	Bernardine
Victoria	Cleopatra	Jeannette	Christabel
Violetta	Clothilde	Josephine	Christobel
Violette	Columbina	Katharine	Christiana
Virginia	Columbine	Katherine	Clementina
Vivienne	Constance	Kimberley	Clementine
Winifred	Constancy	Madeleine	Constantia
	Desdemona	Magdalena	Dulcibella
9	Dominique	Magdalene	Ermintrude
Albertina	Elisabeth	Margareta	Ermyntrude
Albertine	Elizabeth	Margarita	Etheldreda
Alexandra	Emmanuela	Melisande	Evangelina
Amaryllis	Ernestine	Millicent	Evangeline
Ambrosina	Esmeralda	Mirabella	Gwendoline
Ambrosine	Francesca	Marabelle	Hildegarde
Anastasia	Francisca	Nicolette	Jacqueline
Angelique	Frederica	Phillippa	Margaretta
Annabella	Frederika	Philomena	Marguerite
Annabelle	Gabriella	Pollyanna	Petronella
Artemisia	Gabrielle	Priscilla	Wilhelmina
Arthurina	Genevieve	Rosabelle	
Arthurine	Georgette	Rosalinda	11
Bathsheba	Georgiana	Rosemarie	Alexandrina
Benedicta	Geraldine	Stephanie	Christiania
Bernadine	Gwendolen		

Heraldic terms

2	3	4	4
or	bar	arms	base
	red	band	bend

4	5	6	7
blue	gules	purple	roundel
enty	gyron	raguly	saltire
fess	lines	sejant	sea lion
fret	molet	shield	shafted
gold	motto	silver	trefoil
lion	party	square	unicorn
orle	rebus	vested	
pale	rings	wivern	8
pall	sable	wyvern	annulets
paly	semée		armorist
paty	torse	7	bevilled
pean	waved	annulet	blazonry
rose		attired	couchant
semé	6	bezanty	crescent
star	argent	billets	dancetty
undy	armory	bordure	emblazon
urdy	bezant	bottony	escallop
vair	billet	chapter	heraldic
vert	blazon	chevron	indented
wavy	border	circles	insignia
	bouche	dolphin	invected
5	buckle	dormant	lozenges
armed	burely	emblaze	Lyon King
azure	canton	embowed	roundles
badge	circle	enarmed	roundlet
barry	dexter	engrail	sea horse
baton	dragon	estoile	sinister
bendy	ermine	fretted	tincture
black	falcon	gironny	tressure
bowed	fillet	griffin	
cable	fitchy	Ich Dien	9
chief	fleury	leopard	banderole
crest	florid	lozenge	blazoning
cross	fretty	martlet	chevronel
eagle	Garter	miniver	embattled
fesse	herald	nombril	engrailed
field	knight	passant	erminites
flank	mascle	potente	estoillee
flory	middle	purpure	fess point
formy	moline	quarter	fountains
green	nebuly	rampant	hatchment

9
potentate
quarterly
regardant

10
coat-of-arms
crosletted
dovetailed
empalement
escalloped

10
escutcheon
fesse point
fleur-de-lis
fleur-de-lys
King-at-Arms
knighthood
pursuivant
surmounted

11
honour point

12
bend sinister
emblazonment
escutcheoned

13
College of Arms

14
heraldic emblem
Lyon King at Arms

Herbs and spices

3
bay
rue

4
balm
dill
mace
mint
sage

5
anise
basil
chive
clary
clove
cocum
cress
cumin
grass
tansy
thyme

6
bennet
betony

6
borage
chilli
chives
cloves
endive
fennel
garlic
ginger
hyssop
lovage
nutmeg
pepper
savory
sesame
sorrel

7
caraway
catmint
cayenne
chervil
chicory
comfrey
dittany
gentian
juniper

7
lettuce
milfoil
mustard
oregano
paprika
parsley
pimento
pot herb
rampion
rosebay
saffron
salsify
succory
tabasco
vanilla

8
allspice
angelica
camomile
cardamom
cardamum
cinnamon
dropwort
feverfew
lungwort

8
marjoram
purslane
rosemary
samphire
spicknel
tarragon
turmeric
wormwood

9
baldmoney
chamomile
chickweed
coriander
fenugreek
horehound
sea fennel
spearmint
sweet herb
tormentil

10
pennyroyal
peppermint
watercress

11
herb of grace
horseradish
oyster plant

11
pot marigold
winter green

12
southernwood

14
medicinal herbs

15
mustard and cress

Horses

3	5	8	9
cob	pinto	carriage	New Forest
rig	Shire	Dartmoor	Percheron
	Welsh	galiceno	
4		Galloway	10
Arab	6	Highland	Andalusian
Barb	albino	Kabardin	Clydesdale
colt	Basuto	Lusitano	Gelderland
foal	Exmoor	palomino	Hanoverian
mare	tarpan	polo pony	Irish draft
polo		Shetland	Lippizaner
pony	7	stallion	
	draught		11
5	gelding	9	Przewalski's
coach	hackney	Appaloosa	
draft	Jutland	Connemara	12
filly	llanero	Khanstrup	Cleveland Bay
	mustang		thoroughbred

Insects

3	4	4	5
ant	cleg	tick	eggar
bee	flea	wasp	egger
bot	gnat		emmet
bug	grig	5	imago
dor	grub	aphid	larva
fly	lice	aphis	louse
nit	mite	brize	midge
	moth	drake	tinea
	pupa	drone	

6	7	8	9
acarid	ant lion	longhorn	dermestes
aphids	aphides	luna moth	dorbeetle
aptera	blowfly	mealy-bug	dragon-fly
bedbug	cricket	mosquito	eggar moth
beetle	diptera	myriapod	egger moth
botfly	epizoon	night fly	fish louse
breeze	firefly	parasite	flying ant
burnet	gallfly	puss moth	forest fly
caddis	katydid	queen ant	gall-midge
capsid	ladybug	queen bee	ground bug
chafer	lady cow	sand flea	gypsy moth
chigoe	microbe	scorpion	hornet fly
chinch	sand-fly	sheep ked	humble-bee
cicada	stylops	silkworm	ichneumon
cicala	termite	stone-fly	lac-insect
cigala	tortrix	water-bug	millepede
cocoon	wax-moth	white ant	millipede
dayfly		white fly	pine aphis
dorfly	**8**	wireworm	plant lice
earwig	acaridan	woodlice	rug weevil
elater	arachnid	wood mite	sheep lice
epeira	black-fly	wood moth	sheep tick
gadfly	book-worm	wood wasp	sugar mite
hopper	cinnabar	woodworm	swift moth
hornet	Colorado		tiger moth
lappet	crane-fly	**9**	tree louse
larvae	drone bee	Amazon ant	tsetse-fly
locust	drone fly	anopheles	turnip fly
looper	ephemera	booklouse	warble-fly
maggot	fruit-fly	bumble-bee	water flea
mantis	gall mite	caddis fly	whirligig
maybug	gall-wasp	carrot fly	wood borer
may-fly	glow-worm	cedar moth	woodlouse
midget	goat-moth	centipede	
saw-fly	green-fly	chinch bug	**10**
scarab	hawk-moth	chrysalis	bark beetle
termes	honey-bee	clavicorn	bark weevil
thrips	horse-fly	cochineal	bluebottle
tsetse	house-fly	cockroach	boll-weevil
weevil	lacewing	corn borer	bombardier
	ladybird	damselfly	bulldog ant

10

burnet moth
cabbage fly
carpet moth
cockchafer
coleoptera
digger wasp
dung beetle
ephemerans
frog-hopper
hairstreak
horse emmet
lantern fly
lappet moth
leaf insect
meal-beetle
phylloxera
plant louse
rice weevil
sheep louse
silver-fish
Spanish fly
stag beetle
veneer moth
wattle moth
winter moth
wolf spider
woolly bear

11

balm cricket
black beetle
cabbage moth
capharis bug
caterpillar
click beetle
clothes moth
codling moth
emperor moth
ephemeridae
grasshopper
green bottle
lepidoptera
mole-cricket
noctuid moth
scorpion-fly
stick-insect
tiger-beetle
tussock-moth
water beetle

12

bent-wing moth
carpenter bee
carpet beetle
cecropia moth
cheese maggot
cinnabar moth

12

ground beetle
ichneumon fly
milk-white ant
peppered moth
scarab beetle
water-boatman

13

daddy-longlegs
goliath-beetle
ichneumon wasp
saturniid moth

14

cabbage-root fly
Colorado beetle
death's-head moth
elephant beetle
Hercules beetle

15

furniture beetle
striped hawk moth

16

cuckoo-spit insect
deathwatch beetle

Butterflies

5

comma

7

monarch
peacock
ringlet
satyrid
skipper

9

brimstone
large blue
orange tip
wall brown

10

fritillary
red admiral

10

small heath

11

painted lady
swallowtail

12

cabbage white
white admiral

13

tortoiseshell

16

Camberwell beauty

Instruments

4	7	9	10
dial	aerator	flow meter	calculator
grid	ammeter	gasometer	calorifier
lens	aneroid	generator	cyclograph
pole	balance	gyroscope	endiometer
tool	bearing	heliostat	heliograph
tube	counter	hodometer	heliometer
	divider	hour glass	helioscope
5	pH meter	magnifier	heliotrope
clock	quadrat	megaphone	hydrometer
fleam	sundial	metronome	hydrophone
flume	t-square	oleometer	hydroscope
gauge	turbine	pedometer	microphone
laser	vernier	periscope	microscope
lever		polygraph	night glass
meter	**8**	rheometer	pentagraph
probe	analyser	rheoscope	phonograph
relay	bioscope	rheotrope	plane-table
ruler	boot-last	set-square	protractor
scale	calipers	slide rule	respirator
toner	computer	steelyard	steam-gauge
valve	detector	tasimeter	thermostat
	diagraph	taximeter	transistor
6	gasmeter	telegraph	tuning-fork
abacus	odometer	telephone	typewriter
camera	quadrant	telescope	viscometer
dynamo	receiver	televisor	water-gauge
filter	recorder	tide gauge	water-meter
flange	rheostat	wattmeter	
funnel	wireless	wind gauge	**11**
gasket			beam compass
lancet	**9**	**10**	cardiograph
nozzle	aerometer	acetimeter	chronograph
octant	altimeter	acidimeter	chronometer
octile	areometer	astrometer	comptometer
square	barometer	astroscope	depth-finder
	compasses	audiometer	optical lens
	condenser	audiophone	poking stick
	dynameter	binoculars	range-finder

11	12	12	13
seismometer	alcohol meter	opera glasses	pressure gauge
sliding-rule	control valve	perambulator	spring balance
stereoscope	electrometer	sliding scale	
stethoscope	electrophone	spectrometer	14
teleprinter	electroscope	spectroscope	desk calculator
thermometer	ellipsograph	speed-counter	
transformer	elliptograph	weather glass	15
transmitter	field glasses		chemical balance
	kaleidoscope	13	digital computer
	night glasses	Dipping needle	magnifying glass
		electric meter	mariner's compass
		parallel ruler	

International car registration letters

(* former country)

A	Austria
*ADN	Yemen, People's Democratic Republic
AFG	Afghanistan
AL	Albania
AND	Andorra
AUS	Australia

B	Belgium
BD	Bangladesh
BDS	Barbados
BG	Bulgaria
BH	Belize
BR	Brazil
BRN	Bahrain
BRU	Brunei
BS	Bahamas
BUR	Burma

C	Cuba
CDN	Canada
CH	Switzerland
CI	Ivory Coast (Côte d'Ivoire)
CL	Sri Lanka
CO	Colombia
CR	Costa Rica

*CS	Czechoslovakia
CY	Cyprus
D	Germany
*DDR	German Democratic Republic
DK	Denmark
DOM	Dominican Republic
DY	Benin
DZ	Algeria
E	Spain etc.
EAK	Kenya
EAT	Tanzania
EAU	Uganda
EAZ	Zanzibar (Tanzania)
EC	Ecuador
ES	El Salvador
ET	Egypt
ETH	Ethiopia
F	France and territories
FJI	Fiji
FL	Liechtenstein
FR	Faeroe Islands
GB	United Kingdom
GBA	Alderney
GBG	Guernsey
GBJ	Jersey
GBM	Isle of Man
GBZ	Gibraltar
GCA	Guatemala
GH	Ghana
GR	Greece
GUY	Guyana
H	Hungary
HK	Hong Kong
HKJ	Jordan
I	Italy
IL	Israel
IND	India

IR	Iran
IRL	Republic of Ireland
IRQ	Iraq
IS	Iceland
J	Japan
JA	Jamaica
K	Cambodia
KWT	Kuwait
L	Luxembourg
LAO	Laos
LAR	Libya
LB	Liberia
LS	Lesotho
M	Malta
MA	Morocco
MAL	Malaysia
MC	Monaco
MEX	Mexico
MS	Mauritius
MW	Malawi
N	Norway
NA	Netherlands Antilles
NIC	Nicaragua
NL	Netherlands
NZ	New Zealand
P	Portugal etc.
PA	Panama
PAK	Pakistan
PE	Peru
PL	Poland
PNG	Papua New Guinea
PY	Paraguay
RA	Argentina
RB	Botswana
RC	Taiwan

RCA	Central African Republic
RCB	Congo
RCH	Chile
RH	Haiti
RI	Indonesia
RIM	Mauritania
RL	Lebanon
RM	Madagascar
RMM	Mali
RN	Niger
RO	Romania
ROK	South Korea
ROU	Uruguay
RP	Philippines
RSM	San Marino
RU	Burundi
RWA	Rwanda
S	Sweden
SD	Swaziland
SF	Finland
SGP	Singapore
SME	Suriname
SN	Senegal
*SU	Union of Soviet Socialist Republics
SWA	Namibia
SY	Seychelles
SYR	Syria
T	Thailand
TG	Togo
TN	Tunisia
TR	Turkey
TT	Trinidad and Tobago
USA	United States of America
V	Vatican City
VN	Vietnam
WAG	Gambia
WAL	Sierra Leone

WAN	Nigeria
WD	Dominica
WG	Grenada
WL	St Lucia
WS	Western Samoa
WV,	St Vincent and the Grenadines
YU	Yugoslavia
YV	Venezuela
Z	Zambia
ZA	South Africa
ZRE	Zaïre
ZW	Zimbabwe

Islands

2	4	5	5
Ré	Java	Crete	Malta
	Jura	Dabaz	Melos
3	Long	Delos	Naxos
Hoy	Milo	Disco	Oesel
Rum	Oahu	Ellis	Ormuz
Yap	Saba	Farne	Panay
	Sark	Faroe	Paros
4	Skye	Fayal	Pemba
Aran	Sula	Ferro	Perim
Bali	Sulu	Foula	Pines
Bute	Tory	Funen	Rugen
Coll	Ulva	Goree	Sable
Cook	Unst	Haiti	Samar
Cuba	Yell	Hart's	Samos
Edge		Hydra	Texel
Eigg	5	Ibiza	Timor
Elba	Arran	Islay	Tonga
Fiji	Banks	Ivica	
Gozo	Caldy	Lewis	6
Guam	Capri	Leyte	Achill
Herm	Ceram	Lissa	Aegina
Holy	Corfu	Lundy	Andros
Iona	Corvo	Luzon	Baffin

6	6	7	8
Borkum	Tobago	Roanoke	Somerset
Borneo	Tresco	Rockall	Sri Lanka
Bounty	Usedom	St Kilda	Sulawesi
Burray	Ushant	St Lucia	Tasmania
Canary		Salamis	Tenerife
Cerigo	7	São Tomé	Trinidad
Chiloe	Anambas	Socotra	Ulalaska
Chusan	Bahrain	Stewart	Valentia
Comoro	Barents	Sumatra	Victoria
Cyprus	Bermuda	Sumbawa	Viti Levu
Easter	Capraja	Ternate	Zanzibar
Flores	Caprera	Wrangel	
Gomera	Celebes		9
Hainan	Chatham	8	Anticosti
Hawaii	Corsica	Alderney	Ascension
Honshu	Curaçao	Anglesey	Australia
Ionian	Falster	Barbados	Belle Isle
Jersey	Fanning	Bornholm	Christmas
Kodiak	Fehmern	Colonsay	Elephanta
Kyushu	Formosa	Desirade	Ellesmere
Labuan	Gotland	Dominica	Galapagos
Lemnos	Grenada	Fair Isle	Greenland
Lipari	Hayling	Flinders	Halmahera
Lombok	Iceland	Friendly	Isle of Man
Madura	Ichaboe	Guernsey	Lampedusa
Negros	Ireland	Hokkaido	Manhattan
Patmos	Jamaica	Hong Kong	Margarita
Penang	Johanna	Kangaroo	Marquesas
Philae	Laaland	Krakatoa	Mauritius
Pomona	Madeira	Lord Howe	Nantucket
Rhodes	Majorca	Malagasy	New Guinea
Robben	Massowa	Mallorca	Norderney
St John	Mayotte	Melville	Polynesia
St Paul	Mindoro	Mindanao	Raratonga
Savage	Minorca	Pitcairn	Rodrigues
Scarba	Mombasa	Rothesay	Ronaldsay
Sicily	Norfolk	St Helena	St Vincent
Staffa	Nossi Be	St Martin	Singapore
Staten	Okinawa	St Thomas	Stromboli
Tahiti	Palawan	Sakhalin	Teneriffe
Taiwan	Purbeck	Salsette	Vancouver
Thanet	Réunion	Sardinia	Walcheren

10
Ailsa Craig
Cape Breton
Dirk Hartog
Great Abaco
Guadeloupe
Heligoland
Hispaniola
Holy Island
Isle of Dogs
Isle of Mull
Isle of Skye
Kuria Muria
Laccadives
Long Island
Madagascar
Martinique
Micronesia
Montserrat
New Britain
New Ireland
New Zealand
Puerto Rico

11
Axel Heiberg
Grand Canary

11
Guadalcanal
Hart's Island
Isle of Pines
Isle of Wight
Lindisfarne
Little Abaco
Lundy Island
Monte Cristo
Pantelleria
Rhode Island
Sable Island
Scilly Isles
Southampton
Spitsbergen

12
Bougainville
British Isles
Great Britain
Great Cumbrae
New Caledonia
Newfoundland
Novaya Zemlya
Prince Edward
Savage Island

12
South Georgia
Staten Island

13
Juan Fernandez
Little Cumbrae
North East Land
Norfolk Island
Prince of Wales
Prince Patrick
St Bartholomew
Santa Catalina
Stewart Island

14
Melville Island
Tierra del Fuego
Tristan da Cunha

15
Martha's Vineyard
West Spitsbergen

18
Prince Edward Island

Jewellery, gems, etc.

3	4	5	5
gem	sard	bugle	topaz
jet	stud	cameo	watch
		carat	
4	**5**	clasp	**6**
bead	agate	coral	albert
clip	aglet	crown	amulet
gaud	amber	jewel	anklet
jade	badge	lapis	armlet
onyx	beads	links	bangle
opal	beryl	paste	bauble
ring	bezel	pearl	brooch
ruby	bijou	tiara	collar

6	7	9	11
diadem	sardius	cufflinks	aiguillette
enamel	sceptre	gold watch	alexandrite
fibula	spangle	jadestone	cameo brooch
garnet	trinket	jewellery	chrysoberyl
locket		marcasite	chrysoprase
pearls	8	medallion	lapis lazuli
pyrope	amethyst	moonstone	rock crystal
quartz	carcanet	moss agate	slave bangle
spinel	corundum	paillette	wedding ring
tiepin	filigree	press stud	
torque	hallmark	seed pearl	12
wampum	hyacinth	starstone	bead necklace
zircon	intaglio	trinketry	eternity ring
	necklace	turquoise	link bracelet
7	pectoral		mourning ring
adamant	sapphire	10	star sapphire
annulet	sardonyx	amber beads	
cat's eye	scarf-pin	aquamarine	13
chaplet	shirt-pin	black pearl	chain bracelet
coronet	sunstone	bloodstone	coral necklace
crystal		chalcedony	mother-of-pearl
diamond	9	chrysolite	oriental topaz
eardrop	armillary	coral beads	pearl necklace
earring	balas ruby	glass beads	precious stone
emerald	black onyx	mocha stone	
jewelry	black opal	rhinestone	14
pendant	breast-pin	signet ring	engagement ring
peridot	brilliant	topazolite	
regalia	carbuncle	tourmaline	15
ringlet	carnelian	watch-chain	crystal necklace
sardine	cornelian	watch-strap	
		wrist-watch	

Journalism, printing and publishing

2	2	3	3
ad	S.C.	ads	pie
em	S.F.	CRC	run
en	W.F.	die	set
O.P.		EDP	web

4	5	6	7
body	click	ascend	antique
bold	cloth	back-up	article
bulk	crown	banner	artwork
caps	daily	boards	binding
copy	draft	Bodoni	bled off
dash	dummy	ceriph	brevier
demy	flong	cliché	capital
edit	folio	coated	caption
etch	forme	column	cast off
face	fount	delete	diamond
film	fudge	editor	display
flap	gloss	flimsy	edition
grid	index	format	English
lead	leads	galley	engrave
news	libel	indent	etching
open	linen	italic	feature
page	litho	jacket	full out
pica	pearl	keep up	gripper
pull	plate	layout	imprint
quad	point	leader	Italian
ream	print	linage	justify
ruby	proof	makeup	leading
rule	punch	marked	literal
sewn	quire	masked	masking
slug	quote	matrix	measure
stet	recto	minion	monthly
take	reset	modern	mortice
trim	roman	morgue	net sale
type	rough	offset	overrun
	royal	quotes	overset
5	run-on	random	Plantin
black	scoop	review	preface
bleed	serif	revise	prelims
block	solid	rotary	printer
blurb	sorts	screen	publish
cameo	spine	serial	release
canon	story	series	reprint
caret	title	set-off	rewrite
cased	verso	sketch	sits vac
chase	xerox	splash	sub-edit
chill		weekly	tabloid

7
typeset
woodcut

8
art board
bleeding
boldface
colophon
cut flush
dateline
deadline
designer
endpaper
footnote
fournier
Garamond
hairline
halftone
hardback
headband
headline
hot metal
imperial
keyboard
Linotype
Monotype
obituary
on-screen
photoset
print run
register
reporter
softback
tailband
turnover
type area
verbatim
woodpulp

9
art editor
bookplate
bourgeois
box number
brilliant
broadside
casebound
co-edition
collating
columnist
copypaper
copyright
crossword
editorial
exclusive
facsimile
freelance
laminated
lineblock
lower case
make ready
newspaper
newsprint
nonpareil
overprint
pageproof
paperback
paragraph
photocopy
photostat
pseudonym
publisher
quarterly
signature
small pica
sub-editor
symposium
upper case
watermark
web offset
woodblock

10
assembling
annotation
blockmaker
body matter
broadsheet
catch title
city editor
compositor
copy-editor
copyholder
copywriter
desk editor
film critic
four colour
imposition
impression
interleave
journalism
journalist
lamination
leader page
lithograph
long primer
monochrome
news agency
news editor
nom-de-plume
overmatter
paraphrase
press agent
separation
short story
stereotype
supplement
title verso
trade paper
typesetter
typography

11
Advance copy
advertising
agony column
Baskerville
bold old face
circulation
copyfitting
crown octavo
cub reporter
display type
galley proof
great primer
half measure
house editor
letterpress
line drawing
lithography
night editor
platemaking
proof-reader

12
block letters
book reviewer
bromide paper
crossheading
facing matter
feature story
illustration
leader writer
London editor
magazine page
perfect bound
photogravure
sports editor

13
advertisement
Caslon old face
Centaur italic
composing room

13
editor-in-chief
foreign editor
justification
literary agent
spiral binding
stop-press news

14
banner headline
dramatic critic
features editor
Garamond italic
literary editor
managing editor
offset printing

14
perfect binding
personal column

16
Cheltenham italic
colour separation
photolithography

Kings and queens of England (from 1066), Great Britain (from 1603)

William I (the Conqueror) (1066–87)
William II (Rufus) (1087–1100)
Henry I (1100–35)
Stephen (1135–54)
Matilda (1141–48)
Henry II (1154–89)
Richard I (1189–99)
John (1199–1216)
Henry III (1216–72)
Edward I (1272–1307)
Edward II (1307–27)
Edward III (1327–77)
Richard II (1377–99)
Henry IV (1399–1413)
Henry V (1413–22)
Henry VI (1422–61)
Edward IV (1461–83)
Edward V (1483)
Richard III (1483–85)
Henry VII (1485–1509)
Henry VIII (1509–47)
Edward VI (1547–53)
Jane (Lady Jane Grey) (1553)
Mary (1553–58)
Elizabeth I (1558–1603)
James I (1603–25 (James VI of Scotland (1567–1625))
Charles I (1625–49)
Charles II (1660–85)
James II (1685–88)
Mary II (1689–94)

William III (1689–1702)
Anne (1702–14)
George I (1714–27)
George II (1727–60)
George III (1760–1820)
George IV (1820–30)
William IV (1830–37)
Victoria (1837–1901)
Edward VII (1901–10)
George V (1910–36)
Edward VIII (1936)
George VI (1936–52)
Elizabeth II (1952–   )

Kitchen utensils and tableware

3	4	5	5
bin	grid	crock	whisk
can	hook	cruet	wiper
cup	iron	doily	
hob	mill	drier	6
jar	oven	glass	ash pan
jug	pail	grill	basket
lid	rack	hatch	beaker
mop	sink	knife	beater
mug	soap	ladle	boiler
pan	soda	match	bottle
pot	spit	mixer	bucket
tap	tray	mould	burner
tin		plate	candle
tub	5	poker	carafe
urn	airer	range	carver
wok	basin	scoop	cooker
	besom	shelf	cooler
4	board	sieve	copper
bowl	broom	spoon	drawer
coal	brush	stove	duster
cosy	caddy	table	eggbox
dish	china	timer	egg-cup
ewer	churn	tongs	fender
fork	cover	towel	filter

6

flagon
funnel
gas jet
geyser
goblet
grater
heater
ice box
juicer
kettle
mangle
mincer
mortar
muslin
pestle
salver
saucer
scales
shaker
shears
shovel
sifter
siphon
skewer
slicer
string
syphon
tea cup
tea pot
tea urn
trivet
tureen
vessel

7

blender
broiler
cake tin
chip pan
chopper
coal bin

7

coal box
cutlery
dishmat
dishmop
drainer
dredger
dresser
dustbin
dustpan
freezer
griller
grinder
infuser
kneader
kneeler
milk jug
pie dish
pitcher
platter
ramekin
rondeau
salt pot
scuttle
skillet
skimmer
spatula
steamer
stewpan
syringe
tea cosy
tea tray
toaster
tumbler
wash-tub

8

bread bin
canister
cauldron
colander
cream jug

8

crepe pan
crockery
cupboard
dish rack
egg slice
egg spoon
egg timer
egg whisk
fish fork
flan ring
flat iron
gas stove
gridiron
hotplate
matchbox
meatsafe
oilstove
saucepan
sauté pan
scissors
shoe box
slop bowl
stockpot
strainer
tart ring
tea caddy
teacloth
teaplate
teaspoon
water jug

9

baking tin
can opener
casserole
chinaware
coffee cup
coffee pot
corkscrew
crumb tray
dishcloth

9

dish cover
egg beater
fire irons
fireplace
fish knife
fish plate
flue brush
fruit bowl
fruit dish
frying pan
gas burner
gas cooker
gas geyser
gravy boat
kilner jar
pepper pot
piping bag
plate rack
salad bowl
sauceboat
sharpener
slop basin
soup spoon
sugar bowl
tin opener
wineglass

10

apple corer
biscuit box
bread board
bread knife
broomstick
butter dish
chopsticks
coffee mill
cruet stand
dishwasher
egg poacher
fish kettle
floorcloth

10
gas lighter
jelly mould
knife board
liquidiser
liquidizer
milk boiler
mustard pot
pan scourer
pepper mill
percolator
rolling pin
salt cellar
slow cooker
steriliser
sterilizer
tablecloth
tablespoon
waffle iron

11
baking sheet
braising pan

11
bread grater
butter knife
cheesecloth
cheese knife
coal scuttle
coffee maker
dinner plate
dripping pan
flour dredge
fruit stoner
meat chopper
nutcrackers
paring knife
pastry brush
pastry wheel
pudding bowl
serving dish
sugar dredge
tea canister
thermometer
water filter
yogurt maker

12
breakfast cup
carving knife
deep-fat fryer
dessert spoon
fish-strainer
flour dredger
ironing board
kitchen range
measuring cup
measuring jug
nutmeg grater
palette knife
pastry cutter
porridge bowl
potato masher
potato peeler
pudding basin
pudding cloth
refrigerator
thermos flask
toasting fork

13
Butcher's block
chopping board
coffee grinder
food processor
ice-cream maker
kitchen scales
lemon squeezer
preserving jar
vegetable dish
water softener

14
galvanised pail
galvanized pail
juice extractor
knife sharpener
mincing machine
pressure cooker
scrubbing brush

Lakes, lochs, etc.

(* = former name)

3
Awe (Scot)
Van (Turk)

4
Tana (Ethiopia)
Utah (USA)

5
Taupo (NZ)
Urmia (Iran)

4
Bala (Wales)
Chad (W Africa)
Como (Italy)
Erie (Can/USA)
Eyre (Aust)
Kivu (cent. Africa)
Nemi (Italy)
Ness (Scot)

5
Garda (Italy)
Huron (Can/USA)
Leven (Scot)
Lochy (Scot)
Maree (Scot)
Neagh (NI)
Nevis (Scot)
Nyasa (cent. Africa)
Onega (Rus)

6
*Albert (cent. Africa)
Baikal (Rus)
*Edward (cent. Africa)
Geneva (Switz)
Kariba (cent. Africa)
Ladoga (Rus)
Lomond (Scot)
Lugano (Switz)
Malawi (cent. Africa)

6	7	8
Nasser (Egypt)	Torrens (Aust)	Wakatipu (NZ)
Peipus (Est/Rus)	Turkana (E Africa)	Winnipeg (Can)
*Rudolf (E Africa)		
Vänern (Swed)	8	9
Zurich (Switz)	Balkhash (Kazakh)	Athabasca (Can)
	Coniston (Eng)	Bangweulu (Zambia)
7	Grasmere (Eng)	Champlain (USA)
Balaton (Hun)	Issyk Kul (Kyrgyz)	Ennerdale (Eng)
Derwent (Eng)	Maggiore (Italy)	Great Bear (Can)
Katrine (Scot)	Manitoba (Can)	Great Salt (USA)
Koko Nor (China)	Michigan (USA)	Lochinvar (Scot)
Lucerne (Switz)	Superior (Can/USA)	Maracaibo (Venez)
Ontario (Can/USA)	Titicaca (Peru)	Thirlmere (Eng)
	Tung-T'ing (China)	Trasimeno (Italy)
	Victoria (E Africa)	Ullswater (Eng)
		Wastwater (Eng)

10	11
Buttermere (Eng)	Yellowstone (USA)
Great Slave (Can)	
Hawes Water (Eng)	12
Serpentine (Eng)	Derwentwater (Eng)
Tanganyika (cent. Africa)	
Windermere (Eng)	13
	Coniston Water (Eng)
	Virginia Water (Eng)

Languages, nationalities and races

2	4	4	4
Wu	Arab	Igbo	Pict
	Boer	Kelt	Pole
3	Celt	Kroo	Russ
Hun	Chad	Kurd	Scot
Ibo	Copt	Lapp	Serb
Ido	Dane	Lett	Sikh
Jew	Dyak	Manx	Slav
Kru	Erse	Moor	Thai
Min	Finn	Naga	Turk
	Gaul	Pali	Urdu

4	5	6	7
Wend	Swede	Jewish	African
Zulu	Swiss	Judaic	Amharic
	Tamil	Kabyle	Arabian
5	Turki	Kaffir	Aramaic
Aryan	Uzbeg	Korean	Asiatic
Asian	Uzbek	Kyrgyz	Bedouin
Attic	Welsh	Libyan	Belgian
Bantu	Xhosa	Manchu	Bengali
Carib		Mongol	British
Croat	**6**	Navaho	Burmese
Cuban	Aeolic	Navajo	Catalan
Czech	Afghan	Nepali	Chilean
Dayak	Arabic	Norman	Chinese
Doric	Baltic	Parian	Cornish
Dutch	Basque	Parsee	Cypriot
Fante	Bengal	patois	dialect
Fanti	Berber	pidgin	English
Frank	Bihari	Polish	Finnish
Galla	Breton	Pushtu	Fleming
Gipsy	Briton	Rajput	Flemish
Greek	Bulgar	Romaic	Frisian
Gypsy	Celtic	Romany	Gambian
Hausa	Coptic	Sabine	Gaulish
Hindi	Creole	Samian	Gaurani
Indic	Cymric	Samoan	Hamitic
Inuit	Danish	Sindhi	Hebraic
Ionic	Dorian	Slavic	Hellene
Iraqi	Eskimo	Slovak	Hessian
Irish	Fantee	Somali	Hittite
Khmer	French	Soviet	Iberian
Latin	Gaelic	Syrian	Iranian
Malay	Gallic	Telugu	Israeli
Maori	Gascon	Teuton	Italian
Negro	German	Theban	Kirghiz
Norse	Goidel	Trojan	Kurdish
Oriya	Gothic	Tswana	Laotian
Oscan	Hamite	Tuscan	Lappish
Punic	Indian	Viking	Latvian
Roman	Ionian	Yankee	Lombard
Saudi	Italic	Yoruba	Maltese
Scots	Jewess		Marathi
Swazi			

7	8	8	9
Mexican	Albanian	Malagasy	Cambodian
Moorish	Algerian	Mandarin	Cantonese
Morisco	American	Moroccan	Caucasian
mulatto	Antiguan	Negrillo	Ceylonese
Nahuatl	Armenian	Nigerian	Colombian
Negress	Assamese	octoroon	Congolese
Negreto	Assyrian	Parthian	Dravidian
Negroid	Austrian	Peruvian	Esperanto
Nilotic	Balinese	Phrygian	Esquimaux
Ottoman	Batavian	Prussian	Ethiopian
Pahlavi	Bavarian	quadroon	Frenchman
Persian	Bermudan	Romanian	Helvetian
Prakrit	Bohemian	Romansch	Hibernian
Punjabi	Bolivian	Rumanian	Hispanic
Quechua	Cambrian	Sanskrit	Hottentot
Rajpoot	Canadian	Scotsman	Hungarian
Romance	Chaldean	Scottish	Icelander
Romansh	Cherokee	Sicilian	Icelandic
Russian	Corsican	Slavonic	Indo-Aryan
Rwandan	Dutchman	Spaniard	Israelite
Samoyed	Egyptian	Sudanese	Jordanian
Semitic	Esquimau	Sumerian	Kannarese
Serbian	Estonian	Teutonic	Low German
Siamese	Ethiopic	Tunisian	Malayalam
Slovene	Etruscan	Turanian	Mauritian
Spanish	Eurasian	Turcoman	Mongolian
Spartan	Gallican	Turkoman	Norwegian
Swahili	Georgian	Ukranian	Ostrogoth
Swedish	Germanic	Venetian	Pakistani
Tagalog	Goidelic	Visigoth	Provençal
Tibetan	Gujarati	Welshman	Red Indian
Turkish	Hawaiian		Rhodesian
Turkman	Hellenic	9	Roumanian
Turkmen	Hispanic	Afrikaans	Samaritan
Ugandan	Irishman	Afrikaner	Sardinian
Umbrian	Japanese	Afro-Asian	Sinhalese
Walloon	Javanese	Barbadian	Sri Lankan
Yiddish	Kashmiri	Brazilian	Sundanese
	Lebanese	Bulgarian	Taiwanese
8	Liberian	Byzantian	Tanzanian
Accadian	Madurese	Byzantine	Ukrainian
Akkadian			

10	10	11	12
Abyssinian	Lithuanian	Afro-Asiatic	Indo-Germanic
Afrikander	Nicaraguan	Argentinian	King's English
Amerindian	Panamanian	Bush English	lingua franca
Anglo-Saxon	Papiamento	Greenlander	mother tongue
Australian	Paraguayan	Indo-Chinese	New Zealander
Babylonian	Philippine	Indo-Iranian	Scandinavian
Circassian	Philistine	Palestinian	
Costa Rican	Polynesian	Scots Gaelic	13
Englishman	Portuguese		Latin American
Florentine	Rajasthani	12	pidgin English
Guatemalan	Serbo-Croat	Afro-American	Queen's English
High German	Venezuelan	Basic English	Serbo-Croatian
Hindustani	Vietnamese	Indo-European	
Indonesian			

Latin phrases

4

a die (from that day)
in re (in the matter of)
stet (let it stand)

5

ad hoc (for this special purpose)
ad lib (without preparation)
ad rem (to the point)
circa (about)

6

in situ (in its original position)

7

ad finem (towards or at the end)
cui bono? (for whose benefit?)
de facto (in fact; in reality)
fiat lux (let there be light)
per diem (by the day)
sine die (without a day being appointed)
sub rosa (confidential)

8

ab initio (from the beginning)
alter ego (another self)
bona fide (in good faith)
mea culpa (my fault)
nota bene (note well)
pro forma (for the sake of form)

9

ad interim (in the meantime)
ad nauseam (to a disgusting extent)
Dei gratia (by God's grace)
ex officio (in virtue of his office)
hic et nunc (here and now)
inter alia (among other things)
pro patria (for our country)
status quo (the existing state of affairs)
sub judice (under judicial consideration)
vice versa (the other way round)
vox populi (popular opinion)

10

a Deo et rege (from God and the king)
anno Domini (in the year of our Lord)
Deo gratias (thanks be to God)
ex cathedra (with authority)
in extremis (at the point of death)
in memoriam (to the memory of)
prima facie (at first sight)
pro tempore (for the time being)
sine qua non (indispensable condition)
terra firma (solid ground)

11

ad infinitum (to infinity)
anno Christi (in the year of Christ)
de die in diem (from day to day)
de profundis (from the depths of misery)
ex post facto (after the event)
fide et amore (by faith and love)
gloria Patri (glory to the Father)
non sequitur (an unwarranted conclusion)

11

pax vobiscum (peace be with you)
tempus fugit (time flies)

12

ante meridiem (before noon)
compos mentis (sound of mind)
festina lente (hasten slowly)
jacta est alea (the die is cast)
post meridiem (after noon)
servabo fidem (I will keep faith)
veni, vidi, vici (I came, I saw, I conquered)
volo non valeo (I am willing but unable)

13

corpus delicti (body of facts that constitute an offence)
dum spiro, spero (while I breathe. I hope)
fidei defensor (defender of the faith)
in vino, veritas (there is truth in wine)
modus operandi (manner of working)
vincit veritas (truth conquers)

14

ceteris paribus (other things being equal)
in loco parentis (in place of a parent)
nil desperandum (there is no reason to despair)

15

infra dignitatem (beneath one's dignity)
non compos mentis (not of sound mind)
omnia vincit amor (love conquers all things)

17

nunquam non paratus (always ready)
ver non semper viret (spring is not always green)

18

reductio ad absurdum (a reduction to an absurdity)

19

candide et constanter (fairly and firmly)
gloria in excelsis Deo (glory to God in the highest)

20
Fortuna favet fortibus (Fortune favours the bold)

21
quod erat demonstrandum (which was to be proved (or demonstrated))
vivit post funera virtus (virtue survives the grave)

Law sittings

(in chronological order)
Hilary
Easter
Trinity
Michaelmas

Legal terms

2	4	5	5
J.P.	jury	costs	steal
K.C.	lien	court	trial
Q.C.	oath	crime	trust
	plea	estop	usher
3	quit	false	usury
act	rape	forge	valid
bar	rent	fraud	
fee	riot	guilt	6
law	seal	judge	access
rob	stay	juror	action
sue	suit	legal	affirm
use	tort	libel	appeal
	will	minor	arrest
4	writ	mulct	bigamy
abet		order	breach
bail	5	penal	charge
bars	alien	plead	commit
case	arson	poach	deceit
dock	award	proof	disbar
fair	bench	quash	duress
fine	birch	right	equity
gaol	clerk	rules	estate

6	7	8	8
felony	damages	absolute	reprieve
fiscal	defence	abstract	sentence
forger	divorce	act of God	Shops Act
guilty	exhibit	act of law	stealing
incest	faculty	advocate	subpoena
injury	forgery	attorney	testator
insult	hanging	burglary	trespass
junior	harming	Chancery	tribunal
legacy	hearsay	civil law	unlawful
motion	illegal	coercion	validity
murder	impeach	contract	
pardon	inquest	covenant	9
parole	justice	criminal	abduction
police	land tax	deed poll	accessory
prison	larceny	disorder	acquittal
puisne	lawless	distress	agreement
remand	lawsuit	entailed	allotment
repeal	licence	eviction	annulment
revoke	license	evidence	barrister
surety	offence	executor	blackmail
	penalty	fidelity	bona fides
7	perjury	forensic	code of law
accused	precept	guardian	collusion
alimony	probate	homicide	common law
assault	proving	in camera	copyright
assizes	release	indecent	defendant
bailiff	Riot Act	judgment	deviation
bequest	robbery	judicial	discharge
borstal	service	law agent	dismissal
bribery	sheriff	Law Lords	endowment
capital	slander	legal aid	equitable
caution	statute	licensee	execution
circuit	summary	litigant	executrix
codicil	summons	majority	extortion
consent	suspect	murderer	fee simple
control	treason	perjurer	feoffment
convict	trustee	petition	Gaming Act
coroner	verdict	pleading	good faith
counsel	warrant	prisoner	grand jury
cruelty	witness	receiver	guarantee
custody		recorder	guarantor

9

high court
indemnity
innocence
intestacy
intestate
judiciary
land court
licensing
litigious
mandatory
murderous
not guilty
not proven
Old Bailey
plaintiff
precedent
probation
procedure
registrar
remission
solicitor
statutory
summing up
surrender
testament
testimony

10

appearance
assessment
assignment
bankruptcy
common riot
confession
connivance
conspiracy
conveyance
corruption
decree nisi
deed of gift
defamation

10

disclaimer
enticement
estate duty
eye witness
Finance Act
forfeiture
fraudulent
gaming acts
government
gun licence
hard labour
illegality
impediment
in chambers
indictment
injunction
judicature
King's Bench
land tenure
law sitting
Law Society
legitimacy
limitation
liquor laws
litigation
magistrate
misconduct
negligence
Parliament
Poor Law Act
post mortem
procurator
prosecutor
respondent
separation
settlement
trespasser

11

advancement
affiliation

11

appointment
arbitration
arrangement
assize court
attestation
Children Act
civil rights
concealment
condonation
county court
criminal law
death duties
debtors' acts
deportation
dissolution
disturbance
enforcement
engrossment
examination
extenuating
extradition
fair comment
foreclosure
high treason
impeachment
infanticide
issue of writ
King's pardon
maintenance
market overt
obstruction
prerogative
prosecution
Queen's Bench
regulations
requisition
restitution
root of title
royal assent
Sheriffs' Act
stamp duties

11

stipendiary
suicide pact
third degree
trespassing
Vagrancy Act
vesting deed

12

adjudication
Companies Act
compensation
constabulary
conveyancing
co-respondent
cross examine
crown witness
death penalty
embezzlement
encroachment
guardianship
Habeas Corpus
imprisonment
infringement
intimidation
joint tenancy
king's proctor
land transfer
Lord Advocate
Lord of Appeal
manslaughter
misbehaviour
misdemeanour
misdirection
oral evidence
Privy Council
prostitution
Queen's Pardon
ratification
royal charter
royal warrant

12
supreme court
testamentary

13
administrator
act of marriage
apportionment
common assault
court of appeal
criminal libel
ejection order
hereditaments
housebreaking
illegal action
Judge Advocate
justification
law of property
Lord President
parliamentary
petty sessions
public trustee
right of appeal

13
search warrant
simple larceny
trial by ordeal

14
act of indemnity
administration
administratrix
Admiralty Court
common nuisance
concealed fraud
conjugal rights
county judgment
court of justice
criminal appeal
default summons
false pretences
identification
identity parade
local authority
Lord Chancellor
naturalization

14
penal servitude
Queen's evidence
Queen's pleasure
special licence
wrongful arrest

15
act of bankruptcy
Act of Parliament
Act of Settlement
Attorney General
charitable trust
compound a felony
compound larceny
contempt of court
local government
marriage licence
official secrets
power of attorney
quarter sessions
written evidence

Legislatures

4	7	9	11
Dail	Lagting	Odelsting	Nationalrat
Diet	Riksdag	Panchayat	Volkskammer
Sejm	Sangi-in	Standerat	
	Shugi-in		12
6		10	First Chamber
Cortes	8	Lower House	House of Lords
Majlis	Assembly	Oireachtas	Orszaggyules
Seanad	Congress	Parliament	
Senate	Lok Sabha	Rajya Sabha	13
Shengo	Storting	Upper House	Second Chamber
7	9	11	14
Althing	Bundesrat	Dewan Negara	Council of State
Chamber	Bundestag	Newan Ra'ayat	Federal Chamber
Knesset	Folketing	Federal Diet	Federal Council

14
House of Commons
Kuvend Popullor
People's Chamber
People's Council
Staten-Generaal

15
Council of States
Federal Assembly
General Congress
House of Assembly

15
House of Deputies
National Council
People's Assembly

16
Central Committee
Executive Council
House of Delegates
House of the People
National Assembly
National Congress

17
Chamber of Deputies
Council of the Union
Federal Parliament
House of the Nations

18
Congress of Deputies
Eduskunta-Riksdagen
Great People's Khural
House of Councillors
Legislative Council

19
Legislative Assembly

21
Assembly of the Republic
Grand National Assembly
People's Supreme Council

22
Council of Nationalities
General People's Congress
House of Representatives
Supreme People's Assembly

23
National People's Assembly
National People's Congress

24
Chamber of Representatives

25
National Resistance Council

26
National Legislative Council

27
Islamic Consultative Assembly
People's Consultative Assembly

33
Provisional National Defence
Council

40
Chamber of Republics and
   Autonomous Provinces

Literary terms

3	4	5	5
ode	foot	canto	genre
	iamb	drama	ictus
4	myth	elegy	irony
epic	play	fable	lyric

5
metre
novel
octet
prose
rhyme
style
theme
verse

6
ballad
cliché
comedy
dactyl
hubris
lament
monody
octave
parody
pathos
satire
school
septet
sestet
sextet
simile
sonnet
stanza

6
stress
symbol

7
almanac
anagram
couplet
diction
elision
epigram
epistle
epitaph
euphony
fabliau
imagery
paradox
prosody
realism
sarcasm
spondee
tragedy
trochee

8
acrostic
addendum
allegory
anecdote
aphorism
didactic

8
dramatic
eye rhyme
metaphor
oxymoron
pastoral
quatrain
rhetoric
scansion
syllable

9
anthology
assonance
biography
burlesque
catharsis
classical
free verse
half rhyme
tautology
terza rima

10
annotation
blank verse
caricature
denouement
mock heroic
picaresque

10
spoonerism
subjective

11
anachronism
malapropism
noble savage
objectivity
tragicomedy

12
alliteration
onomatopoeia

13
autobiography
belles lettres
heroic couplet

14
Miltonic sonnet
Romantic poetry
sentimentality

15
abridged edition
personification

16
Petrarchan sonnet
Spenserian sonnet

Marine growths, etc.

4
kelp
tang

5
algae
coral

5
dulse
fungi
laver
varec
wrack

6
fungus
sponge
tangle

7
actinia
blubber

7
porifer
sea moss
seaweed

8
agar agar
barnacle

8	9	11
gulf-weed	blue algae	bladder kelp
red algae	madrepore	
red coral	nullipore	12
sargasso	pink coral	bladder wrack
seawrack	sea nettle	marine plants
9	10	13
alcyonite	brown algae	acorn barnacle
bathybius	sea anemone	goose barnacle

Mathematics

3	5	6	7
add	plane	oblong	percent
arc	point	obtuse	polygon
	probe	radial	problem
4	radii	radian	pyramid
axis	range	square	rhombic
base	ratio	vector	rhombus
cone	solid	vertex	section
cube		volume	segment
plus	6		tangent
unit	centre	7	theorem
zero	circle	algebra	
	conics	average	8
5	conoid	complex	abscissa
acute	convex	concave	addition
angle	cosine	conical	analysis
conic	cuboid	cycloid	bisector
cubic	degree	ellipse	calculus
curve	divide	evolute	catenary
equal	equals	hexagon	circular
focal	factor	indices	constant
focus	height	inverse	converse
graph	matrix	maximum	cube root
group	maxima	minimum	cylinder
index	minima	modulus	diagonal
limit	minute	numeral	diameter
maths	modulo	oblique	function
minus	number	octagon	geometry

8	8	10	11
gradient	triangle	arithmetic	denominator
heptagon	variable	continuity	equilateral
infinity		dimensions	equilibrium
involute	**9**	equivalent	geometrical
matrices	cotangent	hyperbolic	permutation
multiply	expansion	hypothesis	probability
negative	frequency	kinematics	symmetrical
ordinate	geometric	multiplier	tetrahedron
parallel	hexagonal	paraboloid	translation
pentagon	hyperbola	percentage	
positive	intersect	proportion	**12**
quadrant	logarithm	right-angle	conic section
quartile	numerator	semicircle	differential
quotient	numerical	square root	intersection
rhomboid	primitive	statistics	number theory
sequence	quadratic		semicircular
subtract	rectangle	**11**	straight line
symmetry	remainder	approximate	trigonometry
		combination	

13	13	14
circumference	perpendicular	complex numbers
linear algebra	plane geometry	multiplication
parallelogram	quadrilateral	
	solid geometry	**17**
		Euclidean geometry

Medical terms

3	3	3	4
arm	ill	toe	back
ear	jaw	wen	bile
ECG	leg		bleb
ECT	lip	**4**	boil
ENT	LSD	ache	bone
eye	pox	acne	burn
fit	pus	ACTH	chin
flu	rib	ague	clap
gut	RSI	AIDS	clot
hip	tic	anus	cold

4	4	5	5
corn	vein	nasal	ulcer
cure	ward	navel	unfit
cyst	wart	nerve	urine
diet	weal	nurse	uvula
disc	womb	opium	valve
gall	X-ray	optic	virus
germ		ovary	wound
gore	**5**	pubic	wrist
gout	ankle	pulse	X-rays
hand	aorta	pupil	
head	belly	reins	**6**
heal	blood	rheum	ailing
heel	bowel	rigor	angina
iris	brain	salts	artery
knee	cheek	salve	biceps
lame	chest	scald	bruise
lens	chill	scalp	bunion
limb	chyle	scurf	cancer
lint	colon	semen	canker
lobe	cough	senna	chorea
lung	cramp	sense	clinic
mole	croup	serum	coccyx
nail	dress	sinew	cornea
neck	drops	sinus	dermis
nose	elbow	skull	doctor
otic	ether	sleep	dosage
ovum	faint	sling	dropsy
pain	femur	spasm	eczema
pang	fever	sperm	elixir
pill	gland	spine	emetic
râle	heart	stone	fester
rash	ilium	stool	fibula
scab	incus	swoon	finger
scar	joint	teeth	gargle
shin	lance	thigh	gather
sick	liver	thumb	goitre
skin	lymph	tibia	gripes
sore	mouth	tonic	growth
stye	mucus	torso	gullet
swab	mumps	toxin	healer
ulna	myopy	truss	health

6	6	7	7
heroin	stupor	bladder	humerus
herpes	tablet	blister	hygiene
hiccup	temple	boracic	illness
infect	tendon	bromide	insulin
infirm	thorax	cardiac	invalid
insane	throat	carotid	jugular
iodine	thrush	cautery	knuckle
kidney	thymol	chafing	lacteal
larynx	tissue	chloral	leprosy
lesion	tongue	choking	leprous
lotion	tonsil	cholera	linctus
lunacy	torpor	chronic	lockjaw
maimed	trance	cocaine	lozenge
malady	tremor	cochlea	lumbago
maniac	tumour	cranium	lunatic
matron	typhus	culture	malaria
matter	unwell	curable	massage
muscle	ureter	cuticle	measles
myopia	uterus	deltoid	medical
opiate	vagina	dentist	menthol
oxygen		dietary	microbe
pelvis	7	dieting	mixture
pepsin	abdomen	disease	morphia
phenol	abscess	dissect	nervous
phenyl	acidity	dresser	nostril
physic	aconite	dysopsy	oculist
pimple	adenoid	earache	operate
plague	ailment	eardrum	organic
poison	albumen	endemic	patella
potion	allergy	enteric	phalanx
radium	amnesia	fasting	pharynx
rectum	anaemia	forceps	pillbox
reflex	anatomy	forearm	plaster
remedy	anodyne	formula	polypus
retina	antacid	gastric	quinine
saliva	anthrax	glottis	recover
scurvy	arsenic	gumboil	rickets
spleen	aspirin	harelip	scabies
splint	autopsy	healing	scalpel
sprain	bandage	healthy	scapula
stitch	bilious	hormone	seasick

7	8	8	8
sensory	bacteria	hygienic	sedative
sick-bay	baldness	hypnotic	shingles
stamina	beri beri	hysteria	shoulder
starved	bile duct	impetigo	sickness
sterile	botulism	incision	sickroom
sternum	caffeine	infected	sneezing
stomach	cataract	inflamed	surgical
stunned	clavicle	insanity	swelling
styptic	club foot	irritant	tapeworm
sunburn	coronary	jaundice	terminal
surgeon	dandruff	lameness	tincture
surgery	deafness	laxative	toxaemia
symptom	debility	lethargy	underfed
syringe	deceased	ligament	uric acid
tetanus	deformed	ligature	varicose
therapy	delirium	liniment	vertebra
thyroid	delivery	magnesia	vomiting
trachea	demented	medicine	wheezing
triceps	diabetes	membrane	windpipe
typhoid	diagnose	migraine	
urethra	diseased	morphine	9
vaccine	dressing	narcosis	adrenalin
veronal	dyslexia	narcotic	alleviate
vertigo	epidemic	neuritis	ambulance
whitlow	epilepsy	neurotic	analgesic
	eye-drops	ointment	antitoxin
8	fainting	overdose	arthritis
abortion	feverish	pancreas	asthmatic
abrasion	first aid	paroxysm	bedridden
acidosis	flat feet	pastille	blindness
adenoids	forehead	pleurisy	caesarean
amputate	fracture	poisoned	carbuncle
antibody	freckles	poultice	cartilage
antidote	ganglion	ptomaine	castor oil
apoplexy	gangrene	recovery	cauterise
appendix	hay fever	Red Cross	cauterize
Asian flu	headache	remedial	chilblain
asphyxia	heat spot	rest care	cirrhosis
atropine	hiccough	ringworm	cortisone
backache	hip joint	sanitary	cuneiform
backbone	hospital	sciatica	curvature
			deformity

9

delirious
dentistry
deodorant
diagnosis
diaphragm
digestion
digestive
disinfect
dislocate
dissector
doctoring
dysentery
dyspepsia
emaciated
emollient
endocrine
epicardia
epidermis
epileptic
eye lotion
eye-strain
faintness
frost-bite
gastritis
germicide
giddiness
glycerine
hamstring
heartburn
hepatitis
hunchback
hypnotism
hypnotist
hysterics
infirmary
influenza
inoculate
invalided
isolation
lachrymal
leukaemia

9

lymph node
medicated
medicinal
menopause
neuralgia
nostalgia
open-heart
operation
osteopath
pacemaker
paralysis
paralytic
phlebitis
physician
pneumonia
poisoning
poisonous
pregnancy
pulmonary
pyorrhoea
rheumatic
sclerosis
squinting
sterilise
sterilize
stiff-neck
stiffness
stimulant
stone deaf
stretcher
sunstroke
taste buds
toothache
treatment
unhealthy
vaccinate
vasectomy

10

Adam's apple
adrenaline

10

amputation
antibiotic
anti-poison
antiseptic
apoplectic
apothecary
blood count
brain fever
breastbone
bronchitis
cerebellum
chicken pox
chloroform
collar bone
concussion
congestion
contortion
convalesce
convulsion
cotton wool
depression
diphtheria
dipsomania
disability
dispensary
dispensing
dissecting
dissection
emaciation
epicardium
epidemical
epiglottis
Epsom salts
eucalyptus
euthanasia
fibrositis
flatulence
grey matter
heat stroke
homoeopath
hypodermic

10

incubation
indisposed
knock-kneed
laryngitis
lung cancer
medicament
meningitis
metabolism
nettle rash
ophthalmia
osteopathy
out-patient
oxygen tent
penicillin
post mortem
psychiatry
quarantine
recuperate
relaxation
rheumatism
sanatorium
sanitarium
shell-shock
specialist
spinal cord
stammering
starvation
strengthen
strychnine
stuttering
tourniquet
transplant

11

acupuncture
anaesthetic
asthmatical
bandy-legged
barbiturate
biliousness
catheterise

11

catheterize
circulation
cod-liver oil
colour-blind
consumption
consumptive
corn plaster
disablement
dislocation
embrocation
face-lifting
finger stall
gall bladder
haemophilia
haemorrhage
homoeopathy
hydrophobia
hypothermia
inoculation
intravenous
long sighted
mustard bath
nursing home
palpitation
peritonitis
prickly heat
psittacosis
radiography
restorative
sal volatile

11

seasickness
spina bifida
stethoscope
stomach-pump
temperature
tennis elbow
thalidomide
therapeutic
tonsillitis
tracheotomy
transfusion
typhus fever
unconscious
vaccination
vivisection
yellow fever

12

appendicitis
carbolic acid
chemotherapy
convalescent
cough lozenge
cough mixture
degeneration
disinfectant
disinfection
friar's balsam
gastric fever
group therapy

12

growing pains
heart disease
hospital care
homoeopathic
hypertension
hyperthermia
hysterectomy
immunisation
immunization
menstruation
prescription
psychiatrist
radiotherapy
recuperation
recuperative
scarlet fever
sciatic nerve
short sighted
skin-grafting
spinal column
thyroid gland
tuberculosis
typhoid fever
zinc ointment

13

anti-spasmodic
blood pressure
bubonic plague
contraception

13

convalescence
duodenal ulcer
eucalyptus oil
fever hospital
German measles
indisposition
lead poisoning
medical school
medicine glass
nervous system
non-contagious
osteomyelitis
pharmacopoeia
poliomyelitis
radioactivity
St Vitus's dance
schizophrenia
shooting pains
shoulder blade
smelling salts
sterilisation
sterilization
stretcher case
tranquilliser
tranquillizer
varicose veins
whooping cough

14

Achilles' tendon
angina pectoris
blood poisoning
Bright's disease
conjunctivitis
floating kidney
hallucinations

14

housemaid's knee
medical student
medicine bottle
mucous membrane
organic disease
plastic surgery
psychoanalysis

15

Addison's disease
adhesive plaster
alimentary canal
radium treatment
unconsciousness
water on the brain

Bones in the human body

3	6	7	8
rib	carpal	maxilla	temporal
toe	coccyx	patella	vertebra
	fibula	scapula	
4	finger	sternum	9
ulna	pelvis		occipital
	radius	8	
5	sacrum	clavicle	10
femur	tarsal	mandible	metacarpal
nasal		parietal	metatarsal
skull	7	phalange	
tibia	frontal		
	humerus		

Military leaders

3

Lee, Robert E. (American Confederate general)
Ney, Michel (French general)

4

Foch, Ferdinand (French field marshal)
Haig, Douglas, 1st Earl (British field marshal)
Hood, Samuel, 1st Viscount (British admiral)
Howe, Richard, 1st Earl (British admiral)
Slim, William, 1st Viscount (British general)

5

Anson, George, Baron (English admiral)
Blake, Robert (English admiral)
Bligh, William (British admiral)
Cimon (Athenian general and statesman)
Drake, Sir Francis (English navigator and admiral)
Hawke, Edward, 1st Baron (English admiral)
Moore, Sir John (British general)
Wolfe, James (British general)

6

Beatty, David, 1st Earl (British admiral)
French, Sir John, 1st Earl of Ypres (British field marshal)

6

Joffre, Joseph Jacques Cesaire (French field marshal)
Koniev, Ivan Stepanovich (Russian general)
Marius, Gaius (Roman general)
Moltke, Helmuth, Count von (Prussian general)
Nelson, Horatio, Viscount (British admiral)
Nimitz, Chester William (American admiral)
Pétain, Henri Philippe (French field marshal)
Rodney, George, 1st Baron (English admiral)
Rommel, Erwin (German field marshal)
Ruyter, Michiel Adrianszoon de (Dutch admiral)
Scipio, Publius Cornelius (Roman general)
Tedder, Arthur William, 1st Baron (British air marshal)
Wavell, Archibald Percival, 1st Earl (British field marshal)
Zhukov, Georgi Konstantinovich (Soviet general)

7

Agrippa, Marcus Vipsanius (Roman general)
Allenby, Edmund Henry Hynman, 1st Viscount (British field marshal)
Blücher, Gebhard Leberecht von (Prussian general)
Bradley, Omar Nelson (American general)
Cassius Longinus, Gaius (Roman general)
Dowding, Hugh Caswell Tremenheere, 1st Baron (British air chief
  marshal)
Fairfax, Thomas, 3rd Baron (English general)
Jackson, Andrew (American general)
Jackson, Thomas Jonathan (Stonewall) (American general)
Phillip, Arthur (British admiral)
Roberts of Kandahar, Frederick Sleigh, 1st Earl (British field marshal)
Turenne, Henri de la Tour d'Auvergne, Vicomte de (French commander)
Wingate, Orde Charles (British general)

8

Agricola, Gnaeus Julius (Roman governor of Britain)
Campbell, Colin, 1st Baron Clyde (Scottish general)
Cochrane, Thomas, 10th Earl of Dundonald (British admiral)
Cromwell, Oliver (English soldier and statesman)
Hannibal (Carthaginian general)
Jellicoe, John Rushworth, 1st Earl (British admiral)
Marshall, George Catlett (American general)

9
Aristides (the Just) (Athenian general)
Bonaparte, Napoleon (French emperor and soldier)
Grenville, Sir Richard (English sea captain)
Kitchener of Khartoum, Horatio Herbert, 1st Earl (British field marshal)
MacArthur, Douglas (American general)
Miltiades (Athenian general)
Trenchard, Hugh Montague, 1st Viscount (British air marshal)

10
Alanbrooke, Alan Francis Brooke, 1st Viscount (British field marshal)
Alcibiades (Athenian general and statesman)
Auchinleck, Sir Claude John Eyre (British field marshal)
Belisarius (Roman general)
Bernadotte, Jean Baptiste (French field marshal)
Cornwallis, Charles, 1st Marquess (British general)
Hindenburg, Paul von (German field marshal)
Kublai Khan (Mongol conqueror of China)
Montgomery of Alamein, Bernard Law, 1st Viscount (British field
  marshal)
Villeneuve, Pierre de (French admiral)
Wellington, Arthur Wellesley, 1st Duke of (British general)

11
Collingwood, Cuthbert, 1st Baron (British admiral)
Marlborough, John Churchill, 1st Duke of (English general)
Wallenstein, Albrecht von (German soldier and statesman)

16
Alexander of Tunis, Earl, Harold Leofric George (British field marshal)

Military terms

3	3	4	4
aim	man	arms	fife
arm	P.O.W.	army	file
foe	war	A.W.O.L.	fire
gas		band	flag
gun	4	base	foot
hut	ally	camp	form
kit	ammo	duel	fort

4	5	5	6
halt	depth	scale	charge
host	ditch	seize	colour
jeep	draft	shako	column
line	drawn	shell	combat
mess	dress	shift	convoy
mine	drill	shock	cordon
moat	enemy	shoot	curfew
plan	enrol	siege	dagger
post	equip	SNAFU	debris
raid	field	snipe	decamp
rank	fight	squad	defeat
ruse	flank	staff	defend
shot	flare	stand	defile
slay	foray	storm	deploy
slug	front	strap	desert
spot	guard	track	detach
spur	guide	troop	detail
tank	horse	truce	disarm
tent	khaki	unarm	dug-out
trap	lance	wheel	embark
unit	lines	wound	embody
ward	march	yield	encamp
wing	medal		engage
zero	melee		enlist
	mount	**6**	enmity
5	mufti	ack-ack	ensign
agent	onset	action	escape
alarm	order	affray	escort
alert	party	allies	firing
annex	peace	ambush	foeman
armed	radar	archer	guards
array	rally	armour	helmet
baton	range	assail	impact
beret	ranks	attack	inroad
busby	relay	battle	invade
cadre	repel	beaten	kitbag
cells	rifle	billet	legion
clean	round	blow-up	limber
corps	route	brevet	marker
decoy	royal	bunker	mining
depot	salvo	castle	mobile
		centre	

6

muster
mutiny
number
occupy
oppose
orders
outfit
parade
parley
parole
patrol
permit
picket
primer
pursue
raider
ransom
ration
ravage
rebuff
recall
recoil
reduce
relief
report
resist
retake
retire
review
roster
saddle
salute
sensor
signal
sketch
sortie
stores
strife
strike
stripe
stroke

6

submit
supply
target
tattoo
thrust
trench
trophy
umpire
valour
victor
walled
war-cry

7

advance
airlift
air-raid
archery
armoury
arsenal
assault
baggage
barrack
barrage
basenet
bastion
battery
battled
besiege
bombard
brigade
canteen
cavalry
charger
chevron
citadel
Cold War
colours
command
company
conquer

7

counter
crusade
debouch
defence
defiant
degrade
destroy
disband
dismiss
dungeon
echelon
epaulet
fall-out
fanfare
fatigue
fortify
forward
foxhole
gallery
gunfire
gunnery
gun-shot
half-pay
harness
holster
hostage
hostile
kremlin
landing
liaison
mounted
neutral
nuclear
on guard
outpost
overrun
parapet
pennant
pitfall
platoon
postern

7

protect
Provost
prowess
pursuit
rampart
rations
refugee
regular
repulse
reserve
retreat
reverse
Riot Act
sandbag
section
service
sniping
spurred
stand-by
support
tactics
trailer
triumph
unarmed
uniform
valiant
venture
victory
ward off
warfare
wargame
warlike
warpath
wounded

8

accoutre
advanced
Air Force
alarm gun
armament

8	8	8	9
armature	hang-fire	saluting	atomic war
armorial	invasion	security	ballistic
barracks	knapsack	shelling	bandolier
bearskin	last post	shooting	barricade
billeted	lay siege	skirmish	battalion
blockade	lay waste	spotting	batteries
bull's eye	limber up	squadron	battle-cry
campaign	magazine	stampede	billeting
casualty	marching	standard	bodyguard
chivalry	militant	stockade	bugle call
civil war	military	stoppage	bulldozer
collapse	mobilise	storming	cannonade
conquest	mobilize	straddle	captaincy
Crusader	movement	strategy	cavalcade
decisive	musketry	strength	ceasefire
defended	on parade	struggle	challenge
defender	on parole	supplies	chevalier
defiance	opponent	supports	conqueror
demolish	ordnance	surround	crossfire
despatch	overcome	tactical	defection
detonate	palisade	time-fuse	defensive
disarray	passport	training	desertion
dismount	password	transfer	discharge
distance	pavilion	unallied	disembody
division	Pay Corps	unbeaten	disengage
duelling	prisoner	uprising	dismantle
embattle	quarters	vanguard	encompass
embodied	ramparts	vanquish	encounter
entrench	rear line	vincible	enrolment
escalade	recharge	warfarer	epaulette
eyes left	re-embark	warhorse	equipment
field day	re-embody	warpaint	espionage
fighting	regiment	yeomanry	esplanade
flagpost	remounts	zero hour	eyes front
flanking	reprisal		eyes right
fortress	reveille	9	fire-drill
furlough	ricochet	aggressor	flagstaff
garrison	rifle-pit	armistice	forage cap
gauntlet	roll-call	army corps	fortalice
gendarme	sabotage	artillery	fortifier
guerilla	saboteur	assailant	fortilage

9	9	10	10
fusillade	stand-fast	demolition	resistance
gas attack	stand fire	deployment	respirator
gladiator	stand firm	despatches	retirement
guardroom	strategic	detachment	revolution
guerrilla	subaltern	detonation	rifle range
haversack	subjugate	direct fire	route march
hostility	surrender	dismounted	sentry duty
incursion	task force	drawbridge	sentry post
irregular	terrorist	embodiment	shell-proof
land force	transport	encampment	signal fire
legionary	treachery	engagement	signalling
lifeguard	tricolour	enlistment	skirmisher
logistics	undaunted	expedition	squad drill
mercenary	unguarded	glasshouse	state of war
militancy	uniformed	guardhouse	stronghold
objective	unopposed	inspection	submission
offensive	unscathed	investment	submissive
officiate	vigilance	invincible	surrounded
onslaught	War Office	leadership	triumphant
operation	watchword	line of fire	vanquisher
overpower	white flag	manoeuvres	victorious
overthrow		map-reading	volunteers
overwhelm	10	martial law	vulnerable
pack drill	aggressive	mortar bomb	
pack train	aide-de-camp	musketeers	11
parachute	air-defence	night-watch	action front
press-gang	ammunition	no man's land	aides-de-camp
projector	annihilate	nuclear war	barrack room
promotion	camouflage	occupation	battledress
protector	capitulate	operations	battlefield
provendor	ceremonial	opposition	battle royal
rear-guard	challenger	patrolling	belligerent
rebellion	commandeer	point blank	bombardment
red ensign	commissary	prison camp	bullet-proof
reinforce	commission	protection	conquerable
reprimand	contraband	provisions	co-operation
safeguard	decampment	quick march	defenceless
semaphore	defendable	recruiting	devastation
sentry-box	defensible	regimental	disarmament
slaughter	demobilise	rendezvous	disbandment
slow march	demobilize	reparation	drawn swords
			dress parade

11

embarkation
fatigue duty
firing party
firing squad
flying squad
foot soldier
forlorn hope
fortifiable
guerilla war
impregnable
indefensive
orderly room
penetration
present arms
protagonist
range finder
rank and file
reconnoitre
recruitment
redoubtable
royal salute
safe conduct

11

searchlight
skirmishing
smokescreen
stand-to-arms
trumpet call
unconquered
war memorial

12

annihilation
anti-aircraft
bailey bridge
capitulation
civil defence
commissariat
commissioned
conscription
court-martial
covering fire
fatigue party
field colours

12

guerrilla war
headquarters
heavy brigade
indefensible
indirect fire
intelligence
landing party
light brigade
light cavalry
line of battle
outmanoeuvre
platoon drill
shock tactics
shoulder belt
shoulder knot
siege tactics
siege warfare
staff college
surveillance
unobstructed
vanquishable

12

white feather
working party

13

accoutrements
advanced guard
carrier pigeon
counter-attack
flying colours
fortification
mass formation
mounted police
ordnance depot
rallying point
regular troops
reinforcement
shoulder strap
squadron drill
storming party
strategically
swordsmanship
trench warfare
War Department

14

ammunition dump
auxiliary force
demobilisation
demobilization
field allowance
general reserve
medical officer
military school
nuclear warfare
reconnaissance
reinforcements

14

reorganisation
reorganization
standing orders
supreme command

15

auxiliary forces
casualty station
clearing station
counter approach
discharge papers

15

flying artillery
guerilla warfare
married quarters
military academy
military college
military funeral
non-commissioned
observation post

16

guerrilla warfare

Molluscs

3	6	7	9
mya	limpet	piddock	gastropod
	loligo	purpura	giant clam
4	mantle	quahaug	land snail
clam	mussel	scallop	littorina
crab	ostrea	scollop	planorbis
slug	oyster	sea hare	shellfish
spat	pecten		
	quahog	8	10
5	sea ear	anodonta	amphineura
gaper	teredo	argonaut	cephalopod
helix	tethys	decapoda	cuttlefish
limax	triton	doridoid	gasteropod
murex	voluta	haliotis	hermit crab
sepia	winkle	mollusca	periwinkle
snail		nauplius	razorshell
solen	7	nautilus	scaphopoda
squid	abalone	pagurian	stone borer
whelk	ascidia	pteropod	stone eater
	bivalve	sea lemon	
6	lobster	shipworm	11
chiton	mytilus	strombus	pearl oyster
cockle	octopod		
cuttle	octopus	9	13
isopod	patella	buccinium	lamellibranch
		dentalium	

Motoring terms

2	3	3	3
A.A.	car	M.O.T.	rod
c.c.	cog	nut	run
h.p.	fan	oil	top
	fit	pin	
3	gas	pit	4
air	hub	R.A.C.	axle
cam	jam	rev	boot
cap	jet	rim	bulb

4

bush
clip
coil
dash
disc
door
flat
fuse
gear
hood
hoot
horn
jack
lane
lock
pump
road
rope
seat
skid
sump
tail
tank
test
tour
tube
tyre
veer
wing

5

brake
cable
chain
chart
choke
clamp
coupé
cover
crank
cut-in

5

drive
frame
gauge
joint
knock
lay-by
level
lever
model
motor
on tow
pedal
rally
rev-up
rivet
rotor
route
screw
sedan
shaft
spark
speed
spoke
stall
start
tools
tread
U-turn
valve
wheel
wiper

6

adjust
big-end
bonnet
bumper
by-pass
camber
car tax
charge

6

clutch
cut-out
damper
dazzle
de-coke
de-icer
de-luxe
detour
dickey
divert
driver
dynamo
engine
filter
fitter
flange
funnel
gasket
heater
hooter
hot rod
hub cap
idling
klaxon
lock-up
mascot
milage
mirror
octane
oilcan
one-way
petrol
pile-up
pinion
piston
saloon
signal
spokes
spring
swerve
switch

6

tappet
timing
torque
tuning

7

air hose
airlock
axle-box
battery
bearing
blowout
bollard
bracket
build-up
bus lane
bus stop
carpark
carport
cat's eye
chassis
contact
control
cooling
dipping
drive-in
exhaust
fanbelt
flyover
gearbox
give-way
goggles
hardtop
highway
joyride
L driver
L plates
licence
log book
luggage
mileage

7

misfire
offside
oil-feed
oil seal
parking
pillion
pull-out
reverse
roadhog
roadmap
road tax
rolling
run into
service
skidpan
spindle
springs
starter
test run
toolkit
top gear
touring
towrope
traffic
trailer
viaduct
warning

8

air brake
air inlet
airtight
autobahn
backfire
back seat
bodywork
brake pad
brake rod
bulkhead
camshaft
cat's eyes

8

clearway
coasting
coned off
converge
coupling
crankpin
cross-ply
cruising
cylinder
declutch
dipstick
driveway
fast lane
feed pipe
feed pump
flat tyre
flywheel
foglight
footpump
friction
fuel pipe
fuel pump
fuel tank
garaging
gasoline
gradient
ignition
joyrider
knocking
manifold
missfire
motoring
motorist
motorway
mounting
mudguard
nearside
oil gauge
oncoming
open road
overhaul

8

overtake
overturn
pavement
puncture
radiator
rattling
rear axle
rear lamp
ring road
roadside
road sign
road test
roof-rack
rotor arm
rush-hour
selector
side road
silencer
skidding
skid mark
slip road
slow down
slow lane
small-end
speeding
squad car
steering
stock car
tail skid
taxi rank
throttle
tyre pump

9

air filter
alignment
anti-glare
back wheel
ball-valve
batteries
brakedrum

9

brakeshoe
breakdown
car polish
chauffeur
coachwork
condenser
cotter pin
crank axle
crank case
de-froster
dipswitch
direction
dirt track
disc brake
diversion
estate car
footbrake
framework
free-wheel
front axle
front seat
fuel gauge
gear lever
gear stick
generator
grand prix
grease-box
grease-gun
half-shaft
handbrake
headlight
hit-and-run
inner tube
insurance
limousine
lubricate
misfiring
motorbike
motorcade
motor show
oil filter

9

overdrive
passenger
patrol car
petrol can
piston rod
point duty
police car
prop shaft
racing car
rear light
reflector
revving-up
road sense
road works
saloon car
spare tyre
spark plug
sports car
spotlight
switch off
taximeter
third gear
T-junction
tramlines
trunk road
two-seater
tyre lever
underseal
wheel base
wheel spin
white line

10

access road
adjustment
anti-dazzle
antifreeze
brake fluid
brake pedal
broken-down
car licence

10

combustion
contraflow
crankshaft
crossroads
detonation
dickey seat
drive shaft
dry battery
four-seater
front wheel
gear casing
gear change
gudgeon pin
headlights
horsepower
inlet valve
insulation
lighting-up
low-tension
lubricator
motorcycle
overtaking
petrol pump
petrol tank
piston ring
private car
radial tyre
rear mirror
rev counter
right of way
roadworthy
roundabout
safety belt
signalling
spare wheel
speed limit
streamline
suspension
tachometer
third-party
three-speed

10

toll bridge
traffic cop
traffic jam
two wheeler
upholstery
ventilator
wheelbrace
windscreen
wing mirror

11

accelerator
accessories
blind corner
brake-lining
built-up area
carburettor
carriageway
clutch pedal
compression
convertible
distributor
driving test
exhaust pipe
front lights
highway code
ignition key
lorry driver
lubrication
luggage rack
number plate
oil pressure
overhauling
overheating
over-revving
owner-driver
petrol gauge
racing model
radiator cap
request stop
reverse gear

11

reverse turn
rotary valve
screen-wiper
self-starter
sliding roof
speedometer
sports model
streamlined
synchromesh
tappet valve
through road
ticking-over
trafficator
vacuum brake

12

acceleration
approach road
arterial road
ball-bearings
breakdown van
clutch-spring
coachbuilder
cylinder head
diesel engine
differential
double-decker
exhaust valve
free-wheeling
gear changing
lock-up garage
miles per hour
motor scooter
motor vehicle
motorcyclist
pillion rider
racing driver
ratchet-wheel
registration
repair outfit
road junction

12

running-board
single-decker
sparking plug
sunshine roof
transmission
turbo-charger
two-speed gear
warning light

13

cooling system
driving mirror
fuel injection
hydraulic jack
inspection pit
licence-holder
pillion-riding
power steering
pressure-gauge
rack-and-pinion
servo-assisted

13

shock absorber
shooting brake
speed merchant
starting motor
steering wheel
traffic lights
traffic signal

14

compression tap
double-declutch
driving licence
exhaust-cam axle
filling station
four-wheel drive
grease-injector
lighting-up time
lubricating oil
miles per gallon
propeller shaft
reclining seats

14

reversing light
service station
starting handle
steering column
third-party risk
three-speed gear
universal joint

15

carriage-builder
dual carriageway
front-wheel drive
hydraulic system
petrol injection

17

revolution counter

21

automatic transmission
power-assisted steering

Mountains, hills and volcanoes

(H = hills; M = mountains; V = volcanoes)

3

Ida (M) (Turk)

4

Alps (M) (Europe)
Blue (M) (Aust)
Cook (M) (NZ)
Etna (V) (Sicily)
Harz (M) (Ger)
Jura (M) (Fr/Switz)
Rigi (M) (Switz)
Ural (M) (Rus)

5

Altai (M) (Kazakh)
Andes (M) (S. Am)
Athos (M) (Gr)
Atlas (M) (Alg/Moroc)
Black (M) (Wales)
Eiger (M) (Switz)
Elgon (M) (Kenya/Uganda)
Ghats (M) (India)
Hekla (V) (Ice)
Kamet (M) (China/India)
Kenya (M) (Kenya)
Logan (M) (Can)
Ochil (H) (Scot)
Pelée (V) (Martin)

5

Rocky (M) (Can/USA)
Weald (H) (Eng)
Wolds (H) (Eng)

6

Ararat (M) (Turk)
Balkan (M) (Bulg)
Carmel (M) (Israel)
Egmont (M) (NZ)
Elbert (M) (USA)
Elbrus (M) (Geo)
Erebus (V) Antarc
Hermon (M) (Leban/Syria)
Kun Lun (M) (China)
Lascar (V) (Chile)
Mendip (H) (Eng)
Mourne (M) (NI)
Olives (M. of) (Israel)
Pamirs (M) (Afghan/China/Tajik)
Pindus (M) (Gr)
Purace (V) (Colomb)
Sangay (V) (Ecuad)
Semeru (V) (Indon)
Sidlaw (H) (Scot)
Slamat (V) (Indon)
Tacana (V) (Guat)
Tasman (M) (NZ)
Tatras (M) (Pol/Slovak)
Taunus (M) (Ger)
Taurus (M) (Turk)
Zagros (M) (Iran)

7

Bernina (M) (Switz)
Big Horn (M) (USA)
Bow Fell (M) (Eng)
Brocken (M) (Ger)
Cheviot (H) (Eng)
Everest (M) (Nepal/Tibet)
Jolluro (V) (Mex)
Kilauea (V) (USA)
Lebanon (M) (Leban)

7

Malvern (H) (Eng)
Olympus (M) (Gr)
Rainier (M) (USA)
Roraima (M) (Braz/Guyana/Venez)
St Elias (M) (Can/USA)
Scafell (M) (Eng)
Skiddaw (M) (Eng)
Snowdon (M) (Wales)
Vulcano (V) (Italy)

8

Ben Nevis (M) (Scot)
Ben Wyvis (M) (Scot)
Cambrian (M) (Wales)
Cameroon (V) (Cameroon)
Cotopaxi (V) (Ecuad)
Cotswold (H) (Eng)
Edgehill (H) (Eng)
Flinders (M) (Aust)
Fujiyama (V) (Japan)
Goatfell (M) (Scot)
Jungfrau (M) (Switz)
Krakatoa (V) (Indon)
Mauna Loa (V) (USA)
Pennines (H) (Eng)
Pentland (H) (Scot)
Pinatubo (V) (Phil)
Pyrenees (M) (Europe)
Quantock (H) (Eng)
Rindjani (V) (Indon)
St Helens (V) (USA)
Santorin (V) (Gr)
Snaefell (M) (I of M)
Vesuvius (V) (Italy)

9

Aconcagua (V) (Arg)
Allegheny (M) (USA)
Annapurna (M) (Nepal)
Apennines (M) (Italy)
Blue Ridge (M) (USA)

9

Cairngorm (M) (Scot)
Chilterns (H) (Eng)
Cleveland (V) (USA)
Cotswolds (H) (Eng)
Dolomites (M) (Italy)
Grampians (M) (Scot)
Helvellyn (M) (Eng)
Himalayas (M) (S. Asia)
Hindu Kush (M) (Cen. Asia)
Karakoram (M)
 (China/India/Pakist)
Kosciusko (M) (Aust)
Mont Blanc (M) (Fr/Italy)
Parícutin (V) (Mex)
Parnassus (M) (Gr)
Ruwenzori (M) (Uganda/Zaïre)
St Gothard (M) (Switz)
Santorini (V) (Gr)
Stromboli (V) (Italy)

10

Adirondack (M) (USA)
Cader Idris (M) (Wales)
Cantabrian (M) (Sp)
Carpathian (M)
 (Czech/Pol/Rom/Slovak/Ukr)
Chimborazo (M) (Ecuad)
Dhaulagiri (M) (Nepal)
Erz Gebirge (M) (Ger)
Guallatiri (V) (Chile)
Lammermuir (H) (Scot)
Matterhorn (M) (Italy/Switz)
North Downs (H) (Eng)

10

Nyamlagira (V) (Zaïre)
South Downs (H) (Eng)

11

Anti-Lebanon (M) (Leban/Syria)
Appalachian (M) (USA)
Bernese Alps (M) (Switz)
Drakensberg (M) (S. Af)
Kilimanjaro (M) (Tanz)
La Soufrière (V) (WI)
Nanga Parbat (M) (Pakist)
Scafell Pike (M) (Eng)
Sierra Madre (M) (Mex)
Tipungatito (V) (Chile)

12

Godwin Austen (M) (Pakist)
Ingleborough (M) (Eng)
Kanchenjunga (M) (Nepal)
Peak District (H) (Eng)
Popocatepetl (V) (Mex)
Sierra Morena (M) (Sp)
Sierra Nevada (M) (USA)

13

Carrantuohill (M) (Ire)
Grossglockner (M) (Austria)
Klyuchevskaya (V) (Rus)

14

Fichtelgebirge (M) (Ger)
Finsteraarhorn (M) (Switz)

15

Bernese Oberland (M) (Switz)

Music and musical terms

1	4	5	5
f	duet	accel	march
p	echo	acuta	metre
	fine	ad lib	mezzo
2	flat	arsis	minim
ff	glee	assai	minor
mf	high	atone	molto
pp	hold	baton	mosso
	hymn	bebop	motet
3	jazz	blare	nonet
air	lead	blues	notes
bar	Lied	bones	octet
bis	lilt	brass	opera
bow	mass	breve	pause
cue	mode	canto	pedal
dim	mood	carol	piano
duo	mute	chant	piper
hum	note	chime	pitch
key	opus	choir	polka
lay	part	chord	primo
low	peal	clang	rondo
più	rall	croon	round
pop	reed	dance	scale
rag	rest	dirge	score
rit	sign	ditty	senza
run	sing	dolce	sharp
ten	sino	drone	sixth
tie	slur	duple	slide
	solo	elegy	soave
4	song	etude	sol-fa
alto	stop	forte	sound
aria	time	fugal	stave
band	tone	fugue	strum
bass	trio	knell	suite
beat	tune	kyrie	swell
bell	vamp	largo	swing
brio	voce	lento	tacet
clef	wind	lyric	tanto
coda	wood	major	tempo

5	6	7	7
tenor	medley	cadence	triplet
theme	melody	cadenza	tuneful
third	minuet	calando	upright
tonic	nobile	chanson	vespers
triad	octave	chanter	vibrato
trill	off-key	chorale	warbler
tuner	phrase	con brio	
tutti	player	concert	**8**
twang	presto	conduct	alto-clef
valse	quaver	crooner	arpeggio
vibes	record	descant	baritone
vocal	rhythm	descend	brillant
voice	rounds	descent	canticle
yodel	scales	discord	composer
	sempre	drummer	con amore
6	septet	fanfare	concerto
accent	sestet	furioso	continuo
adagio	sextet	G-string	crotchet
al fine	shanty	harmony	diminish
anthem	singer	juke-box	dominant
attune	sonata	keynote	down-beat
ballad	stanza	maestro	ensemble
bolero	string	melodic	entr'acte
bugler	subito	musical	falsetto
cadent	tenuto	natural	fantasie
cantor	treble	offbeat	folk-song
chimes	tune-up	pesante	grazioso
choral	unison	poco rit	half-note
chorus	up-beat	prelude	in modo di
da capo	veloce	ragtime	interval
dulcet	vivace	quartet	intonate
eighth	volume	quintet	keyboard
encore	warble	recital	libretto
facile		refrain	lutanist
fading	**7**	reprise	lutenist
finale	agitato	requiem	madrigal
jingle	allegro	rondeau	maestoso
legato	amoroso	scherzo	major key
Lieder	andante	scoring	minor key
litany	animato	seventh	minstrel
lutist	bellows	singing	moderato
		stretto	movement

8

musician
nocturne
notation
operatic
operetta
oratorio
organist
overture
part-song
pastoral
phrasing
plectrum
register
resonant
rhapsody
ritenuto
semitone
septette
sequence
serenade
serenata
sonatina
songster
spiccato
staccato
symmetry
symphony
tone-down
vigoroso
virtuoso
vocalist
warbling

9

acoustics
adagietto
andantino
arabesque
barcarole
cantabile
cantilena

9

conductor
contralto
crescendo
dissonant
dulcitone
folk-music
glissando
high-pitch
high-toned
impromptu
improvise
in harmony
interlude
inversion
irregular
jazz music
leger-line
melodious
meno mosso
metronome
mezzo voce
obbligato
orchestra
part music
pastorale
phonetics
pizzicato
plainsong
polonaise
quartette
quintette
recording
rehearsal
resonance
roundelay
semibreve
sforzando
sin'al fine
slow march
soft pedal
sostenuto

9

sotto voce
spiritoso
syncopate
tenor clef
variation

10

accidental
adaptation
affettuoso
allegretto
bandmaster
comic opera
con spirito
continuato
cor anglais
dance-music
diminuendo
discordant
disharmony
dolcemente
dulcet-tone
folk-singer
fortissimo
grand opera
incidental
instrument
intermezzo
intonation
light opera
major chord
major scale
mezzoforte
minor chord
minor scale
mouth-piece
opera buffa
orchestral
pianissimo
pianoforte
portamento
prima donna

10

recitative
ritardando
semiquaver
string-band
stringendo
syncopated
tonic chord
tonic major
tonic minor
tonic-sol-fa
triple-time
tuning fork
vocal music

11

accelerando
arrangement
canned music
church music
composition
counterpart
discordance
harmonising
harmonizing
incantation
madrigalist
music master
orchestrate
prestissimo
rallentando
rock-and-roll
sacred music
string music
syncopation
transposing

12

allegrissimo
appassionata
augmentation
bass baritone
boogie-woogie

12
chamber music
concert-pitch
double-octave
funeral march
instrumental
mezzo-soprano
military band
opéra comique
orchestrator
organ recital
philharmonic

13
accompaniment
choral singing
conservatoire
harmonic chord
musical comedy
music festival
operatic music
orchestration
sacred concert
string quartet

14
demisemiquaver
direct interval

14
regimental band
wind instrument

15
brass instrument
electronic music
fife-and-drum band
instrumentalist
instrumentation
musical director
string quartette
symphony concert

Tonic sol-fa

doh, do
ray, re
me, mi
fah, fa
soh, so
lah, la
te, ti

Musical instruments

3	4	5	6
kit	pipe	rebec	tam-tam
lur	vina	shawm	tom-tom
	viol	sitar	vielle
4		tabor	violin
drum	5	viola	zither
fife	banjo		
gong	bells	6	7
harp	bugle	cornet	alphorn
horn	cello	fiddle	bagpipe
koto	chime	guitar	baryton
lute	clave	rattle	bassoon
lyre	flute	spinet	celeste
oboe	organ	spoons	cittern
			cornett

7	8	9	10
cowbell	carillon	castanets	kettledrum
cymbals	chime bar	componium	mouth organ
maracas	clappers	cornopean	ophicleide
musette	clarinet	euphonium	sousaphone
ocarina	clavicor	flageolet	symphonium
pandora	dulcimer	harmonica	tambourine
panpipe	handbell	harmonium	tin whistle
piccolo	jew's-harp	mandoline	
piffaro	mandolin	morin-chur	11
sackbut	melodeon	saxophone	aeolian harp
saxhorn	melodica	Wurlitzer	barrel organ
serpent	mirliton	xylophone	harpsichord
sistrum	psaltery		sleigh bells
sordine	recorder	10	synthesiser
tambura	side drum	basset horn	synthesizer
theorbo	theremin	bongo drums	viola d'amore
timpani	triangle	clavichord	violoncello
trumpet	trombone	claviorgan	
ukulele	violetta	contrabass	12
whistle	virginal	cor anglais	glockenspiel
		didgeridoo	Stradivarius
8	9	double bass	viola da gamba
autoharp	accordion	flugelhorn	
bass drum	balalaika	French horn	13
bass horn	bombardon	grand piano	ondes martenot

Musicals

4

Cats (Sir Andrew Lloyd Webber)

5

Annie (Charles Strouse)
Chess (Tim Rice)
Evita (Sir Andrew Lloyd Webber)

6

Kismet (Robert Wright and George Forrest)
Oliver (Lionel Bart)

7
Camelot (Frederick Loewe)

8
Carousel (Richard Rodgers)
Oklahoma (Richard Rodgers)
Show Boat (Jerome Kern)
Tom Jones (Edward German)

9
Brigadoon (Frederick Loewe)
Lilac Time (Franz Schubert)

10
42nd Street (Harry Warren)
Hello Dolly (Jerry Herman)
My Fair Lady (Frederick Loewe)
The New Moon (Sigmund Romberg)

11
A Chorus Line (Marvin Hamlisch)
Call Me Madam (Irving Berlin)
The King and I (Richard Rodgers)
The Music Man (Meredith Willson)

12
Calamity Jane (Sammy Fain)
Guys and Dolls (Frank Loesser)
Song of Norway (Grieg/Robert Wright and George Forrest)
South Pacific (Richard Rodgers)
The Boy Friend (Sandy Wilson)

13
Aspects of Love (Sir Andrew Lloyd Webber)
Half a Sixpence (David Heneker)
La Belle Hélène (Jacques Offenbach)
Les Misérables (Claude-Michel Schonberg)
Merrie England (Edward German)
The Gypsy Baron (Johann Strauss)
The Merry Widow (Franz Lehar)
The Pajama Game (Richard Adler and Jerry Ross)
West Side Story (Leonard Bernstein)

13
White Horse Inn (Ralph Benatzky and Robert Stolz)

14
Finian's Rainbow (Burton Lane)
Flower Drum Song (Richard Rodgers)
Paint Your Wagon (Frederick Loewe)
The Fantasticks (Harvey Schmidt)

15
La Cage Aux Folles (Jerry Herman)
The Land of Smiles (Franz Lehar)
The Sound of Music (Richard Rodgers)

16
Fiddler on the Roof (Jerry Bock)
The Student Prince (Sigmund Romberg)

17
The Most Happy Fella (Frank Loesser)

20
The Phantom of the Opera (Sir Andrew Lloyd Webber)

39
Joseph and the Amazing Technicolor Dreamcoat (Sir Andrew Lloyd Webber)

Musicians

4
Bing, Sir Rudolph
Bull, John
Hess, Dame Myra
Lill, John

5
Alkan, Charles Henri Valentin
Arrau, Claudio
Boehm, Theobald
Bream, Julian Alexander
Bülow, Hans Guido von

5
Dupré, Marcel
Fauré, Gabriel
Field, John
Friml, Rudolph
Grove, Sir George
Halle, Sir Charles
Liszt, Franz
Moore, Gerald
Ogdon, John
Reger, Max
Sharp, Cecil

5

Sousa, John Philip
Spohr, Louis
Stern, Isaac
Widor, Charles Marie

6

Burney, Charles
Busoni, Ferruccio
Casals, Pablo
Clarke, Jeremiah
Cortot, Alfred
Curwen, John
Curzon, Sir Clifford
Enesco, Georges
Franck, César Auguste
Galway, James
Glinka, Mikhail Ivanovich
Hummel, Johann Nepomuk
Morley, Thomas

7

Albéniz, Isaac Manuel Francisco
Brendel, Alfred
Britten, Benjamin, Baron
Corelli, Arcangelo
Dowland, John
Gibbons, Orlando
Hofmann, Joseph Casimir
Joachim, Joseph
Malcolm, George John
Menuhin, Sir Yehudi
Purcell, Henry
Richter, Sviatoslav
Segovia, Andrés
Solomon
Stainer, Sir John
Thibaud, Jacques
Vivaldi, Antonio
Warlock, Peter
Weelkes, Thomas

8

Bruckner, Anton
Clementi, Muzio
Dohnányi, Erno
Grainger, Percy Aldridge
Granados, Enrique
Horowitz, Vladimir
Kreisler, Fritz
Messiaen, Olivier
Milstein, Nathan
Oistrakh, David
Paganini, Niccolò
Philidor, André Danican
Schnabel, Artur
Scriabin, Alexander
Williams, John
Zabaleta, Nicanor

9

Barenboim, Daniel
Bernstein, Leonard
Boulanger, Nadia
Buxtehude, Dietrich
Dolmetsch, Arnold
Hindemith, Paul
Landowska, Wanda
Malipiero, Gian Francesco
Meyerbeer, Giacomo
Scarletti, Domenico
Tortelier, Paul

10

Boccherini, Luigi
Paderewski, Ignacy
Rubinstein, Anton
Rubinstein, Artur
Saint-Saëns, Camille
Stradivari, Antonio

11

Leschetizky, Theodor
Rachmaninov, Sergei

12	17
Dallapiccola, Luigi	Strauss the Younger, Johann
Guido d'Arezzo	

Mythology

Egyptian

2	4	5	6
Ra	Isis	Horus	Osiris
	Maat	Neheh	Renpet
3	Mont	Thoth	Tefnut
Bes	Ptah		Upuaut
Geb		6	
Nut		Amon-Ra	7
Shu		Hathor	Imhotep
			Sekhmet

Greek and Roman

3	4	5	5
Aon	Mors	Cupid	Siren
Ate	Muse	Diana	sylph
Eos	myth	Dryad	Titan
Pan	Rhea	Erato	Venus
Pax	Styx	Fates	Vesta
Sol	Troy	Hades	
	Zeus	Helen	6
4		Hydra	Acamus
Acis	5	Janus	Adonis
Ajax	Aegis	Jason	Aegeus
Ares	Aeson	Lethe	Aeolus
Argo	Amata	Midas	Aerope
Echo	Ammon	Muses	Agenor
Eros	Arete	Naiad	Amycus
Faun	Argos	nymph	Apollo
Fury	Argus	Oread	Athene
Hebe	Ariel	Orion	Athens
Hera	Arion	Paris	Castor
Iris	Atlas	Pluto	Charon
Juno	Ceres	Priam	Crocus
Leda	Circe	satyr	Cronus
Mars	Crete	Sibyl	Daphne

6

Europa
Faunus
Furies
Gorgon
Graces
Hecate
Helios
Hermes
Hestia
Hypnos
Icarus
Medusa
nectar
Nestor
Oberon
Saturn
Scylla
Selene
Vulcan

7

Abderus
Acestes
Alpheus
Amazons
Amphion
Amyntor

7

Antiope
Arachne
Ariadne
Artemis
Asteria
Bacchus
Cyclops
Cythera
Demeter
Electra
Helenus
Jupiter
Lapiths
Mercury
Minerva
Nemesis
Neptune
Oedipus
Olympia
Olympus
Orestes
Orpheus
Pandora
Pegasus
Perseus
Pluvius
Romulus

7

sylphid
Theseus
Ulysses

8

Absyrtus
Achilles
Alcestis
Alcimede
Amalthea
ambrosia
Atalanta
Atlantis
Calliope
Centaurs
Cerberus
Charites
Cytherea
Daedalus
Damocles
Dionysus
Heracles
Hercules
Menelaus
Minotaur
Odysseus
Olympian
Thanatos

9

Aegisthus
Agamemnon
Alcathous
Androcles
Andromeda
Aphrodite
Argonauts
Asclepius
Charybdis
Narcissus

10

Amphiaraus
Amphitrite
Amphitryon
Persephone
Polyphemus

11

Bellerophon
Helen of Troy

12

Golden Fleece
Mount Olympus

Hindu deities

4

Agni
Bali
Soma
Vayu
Yama

5

Aditi
Durga

5

Indra
Shiva
Surya

6

Brahma
Kubera
Manasa

6

Varuna
Vishnu

7

Ganesha
Jyestha
Krishna

7

Saranyu
Sugriva

8

Prithivi

10

Gandharvas

Norse

3	5	6	9
Bor	Aegir	Baldur	Valkyries
Hel	Bragi	Freyja	Yggdrasil
Sif	Freyr		
	Frigg	8	10
4	Hoder	Heimdall	Yggdrasill
Loki	Idunn		
Odin			
Thor			

The nine Muses

Calliope (epic poetry)
Clio (history)
Erato (erotic poetry)
Euterpe (lyric poetry)
Melpomene (tragedy)
Polyhymnia (religious song)
Terpsichore (dance)
Thalia (comedy)
Urania (Astronomy)

The twelve labours of Hercules

The Nemean Lion
The Lernean Hydra
The Arcadian Deer
The Erymanthian Boar
The Augean Stables
The Stymphalean Birds
The Cretan Bull
The Horses of Diomedes
The Girdle of Hippolyta
The Flock of Geryon
The Apples of the Hesperides
The Capture of Cerberus

Nautical terms

2	3	3	4
Al	fid	rum	back
	fog	run	beam
3	guy	sag	beat
aft	H.M.S.	sea	bend
bay	jib	tar	bitt
bow	lee	tow	boom
box	log	way	bows
cat	man		brig
cox	nut	4	bunk
ebb	oar	ahoy	buoy
fay	rig	alee	calm

4

crew
down
east
eddy
flag
flow
foam
fore
furl
gale
gang
gear
haul
hazy
head
helm
hold
hull
jack
keel
knot
land
last
lead
leak
line
list
load
mast
mate
mess
mine
mist
moor
navy
neap
oars
pier
poop
port
prow

4

punt
quay
raft
rank
rate
rear
reef
rung
sail
ship
sink
slip
stay
stem
surf
swab
taut
tide
tilt
toss
trim
trip
veer
waft
wake
warp
wave
west
wind
wing
yard
yarn

5

aback
abaft
abeam
afore
ahead
aloft
avast

5

awash
beach
belay
bells
below
berth
bight
bilge
bosun
briny
cabin
cable
cadet
canal
cargo
caulk
chain
chart
cleat
craft
crank
davit
depth
diver
drift
fleet
float
foggy
gauge
hands
hatch
haven
hawse
hoist
jetty
misty
naval
north
ocean
orlop
radar

5

radio
sands
screw
sheet
shore
siren
sound
steer
stern
storm
surge
swell
tidal
truck
waist
watch
weigh
wharf
wheel
winch
windy
wreck

6

aboard
adrift
afloat
anchor
armada
ashore
astern
beacon
bridge
bunker
convoy
course
cruise
diving
embark
engine
ensign

6	6	7	7
escort	splice	fogbank	rostrum
fathom	squall	foghorn	sailing
fender	stormy	forward	salvage
fo'c'sle	stream	freight	scupper
for'ard	tiller	gangway	scuttle
funnel	unfurl	go below	shallow
furled	unload	grapnel	shipper
galley	vessel	gudgeon	shipway
hawser	voyage	gun-room	shrouds
jetsam		gunwale	sick-bay
jigger	7	guy-rope	sinking
launch	aground	halyard	skipper
league	bale out	harbour	slipway
leeway	ballast	harpoon	squally
locker	bearing	haul-off	steward
marina	bobstay	inboard	tacking
marine	bollard	inshore	tackled
maroon	bowline	Jack Tar	tactics
mayday	breaker	landing	tempest
mid-sea	bulwark	laniard	tonnage
moored	capsize	lanyard	top deck
mutiny	capstan	lee-side	top mast
nautic	captain	leeward	topsail
offing	cat's-paw	loading	topside
on deck	catwalk	logbook	tornado
paddle	channel	look-out	torpedo
patrol	charter	mariner	towline
purser	coaming	marines	towpath
reefer	cockpit	mistral	towrope
rigged	compass	monsoon	typhoon
rigger	corsair	mooring	veering
rudder	cyclone	mudhook	warping
sailor	deadeye	oarsman	watches
saloon	deep-sea	old salt	whistle
salute	draught	on board	wrecked
sculls	dry-dock	outport	
seaman	ebb-tide	pennant	8
seaway	embargo	rations	anchored
sheets	fairway	rigging	approach
shroud	fishery	rollers	armament
signal	flotsam	rolling	at anchor

8	8	8	9
backwash	leeboard	stranded	hurricane
barnacle	lifebelt	submerge	land ahead
beam-ends	lifebuoy	taffrail	lower deck
binnacle	lifeline	vanguard	maelstrom
bolt-rope	long haul	waterway	mainbrace
bowsprit	low water	westerly	mainsheet
bulkhead	magazine	westward	manoeuvre
bulwarks	mainboom	west wind	midstream
castaway	main deck	windlass	minefield
coasting	main mast	wind-sail	navigator
coxswain	mainsail	windward	northerly
crossing	mainstay	wreckage	northward
cruising	mainyard	yachting	north wind
deadwood	maritime		orlop deck
deckhand	masthead	**9**	outrigger
ditty-box	messmate	admiralty	overboard
dockyard	midships	alongside	periscope
dogwatch	moorings	amidships	press-gang
drifting	mutineer	anchorage	royal mast
driftway	mutinous	anchoring	Royal Navy
easterly	nautical	back-stays	sailcloth
eastward	navigate	bargepole	seafaring
even keel	neap tide	barnacles	sea-robber
floating	outboard	below deck	seaworthy
flotilla	overseas	blue peter	semaphore
fogbound	pitching	boatswain	ship's bell
foot-rope	porthole	crosswind	ship's crew
foremast	portside	crow's nest	shipshape
go aboard	put-to-sea	Davy Jones	shipwreck
go ashore	quarters	departure	southerly
hard-alee	reef-knot	driftwood	southward
hatchway	salvager	firedrill	south wind
headwind	sandbank	floodmark	sou'wester
helmsman	scudding	flood-tide	spinnaker
high seas	sea-chest	flying jib	starboard
high tide	seafarer	foreshore	stateroom
hornpipe	sea-rover	foundered	tarpaulin
icebound	spy-glass	gangplank	telescope
jettison	squadron	half-hitch	tide-table
keel-over	standard	high water	trade wind
land ahoy!	stowaway	hoist sail	upper deck

9	10	10	11
water-line	engine room	midshipman	belaying pin
whirlwind	fathomless	nightwatch	middle-watch
yachtsman	fore-and-aft	port of call	quarterdeck
	forecastle	quarantine	range-finder
10	forge ahead	rope-ladder	searchlight
aboard ship	freshwater	shipwright	seasickness
batten down	heavy-laden	signalling	sheet anchor
blue ensign	Jolly Roger	spring-tide	ship's doctor
bootlegger	landlubber	tidal river	ship's papers
breakwater	life-jacket	watertight	south-wester
cast anchor	lighthouse		spring a leak
deadlights	lookout-man	**11**	storm signal
downstream	manoeuvres	abandon ship	three-masted
drop anchor	middle deck	beachcomber	tidal waters

12	12	12
bill of lading	man overboard	Trinity House
change course	marline-spike	undercurrent
companionway	nautical mile	
displacement	naval command	**13**
fishing fleet	outward-bound	quartermaster
Jacob's ladder	Plimsoll line	
maiden voyage	ride at anchor	**15**
	tourist class	Davy Jones' locker

Naval ranks

4	6	7	8
Cook	Cooper	Admiral	Armourer
Mate	Ensign	Captain	cabin boy
Wren	Marine	Deckboy	Chaplain
	Master	Fireman	Coxswain
5	Purser	Greaser	Engineer
Bosun	Rating	Jack Tar	Flag Rank
Cadet	Reefer	look-out	Helmsman
Diver	Seaman	recruit	messmate
Middy	Stoker	Skipper	
Pilot	Topman	Steward	**9**
		Surgeon	Boatswain
			Commander

9	10	12	12
Commodore	Midshipman	Cabin Steward	Telegraphist
Engineman	Shipwright	Chief Officer	Third Officer
Paymaster		Chief Skipper	
Ship's Cook	11	Chief Steward	13
Signalman	Air Mechanic	First Officer	Chief Engineer
	Chief Stoker	Junior Seaman	Harbourmaster
10	Electrician	Master Gunner	Leading Seaman
Able Seaman	Flag Officer	Petty Officer	Marine Officer
Apprentice	Leading Wren	P.T. Instructor	Quartermaster
Coastguard	Rear Admiral	Second Master	Radio Operator
Gun Captain	Ship's Doctor	Senior Purser	Second Officer
Instructor	Vice Admiral	Ship's Surgeon	Signal Officer
Lieutenant	Watchkeeper		Sub-Lieutenant
			Third Engineer

14	15	17
Boatswain's Mate	Boarding Officer	Admiral of the Fleet
Flag-Lieutenant	First Lieutenant	Chief Petty Officer
Leading Steward	Officer's Steward	
Ordinary Seaman		19
Second Engineer	16	Lieutenant-Commander
Ship's Carpenter	Flight Lieutenant	
Warrant Officer		

Nobel prize winners

Chemistry

1901	J.H. van't Hoff (Neth)	1913	A. Werner (Switz)
1902	E. Fischer (Ger)	1914	T.W. Richards (USA)
1903	S. Arrhenius (Swed)	1915	R. Willstätter (Ger)
1904	W. Ramsay (GB)	1916	No award
1905	A. von Bayer (Ger)	1917	No award
1906	H. Moissan (Fr)	1918	F. Haber (Ger)
1907	E. Buchner (Ger)	1919	No award
1908	E. Rutherford (GB)	1920	W. Nernst (Ger)
1909	W. Ostwald (Ger)	1921	F. Soddy (GB)
1910	O. Wallach (Ger)	1922	F.W. Aston (GB)
1911	Marie Curie (Fr)	1923	F. Pregl (Austria)
1912	V. Grignard (Fr)	1924	No award
	P. Sabatier (Fr)	1925	R. Zsigmondy (Ger)

1926 T. Svedberg (Swed)
1927 H. Wieland (Ger)
1928 A. Windaus (Ger)
1929 A. Harden (GB)
      H. von Euler-Chelpin (Swed)
1930 H. Fischer (Ger)
1931 F. Bergius (Ger)
      K. Bosch (Ger)
1932 I. Langmuir (USA)
1933 No award
1934 H. Urey (USA)
1935 F. Joliot (Fr)
      I. Joliot-Curie (Fr)
1936 P. Debye (Neth)
1937 W.N. Haworth (GB)
      P. Karrer (Switz)
1938 R. Kuhn (Ger)
1939 A. Butenandt (Ger)
      L. Ruzicka (Switz)
1943 G. Hevesy (Hung)
1944 O. Hahn (Ger)
1945 A. Virtanen (Fin)
1946 J.H. Northrop (USA)
      W.M. Stanley (USA)
      J.B. Sumner (USA)
1947 Sir R. Robinson (GB)
1948 A. Tiselius (Swed)
1949 W. Giauque (USA)
1950 K. Alder (Ger)
      Otto P.H. Diels (Ger)
1951 E.M. McMillan (USA)
      G.T. Seaborg (USA)
1952 A.J.P. Martin (GB)
      R.L.M. Synge (GB)
1953 H. Staudinger (Ger)
1954 L.C. Pauling (USA)
1955 V. du Vigneaud (USA)
1956 N.N. Semenov (USSR)
      Sir C.N. Hinshelwood (GB)
1957 Sir A.R. Todd (GB)
1958 F. Sanger (GB)
1959 J. Heyrovsky (Czech)

1960 W.F. Libby (USA)
1961 M. Calvin (USA)
1962 J.C. Kendrew (GB)
      M.F. Perutz (GB)
1963 G. Natta (Italy)
      K. Ziegler (Ger)
1964 D.C. Hodgkin (GB)
1965 R.B. Woodward (USA)
1966 R.S. Mulliken (USA)
1967 M. Eigen (Ger)
      R.G.W. Norrish (GB)
      G. Porter (GB)
1968 L. Onsager (USA)
1969 D.H.R. Barton (GB)
      O. Hassel (Nor)
1970 L.F. Leloir (Arg)
1971 G. Herzberg (Can)
1972 C.B. Anfinsen (USA)
      S. Moore (USA)
      W.H. Stein (USA)
1973 E.O. Fischer (Ger)
      G. Wilkinson (GB)
1974 P.J. Flory (USA)
1975 J.W. Cornforth (Austr-GB)
      V. Prelog (Yugo-Switz)
1976 W.N. Lipscomb (USA)
1977 I. Prigogine (Belg)
1978 P. Mitchell (GB)
1979 H.C. Brown (USA)
      G. Wittig (Ger)
1980 P. Berg (USA)
      W. Gilbert (USA)
      F. Sanger (GB)
1981 K. Fukui (Japan)
      R. Hoffman (USA)
1982 A. Klug (S. Af.)
1983 H. Taube (USA)
1984 R.B. Merrifield (USA)
1985 H.A. Hauptman (USA)
      J. Karle (USA)
1986 D. Herschbach (USA)
      Y.T. Lee (USA)
      J. Polanyi (Can)

1987 D.J. Cram (USA)
     J.M. Lehn (Fr)
     C.D. Pedersen (USA)
1988 J. Diesenhofer (Ger)
     R. Huber (Ger)
     H. Michel (Ger)

1989 T.R. Cech (USA)
     S. Altman (USA)
1990 E.J. Corey (USA)
1991 R.R. Ernst (Switz)
1992 R. Marcus (USA)

Economics

1969 F. Frisch (Nor)
     J. Tinberger (Neth)
1970 P.A. Simonson (USA)
1971 S. Kuznets (USA)
1972 K.J. Arrow (USA)
     J.R. Hicks (GB)
1973 W. Leontief (USA)
1974 G. Myrdal (Swed)
     F.A. von Hayek (GB)
1975 L.V. Kantorovich (USSR)
     T.C. Koopmans (USA)
1976 M. Friedman (USA)
1977 B. Ohlin (Swed)
     J.E. Meade (GB)
1978 H.A. Simon (USA)
1979 A. Lewis (GB)
     T. Schultz (USA)

1980 L.R. Klein (USA)
1981 J. Tobin (USA)
1982 G.J. Stigler (USA)
1983 G. Debreu (USA)
1984 R. Stone (GB)
1985 F. Modigliani (USA)
1986 J.M. Buchanan (USA)
1987 R.M. Solow (USA)
1988 M. Allais (Fr)
1989 T. Haavelmo (Nor)
1990 H.M. Markowitz (USA)
     M.H. Miller (USA)
     W.F. Sharpe (USA)
1991 R. Coase (USA)
1992 G. Becker (USA)

Literature

1901 R.F.A. Sully Prudhomme (Fr)
1902 T. Mommsen (Ger)
1903 B. Björnson (Nor)
1904 F. Mistral (Fr)
     J. Echegaray (Sp)
1905 H. Sienkiewicz (Pol)
1906 G. Carducci (Italy)
1907 R. Kipling (GB)
1908 R. Eucken (Ger)
1909 S. Lagerlöf (Swed)
1910 P. Heyse (Ger)
1911 M. Maeterlinck (Belg)
1912 G. Hauptmann (Ger)
1913 R. Tagore (India)
1914 No award

1915 R. Roland (Fr)
1916 V. von Heidenstam (Swed)
1917 K. Gjellerup (Den)
     H. Pontoppidan (Den)
1919 G. Spitteler (Switz)
1920 K. Hamsun (Nor)
1921 A. France (Fr)
1922 J. Benavente Martínez (Sp)
1923 W.B. Yeats (Ire)
1924 W.S. Reymont (Pol)
1925 G.B. Shaw (GB)
1926 G. Deledda (Italy)
1927 H. Bergson (Fr)
1928 S. Undset (Nor)
1929 T. Mann (Ger)

1930 S. Lewis (USA)	1964 J.-P. Sartre (declined) (Fr)
1931 E.A. Karlfeldt (Swed)	1965 M. Sholokhov (USSR)
1932 J. Galsworthy (GB)	1966 S.J. Agnon (Israel)
1933 I.A. Bunin (USSR)	N. Sachs (Swed)
1934 L. Pirandello (Italy)	1967 M.A. Asturias (Guat)
1935 No award	1968 Y. Kawabata (Japan)
1936 E. O'Neill (USA)	1969 S. Beckett (Ire)
1937 R. Martin Du Gard (Fr)	1970 A.I. Solzhenitsyn (USSR)
1938 Pearl S. Buck (USA)	1971 P. Neruda (Chile)
1939 F.E. Sillanpaa (Fin)	1972 H. Böll (Ger)
1943 No award	1973 P. White (Aust)
1944 J.V. Jensen (Den)	1974 E. Johnson (Swed)
1945 G. Mistral (Chile)	H.E. Martinson (Swed)
1946 H. Hesse (Switz)	1975 E. Montale (Italy)
1947 A. Gide (Fr)	1976 S. Bellow (USA)
1948 T.S. Eliot (GB)	1977 V. Aleixandre (Sp)
1949 W. Faulkner (USA)	1978 I.B. Singer (USA)
1950 Earl Russell (GB)	1979 O. Elytis (Gr)
1951 P.F. Lagerkvist (Swed)	1980 C. Milosz (USA)
1952 F. Mauriac (Fr)	1981 E. Canetti (Bulg)
1953 Winston Churchill (GB)	1982 G. García Márquez (Colomb)
1954 E. Hemingway (USA)	1983 W. Golding (GB)
1955 H.K. Laxness (Ice)	1984 J. Seifert (Czech)
1956 J.R. Jiménez (Sp)	1985 C. Simon (Fr)
1957 A. Camus (Fr)	1986 W. Soyinka (Nig)
1958 B.L. Pasternak (declined)	1987 J. Brodsky (USA)
(USSR)	1988 N. Mahfouz (Egypt)
1959 S. Quasimodo (Italy)	1989 C.J. Cela (Sp)
1960 S.-J. Perse (Fr)	1990 O. Paz (Mex)
1961 I. Andric (Yugo)	1991 N. Gordimer (S. Afr)
1962 J. Steinbeck (USA)	1992 D. Walcott (St Lucia)
1963 G. Seferis (Gr)	

Peace

1901 H. Dunant (Switz)	1907 E. Moneta (Italy)
F. Passy (Fr)	L. Renault (Fr)
1902 E. Ducommun (Switz)	1908 K.P. Arnoldson (Swed)
A. Gobat (Switz)	1909 Baron D'Estournelles de
1903 Sir W.R. Cremer (GB)	Constant de Rebecque (Fr)
1904 Institut de Droit International	A.M.P. Beernaert (Belg)
1905 Bertha von Suttner (Austria)	1910 Bureau International
1906 T. Roosevelt (USA)	Permanent de la Paix, Berne

1911 T.M.C. Asser (Neth)
     A. Fried (Austria)
1912 E. Root (USA)
1913 H. la Fontaine (Belg)
1914 No award
1915 No award
1916 No award
1917 International Red Cross,
     Geneva
1918 No award
1919 W. Wilson (USA)
1920 L. Bourgeois (Fr)
1921 K.H. Branting (Swed)
     C.L. Lange (Nor)
1922 F. Nansen (Nor)
1923 No award
1924 No award
1925 Sir A. Chamberlain (GB)
     C.G. Dawes (USA)
1926 A. Briand (Fr)
     G. Stresemann (Ger)
1927 F. Buisson (Fr)
     L. Quidde (Ger)
1928 No award
1929 F.B. Kellogg (USA)
1930 L.O.J. Söderblom (Swed)
1931 J. Addams (USA)
     N.M. Butler (USA)
1932 No award
1933 Sir N. Angell (GB)
1934 A. Henderson (GB)
1935 C. von Ossietzky (Ger)
1936 C. de S. Lamas (Arg)
1937 Viscount Cecil of Chelwood
     (GB)
1938 Office International Nansen
     pour les Refugiés
1939 No award
1940 No award
1941 No award
1942 No award
1943 No award

1944 International Red Cross,
     General
1945 C. Hull (USA)
1946 E.G. Balch (USA)
     J.R. Mott (USA)
1947 American and British Quaker
     organizations
1948 No award
1949 Lord Boyd-Orr (GB)
1950 R. Bunche (USA)
1951 L. Jouhaux (Fr)
1952 A. Schweitzer (Fr)
1953 Gen. G. Marshall (USA)
1954 U.N. High Commissioner for
     Refugees
1955 No award
1956 No award
1957 L.B. Pearson (Can)
1958 Father Georges Pire (Belg)
1959 P.J. Noel-Baker (GB)
1960 A.J. Luthuli (S. Af)
1961 D. Hammarskjöld (Swed)
1962 L. Pauling (USA)
1963 International Red Cross
     Committee and the
     International League of Red
     Cross Societies
1964 Martin Luther King, Jr (USA)
1965 UNICEF
1966 No award
1967 No award
1968 R. Cassin (Fr)
1969 International Labour
     Organization
1970 N.E. Borlaug (USA)
1971 W. Brandt (Ger)
1972 No award
1973 H. Kissinger (USA)
     Le Duc Tho (Nth Viet)
1974 S. MacBride (Ire)
     E. Sato (Japan)
1975 A.S. Sakharov (USSR)

1976 B. Williams (NI)
     M. Corrigan (NI)
1977 Amnesty International
1978 M. Begin (Israel)
     A. Sadat (Egypt)
1979 Mother Teresa (Ind)
1980 A. Pérez Esquivel (Arg)
1981 U.N. High Commissioner for
     Refugees
1982 A. García Robles (Mex)
     A. Myrdal (Swed)
1983 L. Walesa (Pol)
1984 Bishop D. Tutu (S. Af.)

1985 International Physicians for
     the Prevention of Nuclear
     War
1986 E. Wiesel (USA)
1987 O. Arias Sánchez (Costa R)
1988 United Nations Peacekeeping
     Forces
1989 The Dalai Lama (Tibet)
1990 M. Gorbachev (USSR)
1991 Daw Aung San Suu Kyi
     (Burma)
1992 R. Menchú (Guat)

Physics

1901 W. Röntgen (Ger)
1902 H. Antoon Lorentz (Neth)
     P. Zeeman (Neth)
1903 H. Becquerel (Fr)
     P. Curie (Fr)
     Marie Curie (Fr)
1904 Lord Rayleigh (GB)
1905 P. Lenard (Ger)
1906 J.J. Thomson (GB)
1907 A.A. Michelson (USA)
1908 G. Lippmann (Fr)
1909 G. Marconi (Italy)
     F. Braun (Ger)
1910 J.D. van der Waals (Neth)
1911 W. Wien (Ger)
1912 G. Dalén (Swed)
1913 H. Kamerlingh-Onnes (Neth)
1914 M. von Laue (Ger)
1915 W.H. Bragg (GB)
     W.L. Bragg (GB)
1916 No award
1917 C.G. Barkla (GB)
1918 M. Planck (Ger)
1919 J. Stark (Ger)
1920 C.E. Guillaume (Switz)
1921 A. Einstein (Ger)
1922 N. Bohr (Den)

1923 R. Millikan (USA)
1924 K. Siegbahn (Swed)
1925 J. Franck (Ger)
     G. Hertz (Ger)
1926 J. Perrin (Fr)
1927 A.H. Compton (USA)
     C.T.R. Wilson (GB)
1928 O.W. Richardson (GB)
1929 L. de Broglie (Fr)
1930 C.V. Raman (India)
1931 No award
1932 W. Heisenberg (Ger)
1933 P.A.M. Dirac (GB)
     E. Schrödinger (Austria)
1934 No award
1935 J. Chadwick (GB)
1936 V. Hess (Austria)
     C.D. Anderson (USA)
1937 C.J. Davisson (USA)
     G.F. Thomson (GB)
1938 E. Fermi (Italy)
1939 E.O. Lawrence (USA)
1940 No award
1941 No award
1942 No award
1943 O. Stern (USA)
1944 I.I. Rabi (USA)

1945 W. Pauli (Austria)
1946 P.W. Bridgman (USA)
1947 Sir E. Appleton (GB)
1948 P.M.S. Blackett (GB)
1949 H. Yukawa (Japan)
1950 C. Powell (GB)
1951 Sir J.D. Cockcroft (GB)
      E.T.S. Walton (Ire)
1952 F. Bloch (USA)
      E.M. Purcell (USA)
1953 F. Zernike (Neth)
1954 M. Born (GB)
      W. Bothe (Ger)
1955 W.E. Lamb Jr. (USA)
      P. Kusch (USA)
1956 W. Shockley (USA)
      J. Bardeen (USA)
      W.H. Brattain (USA)
1957 Tsung-Dao Lee (China)
      C.N. Yang (China)
1958 D.A. Cherenkov (USSR)
      I.M. Frank (USSR)
      I.E.L. Tamm (USSR)
1959 E. Segre (USA)
      O. Chamberlain (USA)
1960 D. Glaser (USA)
1961 R. Hofstadter (USA)
      R. Mössbauer (Ger)
1962 L.D. Landau (USSR)
1963 J.H.D. Jensen (Ger)
      M.G. Mayer (USA)
      E.P. Wigner (USA)
1964 C.H. Townes (USA)
      N.G. Basov (USSR)
      A.M. Prokhorov (USSR)
1965 R.O. Feynman (USA)
      J.S. Schwinger (USA)
      S. Tomonaga (Japan)
1966 A. Kastler (Fr)
1967 H.A. Bethe (USA)
1968 L.W. Alvarez (USA)
1969 M. Gell-Mann (USA)

1970 H. Alfvén (Swed)
      L.E. Néel (Fr)
1971 D. Gabor (GB)
1972 J. Bardeen (USA)
      L.N. Cooper (USA)
      J.R. Schrieffer (USA)
1973 L. Esaki (Japan)
      I. Giaever (USA)
      B. Josephson (GB)
1974 A. Hewish (GB)
      Sir M. Ryle (GB)
1975 A.N. Bohr (Den)
      B. Mottelson (Den)
      J. Rainwater (USA)
1976 B. Richter (USA)
      S. Ting (USA)
1977 P.W. Anderson (USA)
      N.F. Mott (GB)
      J.H. van Vleck (USA)
1978 P.L. Kapitsa (USSR)
      A.A. Penzias (USA)
      R.W. Wilson (USA)
1979 S.L. Glashow (USA)
      A. Salam (Pak)
      S. Weinberg (USA)
1980 J.W. Cronin (USA)
      V.L. Fitch (USA)
1981 N. Bloembergen (USA)
      A. Schawlow (USA)
      K.M. Siegbahn (Swed)
1982 K.G. Wilson (USA)
1983 S. Chandrasekhar (USA)
      W.A. Fowler (USA)
1984 C. Rubbia (Italy)
      S. van der Meer (Neth)
1985 K. von Klitzing (Ger)
1986 G. Binnig (Ger)
      H. Rohrer (Switz)
      E. Ruska (Ger)
1987 G. Bednorz (Ger)
      A. Müller (Switz)

1988 L.M. Lederman (USA)
M. Schwartz (USA)
J. Steinberger (USA)
1989 N.F. Ramsey (USA)
H.G. Dehmelt (USA)
W. Paul (Ger)

1990 J.I. Friedman (USA)
W.H. Kendall (USA)
R.E. Taylor (Can)
1991 P.-G. de Gennes (Fr)
1992 G. Charpak (Fr)

Physiology or medicine

1901 E. von Behring (Ger)
1902 R. Ross (GB)
1903 N.R. Finsen (Den)
1904 I.P. Pavlov (Russia)
1905 R. Koch (Ger)
1906 C. Golgi (Italy)
S. Ramón y Cajal (Sp)
1907 C.L.A. Laveran (Fr)
1908 P. Ehrlich (Ger)
E. Metchnikoff (Russia)
1909 T. Kocher (Switz)
1910 A. Kossel (Ger)
1911 A. Gullstrand (Swed)
1912 A. Carrel (Fr)
1913 C. Richet (Fr)
1914 R. Bárány (Austria)
1915 No award
1916 No award
1917 No award
1918 No award
1919 J. Bordet (Belg)
1920 A. Krogh (Den)
1921 No award
1922 A.V. Hill (GB)
O. Meyerhof (Ger)
1923 F.G. Banting (Can)
J.R. Macleod (GB)
1924 W.E. Einthoven (Neth)
1925 No award
1926 J. Fibiger (Den)
1927 J. Wagner-Jauregg (Austria)
1928 C. Nicolle (Fr)
1929 C. Eijkman (Neth)
F.G. Hopkins (GB)

1930 K. Landsteiner (USA)
1931 O.M. Warburg (Ger)
1932 E.D. Adrian (GB)
C. Sherrington (GB)
1933 T.H. Morgan (USA)
1934 G.R. Minot (USA)
W.C. Murphy (USA)
G.H. Whipple (USA)
1935 H. Spemann (Ger)
1936 Sir H.H. Dale (GB)
O. Loewi (Ger)
1937 A. Szent-Györgyi (Hung)
1938 C. Heymans (Belg)
1939 G. Domagk (Ger)
1940 No award
1941 No award
1942 No award
1943 H. Dam (Den)
E.A. Doisy (USA)
1944 R.J. Erlanger (USA)
H.S. Gasser (USA)
1945 Sir A. Fleming (GB)
E.B. Chain (GB)
E. Florey (GB)
1946 H.J. Muller (USA)
1947 C.F. Cori (USA)
G.T. Cori (USA)
B.A. Houssay (Arg)
1948 P. Muller (Switz)
1949 W.R. Hess (Switz)
A.E. Moniz (Port)
1950 P.S. Hench (USA)
E.C. Kendall (USA)
T. Reischstein (Switz)

1951 M. Theiler (USA)
1952 S.A. Waksman (USA)
1953 F.A. Lipmann (USA)
      H.A. Krebs (GB)
1954 J.F. Enders (USA)
      T.H. Weller (USA)
      F.C. Robbins (USA)
1955 A.H.J. Theorell (Swed)
1956 A.F. Cournand (USA)
      W. Forssmann (Ger)
      D.W. Richards, Jr (USA)
1957 D. Bovet (Italy)
1958 G.W. Beadle (USA)
      E.L. Tatum (USA)
      J. Lederberg (USA)
1959 S. Ochoa (USA)
      A. Kornberg (USA)
1960 F. MacFarlane Burnet (Aust)
      P.B. Medawar (GB)
1961 G. von Bekesy (USA)
1962 F.H.C. Crick (GB)
      J.D. Watson (USA)
      M.H.F. Wilkins (GB)
1963 J.C. Eccles (Aust)
      A.L. Hodgkin (GB)
      A.F. Huxley (GB)
1964 K. Bloch (USA)
      F. Lynen (Ger)
1965 F. Jacob (Fr)
      A. Lwoff (Fr)
      J. Monod (Fr)
1966 C.B. Huggins (USA)
      F.P. Rous (USA)
1967 R.A. Granit (Swed)
      H.K. Hartline (USA)
      G. Wald (USA)
1968 R.W. Holley (USA)
      H.G. Khorana (USA)
      M.W. Nirenberg (USA)
1969 M. Delbruck (USA)
      A.D. Hershey (USA)
      S. Luria (USA)

1970 J. Axelrod (USA)
      Sir B. Katz (GB)
      U. von Euler (Swed)
1971 E.W. Sutherland, Jr. (USA)
1972 G.M. Edelman (USA)
      R.R. Porter (GB)
1973 K. von Frisch (Ger)
      K. Lorenz (Ger/Austria)
      N. Tinbergen (Neth)
1974 A. Claude (USA)
      C. de Duve (Belg)
      G.E. Palade (USA)
1975 D. Baltimore (USA)
      R. Dulbecco (USA)
      H.M. Temin (USA)
1976 B.S. Blumberg (USA)
      D.G. Gajdusek (USA)
1977 R.S. Yalow (USA)
      R.C.L. Guillemin (USA)
      A.V. Schally (USA)
1978 W. Arber (Switz)
      D. Nathans (USA)
      H.O. Smith (USA)
1979 A.M. Cormack (USA)
      G.N. Hounsfield (GB)
1980 B. Benacerraf (USA)
      J. Dausset (Fr)
      G. Snell (USA)
1981 R.W. Sperry (USA)
      D.H. Hubel (USA)
      T.N. Wiesel (Swed)
1982 S. Bergstrom (Swed)
      B. Samuelsson (Swed)
      J.R. Vane (GB)
1983 B. McClintock (USA)
1984 N.K. Jerne (Den)
      G.J.F. Kohler (Ger)
      C. Milstein (GB)
1985 J.L. Goldstein (USA)
      M.S. Brown (USA)
1986 S. Cohen (USA)
      R. Levi-Montalcini (Italy)

1987 S. Tonegawa (Japan)	1990 J. Murray (USA)
1988 Sir J. Black (GB)	E.D. Thomas (USA)
G. Elion (USA)	1991 E. Neher (Ger)
G. Hitchings (USA)	B. Sakmann (Ger)
1989 J.M. Bishop (USA)	1992 E. Krebs (USA)
H.E. Varmus (USA)	E. Fischer (USA)

Numbers

English	French	German	Italian	Spanish
1	un	eins	uno	uno
2	deux	zwei	due	dos
3	trois	drei	tre	tres
4	quatre	vier	quattro	cuatro
5	cinq	fünf	cinque	cinco
6	six	sechs	sei	seis
7	sept	sieben	sette	siete
8	huit	acht	otto	ocho
9	neuf	neun	nove	nueve
10	dix	zehn	dieci	diez

Roman numerals

1	I	20	XX
2	II	30	XXX
3	III	40	XL
4	IV	50	L
5	V	60	LX
6	VI	70	LXX
7	VII	80	LXXX
8	VIII	90	XC
9	IX	100	C
10	X	500	D
11	XI	1000	M

Oceans and seas

O = oceans; S = seas

3	4	4	4
Red (S)	Aral (S)	Java (S)	Ross (S)
	Azov (S of)	Kara (S)	Sava (S)
	Dead (S)		

5	6	7	7
Banda (S)	Aegean (S)	Andaman (S)	Pacific (O)
Black (S)	Arctic (O)	Arabian (S)	Weddell (S)
China (S)	Baltic (S)	Arafura (S)	
Coral (S)	Bering (S)	Barents (S)	8
Irish (S)	Indian (O)	Behring (S)	Adriatic (S)
Japan (S of)	Ionian (S)	Caspian (S)	Amundsen (S)
North (S)	Laptev (S)	Galilee (S of)	Atlantic (O)
Timor (S)	Tasman (S)	Okhotsk (S of)	Beaufort (S)
White (S)	Yellow (S)		Ligurian (S)
			Sargasso (S)

9	11	14
Antarctic (O)	Persian Gulf (S)	Bellingshausen (S)
Caribbean (S)		English Channel (S)
East China (S)	12	
Hudson Bay (S)	Gulf of Mexico (S)	16
		Gulf of California (S)
10	13	Gulf of St Lawrence (S)
South China (S)	Mediterranean (S)	
Bass Strait (S)		

Officials

2	4	4	5
J.P.	Duke	Tzar	noble
M.C.	Earl	ward	padre
M.P.	Emir		Queen
	head	5	rabbi
3	King	abbot	rajah
Aga	Lady	agent	ruler
Don	Lord	Baron	Sahib
Rex	Miss	Count	sheik
Sir	page	Donna	title
	papa	doyen	vicar
4	peer	elder	wazir
aide	Pope	friar	
Amir	Shah	judge	6
beak	sire	kalif	abbess
Czar	Tsar	laird	caliph
dean		mayor	consul

6

curate
deacon
herald
Kaiser
Knight
Mikado
notary
police
Prince
rector
Regent
sexton
sheikh
squire
sultan
umpire
verger

7

attaché
bailiff
baronet
compere
consort
coroner
curator
Czarina
Dauphin
dowager
Duchess
Emperor
Empress
equerry
hangman
head boy
headman
maestro
Marquis
marshal
monarch
pontiff

7

prefect
prelate
premier
Primate
prophet
Provost
referee
senator
sheriff
skipper
speaker
steward
sultana
Tsarina
Tzarina
viceroy

8

alderman
autocrat
Baroness
black rod
Countess
delegate
dictator
diplomat
director
emissary
guardian
head girl
headsman
maharaja
mandarin
Marquess
Marquise
mayoress
minister
nobleman
overlord
overseer
Tsaritsa
Viscount

9

bodyguard
Càrmelite
centurion
chieftain
chief whip
commander
commodore
constable
deaconess
dignitary
Grand Duke
inspector
lifeguard
liveryman
Lord Mayor
matriarch
Monsignor
ombudsman
Patriarch
policeman
president
principal
registrar
rural dean
secretary
sovereign
statesman
town clerk
town crier
treasurer

10

archdeacon
Chancellor
commandant
commissary
controller
councillor
doorkeeper
headmaster

10

high priest
mace-bearer
postmaster
prebendary
procurator
ringmaster
sea captain

11

aristocracy
chamberlain
cross-bearer
Crown Prince
Lord Provost
Marchioness
policewoman
sword-bearer
tax assessor
tax gatherer
Viscountess

12

armour-bearer
Chief Justice
heir apparent
maid of honour
parish priest
Poet Laureate
Queen Consort
staff officer
tax collector

13

administrator
district judge
judge-advocate
Prime Minister
Prince of Wales
Princess Royal
vice-president

14
Chief Constable
Crown Solicitor
lord of the manor
High Court Judge
King's messenger
Lord Chancellor
Lord Lieutenant
medical officer

14
political agent
Provost-Marshal
superintendent
town councillor
vice-chancellor

15
Astronomer Royal
Attorney-General

15
Cabinet minister
district officer
Governor-General
heir-presumptive
Privy Councillor
Queen's messenger
Vice-chamberlain

Operas

5
Faust (Charles François Gounod)
Tosca (Giacomo Puccini)

6
Carmen (Georges Bizet)
Otello (Giuseppe Verdi)
Salome (Richard Strauss)

7
Arianna (Claudio Monteverdi)
Fidelio (Ludwig van Beethoven)

8
Falstaff (Giuseppe Verdi)
La Bohème (Giacomo Puccini)
Parsifal (Richard Wagner)
Turandot (Giacomo Puccini)

9
Billy Budd (Benjamin Britten)
Lohengrin (Richard Wagner)
Rigoletto (Giuseppe Verdi)
Siegfried (Richard Wagner)

10
Die Walküre (Richard Wagner)
I Pagliacci (Ruggiero Leoncavallo)

10
La Traviata (Giuseppe Verdi)
Prince Igor (Alexander Borodin)

11
Doktor Faust (Ferruccio Busoni)
Don Giovanni (Wolfgang Amadeus Mozart)
Peter Grimes (Benjamin Britten)
William Tell (Gioacchino Rossini)

12
Boris Godunov (Modest Mussorgsky)
Cosi Fan Tutte (Wolfgang Amadeus Mozart)
Das Rheingold (Richard Wagner)
La Gazza Ladra (Gioacchino Rossini)
Porgy and Bess (George Gershwin)
The Ring Cycle (Richard Wagner)

13
Dido and Aeneas (Henry Purcell)
Die Fledermaus (Johann Strauss)
The Magic Flute (Wolfgang Amadeus Mozart)

14
La Favola d'Orfeo (Claudio Monteverdi)
Venus and Adonis (John Blow)

15
Götterdämmerung (Richard Wagner)
Hansel and Gretel (Engelbert Humperdinck)
Le Nozze di Figaro (Wolfgang Amadeus Mozart)
Madame Butterfly (Giacomo Puccini)
The Beggar's Opera (John Gay)

16
Der Rosenkavalier (Richard Strauss)
Die Meistersinger (Richard Wagner)
Tristan and Isolde (Richard Wagner)

17
The Rape of Lucretia (Benjamin Britten)

18
The Barber of Seville (Gioacchino Rossini)

19
Cavalleria Rusticana (Pietro Mascagni)

Operatic and classical singers

4	5	7
Butt, Dame Clara	Pears, Sir Peter	Domingo, Plácido
Lind, Jenny	Teyte, Dame Maggie	Ferrier, Kathleen
Popp, Lucia		Hammond, Dame Joan
	6	Lehmann, Lilli
5	Callas, Maria	Lehmann, Lotte
Baker, Dame Janet	Caruso, Enrico	Nilsson, Birgit
Evans, Sir Geraint	Hotter, Hans	
Gigli, Beniamino	Hunter, Rita	**8**
Gobbi, Tito		Carreras, José
Jones, Dame Gwyneth	**7**	Flagstad, Kirsten
Melba, Dame Nellie	Baillie, Isobel	Melchior, Lauritz
Patti, Adelina	Caballe, Montserrat	Schumann, Elisabeth
	Caccini, Giulio	Te Kanawa, Dame Kiri

9
Chaliapin, Feodor
Christoff, Boris
Pavarotti, Luciano

10
Galli-Curci, Amelita
Los Angeles, Victoria de

10
Sutherland, Dame Joan
Tetrazzini, Luisa

11
Schwarzkopf, Dame Elisabeth

14
Fischer-Dieskau, Dietrich

Painters

3
Arp, Jean
Dix, Otto
Dou, Gerrit
Fry, Roger
Ray, Man

4
Cuyp, Aelbert Jacobsz
Dadd, Richard
Dalí, Salvador
Doré, Gustave
Dufy, Raoul
Etty, William
Goes, Hugo van der
Goya, Francisco de
Gris, Juan
Gros, Antoine Jean
Hals, Frans

4
Hill, David Octavius
Hunt, William Holman
John, Augustus Edwin
John, Gwen
Klee, Paul
Lamb, Henry
Lely, Sir Peter
Maes, Nicolas
Marc, Franz
Miró, Joan
Nash, Paul
Neer, Aert van der
Opie, John
Reni, Guido
Rosa, Salvator
West, Benjamin
Wood, Christopher
Zorn, Anders

5
Appel, Karel
Bacon, Francis
Bakst, Leon
Balla, Giacomo
Beuys, Joseph
Blake, Peter
Blake, William
Bosch, Hieronymus
Bouts, Dierick
Brown, Ford Madox
Burra, Edward
Carra, Carlo
Corot, Jean-Baptiste
 Camille
Crane, Walter
Crome, John
Dagly, Gerhard
Danby, Francis

5
David, Gerard
David, Jacques Louis
Degas, Hilaire-Germain-Edgar
Denis, Maurice
Dürer, Albrecht
Ensor, James
Ernst, Max
Freud, Lucian

5
Gaddi, Taddeo
Gorky, Arshile
Goyen, Jan Josephszoon van
Grant, Duncan James
Grosz, George
Homer, Winslow
Hooch, Pieter de
Johns, Jasper

5

Keene, Charles Samuel
Klimt, Gustav
Kupka, Frantisek
Léger, Fernand
Lippi, Fra Filippo
Lotto, Lorenzo
Lowry, L.S.
Macke, August
Manet, Edouard
Mengs, Anton Raphael
Metsu, Gabriel,
Monet, Claude
Moses, Anna Mary Robertson
Munch, Edvard
Nolan, Sir Sydney
Nolde, Emil
Oudry, Jean-Baptiste
Piper, John
Redon, Odilon
Ricci, Sebastiano
Riley, Dame Bridget Louise
Shahn, Ben
Smith, Sir Matthew
Staël, Nicholas de
Steen, Jan
Tobey, Mark
Watts, George Frederick
Wyeth, Andrew

6

Albers, Josef
Benton, Thomas Hart
Boudin, Eugène
Braque, Georges
Bratby, John
Buffet, Bernard
Callot, Jacques
Clouet, Jean
Cooper, Samuel
Cosway, Richard
Cotman, John Sell

6

Derain, Andre
De Wint, Peter
Dobson, William
Dongen, Kees van
Eakins, Thomas
Floris, Cornelis
Floris, Frans
Fuseli, Henry
Gérard, François
Girtin, Thomas
Greuze, Jean-Baptiste
Guardi, Francesco
Hollar, Wenceslaus
Ingres, Jean-Auguste-Dominique
Isabey, Jean-Baptiste
Knight, Dame Laura
La Tour, George de
La Tour, Maurice-Quentin de
Le Brun, Charles
Le Nain, Antoine
Le Nain, Louis
Le Nain, Mathieu
Leyden, Lucas van
Longhi, Pietro
Lurcat, Jean
Marini, Marino
Martin, John
Massys, Quentin
Millet, Jean François
Moreau, Gustave
Moroni, Giovanni Battista
Morris, William
Oliver, Isaac
Orozco, José Clemente
Ostade, Adrian van
Palmer, Samuel
Ramsay, Allan
Renoir, Pierre Auguste
Ribera, José de
Rigaud, Hyacinthe
Rivera, Diego

6

Romney, George
Rothko, Mark
Rubens, Peter Paul
Sesshu, Sesshu Toyo
Seurat, Georges
Signac, Paul
Sisley, Alfred
Stubbs, George
Tanguy, Yves
Tissot, James Joseph Jacques
Titian (Tiziano Vecellio)
Turner, Joseph Mallord William
Vasari, Giorgio
Warhol, Andy
Wilkie, Sir David
Wilson, Richard
Xia Gui

7

Allston, Washington
Audubon, John James
Bassano, Jacopo
Bellini, Jacopo
Bonnard, Pierre
Boucher, François
Brouwer, Adriaen
Cassatt, Mary
Cennini, Cennino
Cézanne, Paul
Chagall, Marc
Chardin, Jean-Baptiste-Siméon
Chirico, Giorgio de
Cimabue, Giovanni
Courbet, Gustave
Cranach, Lucas (The Elder)
Daumier, Honoré
Delvaux, Paul
Duchamp, Marcel
El Greco (Domenikos
  Theotokopoulos)
Fouquet, Jean

7

Gauguin, Paul
Gozzoli, Benozzo
Hassall, John
Herrera, Francisco de (the Younger)
Hobbema, Meindert
Hockney, David
Hogarth, William
Hokusai, Katsushika
Holbein, Hans (the Younger)
Hoppner, John
Johnson, Cornelius
Kneller, Sir Godfrey
Limosin, Leonard
Lochner, Stefan
Lorrain, Claude
Maclise, Daniel
Martini, Simone
Matisse, Henri
Memlinc, Hans
Millais, Sir John Everett
Morandi, Giorgio
Morisot, Berthe
Morland, George
Murillo, Bartholomé Esteban
O'Keeffe, Georgia
Orcagna, Andrea
Pasmore, Victor
Patinir, Joachim
Pevsner, Antoine
Picabia, Francis
Picasso, Pablo
Pollock, Jackson
Poussin, Nicolas
Prud'hon, Pierre Paul
Rackham, Arthur
Raeburn, Sir Henry
Raphael (Raffaello Santi)
Redouté, Pierre Joseph
Roberts, Tom
Rouault, Georges
Rublyov, Andrei

7

Sargent, John Singer
Schiele, Egon
Seghers, Hercules Pieterzoon
Shepard, Ernest Howard
Sickert, Walter Richard
Snyders, Frans
Soutine, Chaim
Spencer, Sir Stanley
Teniers, David (the Younger)
Tibaldi, Pellegrino
Tiepolo, Giovanni Battista
Uccello, Paolo
Utamaro, Kitagawa
Utrillo, Maurice
Van Dyke, Sir Anthony
Van Eyck, Hubert
Van Eyck, Jan
Van Gogh, Vincent
Vermeer, Jan
Watteau, Antoine
Zoffany, Johann
Zuccaro, Federico
Zuccaro, Taddeo

8

Angelico, Fra
Annigoni, Pietro
Auerbach, Frank
Beckmann, Max
Boccioni, Umberto
Brueghel, Jan
Brueghel, Pieter (the Elder)
Carracci, Annibale
Castagno, Andrea del
Crivelli, Carlo
Daubigny, Charles-François
Delaunay, Robert
Drysdale, Sir Russell
Dubuffet, Jean
Giordano, Luca
Gossaert, Jan

8

Guercino, Giovanni
Hamilton, Richard
Hilliard, Nicholas
Jongkind, Johan Barthold
Jordaens, Jacob
Kirchner, Ernst Ludwig
Landseer, Sir Edwin
Lawrence, Sir Thomas
Lorraine, Claude
Magritte, René
Malevich, Kazimir
Mantegna, Andrea
Meegeren, Hans van
Mondrian, Piet
Mulready, William
Munnings, Sir Alfred
Piranesi, Giambattista
Pissarro, Camille
Pontormo, Jacopo da
Reynolds, Sir Joshua
Rossetti, Dante Gabriel
Rousseau, Henri Julien
Rousseau, Théodore
Ruisdael, Jacob van
Sassetta, Stefano di Giovanni
Severini, Gino
Terborch, Gerard
Vasarély, Victor
Veronese, Paolo
Vlaminck, Maurice de
Vuillard, Edouard
Whistler, James Abbott McNeill
Whistler, Rex
Zurbarán, Francisco de

9

Altdorfer, Albrecht
Bonington, Richard Parkes
Canaletto (Antonio Canal)
Carpaccio, Vittore
Cavallini, Pietro
Constable, John

9

Cornelius, Peter von
Correggio, Antonio Allegri
Da Messina, Antonello
De Kooning, Willem
Delacroix, Eugène
Delaroche, Paul
Fabritius, Carel
Feininger, Lyonel
Fragonard, Jean-Honoré
Francesca, Piero della
Friedrich, Caspar David
Géricault, Théodore
Greenaway, Kate
Grünewald, Matthias
Hiroshige, Ando Tokitaro
Honthorst, Gerard (Gerrit) van
Jawlensky, Alexei von
Kandinsky, Wassily
Kauffmann, Angelica
Kokoschka, Oskar
Lissitzky, El
Nicholson, Ben
Pisanello (Antonio Pisano)
Rembrandt (Rembrandt
  Harmenszoon van Rijn)
Siqueiros, David Alfaro
Thornhill, Sir James
Velázquez, Diego Rodríguez de
  Silva
Wouwerman, Philips

10

Alma-Tadema, Sir Lawrence
Archipenko, Alexander
Arcimboldo, Giuseppe
Berruguete, Alonso
Berruguete, Pedro
Botticelli, Sandro
Burne-Jones, Sir Edward Coley
Caravaggio, Michelangelo Merisi da
Champaigne, Philippe de

10

Cruikshank, George
Giacometti, Alberto
Lorenzetti, Ambrogio
Meissonier, Jean-Louis-Ernest
Modigliani, Amedeo
Moholy-Nagy, Lászó
Motherwell, Robert
Pollaiuolo, Antonio
Pollaiuolo, Piero
Schwitters, Kurt
Signorelli, Luca
Sutherland, Graham Vivian
Tintoretto, Jacopo Robusti
Van de Velde, Henri
Verrocchio, Andrea del
Zuccarelli, Francesco

11

Bartolommeo, Fra
Chodowiecki, Daniel Nikolaus
Domenichino (Domenico Zampieri)
Terbrugghen, Hendrick

12

Fantin-Latour, Henri
Gainsborough, Thomas
Giulio Romano (Giulio Pippi)
Lichtenstein, Roy
Michelangelo (Michelangelo
  Buonarroti)
Palma Vecchio, Jacopo
Parmigianino, (Francesco Mazzola)
Pinturicchio, Bernadino di Betto
Rauschenberg, Robert
Van der Weyden, Rogier
Winterhalter, Franz Xavier

13

Lorenzo Monaco
Piero di Cosimo (Piero di Lorenzo)

15	17
Leonardo da Vinci	Gentile da Fabriano
Toulouse-Lautrec, Henri de	Domenico Veneziano

Peerage

4	7	8
Duke	Duchess	Marquess
Earl	Marquis	Viscount
5	**8**	**11**
Baron	Baroness	Marchioness
	Countess	Viscountess

People words

2	3	4	4
B.A.	she	hero	sage
he	sir	host	team
M.A.	son	idol	them
Ma	sot	Jack	they
Pa	spy	Jill	thug
me	tar	jury	tike
us	you	kith	toff
we		lass	Tory
	4	liar	twin
3	aunt	lout	tyke
ace	bard	maid	tyro
ass	bear	male	user
boy	beau	Mama	waif
B.Sc.	bore	mate	ward
cad	boss	mess	Whig
Dad	brat	minx	wife
gay	drip	Miss	
him	duck	mite	**5**
imp	dupe	monk	adult
kid	folk	mutt	alien
kin	fool	ogre	angel
lad	gang	Papa	Aunty
man	girl	peer	bairn
men	heel	prig	beast
Mum	heir	rake	

5	5	5	6
being	joker	scamp	darner
belle	Judas	scout	debtor
bigot	juror	shark	deputy
bride	knave	shrew	digger
brute	leper	siren	dodger
bully	local	uncle	dragon
cadet	locum	vixen	driver
cheat	loser	voter	drudge
child	magus	wader	duffer
choir	nanny	wench	egoist
chump	Negro	widow	escort
clown	niece	witch	expert
crank	ninny	woman	family
crone	nomad	women	father
dunce	nymph	wooer	fellow
dwarf	owner	yobbo	female
enemy	party	yokel	fencer
exile	pater	youth	fiancé
extra	payee		friend
fence	payer	**6**	gaffer
fiend	pigmy	albino	gossip
flirt	pin-up	allies	Granny
flock	piper	amazon	Granpa
freak	poser	angler	grouch
ghost	proxy	Apache	grower
giant	prude	Auntie	gunman
gipsy	pupil	au pair	gunner
giver	pygmy	backer	healer
goose	quack	bandit	hermit
grass	queen	beater	hippie
groom	queer	beauty	hoaxer
guest	racer	bidder	humbug
guide	raker	boozer	hunter
gypsy	rebel	bowler	infant
heavy	rider	cadger	inmate
hiker	rival	caller	jeerer
hussy	rogue	camper	jerker
idiot	rover	captor	jester
idler	rower	cousin	Jesuit
in-law	sahib	coward	jet-set
issue	saint	damsel	jogger
	saver	dancer	jumper

6	6	6	7
junior	pundit	umpire	breeder
keeper	punter	urchin	brother
lancer	puppet	vandal	buffoon
loafer	purist	vendor	bumpkin
loonie	Quaker	victim	captain
lyrist	rabbit	victor	captive
madcap	rabble	viewer	caveman
madman	racist	viking	chanter
maiden	ragtag	virago	charlie
maniac	raider	virgin	charmer
marine	ranger	votary	cheater
martyr	rapist	walker	checker
master	rascal	wanton	citizen
matron	reader	waster	climber
medium	runner	winner	clipper
member	rustic	wizard	Cockney
mentor	sadist	worker	colonel
midget	savage	wretch	company
minion	scorer	writer	compere
missus	scouse	yeoman	crawler
mister	sender	zealot	creator
mortal	senior	zombie	creeper
mother	sentry		cripple
mugger	shadow		crooner
myself	sheila	7	cry-baby
nagger	sinner	atheist	cuckold
native	sister	athlete	culprit
nephew	sitter	avenger	cyclist
nipper	skater	babbler	damosel
nitwit	smiler	ballboy	darling
nobody	smoker	bastard	dawdler
parent	snorer	batsman	denizen
patron	spouse	beatnik	devotee
pauper	square	bedmate	diarist
peeler	squire	beloved	diehard
peeper	sucker	best man	diviner
penpal	suitor	bigshot	doubter
person	toiler	blabber	dowager
player	tomboy	boarder	dragoon
poseur	truant	boaster	dreamer
public	tyrant	bouncer	drifter
		bounder	

7	7	7	7
dullard	hostage	paddler	shopper
dweller	hostess	paragon	show-off
egghead	hothead	partner	shyster
egotist	husband	patient	sibling
elector	hustler	patriot	skipper
erecter	imposer	peasant	sleeper
exposer	insured	plodder	society
failure	insurer	plotter	soloist
fair sex	invader	plucker	someone
fall-guy	invalid	pranker	soother
fanatic	jackass	presser	soprano
fancier	Jack Tar	private	spender
fascist	Jezebel	protégé	sponger
fathead	Joe Soap	prowler	sponsor
fiancée	jostler	puritan	stinker
fiddler	juggler	pursuer	stirrer
fielder	juryman	puzzler	striker
flapper	killjoy	quitter	student
flasher	kindred	radical	stylist
founder	kingpin	rambler	subject
frisker	kinsman	realist	suspect
gabbler	lesbian	recluse	swagman
gallant	lookout	redhead	sweeper
gambler	lunatic	redskin	swimmer
general	magnate	referee	swinger
gentile	mankind	refugee	tattler
giggler	meddler	regular	taunter
glutton	mobster	rescuer	thinker
gourmet	monitor	retinue	toddler
Grandma	mourner	reviver	tourist
Grandpa	mudlark	roadhog	trainee
grantor	mumbler	royalty	trainer
grasper	negress	ruffian	traitor
haggler	nibbler	rumbler	tripper
half-wit	niggard	runaway	trollop
has-been	nominee	rustler	trooper
heathen	oarsman	scrooge	trouper
heckler	old fogy	sculler	trustee
heiress	old girl	seducer	twister
heroine	old maid	settler	upstart
hoarder	old salt	shooter	voyager
hoodlum	outcast		

7	8	8	8
vulture	bigamist	dirty dog	investor
warbler	big noise	disciple	landsman
wastrel	blackleg	disposer	landsmen
widower	blighter	divorcee	layabout
windbag	bohemian	do-gooder	linesman
wise-guy	bookworm	dogsbody	lingerer
witness	borrower	drunkard	linguist
wolf-cub	Boy Scout	everyone	listener
worrier	braggart	examiner	literate
	brethren	executor	livewire
8	brunette	fatalist	loiterer
abductor	busybody	feminist	loyalist
absentee	callgirl	finalist	maligner
academic	cannibal	finisher	mandarin
achiever	canoeist	follower	man-hater
adjutant	castaway	freshman	mannikin
adulator	Catholic	gadabout	marauder
advocate	celibate	guerilla	marksman
aesthete	champion	harridan	May Queen
agitator	chaperon	helpmate	mediator
agnostic	children	helpmeet	messmate
alarmist	commoner	highbrow	mistress
altruist	commuter	hijacker	molester
ancestor	consumer	homicide	moralist
arranger	convener	hooligan	motorist
assassin	corporal	horseman	murderer
assembly	crackpot	humorist	mutineer
assignee	creditor	humpback	objector
assignor	criminal	idealist	observer
assuager	crusader	idoliser	occupant
attacker	customer	idolizer	occupier
attestor	daughter	idyllist	offender
audience	debutant	imbecile	old-timer
bachelor	deceased	imitator	old woman
bankrupt	deceiver	immortal	onlooker
baritone	defector	imposter	operator
beginner	defender	improver	opponent
beguiler	democrat	inferior	optimist
believer	deserter	informer	outsider
benedict	detector	innocent	pacifist
betrayer	devourer	intended	paleface
		intruder	papalist

8	8	9	9
paramour	spitfire	addressee	constable
parasite	sprinter	adulterer	contender
partaker	squatter	adversary	contralto
partisan	squeaker	applicant	contriver
passer-by	squealer	appraiser	co-patriot
perjurer	stickler	arch-enemy	cover girl
pharisee	stitcher	assailant	crackshot
pilferer	stowaway	associate	cricketer
playmate	stranger	augmenter	daredevil
plebeian	stripper	backbiter	dark horse
poisoner	stroller	barbarian	debutante
prattler	strutter	battle-axe	declaimer
prisoner	suckling	bedfellow	defaulter
prodigal	sufferer	beggarman	defeatist
producer	superior	blockhead	defendant
receiver	superman	bluebeard	dependant
recorder	townsman	blusterer	depositor
redeemer	triplets	boy friend	desperado
reformer	true love	brigadier	dissenter
relation	turncoat	bystander	dissident
reporter	two-timer	cabin crew	dolly bird
resident	underdog	Calvinist	entourage
reveller	vagabond	candidate	epileptic
riffraff	villager	canvasser	everybody
rifleman	wanderer	celebrity	executrix
romancer	wayfarer	chain-gang	exhibitor
Rotarian	Wesleyan	character	exploiter
seafarer	wheedler	charlatan	extractor
selector	whistler	chatterer	extremist
sergeant	whizz-kid	Christian	extrovert
shrinker	wrestler	churchman	family man
sidesman	wriggler	clientele	favourite
sketcher	yodeller	colleague	fire-eater
slattern	yourself	comforter	first born
sluggard		commander	flatterer
small fry	9	committee	forebears
somebody	aborigine	commodore	foreigner
songster	absconder	communist	foster son
son-in-law	abstainer	community	foundling
sorcerer	academist	companion	free agent
spinster	accessory	conspirer	freelance

9	9	9	9
freemason	muscleman	sightseer	womanizer
gainsayer	neighbour	simpleton	womankind
gentleman	next of kin	skin-diver	womenfolk
Girl Guide	nominator	skinflint	wrongdoer
go-between	nonentity	skylarker	yachtsman
groomsman	non-smoker	slanderer	young lady
groveller	numerator	slowcoach	youngster
guerrilla	occultist	socialist	
guest star	offspring	socialite	10
guinea pig	Old Master	sojourner	Anglo-Saxon
half-caste	oppressor	solicitor	antagonist
high-flier	organizer	son-of-a-gun	aristocrat
household	ourselves	spectator	babe-in-arms
housewife	pacemaker	spokesman	baby-sitter
hunchback	panellist	sportsman	bamboozler
ignoramus	part-owner	stammerer	benefactor
immigrant	passenger	stargazer	better-half
informant	pen-friend	star pupil	big brother
inheritor	pen-pusher	straggler	blackguard
initiator	pin-up girl	strangler	black sheep
insolvent	plaintiff	strongman	blasphemer
intestate	plutocrat	stutterer	bobbysoxer
introvert	postulant	swaggerer	bridegroom
inveigler	presenter	temptress	bridesmaid
jay-walker	preserver	terrorist	bureaucrat
job-hunter	pretender	testatrix	campaigner
kidnapper	profiteer	testifier	capitalist
kinswoman	protector	tormenter	caravanner
ladies' man	protester	tormentor	card-player
landowner	purchaser	townsfolk	cavalryman
lay reader	purloiner	traveller	changeling
medallist	pussyfoot	tribesman	chatterbox
Methodist	ratepayer	trickster	chauvinist
middleman	recipient	underling	churchgoer
mitigator	Samaritan	valentine	cinderella
moderator	Sassenach	Victorian	clodhopper
moraliser	scapegoat	vigilante	cohabitant
moralizer	scarecrow	volunteer	competitor
mortgagee	schoolboy	warmonger	councillor
mortgagor	scoundrel	whosoever	counsellor
multitude	scribbler	womaniser	countryman

10	10	10	10
crosspatch	grass widow	originator	tweedledee
daydreamer	half-sister	out-patient	tweedledum
day-tripper	harmoniser	peeping Tom	unbeliever
delinquent	harmonizer	persecutor	undertaker
demoiselle	hatchet man	petitioner	unemployed
deputation	head hunter	pinchpenny	wallflower
descendant	highjacker	polo player	well-wisher
dilettante	hitch-hiker	population	White Friar
discoverer	human being	proprietor	whomsoever
dissembler	individual	prosecutor	woman-hater
drug addict	inhabitant	Protestant	worshipper
drug pusher	inquisitor	psychopath	young blood
dunderhead	kith-and-kin	ragamuffin	yourselves
Dutch uncle	lady-killer	reclaimant	
early riser	land-holder	republican	11
elaborator	landlubber	repudiator	academician
electorate	languisher	ringleader	adventuress
Englishman	lawbreaker	scrutineer	animal lover
enthusiast	left-winger	son-and-heir	aristocracy
eye-witness	licentiate	soothsayer	association
fabricator	lieutenant	speculator	beauty queen
fire-raiser	lotus-eater	spoilsport	beneficiary
fly-by-night	lower class	squanderer	bible reader
footballer	maiden aunt	stepfather	blackmailer
forefather	maiden lady	stepmother	blue-eyed boy
forerunner	malingerer	stepsister	blunderhead
fosterling	man of straw	subscriber	breadwinner
fraternity	married man	substitute	brotherhood
freeholder	mastermind	sugar daddy	cave-dweller
free-trader	matchmaker	supplicant	centenarian
fuddy-duddy	merrymaker	sweetheart	cheer leader
fund-raiser	Methuselah	sworn enemy	clairvoyant
gastronome	mind-reader	tale-bearer	commentator
gentlefolk	moneyed man	tale-teller	connoisseur
girl friend	mountebank	taskmaster	conspirator
goalkeeper	mouthpiece	tea-drinker	constituent
gold-digger	namby-pamby	tenderfoot	distributor
good fellow	ne'er-do-well	themselves	double-agent
grandchild	neutralist	third party	drug peddlar
Grandmamma	nincompoop	trespasser	eager beaver
grand-uncle	non-starter	troubadour	electioneer
	old soldier		

11	11	12	12
embroiderer	non-resident	acquaintance	leading light
enchantress	nosey-parker	artful dodger	letter-writer
entertainer	opportunist	assassinator	lounge-lizard
exaggerator	panic-monger	bachelor girl	Mademoiselle
father-in-law	parishioner	benefactress	man-about-town
fault-finder	participant	bible-thumper	married woman
femme fatale	pearly queen	blood brother	mezzo-soprano
fighting man	perpetrator	bluestocking	modest violet
first cousin	personality	brother-in-law	morris dancer
flat dweller	philosopher	chief mourner	natural child
flying squad	predecessor	church-member	near relation
foot soldier	prize-winner	commiserator	nonagenarian
forestaller	probationer	conservative	octogenarian
foster-child	rank-and-file	contemplator	old gentleman
freethinker	rapscallion	convalescent	participator
galley slave	rationalist	co-respondent	proprietress
gatecrasher	right-winger	cosmopolitan	public figure
gentlewoman	Royal Family	demonstrator	remonstrator
god-daughter	rugby player	double-dealer	resuscitator
grandfather	scaremonger	eavesdropper	roller-skater
grandmother	scoutmaster	exterminator	rolling stone
grand-nephew	scrutiniser	featherbrain	scatterbrain
grandparent	scrutinizer	foster-father	schoolfellow
guttersnipe	search party	foster-mother	second cousin
half-brother	shareholder	foster-parent	second fiddle
infantryman	sister-in-law	foster-sister	sequestrator
interceptor	sleepwalker	globe-trotter	sexagenarian
interviewer	spendthrift	guest speaker	single person
intimidator	stepbrother	head-shrinker	sole occupant
joint-tenant	stockholder	heir-apparent	spiritualist
manipulator	story teller	holidaymaker	stepdaughter
masquerader	subordinate	humanitarian	street-urchin
materialist	suffragette	impersonator	stuffed shirt
middle class	sworn friend	inseparables	sub-committee
millionaire	sympathizer	intellectual	swashbuckler
misanthrope	teetotaller	intermediary	sworn enemies
moonlighter	telepathist	interrogator	tennis player
mother-in-law	torch-bearer	investigator	transgressor
name-dropper	town-dweller	kleptomaniac	troublemaker
nationalist		knight-errant	ugly customer
night-walker		landed gentry	ugly duckling

12	13	13	13
village idiot	daughter-in-law	high churchman	speed merchant
wicket keeper	exhibitionist	hypochondriac	undergraduate
wool gatherer	experimentist	Job's comforter	
working class	fashion-monger	laughing stock	**14**
	first offender	machiavellian	good-for-nothing
13	fortune-hunter	miracle-worker	philanthropist
blood relation	foster-brother	misanthropist	sensationalist
conventionist	fresh-air fiend	mischief-maker	sentimentalist
correspondent	grand-daughter	nonconformist	septuagenarian
		perfectionist	skittles-player
			stamp-collector

Phobias

9
zoophobia (animals)

10
acrophobia (heights)
aerophobia (flying)
altophobia (heights)
ergophobia (work)
gatophobia (cats)
gynophobia (women)
koniphobia (dust)
musophobia (mice)
pyrophobia (fire)
xenophobia (strangers)

11
agoraphobia (open spaces)
androphobia (men)
anemophobia (draughts)
hippophobia (horses)
hydrophobia (water)
hypsophobia (high places)
limnophobia (lakes)
ochlophobia (crowds)
thixophobia (touching)

12
achluophobia (night; darkness)
ailurophobia (cats)
amathophobia (dust)

13
ailourophobia (cats)
arachnophobia (spiders)
gephyrophobia (crossing a bridge)
ichthyophobia (fish)
melissophobia (bees)
ophidiophobia (snakes)
ornithophobia (birds)
pnigerophobia (smothering; choking)
pteronophobia (feathers)
spheksophobia (wasps)

14
alektorophobia (chickens)
thalassophobia (sea)

17
triskaidekaphobia (number 13)

Physics

3
bar
erg
gas
ion
lux
mil
ohm
rad

4
atom
cell
flux
gain
heat
lens
Mach
mass
mole
node
pole
rays
spin
tone
tube
volt
watt
wave
work
X-ray

5
anion
anode
curie
cycle
decay
diode

5
earth
farad
field
fluid
force
hertz
joule
laser
light
lumen
maser
motor
orbit
phase
pitch
power
prism
speed
valve

6
ampere
atomic
charge
convex
energy
fusion
impact
isobar
kelvin
magnet
moment
newton
optics
pascal
period
plasma
proton

6
second
shells
strain
stress
triode
vacuum
vapour
vector
weight

7
ammeter
aneroid
beta ray
calorie
candela
cathode
Celsius
circuit
concave
current
decibel
density
dry cell
element
entropy
fission
lattice
neutron
nuclear
nucleon
nucleus
osmosis
reactor
spectra

8
beta rays
betatron

7
Brownian
cohesion
dynamics
electric
electron
enthalpy
fluidics
free fall
friction
graviton
half-life
harmonic
heat pump
infra-red
isotopes
magneton
molecule
momentum
parallax
particle
pendulum
positive
positron
pressure
rheology
solenoid
specific
spectrum
velocity

9
acoustics
allotropy
alpha rays
barometer
black body
Boyle's law
capacitor
condenser

9

conductor
cyclotron
diffusion
discharge
electrode
frequency
gamma rays
generator
harmonics
induction
magnetism
magnetron
mechanics
microwave
radiation
rectifier
resonance
telescope
tribology

10

absorption
cathode ray
Centigrade
conduction
convection
cosmic rays
cryogenics
dielectric
dispersion
efficiency
electrical
Fahrenheit
holography

10

latent heat
Mach number
mass number
microscope
Planck's law
pneumatics
radiopaque
radio waves
reflection
refraction
relativity
resistance
scattering
sinusoidal
supersonic
transducer
transistor
wavelength

11

accelerator
calorimeter
capacitance
capillarity
centrifugal
centripetal
compression
diffraction
electricity
electrolite
electronics
evaporation
fibre optics
gravitation

11

laminar flow
neutron star
oscillation
radioactive
radio-opaque
resistivity
temperature
transformer
transuranic
triple point
ultrasonics

12

absolute zero
acceleration
atomic number
atomic weight
beta particle
boiling point
Celsius scale
centre of mass
cloud chamber
conductivity
critical mass
densitometer
Einstein's law
electrolysis
electroscope
fluorescence
galvanometer
infra-red rays
interference
Newton's rings
permeability

12

polarization
specific heat
spectrograph
spectrometer

13

alpha particle
Becquerel rays
bubble chamber
direct current
discharge tube
Doppler effect
freezing point
geiger counter
kinetic energy
magnetic field
neutron number
nuclear fusion
nuclear isomer
quantum theory
radioactivity
scintillation
semiconductor

14

atomic mass unit
breeder reactor
cathode ray tube
diffractometer
electric energy
ferromagnetism
nuclear fission
nuclear reactor
transverse rays

15

centre of gravity
electric current
Fahrenheit scale
Planck's constant
potential energy

15

saturated vapour
specific gravity
visible spectrum

16

Brownian movement
centrifugal force
centripetal force
mass spectrometer

16
Pascal's principle
valence electrons

17
integrated circuit

18
absorption spectrum
alternating current
elementary particle

19
Archimedes' principle
Avogadro's hypothesis

19
background radiation
potential difference

20
ultraviolet radiation

Pigs

5
Duroc
Welsh

8
Landrace
Pietrain
Tamworth

9
Berkshire
Hampshire

10
Large White

15
Swedish Landrace

17
British Saddleback
Gloucester Old Spot

20
Vietnamese Pot-bellied

Plants and flowers

3	4	5	5
hop	musk	erica	tulip
ivy	pink	flora	viola
may	rape	gorse	
rye	reed	henna	6
	rice	lilac	acacia
4	rose	lotus	alpine
aloe	rush	lupin	arnica
arum	tare	oxlip	azalea
dock	woad	pansy	bryony
fern		peony	cactus
flag	5	phlox	clover
flax	agave	poppy	coleus
hemp	aster	sedge	cotton
iris	briar	senna	crocus
jute	broom	stock	dahlia
lily	daisy		darnel

6	7	8	8
fennel	freesia	camellia	sainfoin
fescue	fuchsia	cat's tail	saltwort
hyssop	gentian	charlock	scabious
madder	heather	clematis	shamrock
millet	hemlock	cockspur	snowdrop
mimosa	henbane	cyclamen	soapwort
myrtle	honesty	daffodil	sweet pea
nettle	jacinth	dianthus	tuberose
orchid	jasmine	dropwort	valerian
rattan	jonquil	eggplant	veronica
salvia	kingcup	fleabane	wild rose
scilla	lobelia	fleawort	wistaria
sesame	lupinus	foxglove	wisteria
spurge	may lily	fumitory	woodbine
squill	milfoil	gardenia	woodrush
sundew	mustard	geranium	wormwood
teasel	opuntia	gladiola	xanthium
thrift	papyrus	gloxinia	
twitch	petunia	harebell	9
violet	primula	hawkweed	aaron's rod
yarrow	ragwort	helenium	amaryllis
zinnia	rambler	hibiscus	aquilegia
	sanicle	hyacinth	arrowfoot
7	sea pink	japonica	bluegrass
aconite	tea rose	knapweed	broomrape
anemone	thistle	laburnum	buckwheat
begonia	tobacco	larkspur	buttercup
bistort	trefoil	lavender	campanula
blossom	verbena	lungwort	candytuft
bracken	vervain	magnolia	carnation
bugloss		marigold	celandine
bulrush	8	milkweed	chickweed
burdock	acanthus	milkwort	cineraria
campion	agrimony	moss pink	coltsfoot
catmint	arum lily	musk rose	columbine
chicory	asphodel	oleander	corn-poppy
clarkia	aubretia	plumbago	dandelion
cowslip	auricula	pond lily	dog violet
day lily	bedstraw	primrose	edelweiss
dogbane	bindweed	puffball	eglantine
dog rose	bluebell	rock rose	eyebright

9

forsythia
germander
gladiolus
glasswort
goldenrod
ground ivy
groundsel
hellebore
hollyhock
hydrangea
moneywort
monkshood
narcissus
patchouli
pimpernel
pyrethrum
safflower
saxifrage
snakeroot
speedwell
spikenard
stonecrop
sunflower
sweet flag
tiger lily
tormentil
verbascum
water lily
wolf's bane
woundwort

10

agapanthus
amaranthus
aspidistra
belladonna
busy lizzie

10

bitterwort
cinquefoil
corncockle
cornflower
couch grass
cow parsley
cranesbill
cuckoopint
damask rose
delphinium
Easter lily
fritillary
gaillardia
goosegrass
gypsophila
heart's-ease
heliotrope
lady's smock
marguerite
mignonette
nasturtium
opium poppy
oxeye daisy
pennyroyal
periwinkle
poinsettia
polyanthus
snapdragon
spleenwort
stitchwort
sweet briar
thorn apple
touch-me-not
wallflower
willowherb
wind flower
wood sorrel

11

antirrhinum
bishop's weed
bittersweet
canary grass
convolvulus
fig marigold
forget-me-not
gillyflower
globe flower
helleborine
honeysuckle
ipecacuanha
London pride
love-in-a-mist
marram grass
marsh mallow
meadowsweet
pampas grass
prickly pear
ragged robin
rambler rose
red-hot poker
rubber plant
sea lavender
wintergreen
wood anemone

12

autumn crocus
compass plant
globe thistle
Jacob's-ladder
lady's slipper
old man's beard
pitcher plant
quaking grass
rhododendron

12

Solomon's-seal
sweet william
venus flytrap

13

African violet
bleeding heart
Christmas rose
chrysanthemum
creeping jenny
crown imperial
elephant grass
grape hyacinth
marsh marigold
meadow saffron
passion flower
slipper orchid
traveller's joy
winter aconite

14

bougainvillaea
Canterbury bell
castor-oil plant
lords-and-ladies

15

lily-of-the-valley
Michaelmas daisy
star-of-Bethlehem
Virginia creeper
woody nightshade

16

deadly nightshade
love-lies-bleeding

Play titles

4

Loot (Joe Orton)
Ross (Terence Rattigan)

5

Caste (T.W. Robertson)
Faust (Goethe)
Roots (Arnold Wesker)

6

Ghosts (Henrik Ibsen)
Plenty (David Hare)
Salome (Oscar Wilde)
Strife (John Galsworthy)
The Fan (Carlo Goldoni)

7

Amadeus (Peter Shaffer)
Candida (G.B. Shaw)
Electra (Sophocles)
Jumpers (Tom Stoppard)
The Lark (Jean Anouilh)
The Room (Harold Pinter)
Volpone (Ben Jonson)

8

Hay Fever (Noel Coward)
Peter Pan (J.M. Barrie)
The Birds (Aristophanes)
The Frogs (Aristophanes)

9

All My Sons (Arthur Miller)
Cavalcade (Noel Coward)
Dr Faustus (Christopher Marlowe)
Flare Path (Terence Rattigan)
Golden Boy (Clifford Odets)
Happy Days (Samuel Beckett)
Pygmalion (G.B. Shaw)
The Circle (W. Somerset Maugham)

9

The Critic (R.B. Sheridan)
The Rivals (R.B. Sheridan)

10

All For Love (John Dryden)
I Am a Camera (John Van Druten)
Lysistrata (Aristophanes)
The Balcony (Jean Genet)
The Hostage (Brendan Behan)
The Seagull (Anton Chekhov)

11

A Doll's House (Henrik Ibsen)
Hedda Gabler (Henrik Ibsen)
Journeys' End (R.C. Sherriff)
Love For Love (William Congreve)
Tamburlaine (Christopher Marlowe)
The Bankrupt (Alexander Ostrovsky)
The Crucible (Arthur Miller)
The Wild Duck (Henrik Ibsen)

12

After the Fall (Arthur Miller)
Bedroom Farce (Alan Ayckbourn)
Blithe Spirit (Noel Coward)
Charley's Aunt (Brandon Thomas)
Duel of Angels (Jean Giraudoux)
Major Barbara (G.B. Shaw)
The Caretaker (Harold Pinter)
The Mousetrap (Agatha Christie)
Three Sisters (Anton Chekhov)

13

A Taste of Honey (Shelagh
  Delaney)
Arms and the Man (G.B. Shaw)
Hobson's Choice (Harold Brighouse)
Quality Street (J.M. Barrie)
The Dumb Waiter (Harold Pinter)
The Linden Tree (J.B. Priestley)

13

The Magistrate (A.W. Pinero)
The Winslow Boy (Terence Rattigan)
Under Milk Wood (Dylan Thomas)

14

An Ideal Husband (Oscar Wilde)
Man and Superman (G.B. Shaw)
Separate Tables (Terence Rattigan)
The Corn is Green (Emlyn Williams)
The Deep Blue Sea (Terence Rattigan)
The Entertainer (John Osborne)
The Old Bachelor (William Congreve)
The Philanderer (G.B. Shaw)
This Happy Breed (Noel Coward)

15

Bartholomew Fair (Ben Jonson)
Dangerous Corner (J.B. Priestley)
Design for Living (Noel Coward)
Heartbreak House (G.B. Shaw)
Look Back in Anger (John Osborne)
Present Laughter (Noel Coward)
The Constant Wife (W. Somerset Maugham)
Waiting for Godot (Samuel Beckett)

16

A Cuckoo in the Nest (Ben Travers)
An Inspector Calls (J.B. Priestley)
Death of a Salesman (Arthur Miller)
Pillars of Society (Henrik Ibsen)
The Adding Machine (Elmer Rice)
The Birthday Party (Harold Pinter)
The Cherry Orchard (Anton Chekhov)
The Cocktail Party (T.S. Eliot)
The Family Reunion (T.S. Eliot)
The Master Builder (Henrik Ibsen)

16

The Way of the World (William Congreve)
What the Butler Saw (Joe Orton)
When We are Married (J.B. Priestley)

17

A Man for All Seasons (Robert Bolt)
Arsenic and Old Lace (Joseph Kesselring)
Romanoff and Juliet (Peter Ustinov)
The Constant Couple (George Farquhar)
The Devil's Disciple (G.B. Shaw)
The Glass Menagerie (Tennessee Williams)
The Good Natured Man (Oliver Goldsmith)
'Tis Pity She's a Whore (John Ford)

18

An Enemy of the People (Henrik Ibsen)
Caesar and Cleopatra (G.B. Shaw)
Five Finger Exercise (Peter Shaffer)
French without Tears (Terence Rattigan)
Lady Windermere's Fan (Oscar Wilde)
She Stoops to Conquer (Oliver Goldsmith)
Suddenly Last Summer (Tennessee Williams)
The Browning Version (Terence Rattigan)

19

Androcles and the Lion (G.B. Shaw)
Chips with Everything (Arnold Wesker)

19
Every Man in his Humour
  (Ben Jonson)
The Inspector General (Nikolai
  Gogol)
The School for Scandal
  (R.B. Sheridan)
What Every Woman Knows
  (J.M. Barrie)

20
A Woman of No Importance
  (Oscar Wilde)
Entertaining Mr Sloane
  (Joe Orton)
Murder in the Cathedral
  (T.S. Eliot)
The Admirable Crichton
  (J.M. Barrie)
The Recruiting Officer (George
  Farquhar)

21
A Streetcar Named Desire
  (Tennessee Williams)
The Second Mrs Tanqueray
  (A.W. Pinero)

22
Every Man out of his Humour
  (Ben Jonson)

25
Who's Afraid of Virginia Woolf?
  (Edward Albee)

26
The Barretts of Wimpole Street
  (Rudolf Besier)

27
The Importance of Being Earnest
  (Oscar Wilde)

Poetry, prose and grammar

3	4	5	5
ego	myth	blurb	index
lay	noun	canto	lyric
ode	past	carol	maxim
pun	play	colon	metre
	plot	comma	motif
4	poem	dirge	novel
bard	quip	ditty	paean
coda	rule	drama	prose
copy	saga	elegy	psalm
dual	scan	essay	quote
epic	song	fable	rhyme
foot	tone	farce	rondo
form	verb	folio	scene
glee	work	idyll	shift
mime		iliad	slang
mood		image	style

5

tense
theme
triad
verse
vowel

6

accent
active
adverb
annals
ballad
chorus
clause
cliché
comedy
critic
define
derive
ending
future
hiatus
homily
humour
hyphen
iambic
jargon
legend
lyrist
number
object
parody
pathos
period
person
phrase
plural
poetic
prefix
review
rhythm

6

riddle
satire
simile
sketch
slogan
sonnet
stanza
stress
suffix
symbol
thesis
verbal

7

adjunct
anagram
analogy
analyse
antonym
article
cadence
cantata
collate
content
context
couplet
descant
diction
edition
epistle
epitaph
fantasy
fiction
harmony
idyllic
inflect
introit
lexicon
lyrical
nemesis
odyssey

7

paradox
parsing
passive
perfect
persona
present
pronoun
prosaic
proverb
quartet
refrain
regular
requiem
setting
subject
tragedy
trilogy
triolet
triplet

8

acrostic
allusion
alphabet
analysis
asterisk
canticle
contrast
definite
dialogue
doggerel
dramatic
epic poem
epigraph
epilogue
footnote
full stop
generate
glossary
guttural
language

8

laureate
libretto
limerick
madrigal
metaphor
metrical
mock epic
negative
nonsense
particle
pastoral
phonetic
poetical
positive
prologue
quantity
relative
rhapsody
rhetoric
Romantic
scanning
scenario
sentence
singular
suspense
swan song
temporal
thriller
whodunit
word play

9

adjective
ampersand
anonymous
anthology
biography
broadside
burlesque
cacophony
classical

9	9	10	11
conjugate	symbolism	palindrome	superlative
criticism	symposium	paraphrase	tragicomedy
etymology		short story	
facsimile	**10**	subjective	**12**
flashback	apostrophe	tetrameter	alliteration
formative	atmosphere		alphabetical
free verse	avant garde	**11**	bibliography
hyperbole	blank verse	association	metaphorical
imperfect	bowdlerise	ballad style	nursery rhyme
inflexion	bowdlerize	comic relief	Poet Laureate
inversion	caricature	comparative	
irregular	colloquial	concordance	**13**
lyric poem	comparison	conjunction	irregular verb
masculine	definition	conjunctive	lyrical poetry
objective	definitive	descriptive	poetic licence
past tense	derivative	future tense	ungrammatical
platitude	grammarian	ghost writer	
potential	hyphenated	grammatical	**14**
principle	indefinite	lyric poetry	indicative mood
prose poem	infinitive	Miracle play	inverted commas
quartette	inflection	Mystery play	science fiction
quotation	intonation	parenthesis	transformation
roundelay	involution	Passion play	
semicolon	linguistic	preposition	**15**
soliloquy	manuscript	punctuation	definite article
	nom de plume	regular verb	personification
		subordinate	split infinitive

Poets Laureate

3
Pye, Henry James

4
Rowe, Nicholas
Tate, Nahum

6
Austin, Alfred
Cibber, Colley
Dryden, John

6
Eusden, Laurence
Hughes, Ted
Warton, Thomas

7
Bridges, Robert
Southey, Robert

8
Betjeman, Sir John
Day-Lewis, Cecil

8
Shadwell, Thomas
Tennyson, Alfred, Lord

9
Masefield, John
Whitehead, William

10
Wordsworth, William

Poisons

4	7	9	12
acid	cocaine	rat poison	barbiturates
upas	cyanide	toadstool	carbonic acid
	hemlock	veratrine	fool's parsley
5	henbane	wolf's bane	water hemlock
dwale	veronal		
ergot	vitriol	**10**	**13**
fungi		aqua fortis	carbonic oxide
venom	**8**	belladonna	caustic potash
	atropine	chloroform	sulphuric acid
6	botulism	mustard gas	
antiar	chlorine	nitric acid	**14**
curare	ergotine	oxalic acid	carbon monoxide
heroin	hyoscine	picric acid	
iodine	nicotine	salmonella	**15**
phenol	phosgene	snake venom	hydrocyanic acid
	ptomaine	strychnine	irritant poisons
7	ratsbane	weed-killer	narcotic poisons
aconite	thallium		
ammonia		**11**	**16**
aniline	**9**	caustic soda	deadly
arsenic	baneberry	insecticide	nightshade
bromine	colchicum	lead acetate	
coal gas	monkshood	prussic acid	
	nux vomica	sugar of lead	

Political terms

2	3	4	4
E.C.	I.R.A.	ayes	noes
M.P.	K.G.B.	bill	oath
J.P.	law	coup	pact
U.N.	opt	Dail	pass
	P.L.O.	Duma	peer
3	red	gain	poll
act	sit	left	seat
bar	tax	lord	Tory
C.I.S.	T.U.C.	mace	veto
E.E.C.		N.A.T.O.	vote

4
Whig
whip
writ

5
agent
amend
by-law
chair
clerk
count
draft
edict
elect
enact
house
junta
legal
lobby
Nazis
order
paper
party
rally
right
valid
voter

6
assent
backer
ballot
budget
caucus
clause
colony
Cortes
decree
divide
Enosis
Fabian

6
govern
heckle
labour
leader
Maoism
member
motion
nation
picket
policy
quorum
recess
record
reform
report
ruling
secede
senate
speech
strike
summon
teller
tyrant

7
adjourn
anarchy
borough
boycott
cabinet
canvass
censure
chamber
closure
Cold War
Commons
commune
council
deficit
dissent
elector

7
embargo
fascism
fascist
federal
finance
gallery
heckler
hot line
Knesset
liberal
mandate
Marxism
neutral
opening
outvote
pairing
passage
politic
Poor Law
premier
prolong
radical
reading
recount
re-elect
re-enact
Riksdag
senator
session
speaker
statute
tribune
tyranny
vacancy
Zionism
Zionist

8
assembly
Black Rod
blockade

8
chairman
commoner
Congress
democrat
dictator
dissolve
division
dominion
feminism
free vote
home rule
left wing
majority
minister
ministry
minority
national
official
politics
republic
schedule
Storting
Treasury
Unionism
Unionist
Woolsack

9
amendment
anarchism
apartheid
ballot box
Bundestag
coalition
committee
communism
communist
democracy
deterrent
exchequer
First Lord
legislate

9
ombudsman
president
Reichstag
right wing
sanctions
socialism
socialist
terrorism

10
by-election
capitalism
chancellor
collective
conference
devolution
government
guillotine
invalidate
monarchism
opposition

10
parliament
Plaid Cymru
radicalism
referendum
republican
resolution
revolution
scrutineer
third world
trade union
Warsaw Pact
White House
White Paper

11
adjournment
back bencher
ballot paper
casting vote
congressman
constituent

11
co-operative
demarcation
dissolution
divine right
finance bill
imperialist
independent
legislation
legislative
nationalist
party leader
private bill
statute book
suffragette

12
commissioner
Common Market
Commonwealth
conservatism
conservative

12
constituency
constitution
deputy leader
dictatorship
federal union
House of Lords
House of Peers
invalidation
Lord Advocate
Privy Council
welfare state

13
demonstration
Home Secretary
international
Lord Privy Seal
Prime Minister
shadow cabinet
trade unionist
United Nations

14
constitutional
deputy chairman
Lord Chancellor
representative
Social Democrat

15
Attorney General
cabinet minister
general election
Liberal Democrat
minister of state

16
Chiltern Hundreds
Maastricht treaty

Politicians and statesmen

3
Fox, Charles James (British statesman)
Fox, Dr Liam (British politician)
Fox, Sir Marcus (British politician)
Lie, Trygve (Norwegian statesman)

4
Benn, Anthony Wedgwood (British politician)
Blum, Leon (French statesman)

4

Bose, Subhas Chandra (Indian nationalist leader)
Cook, Robin (British politician)
Foot, Sir Michael (British politician)
Howe, Sir (Richard Edward) Geoffrey (British politician)
Hurd, Douglas (British politician)
King, Martin Luther (American civil rights leader)
King, Tom (British politician)
Knox, David (British politician)
Meir, Golda (Israeli Stateswoman)
Owen, David, Baron (British politician)
Rusk, Dean (American Statesman)

5

Agnew, Spiro Theodore (American politician)
Ashby, David (British politician)
Astor, Nancy Witcher, Viscountess (British politician)
Begin, Menachem (Israeli statesman)
Bevan, Aueurin (British politician)
Bevin, Ernest (British statesman)
Botha, Louis (S. African soldier and statesman)
Botha, Pieter Willem (S. African statesman)
De Wit, Jan (Dutch statesman)
Emmet, Robert (Irish patriot)
Gould, Bryan (British politician)
Laval, Pierre (French politician)
Lenin, Vladimir Ilyich (Soviet statesman)
Nehru, Pandit Jawaharlal (Indian statesman)
Nkomo, Joshua (Zimbabwean politician)
Perón, Juan Domingo (Argentinian statesman)
Sadat, Anwar (Egyptian statesman)
Short, Clare (British politician)
Smith, Ian Douglas (Zimbabwean politician)
Smith, John (British politician)
Smuts, Jan Christian (S. African statesman)
Snape, Peter (British politician)
Spaak, Paul Henri (Belgian statesman)
Steel, Sir David (British politician)
Straw, Jack (British politician)
Vance, Cyrus (American statesman)

6

Arafat, Yassir (Palestinian leader)
Bhutto, Benazir (Pakistani politician)
Bhutto, Zulfikar Ali (Pakistani statesman)
Brandt, Willy (German statesman)
Bright, John (radical Quaker statesman)
Butler, Richard Austen, Baron (British statesman)
Castle, Barbara, Baroness (British politician)
Castro, Fidel (Cuban revolutionary and statesman)
Clarke, Kenneth (British politician)
Cobden, Richard (British Politician)
Cripps, Sir Stafford (British statesman)
Crispi, Francesco (Italian statesman)
Currie, Edwina (British politician)
Davitt, Michael (Irish nationalist)
Dubček, Alexander (Czechoslovak statesman)
Dulles, John Foster (American statesman)
Erhard, Ludwig (German statesman)
Fowler, Sir Norman (British politician)
Franco, Francisco (Spanish soldier and dictator)
Gandhi, Indira (Indian stateswoman)
Gandhi, Mohandas Karamchand (Indian religious and political leader)
Healey, Denis Winston, Baron (British statesman)
Kaunda, Kenneth (African statesman)
Lamont, Norman (British politician)
Lilley, Peter (British politician)
Mosley, Sir Oswald (British Fascist)
Nasser, Gamal Abdel (Egyptian statesman)
Petain, Henri Philippe (French soldier and statesman)
Powell, John Enoch (British politician)
Quayle, Dan (American politician)
Rhodes, Cecil John (S. African statesman)
Stalin, Joseph (Soviet statesman)
Thorpe, (John) Jeremy (British politician)
Wilkes, John (British politician)

7

Allende, Salvador (Chilean statesman)
Ashdown, Paddy (British politician)
Atatürk, Kemal (Turkish statesman)
Bolivar, Simon (S. American statesman)
De Klerk, F.W. (S. African statesman)

7
Gaddafi, Moammar Al (Libyan statesman)
Grattan, Henry (Irish statesman)
Grimond, Joseph (British politician)
Gromyko, Andrei (Soviet diplomat)
Jackson, Glenda (British politician)
Jenkins, Roy Harris, Baron (British statesman)
Keating, Paul (Australian politician)
Kinnock, Neil (British politician)
Kosygin, Aleksei (Soviet statesman)
Macleod, Iain Norman (British politician)
Mandela, Nelson (S. African political leader)
Mazzini, Giuseppe (Italian patriot)
Menzies, Sir Robert Gordon (Australian statesman)
Molotov, Vyacheslav (Soviet diplomat)
Nyerere, Julius (Tanzanian statesman)
O'Connor, Thomas Power (Irish nationalist)
Parnell, Charles Stewart (Irish politician)
Pearson, Lester Bowles (Canadian statesman)
Raffles, Sir (Thomas) Stamford (British colonial administrator)
Rifkind, Malcolm (British politician)
Rumbold, Angela (British politician)
Salazar, Antonio de Oliveira (Portuguese dictator)
Schmidt, Helmut (German statesman)
Shastri, Lal Bahadur (Indian statesman)
Trotsky, Leon (Russian revolutionary)
Trudeau, Pierre Eliott (Canadian statesman)
Yeltsin, Boris (Russian statesman)

8
Adenauer, Konrad (German statesman)
Amin Dada, Idi (Ugandan politician)
Ayub Khan Mohammed (Pakistani statesman)
Bismarck, Otto von (German statesman)
Brezhnev, Leonid (Soviet statesman)
Bulganin, Nikolai (Soviet statesman)
Cosgrave, William Thomas (Irish statesman)
Crossman, Richard Howard Stafford (British politician)
De Gaulle, Charles (French soldier and statesman)
De Valera, Eamon (Irish statesman)
Dunwoody, Gwyneth (British politician)
Griffith, Arthur (Irish statesman)

8

Harriman, William Averell (American diplomat)
Hastings, Warren (British colonial administrator)
Hirohito (emperor of Japan)
Holyoake, Sir Keith Jacka (N.Z. statesman)
Kenyatta, Jomo (Kenyan statesman)
Lawrence, Sir Ivan (British politician)
Morrison, Herbert Stanley, Baron (British statesman)
O'Connell, Daniel (Irish national leader)
Poincaré, Raymond Nicolas (French statesman)
Pompidou, Georges (French statesman)
Shephard, Gillian (British politician)
Sikorski, Wladyslaw (Polish soldier and statesman)
Verwoerd, Hendrik Frensch (S. African politician)
Weizmann, Chaim (Israeli statesman)
Williams, Shirley, Baroness (British politician)

9

Ben Gurion, David (Israeli statesman)
Bottomley, Peter (British politician)
Bottomley, Virginia (British politician)
Chou En-lai (Chinese statesman)
Churchill, Lord Randolph Henry Spencer (British politician)
Gaitskell, Hugh Todd Naylor (British politician)
Gorbachev, Mikhail (Soviet statesman)
Henderson, Arthur (British politician)
Heseltine, Michael (British politician)
Ho Chi Minh (Vietnamese statesman)
Kissinger, Henry (American diplomat)
MacDonald, James Ramsay (British statesman)
MacDonald, Sir John (Canadian statesman)
Mussolini, Benito (Italian Fascist dictator)
Nicholson, Emma (British politician)
Stevenson, Adlai (American politician)

10

Carrington, Peter, 6th Baron (British statesman)
Clemenceau, Georges (French statesman)
Hattersley, Roy (British politician)
Khrushchev, Nikita (Soviet statesman)
Mao Tse-tung (Chinese statesman)
Mitterrand, François Maurice (French statesman)
Waldegrave, William (British politician)

11
Castlereagh, Robert Stewart, Viscount (British statesman)

12
Bandaranaike, Solomon (Sri Lankan statesman)
Mendès-France, Pierre (French statesman)

13
Chiang Kai-shek (Chinese soldier and statesman)

14
Heathcoat-Amery, David (British politician)

15
Giscard d'Estaing, Valéry (French statesman)

Popes (from 1492)

Alexander VI (1492)	Clement VIII (1592)	Clement XIII (1758)
Pius III (1503)	Leo XI (1605)	Clement XIV (1769)
Julius II (1503)	Paul V (1605)	Pius VI (1775)
Leo X (1513)	Gregory XV (1621)	Pius VII (1800)
Adrian VI (1522)	Urban VIII (1623)	Leo XII (1823)
Clement VII (1523)	Innocent X (1644)	Pius VIII (1829)
Paul III (1534)	Alexander VII (1655)	Gregory XVI (1831)
Julius III (1550)	Clement IX (1667)	Pius IX (1846)
Marcellus II (1555)	Clement X (1670)	Leo XIII (1878)
Paul IV (1555)	Innocent XI (1676)	Pius X (1903)
Pius IV (1559)	Alexander VIII (1689)	Benedict XV (1914)
Pius V (1566)	Innocent XII (1691)	Pius XI (1922)
Gregory XIII (1572)	Clement XI (1700)	Pius XII (1939)
Sixtus V (1585)	Innocent XIII (1721)	John XXIII (1958)
Urban VII (1590)	Benedict XIII (1724)	Paul VI (1963)
Gregory XIV (1590)	Clement XII (1730)	John Paul I (1978)
Innocent IX (1591)	Benedict XIV (1740)	John Paul II (1978)

Popular musicians and groups

2

U2

3

ABC
Ant, Adam
Day, Doris
Eno, Brian
Jam, The
Lee, Brenda
Lee, Peggy
Mud
O.M.D.
Ono, Yoko
Ray, Johnny
Rea, Chris
UFO
Vee, Bobby
War
Who, The
Yes

4

10CC
Abba
AC/DC
Anka, Paul
Baez, Joan
Ball, Michael
Band, The
Bart, Lionel
Beck, Jeff
Bilk, Acker
Blue, Barry
Bros
Bush, Kate
Byrd, Charlie
Cars, The
Cash, Johnnie
Cher

4

Chic
Cole, Nat 'King'
Como, Perry
Cure, The
Dana
Dion
Dury, Ian
Eddy, Duane
Fame, Georgie
Ford, Tennessee Ernie
Free
Fury, Billy
Gaye, Marvin
Getz, Stan
Idol, Billy
Joel, Billy
John, Elton
Kale, J.J.
Kern, Jerome
Kidd, Johnny
King, B.B.
King, Carole
King, Jonathan
Kiss
Kitt, Eartha
Lowe, Nick
Lulu
Lynn, Vera
Mann, Barry
Maze
Monk, Thelonius
Most, Mickie
Move, The
Nice, The
Paul, Billy
Piaf, Edith
Reed, Lou
Rich, Charlie
Ross, Diana

4

Rush
Sade
Shaw, Artie
Shaw, Sandie
Styx
T Rex
UB40
Wham
Wolf, Howlin'
Wood, Roy
Wray, Link

5

Adler, Larry
Adler, Lou
Aswad
Baker, Peter 'Ginger'
Basie, Count
Berry, Chuck
Berry, Nick
Black, Cilla
Bolan, Marc
Boone, Pat
Bowie, David
Bread
Brown, James
Byrds, The
Chinn, Nicky
Clark, Dave, 5
Clark, Petula
Clash, The
Cliff, Jimmy
Cogan, Alma
Cohen, Leonard
Cooke, Sam
Cream, The
Croce, Jim
Darin, Bobby
Davis, Miles

5

Davis, Sammy, Jnr
Davis, Spencer, Group
Dells, The
Doors, The
Dylan, Bob
Essex, David
Faces, The
Ferry, Bryan
Flack, Roberta
Freed, Alan
Green, Al
Haley, Bill
Handy, William Christopher
Hayes, Isaac
Heart
Hines, Earl
Holly, Buddy
James, Bob
James, Tommy and the Shondells
Jarre, Jean-Michel
Jones, Quincy
Jones, Tom
Kinks, The
Klein, Allen
Laine, Frankie
Lewis, Jerry Lee
Logan, Johnny
Lymon, Frankie and the Teenagers
Mocoy, Van
Moore, Gary
Moyet, Alison
Numan, Gary
O'Jays, The
Perry, Richard
Price, Alan
Proby, P.J.
Queen
Reddy, Helen
Saxon
Sayer, Leo
Scott, Ronnie

5

Seger, Bob
Simon, Carly
Slade
Smith, Bessie
Starr, Ringo
Sting
Sweet, The
Tatum, Art
White, Barry
Wyman, Bill
Yazoo
Young, Neil
Young, Paul
Zappa, Frank
ZZ Top

6

Alpert, Herb
Argent
Atkins, Chet
Atwell, Winifred
Avalon, Frankie
Baldry, Long John
Bassey, Shirley
Bechet, Sidney
Benson, George
Berlin, Irving
Bolden, Buddy
Boney M
Boston
Browne, Jackson
Burdon, Eric
Chapin, Harry
Cocker, Joe
Cooder, Ry
Cooper, Alice
Cougar, John
Creole, Kid and the Coconuts
Crosby, Bing
Damned, The
Dekker, Desmond

6

Denver, John
Domino, Fats
Dr Hook
Eagles, The
Easton, Sheena
Equals, The
Fabian
Family
Fields, Gracie
Fisher, Eddie
Geldof, Bob
Harris, Emmylou
Hooker, John Lee
Hunter, Ian
Jagger, Mick
Jolson, Al
Joplin, Janis
Joplin, Scott
Knight, Gladys and the Pips
Kooper, Al
Korner, Alexis
Kramer, Billy J
Lauper, Cyndi
Leiber, Jerry
Lennon, John
Marley, Bob and the Wailers
Martin, George
Martin, John
Marvin, Lee
Mathis, Johnny
Mayall, John
McLean, Don
Midler, Bette
Miller, Glen
Miller, Steve
Mingus, Charlie
Montez, Chris
Morton, Jelly Roll
Nelson, Ricky
Nelson, Willie
Newman, Randy

6

Nugent, Ted
Osmond, Donny
Palmer, Robert
Parker, Charlie
Parker, Colonel Tom
Parton, Dolly
Paxton, Tom
Pitney, Gene
Police, The
Porter, Cole
Prince
Reeves, Jim
Revere, Paul and the Raiders
Richie, Lionel
Rivers, Johnny
Rogers, Kenny
Sedaka, Neil
Seeger, Pete
Simone, Nina
Sledge, Percy
Summer, Donna
Taupin, Bernie
Taylor, James
Thomas, B.J.
Troggs, The
Turner, Ike and Tina
Twitty, Conway
Valens, Ritchie
Vinton, Bobby
Waller, Fats
Waters, Muddy
Wilson, Jackie
Winter, Edgar
Winter, Johnny
Womack, Bobby
Wonder, Stevie

7

America
Animals, The
Atkins, Chet
Archies

7

Ballard, Hank
Beatles, The
Bee Gees, The
Bennett, Tony
Blondie
Bonjovi
Brubeck, Dave
Calvert, Eddie
Cassidy, David
Chapman, Mike
Charles, Ray
Checker, Chubby
Clapton, Eric
Clooney, Rosemary
Cochran, Eddie
Collins, Judy
Collins, Phil
De Burgh, Chris
Diamond, Neil
Diddley, Bo
Donegan, Lonnie
Donovan
Edmunds, Dave
Epstein, Brian
Francis, Connie
Gabriel, Peter
Genesis
Glitter, Gary
Goodman, Benny
Guthrie, Woody
Hampton, Lionel
Hancock, Herbie
Hendrix, Jimi
Holiday, Billie
Hollies, The
Jackson, Mahalia
Jackson, Michael
Jackson, Millie
Jarreau, Al
Lofgren, Nils
Madness

7

Madonna
Manilow, Barry
Martell, Lena
Martino, Al
Michael, George
Monkees, The
Nilsson
Orbison, Roy
Osmonds, The
Perkins, Carl
Pickett, Wilson
Presley, Elvis
Preston, Billy
Rainbow
Redding, Otis
Richard, Cliff
Richard, Keith
Russell, Leon
Santana
Scraggs, Boz
Seekers, The
Shadows, The
Shankar, Ravi
Shannon, Del
Shapiro, Helen
Sinatra, Frank
Sinatra, Nancy
Spector, Phil
Squeeze
Stevens, Cat
Stewart, Rod
Traffic
Turtles, The
Valance, Ricky
Vaughan, Frankie
Vaughan, Sarah
Vincent, Gene
Wakeman, Rick
Warwick, Dionne
Whitman, Slim
Wizzard

7

Wynette, Tammy
Zombies, The

8

Anderson, Eric
Aznavour, Charles
Campbell, Glen
Chi-lites, The
Coasters, The
Coltrane, John
Crystals, The
Drifters, The
Four Aces, The
Four Tops, The
Frampton, Peter
Franklin, Aretha
Hamlisch, Marvin
Harrison, George
Hawkwind
Heatwave
Ink Spots
Jennings, Waylon
Marsalis, Wynton
Mayfield, Curtis
Meat Loaf
Minnelli, Liza
Miracles, The
Mitchell, Joni
Morrison, Van
Oldfield, Mike
Osbourne, Ozzy
Peterson, Oscar
Platters, The
Rafferty, Gerry
Robinson, Smokey
Ronettes, The
Ronstadt, Linda
Sondheim, Stephen
Specials, The
Stigwood, Robert

8

Stroller, Mike
Supremes, The
Ultravox
Vandross, Luther

9

Air Supply
Armstrong, Louis
Bacharach, Burt
Badfinger
Beach Boys, The
Beefheart, Captain
Belafonte, Harry
Bucks Fizz
Chipmunks, The
Crusaders, The
Ellington, Duke
Faithfull, Marianne
Fogelberg, Dan
Foreigner
Gillespie, Dizzy
Goldsboro, Bobby
Grappelli, Stephane
Leadbelly
Little Eva
Lyttelton, Humphrey
Marmalade
McCartney, Paul
Men at Work
Motorhead
O'Sullivan, Gilbert
Pink Floyd
Reinhardt, Django
Rose Royce
Roxy Music
Scorpions
Searchers, The
Shirelles, The
Simply Red
Status Quo
Steely Dan

9

Streisand, Barbra
Thin Lizzy
Townshend, Pete
Uriah Heep
Yardbirds, The

10

Amen Corner
Bad Company
Bananarama
Carmichael, Hoagy
Carpenters, The
Commodores, The
Deep Purple
Dr Feelgood
Duran Duran
Eurythmics
Fitzgerald, Ella
Highwaymen, The
Iron Maiden
Jethro Tull
Kalin Twins
Little Feat
Long Ryders, The
Moody Blues
Mungo, Jerry
Newton-John, Olivia
Pretenders, The
Scott-Heron, Gill
Sex Pistols, The
Small Faces, The
Stranglers, The
Stylistics, The
Washington, Dinah
Whitesnake

11

Armatrading, Joan
Beiderbecke, Bix
Culture Club
Dire Straits

11

Foundations
Four Seasons, The
Human League
Impressions, The
Jackson Five
Joy Division
King Crimson
Led Zeppelin
Lindisfarne
Manfred Mann
Marvelettes, The
Ohio Players
Overlanders
Pet Shop Boys
Procul Harum
Simple Minds
Springfield, Dusty
Springfield, Rick
Springsteen, Bruce
Temptations, The
Theodorakis, Mikis
Wishbone Ash

12

Black Sabbath
Boomtown Rats
Cockney Rebel
Fleetwood Mac
Grateful Dead
Hall and Oates
Hot Chocolate
Housemartins, The
Sonny and Cher
Style Council
Talking Heads
Young Rascals, The

13

Isley Brothers
Kristofferson, Kris
Little Richard

13
Lovin' Spoonful
Mamas and Papas
Mott the Hoople
Reo Speedwagon
Rolling Stones, The
Spandau Ballet
Staple Singers
Tears for Fears
Three Dog Night
Zager and Evans

14
Allman Brothers
Bay City Rollers
Blue Oyster Cult

19
Barclay James Harvest

20
Dexys Midnight Runners
Emerson Lake and Palmer
KC and the Sunshine Band
Sly and the Family Stone

21
Freddie and the Dreamers
Gerry and the Pacemakers

14
Doobie Brothers
Everly Brothers
Fifth Dimension
Herman's Hermits
Jon and Vangelis
Kool and the Gang
Seals and Crofts

15
Detroit Spinners

16
Average White Band
Booker T and the MG's
Brotherhood of Man

22
Bachman-Turner Overdrive
Electric Light Orchestra
Siouxsie and the Banshees

24
Crosby Stills Nash and Young

26
Creedence Clearwater Revival

16
Earth Wind and Fire
Peter Paul and Mary

17
Grand Funk Railroad
Jefferson Airplane
Righteous Brothers
Simon and Garfunkel
Swinging Blue Jeans

18
Blood Sweat and Tears
Buffalo Springfield
Fairport Convention
Public Image Limited

Ports

3	**4**	**4**	**4**
Bar (Yugo)	Baku (Azer)	Hull (Eng)	Pula (Croat)
Ilo (Peru)	Bari (Italy)	Kiel (Ger)	Riga (Lat)
	Cebu (Philip)	Kobe (Japan)	Safi (Moroc)
4	Cobh (Ire)	Okha (Rus)	Suez (Egypt)
Acre (Israel)	Cork (Ire)	Oran (Alg)	Tain (Scot)
Aden (Yemen)	Elat (Israel)	Oslo (Nor)	Tema (Ghana)
Akko (Israel)	Erie (USA)	Para (Braz)	Wick (Scot)
Amoy (China)			

5	5	5	6
Akyab (Burma)	Izmir (Turk)	Yalta (Ukr)	Chefoo (China)
Arica (Chile)	Kerch (Ukr)	Ystad (Swed)	Cochin (India)
Basra (Iraq)	Kochi (Japan)		Danzig (Pol)
Beira (Mozamb)	Kotor (Yugo)	6	Dieppe (Fr)
Belem (Braz)	Lagos (Nigeria)	Abadan (Iran)	Douala (Camer)
Brest (Fr)	Leith (Scot)	Agadir (Moroc)	Dunbar (Scot)
Canea (Gr)	Lulea (Swed)	Ancona (Italy)	Dundee (Scot)
Ceuta (Moroc)	Malmö (Swed)	Ashdod (Israel)	Durban (S.Af)
Colón (Pan)	Osaka (Japan)	Balboa (Pan)	Ferrol (Sp)
Corfu (Gr)	Ostia (Italy)	Bastia (Cors)	Gdansk (Pol)
Dakar (Seneg)	Palma (Sp)	Beirut (Leban)	Gdynia (Pol)
Delft (Neth)	Palos (Sp)	Bergen (Nor)	Haldia (India)
Dover (Eng)	Pusan (S.Kor)	Bilbao (Sp)	Hankow (China)
Eilat (Israel)	Rabat (Moroc)	Bombay (India)	Izmail (Ukr)
Emden (Ger)	Reval (Eston)	Bremen (Ger)	Jeddah (Saudi A)
Gaeta (Italy)	Scapa (Scot)	Calais (Fr)	Kalmar (Swed)
Galle (Sri L)	Trani (Italy)	Callao (Peru)	Kandla (India)
Genoa (Italy)	Varna (Bulg)	Cannes (Fr)	Larvik (Nor)
Haifa (Israel)	Wisby (Swed)	Chalna (Pak)	Lisbon (Port)

6	6	7
Lobito (Angola)	St Malo (Fr)	Algiers (Alg)
London (Eng)	Santos (Braz)	Antwerp (Belg)
Madras (India)	Sittwe (Burma)	Belfast (NI)
Manila (Philip)	Skikda (Alg)	Bushire (Iran)
Maputo (Mozamb)	Smyrna (Turk)	Cardiff (Wales)
Matadi (Zaïre)	Suakin (Sudan)	Cattaro (Yugo)
Mtwara (Tanz)	Swatow (China)	Cayenne (Fr.Guiana)
Naples (Italy)	Sydney (Aust)	Chatham (Eng)
Narvik (Nor)	Tainan (Taiwan)	Colombo (Sri L)
Nelson (NZ)	Tetuan (Moroc)	Corunna (Sp)
Odense (Den)	Toulon (Fr)	Cotonou (Benin)
Odessa (Ukr)	Tromsö (Nor)	Dampier (Aust)
Oporto (Port)	Venice (Italy)	Detroit (USA)
Ostend (Belg)	Weihai (China)	Donegal (Ire)
Padang (Indon)	Wismar (Ger)	Dundalk (Ire)
Patras (Gr)		Dunkirk (Fr)
Penang (Malay)	7	Foochow (China)
Recife (Braz)	Aalborg (Den)	Funchal (Sp)
Rhodes (Gr)	Abidjan (Iv.Coast)	Geelong (Aust)
Rijeka (Croat)	Ajaccio (Cors)	Grimsby (Eng)

7

Guaymas (Mex)
Halifax (Can)
Hamburg (Ger)
Harwich (Eng)
Horsens (Den)
Houston (USA)
Jakarta (Indon)
Karachi (Pak)
Keelung (Taiwan)
Kitimat (Can)
La Plata (Arg)
Larnaca (Cyprus)
Leghorn (Italy)
Le Havre (Fr)
Livorno (Italy)
Marsala (Italy)
Melilla (Moroc)
Messina (Italy)
Mogador (Moroc)
Mombasa (Kenya)
New York (USA)
Norfolk (USA)
Odhotsk (Rus)
Palermo (Italy)
Piraeus (Gr)
Rangoon (Burma)
Rostock (Ger)
Salerno (Italy)
San Juan (P.Rico)
Seattle (USA)
Stettin (Pol)
Swansea (Wales)
Tallinn (Eston)
Tangier (Moroc)
Tilbury (Eng)
Tobarao (Braz)
Trapani (Italy)
Trieste (Italy)
Tripoli (Libya)
Yingkow (China)
Youghal (Ire)

8

Adelaide (Aust)
Alicante (Sp)
Arrecife (Sp)
Auckland (NZ)
Benghazi (Libya)
Bordeaux (Fr)
Boulogne (Fr)
Brindisi (Italy)
Brisbane (Aust)
Budapest (Hun)
Calcutta (India)
Cape Town (S.Af)
Cocanada (India)
Coquimbo (Chile)
Cuxhaven (Ger)
Damietta (Egypt)
Dunleary (Ire)
Elsinore (Den)
Falmouth (Eng)
Flushing (Neth)
Freetown (Sierra L)
Gisborne (NZ)
Göteborg (Swed)
Greenock (Scot)
Hakodate (Japan)
Halmstad (Swed)
Helsinki (Fin)
Holyhead (Wales)
Honfleur (Fr)
Honolulu (Hawaii)
Istanbul (Turk)
Kakinada (India)
Kingston (Jam)
La Coruña (Sp)
La Guiara (Venez)
Limassol (Cyprus)
Llanelli (Wales)
Macassar (Indon)
Makassar (Indon)
Matarini (Peru)
Montreal (Can)

8

Moulmein (Burma)
Nagasaki (Japan)
Nakhodka (Rus)
Navarino (Gr)
Newhaven (Eng)
Nykoping (Swed)
Paradeep (Indon)
Pechenga (Rus)
Pembroke (Wales)
Penzance (Eng)
Plymouth (Eng)
Portland (Eng)
Port Said (Egypt)
St Helier (Ch.I)
Sandwich (Eng)
Shanghai (China)
Szczecin (Pol)
Taganrog (Rus)
Takoradi (Ghana)
Tamatave (Madag)
Tientsin (China)
Tiksi Bay (Rus)
Vera Cruz (Mex)
Weymouth (Eng)
Yokohama (Japan)

9

Algeciras (Sp)
Amsterdam (Neth)
Archangel (Rus)
Ardrossan (Scot)
Avonmouth (Eng)
Baltimore (USA)
Barcelona (Sp)
Cartagena (Colomb)
Cartagena (Sp)
Cherbourg (Fr)
Churchill (Can)
Constanta (Rom)
Cristobal (Pan)
Devonport (Eng)

9

Dubrovnik (Croat)
Esquimalt (Can)
Essaquira (Moroc)
Europoort (Neth)
Flensburg (Ger)
Fos-sur-mer (Fr)
Galveston (USA)
Gravesend (Eng)
Guayaquil (Ecuad)
Helsingör (Den)
Hiroshima (Japan)
Kagoshima (Japan)
Kaohsiung (Taiwan)
King's Lynn (Eng)
Kolobrzeg (Pol)
Las Palmas (Sp)
Leningrad (Rus)
Liverpool (Eng)
Lyttleton (NZ)
Marseille (Fr)
Mbuji-mayi (Zaïre)
Melbourne (Aust)
Mossel Bay (S.Af)

9

Nantucket (USA)
Newcastle (Aust)
Newcastle (Eng)
Owen Sound (Can)
Pensacola (USA)
Port Arzew (Alg)
Port Klang (Malay)
Port Louis (Maur)
Portmadoc (Wales)
Port Mahon (Sp)
Port Natal (S.Af)
Porto Novo (Benin)
Port Royal (Jam)
Port Sudan (Sudan)
Rotterdam (Neth)
Scapa Flow (Scot)
Sheerness (Eng)
Stavanger (Nor)
Stockholm (Swed)
Stornaway (Scot)
Trondheim (Nor)
Vancouver (Can)
Zeebrugge (Belg)

10

Alexandria (Egypt)
Barnstaple (Eng)
Bridgeport (USA)
Casablanca (Moroc)
Charleston (USA)
Colchester (Eng)
Copenhagen (Den)
East London (S.Af)
Felixstowe (Eng)
Folkestone (Eng)
George Town (Malay)
Gothenburg (Swed)
Hammerfest (Nor)
Hartlepool (Eng)
Jersey City (USA)
La Rochelle (Fr)
Los Angeles (USA)
Marseilles (Fr)
Montego Bay (Jam)
Montevideo (Urug)
New Bedford (USA)
New Orleans (USA)

10

Nouakchott (Mauritania)
Pernambuco (Braz)
Perth Amboy (USA)
Port Arthur (China)
Portsmouth (Eng)
Portsmouth (USA)
San Juan Bay (Peru)
Simonstown (S.Af)
Sunderland (Eng)
Teignmouth (Eng)
Travemünde (Ger)
Valparaiso (Chile)
Vlissingen (Neth)
Whitstable (Eng)

11

Bremerhaven (Ger)
Buenos Aires (Arg)
Christiania (Nor)
Cinque Ports (Eng)
Dar es Salaam (Tanz)
Grangemouth (Scot)
Helsingborg (Swed)
Hermoupolis (Gr)
Masulipatam (India)
Pearl Harbor (Hawaii)
Pondicherry (India)
Port Glasgow (Scot)
Port Jackson (Aust)
Port Moresby (Papua N.G.)
Port-of-Spain (Trin & Tob)
Richard's Bay (S.Af)

11
St Peter Port (Ch.I)
Saint Helier (Ch.I)
Shimonoseki (Japan)
Southampton (Eng)
Three Rivers (Can)
Vladivostok (Rus)

12
Barranquilla (Colomb)
Buenaventura (Colomb)
Dun Laoghaire (Ire)
Kotakinabalu (Malay)
Masulipatnam (India)
Milford Haven (Wales)
Mina Al-Ahmadi (Kuwait)
North Shields (Eng)
Port Adelaide (Aust)
Port Harcourt (Nigeria)

12
Port Sunlight (Eng)
Puerto Hierro (Venez)
Rio de Janeiro (Braz)
St Petersburg (Rus)

13
Christiansund (Nor)
Frederikshavn (Den)
Middlesbrough (Eng)
Petropavlovsk (Rus)
Port Elizabeth (S.Af)
Puerto Cabello (Venez)
Wilhelmshaven (Ger)

14
Constantinople (Turk)
Mina Hassan Tani (Moroc)
Santiago de Cuba (Cuba)

Poultry

4
Buff (goose)

5
Aseel (chicken)
Pearl (guinea fowl)
Pekin (duck)
Roman (goose)
Rouen (duck)
White (guinea fowl)

6
Ancona (chicken)
Bahama (duck)
Canada (goose)
Cochin (chicken)
Embden (goose)
Silkie (chicken)
Sussex (chicken)

7
Chinese (goose)
Crested (duck)
Dorking (chicken)
Gambian (goose)
Leghorn (chicken)
mallard (duck)
Muscovy (duck)

8
barnacle (goose)
Carolina (duck)
mandarin (duck)
Toulouse (goose)

9
Aylesbury (duck)
Careopsis (goose)
Orpington (duck)

9
Welsummer (chicken)
Wyandotte (chicken)

10
Andalusian (chicken)
Bourbon Red (turkey)
Indian Game (chicken)
Sebastopol (goose)

11
Barnevelder (chicken)
Black Cayuga (duck)

12
Black Norfolk (turkey)
Indian Runner (duck)
Japanese teal (duck)
Plymouth Rock (chicken)

13
Blue Orpington (duck)
Buff Orpington (duck)
Khaki Campbell (duck)

14
Black East India (duck)
Rhode Island Red (chicken)

Prehistoric animals

8	10	11	12
eohippus	allosaurus	pterodactyl	brontosaurus
	anchithere	pterosaurus	megalosaurus
9	diplodocus	stegosaurus	velociraptor
iguanodon		triceratops	
pterosaur	11	tyrannosaur	13
	dinotherium		brachiosaurus
	protohippus		tyrannosaurus

Presidents of the United States of America

George Washington (1789–97)	Millard Fillmore (1850–53)
John Adams (1797–1801)	Franklin Pierce (1853–57)
Thomas Jefferson (1801–09)	James Buchanan (1857–61)
James Madison (1809–17)	Abraham Lincoln (1861–65)
James Monroe (1817–25)	Andrew Johnson (1865–69)
John Quincy Adams (1825–29)	Ulysses Simpson Grant (1869–77)
Andrew Jackson (1829–37)	Rutherford Birchard Hayes
Martin Van Buren (1837–41)	(1877–81)
William Henry Harrison (1841)	James Abram Garfield (1881)
John Tyler (1841–45)	Chester Alan Arthur (1881–85)
James Knox Polk (1845–49)	Grover Cleveland (1885–89)
Zachary Taylor (1849–50)	Benjamin Harrison (1889–93)

Grover Cleveland (1893–97)
William McKinley (1897–1901)
Theodore Roosevelt (1901–09)
William Howard Taft (1909–13)
(Thomas) Woodrow Wilson
  (1913–21)
Warren Gamaliel Harding (1921–23)
(John) Calvin Coolidge (1923–29)
Herbert Clark Hoover (1929–33)
Franklin Delano Roosevelt
  (1933–45)

Harry S. Truman (1945–53)
Dwight David Eisenhower (1953–61)
John Fitzgerald Kennedy (1961–63)
Lyndon Baines Johnson (1963–69)
Richard Milhous Nixon (1969–74)
Gerald Rudolph Ford (1974–77)
James Earl Carter (1977–81)
Ronald Wilson Reagan (1981–88)
George Herbert Walker Bush
  (1988–92)
William Jefferson Clinton (1992–

Prime Ministers of Great Britain (from 1721)

Robert Walpole (1721–42)
Spencer Compton, Earl of Wilmington (1742–43)
Henry Pelham (1743–54)
Thomas Pelham-Holles, Duke of Newcastle (1754–56)
William Cavendish, Duke of Devonshire (1756–57)
Thomas Pelham-Holles, Duke of Newcastle (1757–62)
John Stuart, Earl of Bute (1762–63)
George Grenville (1763–65)
Charles Watson-Wentworth, Marquess of Rockingham (1765–66)
William Pitt, Earl of Chatham (1766–68)
Augustus Henry Fitzroy, Duke of Grafton (1768–70)
Frederick North, Lord North (1770–82)
Charles Watson-Wentworth, Marquess of Rockingham (1782)
William Petty, Earl of Shelburne (1782–83)
William Henry Cavendish Bentinck, Duke of Portland (1783)
William Pitt (1783–1801)
Henry Addington (1801–04)
William Pitt (1804–1806)
William Wyndham Grenville, Baron Grenville (1806–07)
William Henry Cavendish Bentinck, Duke of Portland (1807–09)
Spencer Perceval (1809–12)
Robert Banks Jenkinson, Earl of Liverpool (1812–27)
George Canning (1827)
Frederick John Robinson, Viscount Goderich (1827–28)
Arthur Wellesley, Duke of Wellington (1828–30)
Charles Grey, Earl Grey (1830–34)
William Lamb, Viscount Melbourne (1834)
Sir Robert Peel (1834–35)

William Lamb, Viscount Melbourne (1835–41)
Sir Robert Peel (1841–46)
John Russell, Earl Russell (1846–52)
Edward George Geoffrey Smith-Stanley, Earl of Derby (1852)
George Hamilton Gordon, Earl of Aberdeen (1852–55)
Henry John Temple, Viscount Palmerston (1855–58)
Edward George Geoffrey Smith-Stanley, Earl of Derby (1858–59)
Henry John Temple, Viscount Palmerston (1859–65)
John Russell, Earl Russell (1865–66)
Edward George Geoffrey Smith-Stanley, Earl of Derby (1866–68)
Benjamin Disraeli, Earl of Beaconsfield (1868)
William Ewart Gladstone (1868–74)
Benjamin Disraeli, Earl of Beaconsfield (1874–80)
William Ewart Gladstone (1880–85)
Robert Arthur Talbot Gascoyne-Cecil, Marquess of Salisbury (1885–86)
William Ewart Gladstone (1886)
Robert Arthur Talbot Gascoyne-Cecil, Marquess of Salisbury (1886–92)
William Ewart Gladstone (1892–94)
Archibald Philip Primose, Earl of Rosebery (1894–95)
Robert Arthur Talbot Gascoyne-Cecil, Marquess of Salisbury (1895–1902)
Arthur James Balfour (1902–05)
Sir Henry Campbell-Bannerman (1905–08)
Herbert Henry Asquith (1908–16)
David Lloyd George (1916–22)
Andrew Bonar Law (1922–23)
Stanley Baldwin (1923–24)
(James) Ramsay MacDonald (1924)
Stanley Baldwin (1924–29)
(James) Ramsay MacDonald (1929–35)
Stanley Baldwin (1935–37)
Neville Arthur Chamberlain (1937–40)
Sir Winston Leonard Spencer Churchill (1940–45)
Clement Richard Attlee (1945–51)
Sir Winston Leonard Spencer Churchill (1951–55)
Robert Anthony Eden (1955–57)
Maurice Harold Macmillan (1957–63)
Alexander Frederick Douglas–Home (1963–64)
(James) Harold Wilson (1964–70)
Edward Richard George Heath (1970–74)
(James) Harold Wilson (1974–76)
(Leonard) James Callaghan (1976–79)
Margaret Hilda Thatcher (1979–1990)
John Major (1990–   )

Professions, trades and occupations

2	4	5	6
G.P.	tout	leech	bagman
M.D.	ward	luter	bailer
M.O	whip	mason	bandit
P.A.		medic	banker
P.M.		miner	barber
	5	navvy	bargee
	actor	nurse	barker
3	agent	oiler	barman
doc	augur	pilot	batman
don	baker	piper	bearer
pro	boots	pupil	beggar
rep	bosun	quack	binder
spy	caddy	rabbi	boffin
vet	choir	reeve	bookie
	clerk	scout	bowman
4	clown	sewer	brewer
ayah	coach	shoer	broker
bard	comic	slave	bugler
boss	crier	smith	bursar
char	crimp	sower	busker
chef	curer	staff	butler
cook	daily	sweep	cabbie
crew	envoy	tamer	cabman
diva	extra	taxer	canner
dyer	fakir	thief	carter
gang	fence	tiler	carver
hack	fifer	tuner	casual
hand	filer	tutor	censor
head	flier	tyler	clergy
herd	gipsy	usher	cleric
mage	gluer	valet	codist
maid	groom	viner	coiner
mate	guard		comber
mime	guide		conman
page	guild	6	coolie
peon	gypsy	airman	cooper
poet	hakim	archer	copper
seer	harpy	artist	co-star
serf	hirer	author	
thug			

6	6	6	6
coster	hawker	ostler	seaman
cowboy	healer	packer	seizor
cowman	heaver	parson	seller
critic	hodman	pastor	server
cutler	hooper	pavier	setter
cutter	horner	pedlar	sexton
dancer	hosier	penman	singer
dealer	hunter	picker	skivvy
digger	intern	pieman	slater
docker	issuer	pirate	sleuth
doctor	jailer	pitman	snarer
dowser	jobber	plater	sorter
draper	jockey	player	squire
drawer	joiner	porter	stager
driver	jurist	potboy	stoker
drover	keeler	potter	storer
editor	keeper	priest	tabler
fabler	killer	pruner	tailor
factor	lackey	purser	tanner
farmer	lander	ragman	tasker
feller	lawyer	ranger	taster
fisher	lender	ratter	teller
fitter	loader	reader	tester
forger	logman	reaper	tiller
framer	marker	rector	tinker
gaffer	master	regent	tinman
ganger	matron	relief	tinner
gaoler	medico	renter	toller
gaucho	mender	rigger	touter
gigolo	menial	ringer	toy-boy
gilder	mentor	robber	tracer
gillie	mercer	roofer	trader
glazer	milker	rooter	tubman
glover	miller	sacker	turner
graver	minter	sailor	tycoon
grocer	monger	salter	typist
guider	mystic	sapper	usurer
gunman	nailer	sawyer	valuer
gunner	notary	scribe	vamper
harper	nurser	sea-dog	vanman
hatter	oboist	sealer	vender

6	7	7	7
vendor	blaster	doorman	hogherd
verger	blender	dragman	hostler
verser	boatman	drapier	indexer
viewer	bondman	drayman	inlayer
waiter	bookman	dredger	janitor
waller	bottler	dresser	juggler
warden	brigand	drogman	junkman
warder	builder	drummer	juryman
warper	burglar	dustman	knacker
washer	butcher	farrier	knitter
weaver	buttons	fascist	laceman
weeder	callboy	fiddler	lombard
welder	carrier	fireman	mailman
whaler	cashier	florist	maltman
worker	caterer	flunkey	manager
wright	cellist	flutist	mangler
writer	chanter	footboy	marbler
	chapman	footman	marcher
7	chemist	footpad	mariner
abigail	chorist	foreman	marshal
acolyte	cleaner	founder	masseur
acrobat	clipper	frogman	matador
actress	co-agent	fueller	matelot
actuary	coalman	furrier	meat man
alewife	cobbler	gateman	midwife
almoner	collier	glazier	milkman
analyst	co-pilot	gleaner	modiste
arbiter	copyist	gleeman	monitor
artisan	coroner	glosser	moulder
artiste	corsair	grafter	newsboy
assayer	counsel	grainer	oculist
assizer	courier	granger	officer
auditor	cowherd	grantee	orderer
aviator	crofter	grantor	orderly
bailiff	cropper	grazier	pageboy
bandman	curator	grinder	painter
bellboy	currier	gymnast	palmist
bellhop	danseur	hackler	peddler
best boy	dentist	harpist	pianist
best man	dietist	haulier	picador
birdman	ditcher	herbist	planner
		herdman	

7	7	8	8
planter	swabber	boatsman	engraver
plumber	sweeper	bondmaid	enroller
poacher	taxi-man	bondsman	epic poet
poetess	teacher	botanist	essayist
postman	tipster	bowmaker	examiner
presser	tracker	boxmaker	exorcist
printer	trainer	brewster	explorer
rancher	trapper	cabin boy	exporter
realtor	trawler	cellarer	fabulist
refiner	trimmer	ceramist	factotum
riveter	trucker	chandler	falconer
roadman	trustee	choirboy	famulist
roaster	tumbler	coachman	farmhand
rustler	violist	co-author	ferryman
sacrist	wagoner	codifier	figurant
saddler	warrior	collator	filmstar
sampler	webster	comedian	finisher
scourer	weigher	compiler	fishwife
scraper	wheeler	composer	flatfoot
servant	woodman	conclave	flautist
settler	workman	conjurer	fletcher
sharper	wrapper	conjuror	forester
shearer		conveyor	forgeman
shipper	**8**	courtier	fugleman
shopboy	aeronaut	coxswain	gangster
showman	analyser	croupier	gardener
shunter	annalist	dairyman	gavelman
skinner	aphorist	danseuse	gendarme
skipper	apiarist	deckhand	glassman
smelter	arborist	defender	goatherd
snipper	armorist	designer	gossiper
soldier	armourer	director	governor
soloist	arrestor	domestic	guardian
spencer	assessor	dragoman	guerilla
spinner	attorney	druggist	gunsmith
spotter	bagmaker	educator	hammerer
stainer	bagpiper	embalmer	handmaid
stamper	bandsman	emissary	handyman
stapler	bargeman	employee	hatmaker
steward	bedmaker	employer	haymaker
surgeon	bleacher	engineer	head cook

8	8	8	8
headsman	musician	restorer	surveyor
helmsman	newshawk	retailer	swindler
henchman	novelist	retainer	tallyman
herdsman	onion-man	reviewer	taverner
hired man	operator	rewriter	teamster
hireling	optician	rivetter	thatcher
home help	ordainer	romancer	thespian
hotelier	organist	rugmaker	thresher
houseboy	outrider	rumourer	tin miner
huntsman	overseer	salesman	tinsmith
importer	pargeter	satirist	torturer
improver	parodist	sawbones	toymaker
inkmaker	penmaker	scullion	tripeman
inventor	perfumer	sculptor	truckman
jet pilot	pewterer	seamster	turnspit
jeweller	picaroon	sea-rover	tutoress
labourer	plougher	seasoner	unionist
landgirl	polisher	seedsman	valuator
landlady	potmaker	sempster	vintager
landlord	prefacer	servitor	virtuoso
lapidary	preluder	shearman	vocalist
larcener	pressman	shepherd	volumist
lecturer	probator	shipmate	waitress
linesman	procurer	ship's boy	walker-on
lumberer	promoter	shopgirl	wardress
magician	prompter	showgirl	warrener
maltster	prosaist	sidesman	watchman
masseuse	provider	sketcher	waterman
measurer	psalmist	smuggler	wet nurse
mechanic	publican	spaceman	whaleman
medalist	pugilist	spearman	whitener
melodist	purveyor	speedcop	wigmaker
merchant	quarrier	spurrier	winnower
milkmaid	raftsman	starcher	wool-dyer
millgirl	receiver	stitcher	workhand
millhand	re-grater	stockman	wrestler
milliner	relessee	storeman	
minister	relessor	stripper	9
minstrel	repairer	strummer	alchemist
mistress	reporter	stuntman	anatomist
modeller	resetter	supplier	annotator
muralist			

9	9	9	9
announcer	cheapjack	embezzler	gospeller
arbitress	chorister	enameller	governess
arborator	clarifier	engineman	groundman
archeress	clergyman	engrosser	guardsman
architect	clinician	epitomist	guerrilla
archivist	clogmaker	errand boy	guitarist
art critic	coalminer	estimator	gun-runner
art dealer	collector	examinant	harlequin
artificer	colourist	excavator	harmonist
astronaut	columnist	excerptor	harpooner
attendant	concierge	exchanger	harvester
authoress	conductor	exciseman	hellenist
balladist	conserver	executive	herbalist
ballerina	cosmonaut	exorciser	herborist
bank agent	cost clerk	exorcizer	hired hand
barrister	costumier	fabricant	hired help
barrow boy	courtesan	fashioner	historian
beefeater	couturier	felt-maker	homeopath
beekeeper	cowkeeper	figurante	hop-picker
beemaster	cracksman	film actor	hosteller
biologist	craftsman	film extra	housemaid
boatswain	crayonist	financier	housewife
bodyguard	cymbalist	fire-eater	hygienist
boilerman	daily help	fish-curer	hypnotist
bondslave	dairymaid	fisherman	incumbent
bootmaker	decorator	fish-woman	innkeeper
bootblack	desk clerk	flag-maker	inscriber
bootmaker	detective	flyfisher	inspector
buccaneer	dicemaker	freelance	ironsmith
burnisher	die-sinker	freighter	itinerant
bus driver	dietetist	fruiterer	job-master
cab driver	dietician	furbisher	kennel-man
café owner	dietitian	furnisher	lacemaker
cameraman	directrix	galvanist	lacquerer
car driver	dispenser	gasfitter	lady's maid
caretaker	dissector	gazetteer	lampooner
carpenter	distiller	gem-cutter	land agent
casemaker	draftsman	geologist	landreeve
catechist	dramatist	gladiator	larcenist
cellarman	Drum Major	gluemaker	launderer
charwoman	drum-maker	goldsmith	laundress
chauffeur	ecologist	gondolier	legionary

9

9	9	9	9
librarian	osteopath	ropemaker	town clerk
linotyper	outfitter	roundsman	towncrier
lion tamer	paymaster	sacristan	tradesman
liveryman	pedagogue	safemaker	tragedian
loan agent	performer	sailmaker	traveller
lockmaker	physician	scarifier	treasurer
locksmith	physicist	scavenger	tributary
log-roller	plasterer	scenarist	trumpeter
lumberman	ploughboy	scientist	tympanist
machinist	pluralist	scrivener	usherette
magnetist	poetaster	sea-robber	varnisher
major domo	pointsman	secretary	versifier
male model	policeman	shipowner	warranter
male nurse	pop artist	ship's mate	washerman
man-at-arms	portrayer	shoeblack	waxworker
mannequin	portreeve	shoemaker	winemaker
mechanist	postilion	signalman	woodreeve
medallist	postwoman	soapmaker	workwoman
memoirist	practiser	solicitor	zoo keeper
mercenary	precentor	sonneteer	zoologist
mesmerist	preceptor	sorceress	
messenger	predicant	soubrette	10
metallist	prelector	spiderman	Able Seaman
metrician	presenter	stableboy	accountant
middleman	priestess	stableman	advertiser
mill-owner	privateer	stagehand	aerologist
model girl	professor	stationer	agrologist
mortician	profilist	stevedore	agronomist
muffin-man	publicist	sub-editor	air hostess
musketeer	publisher	swineherd	air steward
myologist	pulpiteer	swordsman	algebraist
navigator	puppeteer	syndicate	apothecary
negotiant	qualifier	synoptist	apprentice
neologian	quarryman	tablemaid	arbalister
neologist	racketeer	tailoress	arbitrator
newsagent	railmaker	tea-taster	astrologer
nursemaid	recruiter	tentmaker	astronomer
odd-job man	reformist	test pilot	auctioneer
office boy	rehearser	therapist	audit clerk
operative	ribbonman	timberman	balloonist
ordinator	roadmaker	toolsmith	ballplayer

10	10	10	10
bandmaster	clockmaker	explorator	ironmonger
bank robber	clog dancer	fictionist	ironworker
baseballer	cloth maker	file-cutter	journalist
bassoonist	coachmaker	filibuster	journeyman
beautician	co-assessor	film editor	kennelmaid
bell-ringer	coastguard	firemaster	lady doctor
bibliopole	colloquist	fire-worker	land holder
bill poster	comedienne	fishmonger	land jobber
biochemist	compositor	flight crew	land worker
biographer	compounder	flowergirl	laundryman
blacksmith	concordist	fluvialist	law officer
bladesmith	contractor	folk-dancer	legislator
blockmaker	controller	folk-singer	librettist
bombardier	copyholder	freebooter	linotypist
bondswoman	copywriter	fund raiser	liquidator
bonesetter	counsellor	gamekeeper	lobsterman
bookbinder	cultivator	game warden	lock-keeper
bookholder	customs man	geisha girl	lumberjack
bookkeeper	cytologist	geneticist	magistrate
bookseller	delineator	geographer	manageress
bootlegger	directress	glee-singer	manicurist
bricklayer	disc jockey	glossarist	manservant
brickmaker	discounter	gold-beater	matchmaker
brushmaker	discoverer	gold-digger	medical man
bureaucrat	dishwasher	gold-washer	militiaman
caravaneer	dispatcher	grammarian	millwright
career girl	dockmaster	gunslinger	mineralist
cartoonist	dog breeder	hackney-man	missionary
cartwright	dog-fancier	hall porter	moonshiner
cash-keeper	doorkeeper	handmaiden	naturalist
cat breeder	dressmaker	harvestman	negotiator
cat burglar	drummer-boy	head porter	newscaster
ceramicist	dry cleaner	head waiter	news editor
chair-maker	emblazoner	highwayman	newsvendor
chargehand	emboweller	homoeopath	newswriter
charioteer	enamellist	horn player	night nurse
chorus girl	ephemerist	horologist	nurseryman
chronicler	epitaphist	house agent	obituarist
chucker-out	epitomiser	husbandman	oil painter
circuiteer	epitomizer	inoculator	osteologer
claim agent	evangelist	institutor	overlooker
clapper boy	examinator	instructor	pantrymaid

10	10	10	11
park-keeper	second mate	translator	bank cashier
park-ranger	seminarist	trawlerman	bank manager
pastry-cook	serving-man	troubadour	bargemaster
pathfinder	sexologist	typesetter	basketmaker
pawnbroker	ship broker	undertaker	beachcomber
pearl-diver	ship holder	veterinary	Benedictine
pediatrist	shipmaster	victualler	bill-sticker
pedicurist	shipwright	vocabulist	bird catcher
pharmacist	shopfitter	wage-earner	bird fancier
piano tuner	shopkeeper	wainwright	bird watcher
pickpocket	shopwalker	watchmaker	boatbuilder
platelayer	signwriter	wholesaler	boilermaker
playwright	silk-weaver	winegrower	boilersmith
politician	skirmisher	wine waiter	bondservant
postillion	sneak thief	woodcarver	bootcatcher
postmaster	soap-boiler	woodcutter	broadcaster
prescriber	specialist	woodworker	bullfighter
prima donna	staff nurse	wool-comber	businessman
private eye	stewardess	wool-grower	candlemaker
procurator	stipulator	wool-trader	car salesman
programmer	stone-borer	work fellow	cattle thief
pronouncer	stonemason	work master	chambermaid
proprietor	strategist	work people	chiropodist
prospector	superviser	working man	choirmaster
protractor	surcharger	yardmaster	chronologer
quiz master	surface-man	zinc-worker	cipher clerk
railwayman	swan-keeper	zoographer	clock-setter
rat catcher	symphonist	zymologist	cloth worker
recitalist	tally clerk		coffin maker
researcher	taskmaster	**11**	collar maker
ringmaster	taxi-driver	accompanist	conductress
roadmender	tea-blender	acoustician	confederate
ropedancer	tea planter	adjudicator	congressman
roughrider	technician	annunciator	consecrator
safeblower	theologian	antiquarian	conservator
sales force	theologist	apple-grower	conveyancer
saleswoman	timekeeper	arbitratrix	coppersmith
schoolmarm	tractarian	army officer	cosmologist
scrutineer	traffic cop	arquebusier	crane driver
sculptress	trafficker	artillerist	crime writer
sea-captain	tram driver	audio typist	cub reporter
seamstress	transactor	bag snatcher	cypher clerk
			deliveryman

11	11	11	11
demographer	housemother	neurologist	scrapdealer
dispensator	hymnologist	neurotomist	secret agent
draughtsman	illuminator	night porter	servant girl
duty officer	illusionist	night sister	serving maid
electrician	illustrator	nightworker	share-broker
emblematist	infantryman	numismatist	sheepfarmer
embroiderer	institutist	office staff	shepherdess
entertainer	interpreter	onion seller	shipbreaker
estate agent	interviewer	opera singer	shipbuilder
ethnologist	iron founder	orientalist	ship's master
executioner	ivory carver	pamphleteer	shop steward
extortioner	ivory turner	panel beater	silversmith
factory hand	ivory worker	pantomimist	slaughterer
faith healer	kitchenmaid	paperhanger	slave driver
field worker	lamplighter	parish clerk	smallholder
filing clerk	land steward	parlourmaid	steeplejack
fire brigade	laundrymaid	pathologist	stockbroker
flax dresser	leading lady	pattenmaker	stone cutter
fruit picker	ledger clerk	pearlfisher	storekeeper
galley slave	lifeboatman	pettifogger	stripteaser
genealogist	lightkeeper	philatelist	system-maker
ghostwriter	linen draper	pieceworker	taxidermist
glass bender	lithologist	pork butcher	telegrapher
glass blower	lithotomist	portraitist	telephonist
glass cutter	lorry driver	preceptress	ticket agent
glass worker	madrigalist	probationer	toastmaster
grave digger	maidservant	promulgator	tobacconist
greengrocer	mammalogist	proofreader	tooth drawer
haberdasher	master baker	property man	topographer
hairdresser	medicine man	proprietrix	torch bearer
hair stylist	memorialist	questionary	town planner
hardwareman	merchantman	radiologist	train bearer
head foreman	metal worker	rag merchant	transcriber
head workman	miniaturist	represister	transporter
hierologist	money broker	republisher	travel agent
histologist	money lender	rhetorician	type founder
horse doctor	monographer	roadsweeper	typographer
horse trader	music critic	safebreaker	underbearer
hospitaller	music master	sandwich man	underwriter
hotel keeper	myographist	sanscritist	upholsterer
housekeeper	mythologist	saxophonist	washerwoman
housemaster	needlewoman	scoutmaster	watchkeeper

11	12	12	12
wheel cutter	cosmographer	joint trustee	physiologist
wheelwright	costermonger	king's counsel	plant manager
witchdoctor	crafts master	knife grinder	ploughwright
xylophonist	craniologist	knife thrower	plumber's mate
zoographist	cryptogamist	labouring man	postmistress
	dance hostess	land surveyor	practitioner
12	deep-sea diver	lath-splitter	press officer
accordionist	demonstrator	leader writer	prison warder
actor manager	ecclesiastic	lexicologist	prize fighter
ambulance man	egyptologist	lithographer	professional
anaesthetist	elecutionist	longshoreman	propagandist
artilleryman	engine driver	loss adjuster	proprietress
artist's model	entomologist	lumber dealer	psychiatrist
ballet dancer	entrepreneur	maître d'hôtel	psychologist
ballet master	escapologist	make-up artist	publicity man
bantamweight	experimenter	manual worker	pupil teacher
bellows maker	family doctor	manufacturer	puppet player
bibliologist	farm labourer	mass producer	quarry master
body snatcher	film director	meat salesman	racing driver
booking clerk	film producer	metallurgist	radiographer
bus conductor	first officer	mezzo soprano	receptionist
cabinet maker	flying doctor	microscopist	remembrancer
calligrapher	footplateman	mineralogist	restaurateur
cardiologist	geometrician	miscellanist	riding master
caricaturist	geriatrician	money changer	right-hand man
carpet bagger	glass grinder	morris dancer	rubber grader
carpet fitter	greasemonkey	mosaic artist	sales manager
cartographer	hagiographer	mosaic worker	scene shifter
cheesemonger	haliographer	newspaperman	schoolmaster
chief cashier	harness maker	nutritionist	screenwriter
chimney sweep	head gardener	obstetrician	scriptwriter
chronologist	head shrinker	office junior	scullery maid
churchwarden	homeopathist	orchestrator	seafaring man
circuit rider	horse-breaker	organ builder	seed merchant
civil servant	hotel manager	organ grinder	seismologist
clarinettist	housebreaker	orthographer	sharpshooter
clerk of works	house steward	pattern maker	ship chandler
coach builder	house surgeon	pediatrician	shoe repairer
commissioner	instructress	phonographer	silver beater
confectioner	invoice clerk	photographer	slaughterman
corn chandler	jerry builder	phrenologist	snake charmer

12

social worker
soil mechanic
special agent
speechwriter
spice blender
sportscaster
sportswriter
stage manager
statistician
steel erector
stenographer
stonebreaker
street trader
street walker
sugar refiner
tax collector
technologist
telegraph boy
telegraphist
test engineer
therapeutist
ticket porter
timber trader
toll gatherer
tourist agent
toxicologist
tradespeople
transplanter
trichologist
undermanager
underservant
veterinarian
warehouseman
water diviner
wine merchant
wood engraver
works manager

13

administrator
agriculturist
antique dealer

13

archaeologist
arithmetician
articled clerk
bibliographer
campanologist
cartographist
chartographer
chicken farmer
choreographer
chronographer
civil engineer
coffee-planter
contortionist
contrabandist
cotton spinner
counterfeiter
cryptographer
dancing master
dermatologist
diagnostician
diamond cutter
draughtswoman
drawing master
dress designer
drill sergeant
electroplater
emigrationist
epigrammatist
estate manager
exhibitionist
family butcher
fencing master
fortune teller
freight broker
glyphographer
gynaecologist
harbour master
homoeopathist
hospital nurse
ichthyologist
industrialist
joint executor

13

letter carrier
lexicographer
lighthouse man
maid-of-all-work
master builder
master mariner
mathematician
melodramatist
metaphysician
meteorologist
music mistress
night watchman
ornithologist
orthographist
paediatrician
park attendant
periodicalist
pharmaceutist
physiognomist
physiographer
poultry farmer
psychoanalyst
public speaker
queen's counsel
racing tipster
revolutionary
revolutionist
rubber planter
sailing master
schoolteacher
science master
shop assistant
singing master
station master
stenographist
stereoscopist
stethoscopist
street sweeper
sub-contractor
supernumerary
toll collector
trade unionist

13

tramcar driver
tram conductor
ventriloquist
window cleaner
window dresser
woollen draper
writing master

14

administratrix
anthropologist
autobiographer
bacteriologist
ballet mistress
billiard marker
billiard player
chimney sweeper
classics master
colour sergeant
commissionaire
dancing partner
discount broker
ecclesiologist
educationalist
encyclopaedist
exchange broker
handicraftsman
horticulturist
house decorator
house furnisher
language master
leather dresser
manual labourer
market gardener
medical officer
merchant tailor
miscellanarian
mother superior
music publisher
reception clerk
scenery painter
schoolmistress

14	15	15
ship's carpenter	domestic servant	portrait painter
spectacle maker	gentleman farmer	professional man
superintendent	hackney coachman	programme seller
systems analyst	heart specialist	provision dealer
tallow chandler	hierogrammatist	railway engineer
watercolourist	historiographer	resurrectionist
weather prophet	instrumentalist	scripture reader
	insurance broker	shorhand-typist
15	jack-of-all-trades	sleeping partner
assistant master	musical director	stretcher bearer
Bow Street runner	numismatologist	ticket collector
crustaceologist	ophthalmologist	tightrope walker
dancing mistress	platform speaker	tonsorial artist
diamond merchant		

Pseudonyms

Real name (pseudonym)

Barrie, Sir J.M. (Gavin Ogilvy)
Beecher Stowe, Harriet (Christopher Crowfield)
Boyd, Rev. A.K.H (Country Parson)
Brontë, Anne (Acton Bell)
Brontë, Charlotte (Currer Bell)
Brontë, Emily (Ellis Bell)
Burns, Robert (Sylvander)
Chesterton, G.K. (Arion)
Clemens, Samuel Langhorne (Mark Twain)
Coombe, William (Doctor Syntax)
Cross, Mrs J.W. (George Eliot)
De Quincey, Thomas (English Opium Eater)
Dickens, Charles (Boz/Timothy Sparks)
Dodgson, Rev. C. Lutwidge (Lewis Carroll)
Dudevant, Aurore (George Sand)
Evans, Marian (George Eliot)
Galsworthy, John (John Sinjohn)
Gilbert, W.S. (Bab)
Gladstone, W.E. (Bartholomew Bouverie)
Gower-Robinson, Mrs U.H. (Ursula Bloom)
Grossmith, Mrs George Jr (Adelaide Astor)
Harris, Joel Chandler (Uncle Remus)
Herbert, H.W. (Frank Forrester)

Holdsworth, Mrs. (G.B. Stern)
Hope Hawkins, Anthony (Anthony Hope)
Hughes, Thomas (Tom Brown)
Hugo, Victor (Paul Foucher)
Irving, Mrs H.B. (Dorothy Baird)
Korzeniowski, Joseph C. (Joseph Conrad)
Lamb, Charles (Elia)
Langtry, Lillie (Mr Jersey)
Longfellow, Henry W. (Hans Hammergafferstein)
Lowell, James Russell (Hosea Biglow)
Lyttelton, Hon. Mrs. Alfred (Edith Hamlet)
McNeile, Capt. H.C. (Sapper)
Moore, Thomas (Little Thomas)
Munro, H.H. (Saki)
Olchewitz, M. (Jules Verne)
Philpot, Dr Joseph Henry (Philip Lafargue)
Poe, Edgar Allan (Hans Pfaal)
Proctor, John (Puck)
Rhodes, Mrs (Guy D'Hardelot)
Ruskin, John (Graduate of Oxford)
Savage, Mrs (Ethel M. Dell)
Scott, Sir Walter (Peter Pattison)
Shaw, George Bernard (Corno di Bassetto; Redbarn Wash)
Shelley, Percy Bysshe (John Fitzvictor)
Stern, Laurence (Yorick)
Swinburne, A.C. (Mrs Horace Manners)
Tennyson, Alfred, Lord (Merlin)
Thackeray, W.M. (Arthur Pendennis)
Thibault, Jacques Anatole (Anatole France)
Trollope, Anthony (One of the Firm)
Wood, Mrs Henry (Johnny Ludlow)
Yates, Edmund (The Flaneur)

Religious buildings

4	6	6	7
kirk	ashram	pagoda	chantry
	chapel	priory	convent
5	church	temple	deanery
abbey	mosque		minster
duomo			

8	9	12
basilica	cathedral	chapter house
cloister	monastery	meeting house
lamasery	synagogue	

Religious movements

3	7	7	9
Zen	Bahaism	Sikhism	Adventism
	Friends	Wahabis	Calvinism
5	Gideons	Zionism	Huguenots
Islam	Jainism		Jansenism
Sikhs	Judaism	8	Methodism
	Jumpers	Adamites	pantheism
6	Lamaism	Baptists	
Babism	Mormons	Buddhism	10
Shinto	Muslims	Catholic	Anabaptism
Taoism	Parsees	Hinduism	Buchmanism
Voodoo	Quakers	humanism	
	Shakers	Puritans	

11	13	16
Anglicanism	Mohammedanism	Christian Science
Arminianism	Protestantism	Plymouth Brethren
Covenanters	Roman Catholic	Society of Friends
	Salvation Army	
12		17
Christianity	14	Congregationalism
Presbyterian	fundamentalism	Jehovah's Witnesses
spiritualism		
Unitarianism		

Religious orders

7	9	11
Templar	Carmelite	Augustinian
	Dominican	Benedictine
8		Hospitaller
Capuchin	10	
Salesian	Carthusian	17
Trappist	Cistercian	Premonstratensian
Ursuline	Franciscan	

Religious terms

3	4	5	5
alb	icon	choir	pasch
ark	idol	credo	piety
ave	I.N.R.I.	creed	pious
eve	lama	cross	psalm
God	Lent	deism	rabbi
I.H.S	mace	deist	relic
Jew	mass	deity	saint
lay	nave	demon	Satan
nun	pope	devil	synod
pew	pray	dirge	taboo
pyx	rite	dogma	tract
R.I.P.	sect	druid	vicar
see	sext	elder	vigil
sin	soul	ephod	wafer
vow	text	excat	
	Toc H	faith	6
4	veil	friar	abbacy
abbé	wake	glory	abbess
alms	yoga	godly	Advent
amen	Zion	grace	adytum
apse		grail	anoint
Baal	5	guild	anthem
bier	abbey	Hades	aumbry
cope	abbot	Hindu	banner
cowl	abyss	image	beadle
curé	aisle	Islam	belfry
dean	Allah	karma	bishop
Eden	altar	Koran	Buddha
evil	amice	laity	burial
fast	angel	lauds	cantor
font	banns	manse	censer
hadj	beads	matin	chapel
hajj	Bible	mitre	cherub
halo	bigot	morse	Christ
hell	bless	myrrh	church
holy	canon	niche	cierge
hood	carol	pagan	clergy
host	chant	papal	cleric
hymn			

6	6	7	7
curate	orison	advowee	Genesis
deacon	pagoda	ampulla	gentile
decant	papacy	angelic	glorify
devout	Papism	angelus	godhead
dharma	Papist	apostle	godless
divine	parish	apparel	godlike
Easter	parson	atheism	gradine
Exodus	pastor	atheist	gremial
friary	Popery	aureole	hassock
gloria	prayer	baptise	heathen
gospel	preach	baptism	heretic
hallow	priest	baptist	holy day
heaven	psalms	baptize	hosanna
Hebrew	pulpit	beatify	impiety
hegira	Quaker	biretta	incense
heresy	rector	Calvary	infidel
homily	repent	cassock	Introit
hymnal	ritual	chalice	Jehovah
intone	rochet	chancel	Judaism
Jesuit	rosary	chantry	Lady Day
Jewess	sacred	chaplet	Lamaism
Jewish	sangha	chapter	lectern
Judaic	scribe	charity	liturgy
kismet	seraph	chrisom	low mass
Levite	sermon	collect	Madonna
litany	server	complin	maniple
mantra	Shinto	confirm	mattins
martyr	shrine	convent	messiah
matins	shrive	convert	mid Lent
missal	sinful	cornice	minaret
Mormon	sinner	crosier	minster
mosaic	spirit	crozier	miracle
Moslem	Sunday	crusade	mission
mosque	Te Deum	deanery	mozetta
Muslim	temple	dharani	muezzin
mystic	verger	diocese	mystics
nimbus	vestry	diptych	narthex
novice	virgin	Epistle	nirvana
oblate		eternal	nocturn
oratio	7	faculty	numbers
ordain	acolyte	fasting	nunnery
orders	Adamite	Galilee	oratory

7	8	8	8
ordinal	ablution	diocesan	orthodox
Our Lady	agnostic	disciple	paganism
Our Lord	Agnus Dei	divinity	Passover
penance	alleluia	doctrine	Pharisee
pilgrim	almighty	doxology	preacher
pontiff	Anglican	druidism	predella
prayers	anointed	Ember Day	prophecy
prebend	antiphon	enthrone	prophesy
prelate	antipope	epiphany	Proverbs
primacy	apostate	eternity	psalmist
primate	apparels	ethereal	Ramadhan
profane	Atheneum	evensong	redeemer
prophet	Ave Maria	evermore	religion
psalter	beatific	exorcist	response
puritan	benefice	faithful	reverend
Ramadan	biblical	frontlet	rogation
rebirth	brethren	God's acre	sacristy
rectory	breviary	Hail Mary	Sadducee
requiem	Buddhism	heavenly	sanctify
reredos	Buddhist	hell fire	satanism
retreat	canonise	hierarch	seraphim
sabbath	canonize	high mass	sidesman
sainted	canticle	Holy Name	superior
saintly	cardinal	Holy Week	surplice
sanctum	Catholic	homilies	transept
sanctus	cemetery	hymn book	triptych
Saracen	cenotaph	idolater	unbelief
satanic	cherubim	idolatry	vestment
saviour	christen	immortal	vicarage
service	ciborium	lay clerk	
steeple	cincture	Lord's day	9
stipend	clerical	lychgate	ablutions
tempter	compline	Mass book	All Saints
tonsure	conclave	minister	anointing
trinity	corporal	ministry	Apocrypha
unblest	covenant	Mohammed	apostolic
unction	creation	monastic	archangel
unfrock	credence	Muhammad	archfiend
Vatican	crucifer	nativity	ascension
vespers	crucifix	Nazarene	athenaeum
worship	dalmatic	obituary	atonement
	deaconry	oblation	baptistry
	devotion	offering	beatitude

9	9	10	10
bishopric	offertory	antechapel	Lady Chapel
blasphemy	orthodoxy	Antichrist	Magnificat
Candlemas	Pentecost	Apocalypse	meditation
Carmelite	plainsong	apostolate	missionary
catechism	prayer mat	archbishop	Mohammedan
cathedral	preaching	archdeacon	omnipotent
celestial	presbyter	archpriest	ordination
cerecloth	priestess	assumption	Palm Sunday
Christian	purgatory	Athanasian	pilgrimage
Christmas	Quakerism	baptistery	prayer book
churching	religious	Benedictus	prebendary
clergyman	repentant	Bible class	presbytery
communion	responses	biblically	priesthood
confessor	reverence	Black Friar	Protestant
cremation	rural dean	Carthusian	Puritanism
damnation	sacrament	ceremonial	redemption
deaconess	sacrifice	chronicles	repentance
dedicated	sacrilege	Church Army	revelation
desecrate	sacristan	churchgoer	sacrosanct
Easter Day	salvation	church work	scriptural
Ember Days	sanctuary	churchyard	sepulchral
episcopal	scripture	confession	tabernacle
Eucharist	sepulchre	consecrate	temptation
evangelic	solemnise	devotional	unanointed
genuflect	solemnity	Dominicans	unbeliever
gospeller	solemnize	Eastertide	unorthodox
hierarchy	spiritual	ecumenical	Whit Sunday
Holy Ghost	synagogue	Ember weeks	White Friar
holy water	testament	evangelism	worshipper
incumbent	venerable	evangelist	
induction	vestments	Free Church	11
Lammas day		Good Friday	abomination
lay reader	10	halleluiah	All Souls' Day
Leviticus	absolution	hallelujah	altar screen
Low Church	abstinence	heaven born	Benedictine
Low Sunday	altar bread	heliolatry	benediction
martyrdom	altar cloth	High Church	benedictory
Methodism	altar cross	high priest	bibliolatry
Methodist	altar light	holy orders	blasphemous
moderator	altar steps	Holy Spirit	Catholicism
monastery	altar table	indulgence	celebration
Mormonism	Anabaptist	infallible	Christendom
obeisance	anointment	invocation	christening

11

church mouse
communicant
consecrator
crematorium
crucifixion
desecration
devotionist
divine light
doxological
eternal life
evangelical
evening hymn
everlasting
freethinker
hagiography
hierarchism
hierography
immortality
incarnation
inquisition
intercessor
investiture
irreverence
Lord's Supper
miracle play
mission room
Nicene Creed
parishioner
passion play
Passion Week

11

paternoster
patron saint
pontificate
purificator
Reformation
Roman Church
sacramental
undedicated
unrighteous
Wesleyanism
Whitsuntide

12

All Saints Day
Annunciation
archdeaconry
Ascension Day
Ash Wednesday
Bible Society
choir service
Christianity
Christmas Day
Christmas Eve
church living
church parade
churchwarden
confessional
confirmation
congregation
consecration

12

discipleship
dispensation
Easter Sunday
ecclesiastic
enthronement
frankincense
hot gospeller
intercession
Low Churchman
mission house
New Testament
Nunc Dimittis
Old Testament
Presbyterian
purification
Quadragesima
Resurrection
Rogation Days
Rogation Week
Salvationist
Sanctus bell
Septuagesima
spiritualism
Sunday school
thanksgiving
Unitarianism

13

Anglo-Catholic
antichristian

13

Apostles' Creed
archbishopric
beatification
burial service
burnt offering
Christianlike
church service
confessionary
Corpus Christi
devotionalist
Eastern Church
excommunicate
glorification
High Churchman
Holy Innocents
incense burner
miracle worker
mission church
Mohammedanism
Nonconforming
pectoral cross
prayer meeting
Quinquagesima
Roman Catholic
reincarnation
Salvation Army
Shrove Tuesday
Trinity Sunday
unconsecrated
Way of the Cross

14

burnt sacrifice
church assembly
communion table
Easter offering
ecclesiastical
fundamentalism
Gregorian chant

14

high priesthood
Maundy Thursday
Orthodox Church
Redemptionists
Reformed Church
sanctification
sign of the cross

15

anti-evangelical
excommunication
Harvest Festival
Jehovah's Witness
Mothering Sunday
Transfiguration

Reptiles and amphibians

3
asp
boa
eft
olm

4
frog
newt
toad
worm

5
adder
agama
cobra
gecko
guana
hydra
krait
mamba
snake
viper

6
cayman
dragon
gavial
hydrus
iguana
lizard
moloch
mugger
python
taipan
turtle

6
wyvern
zaltys

7
axolotl
gharial
rattler
reptile
serpent
tadpole
tuatara

8
amphibia
anaconda
basilisk
bullfrog
horn toad
matamata
moccasin
pit viper
rat snake
ringhals
sea snake
slowworm
terrapin
tortoise
tree frog

9
alligator
blindworm
boomslang
chameleon
conger eel
crocodile

9
giant frog
giant toad
king cobra
king snake
puff adder
ring snake
tree snake
water newt
whip snake

10
amphibians
black mamba
black snake
bushmaster
clawed frog
copperhead
coral snake
death adder
fer-de-lance
glass snake
grass snake
green mamba
green snake
hellbender
horned frog
horned toad
natterjack
night adder
river snake
rock python
salamander
sand lizard
sea serpent
wall lizard

10
water snake
worm lizard

11
constrictor
cottonmouth
flying snake
Gaboon viper
gila monster
green lizard
green turtle
horned viper
midwife toad
rattlesnake
smooth snake
water lizard
water python

12
flying lizard
green tree boa
horned iguana
horned lizard
Komodo dragon
pond tortoise

13
aquatic lizard
frilled lizard
giant tortoise
Russell's viper
spadefoot toad
water moccasin

14
boa constrictor
fire salamander

Rivers

2
Ob (Rus)
Po (It)

3
Ain (Fr)
Aln (Eng)
Bug (Pol/Ukr)
Cam (Eng)
Dee (Eng)
Dee (Scot)
Dee (Wales)
Don (Scot)
Ems (Ger)
Exe (Eng)
Fal (Eng)
Fly (Papua N.G.)
Lea (Eng)
Lee (Ire)
Lot (Fr)
Lys (Belg/Fr)
Red (USA)
Rur (Ger)
Rye (Eng)
Tay (Scot)
Ure (Eng)
Usa (Rus)
Usk (Eng/Wales)
Wey (Eng)
Wye (Eng/Wales)
Yeo (Eng)

4
Adda (It)
Adur (Eng)
Aire (Eng)
Aire (Scot)
Alma (Ukr)
Amur (China/Rus)

4
Amur (Mong)
Arno (It)
Arun (Eng)
Arun (Nepal)
Avon (Eng)
Bure (Eng)
Cher (Fr)
Coln (Eng)
Dart (Eng)
Doon (Scot)
Dove (Eng)
Ebro (Sp)
Eden (Eng)
Eden (Scot)
Elbe (Ger)
Erne (Ire)
Isis (Eng)
Juba (E.Af)
Kama (Rus)
Lahn (Ger)
Lech (Ger)
Lena (Rus)
Lune (Eng)
Maas (Neth)
Main (Ger)
Main (N.I.)
Miño (Sp)
Mole (Eng)
Naze (Eng)
Nile (Egypt/Sudan)
Oder (Czech/Ger/Pol)
Ohio (USA)
Oise (Fr)
Ouse (Eng)
Oxus (Asia)
Peel (Aust)
Ravi (India)
Rede (Eng)

4
Ruhr (Ger)
Saar (Fr/Ger)
Spey (Scot)
Taff (Wales)
Tarn (Fr)
Tawe (Wales)
Tees (Eng)
Test (Eng)
Towy (Wales)
Tyne (Eng)
Ural (Rus, Kazakh)
Vaal (S.Af)
Wear (Eng)
Yare (Eng)

5
Aisne (Fr)
Allan (Scot)
Allen (Scot)
Aller (Ger)
Annan (Scot)
Benue (Nigeria)
Brent (Eng)
Camel (Eng)
Clyde (Scot)
Colne (Eng)
Congo (Zaïre)
Douro (Port)
Dovey (Wales)
Drava (Hun)
Duero (Sp)
Forth (Scot)
Foyle (Ire)
Frome (Austral)
Frome (Eng)
Indus (India)
James (USA)
Jumna (India)

5

Kafue (Zambia)
Leven (Scot)
Loire (Fr)
Marne (Fr)
Meuse (Belg)
Minho (Port)
Neath (Wales)
Niger (Nigeria)
Otter (Eng)
Peace (Can)
Purus (Braz)
Rance (Fr)
Rhine (Ger/Neth/Switz)
Rhône (Fr/Switz)
Saale (Ger)
Saône (Fr)
Seine (Fr)
Shiel (Scot)
Snake (USA)
Somme (Fr)
Stour (Eng)
Swale (Eng)
Tagus (Port)
Tamar (Eng)
Teign (Eng)
Teith (Scot)
Tiber (It)
Trent (Eng)
Tweed (Scot)
Volga (Rus)
Volta (Burkina/Ghana)
Weser (Ger)
Xingu (Braz)
Yukon (Can)
Zaïre (Zaïre)

6

Albany (Can)
Allier (Fr)
Amazon (Braz/Peru)

6

Angara (Rus)
Barrow (Ire)
Beauly (Scot)
Calder (Eng)
Chenab (Pak)
Coquet (Eng)
Crouch (Eng)
Danube (Europe)
Fraser (Can)
French (Can)
Gambia (Gambia)
Ganges (India)
Hamble (Eng)
Hudson (USA)
Humber (Eng)
Itchen (Eng)
Japura (Braz)
Jordan (Israel/Jordan)
Kennet (Eng)
Liffey (Ire)
Loddon (Aust)
Medway (Eng)
Mekong (China/Laos)
Mersey (Eng)
Monnow (Eng)
Morava (Czech)
Murray (Aust)
Neckar (Ger)
Neisse (Ger)
Nelson (Can)
Orange (S.Af)
Orwell (Eng)
Paraná (Braz)
Platte (USA)
Ribble (Eng)
Severn (Eng)
Sutlej (India)
Teviot (Scot)
Thames (Eng)
Ticino (Switz)

6

Tigris (Iraq/Turk)
Tugela (S.Af)
Vienne (Fr)
Vltava (Czech)
Wabash (USA)
Weaver (Eng)
Wharfe (Eng)
Witham (Eng)
Yarrow (Scot)
Yellow (China)

7

Cauvery (India)
Darling (Aust)
Derwent (Eng)
Durance (Fr)
Garonne (Fr)
Hooghly (India)
Hwang Ho (China)
Lachlan (Aust)
Limpopo (S.Af)
Lualaba (Zaïre)
Madeira (Braz)
Marañón (Braz/Peru)
Moselle (Ger)
Orontes (Syria)
Pechora (Rus)
Potomac (USA)
Salween (Burma)
Scheldt (Belg)
Senegal (Senegal)
Shannon (Ire)
Sungari (China)
Uruguay (Braz/Uruguay)
Vistula (Pol)
Waikato (NZ)
Waveney (Eng)
Yangtse (China)

7
Yenisei (Rus)
Zambezi (Ang/Mozamb/Zambia/
  Zimb)

8
Amu Darya (Asia)
Arkansas (USA)
Beaulieu (Eng)
Canadian (USA)
Cherwell (Eng)
Colorado (USA)
Columbia (USA)
Delaware (USA)
Demerara (Guyana)
Godavari (India)
Klondike (Can)
Manawatu (NZ)
Missouri (USA)
Paraguay (Para)
Putamayo (Ecuad)
Saguenay (Can)
Suwannee (USA)
Syr Darya (Kazakh)
Torridge (Eng)
Wansbeck (Eng)
Windrush (Eng)

9
Churchill (Can)
Essequibo (Guyana)
Euphrates (Iraq)
Great Ouse (Eng)
Irrawaddy (Burma)
Mackenzie (Can)
Rio Grande (Mex)
Tennessee (USA)

10
Hawkesbury (Aust)
Sacramento (USA)
St Lawrence (Can)
Shenandoah (USA)

11
Brahmaputra (India)
Desaguadero (Boliv)
Mississippi (USA)
Shatt Al-Arab (Iran/Iraq)
Susquehanna (USA)
Yellowstone (USA)

12
Guadalquivir (Sp)
Saskatchewan (Can)

Rocks, minerals and ores

3	4	6	6
tin	talc	albite	humite
	zinc	augite	indium
4		basalt	nickel
gold	**5**	cobalt	pyrope
iron	agate	copper	quartz
lead	beryl	gabbro	radium
mica	emery	galena	rutile
opal	flint	garnet	schorl
ruby	shale	gneiss	silica
	topaz	gypsum	silver

6	8	8	9
sodium	antimony	stibnite	scheelite
sphene	Blue John	stilbite	scolecite
zircon	bronzite	thallium	soapstone
	calamine	titanium	spodumene
7	chlorite	tungsten	strontium
alunite	chromite		sylvanite
anatase	chromium	**9**	tellurium
arsenic	cinnabar	almandine	tremolite
azurite	corundum	aluminium	turquoise
barytes	cryolite	carnalite	wavellite
bauxite	diallage	chabasite	willemite
bismuth	diopside	china clay	witherite
breccia	dioptase	erythrite	
cadmium	dolerite	fluorspar	**10**
calcite	dolomite	gmelinite	actinolite
calcium	epsomite	granulite	cervantite
calomel	feldspar	greywacke	chalcedony
cuprite	fluorite	haematite	chrysolite
diamond	graphite	hornstone	dyscrasite
diorite	hyacinth	limestone	glauberite
emerald	idocrase	lodestone	glauconite
epidote	ilmenite	magnesite	greenstone
felsite	limonite	magnesium	heulandite
granite	meionite	magnetite	hornblende
hessite	melanite	malachite	lepidolite
iridium	mesolite	marcasite	meerschaum
kyanite	mimetite	margarite	molybdenum
lignite	monazite	mispickel	orthoclase
lithium	nephrite	muscovite	phosphorus
mercury	orpiment	natrolite	pyrochlore
olivine	petalite	niccolite	pyrolusite
realgar	platinum	pectolite	sapphirine
syenite	porphyry	periclase	serpentine
thorite	prehnite	phenacite	sphalerite
thorium	psammite	phonolite	staurolite
uranium	pyroxene	potassium	thomsonite
yttrium	rhyolite	proustite	tourmaline
zeolite	rock salt	quartzite	vanadinite
zincite	sapphire	rhodonite	websterite
ziosite	siberite	sandstone	zincblende
	sodalite	scapolite	

11	11	11	11
amblygonite	franklinite	phillipsite	simmimanite
cassiterite	hypersthene	pitchblende	smithsonite
chondrodite	Iceland spar	psilomelane	
chrysoberyl	lapis lazuli	pyrargyrite	12
cobaltbloom	molybdenite	rock crystal	pyromorphite
			tetrahedrite
			wollastonite

Saints

3	5	6	7
Ann	Hilda	Thomas	Swithun
	James	Ursula	Theresa
4	Lucia		William
Anne	Olave	7	
Bede	Peter	Ambrose	8
Joan	Vitus	Anthony	Aloysius
John		Austell	Augustus
Jude	6	Barbara	Barnabas
Just	Agatha	Bernard	Benedict
Lucy	Albert	Bridget	Bernhard
Luke	Andrea	Cecilia	Boniface
Mark	Andrew	Clement	Ignatius
Mary	Anselm	Crispin	Lawrence
Paul	Ansgar	Dominic	Margaret
Rita	Fabian	Dunstan	Nicholas
	Fergus	Etienne	Veronica
5	Gallus	Eustace	Winifred
Agnes	George	Francis	
Aidan	Helena	Germain	9
Alban	Hilary	Gregory	Augustine
André	Jerome	Joachim	Catherine
Asaph	Joseph	Matthew	Christina
Basil	Martha	Michael	Demetrius
Bride	Martin	Nicolas	Elizabeth
Bruno	Michel	Patrick	Joan of Arc
Clair	Monica	Raphael	Sebastian
David	Philip	Saviour	Valentine
Denis	Pierre	Stephen	Wenceslas
Elias	Teresa	Swithin	
Giles			

11	13	14	15
Bartholomew	Mary Magdalene	John the Baptist	Francis of Assisi
Bonaventure	Thomas Aquinas		
Christopher			

Patron saints

Agatha (bell founders)
Andrew (Scotland)
Bernard of Menthon (mountaineers)
Boniface (Germany)
Cecilia (musicians)
Christopher (travellers)
Crispin (shoemakers)
David (Wales)
Denis (France)

George (England)
Jude (hopeless causes)
Luke (physicians and surgeons)
Martha (housewives)
Nicholas (children)
Patrick (Ireland)
Valentine (lovers)
Vitus (epilepsy and nervous
   diseases)
Wenceslas (Bohemia)

Sciences

5	7	8	9
logic	zoology	rheology	micrology
		Sinology	neurology
6	**8**	taxonomy	orography
augury	aerology		pathology
botany	aeronomy	**9**	phonetics
conics	agronomy	acoustics	radiology
optics	biometry	aetiology	sociology
	bryology	astronomy	taxidermy
7	cytology	cartology	zoography
anatomy	dynamics	chemistry	
biology	ethology	chiropody	**10**
cookery	etiology	chorology	biophysics
ecology	forestry	cosmology	cardiology
farming	kinetics	dentistry	craniology
myology	medicine	emetology	demography
orology	mycology	ethnology	Egyptology
otology	nosology	geography	entomology
phonics	ontology	histology	enzymology
physics	penology	horometry	gastrology
science	pharmacy	hydrology	geophysics
statics	pomology	ichnology	homeopathy
surgery	posology	mechanics	hydraulics

10	11	11	13
hydrometry	aerobiology	ornithology	crustaceology
hydropathy	aeronautics	osteography	endocrinology
kinematics	agriculture	paediatrics	hydrodynamics
metallurgy	archaeology	photography	marine biology
microscopy	cartography	radiography	meteorography
morphology	cosmography	stereometry	ophthalmology
oneirology	craniometry		sedimentology
osteopathy	criminology	**12**	
pediatrics	dermatology	biochemistry	**14**
phrenology	electronics	biogeography	chromatography
physiology	entozoology	electropathy	cinematography
psychiatry	gynaecology	epidemiology	natural history
psychology	haematology	horticulture	natural science
seismology	heliography	hydrostatics	
technology	homoeopathy	lexicography	**15**
telegraphy	hydrography	microbiology	computer science
topography	ichthyology	pharmacology	neurophysiology
toxicology	mathematics	physiography	psychopathology
	neurography	pneumatology	thermochemistry
		protozoology	
		trigonometry	

Scientists and inventors

3

Ohm, George Simon
Ray, John

4

Abel, Sir Frederick
Airy, Sir George Biddell
Baer, Karl Ernest von
Bell, Alexander Graham
Benz, Karl
Biro, Laszlo
Bohr, Niels Henrik David
Cohn, Ferdinand Julius
Davy, Sir Humphrey
Hahn, Otto
Howe, Elias
Koch, Robert
Otto, Nikolaus August

4

Todd, Alexander Robertus, Baron
Watt, James

5

Adams, John Couch
Arago, Dominique François Jean
Bacon, Roger
Baird, John Logie
Baker, Sir Benjamin
Banks, Sir Joseph
Black, Joseph
Bondi, Sir Hermann
Boyle, Robert
Bragg, Sir William Henry
Brahe, Tycho
Curie, Marie Sklodowska
Curie, Pierre

5

Dewar, Sir James
Dirac, Paul Adrien Maurice
Euler, Leonhard
Fabre, Jean Henri Casimir
Fermi, Enrico
Gauss, Karl Friedrich
Henry, Joseph
Hertz, Heinrich Rudolf
Hooke, Robert
Joule, James Prescott
Lyell, Sir Charles
Maxim, Sir Hiram Stevens
Morse, Samuel Finley Breese
Nobel, Alfred Bernhard
Pauli, Wolfgang
Raman, Sir Chandrasekhara
  Venkata
Soddy, Frederick
Tesla, Nikola
Volta, Alessandro
Young, Thomas

6

Adrian, Edgar Douglas, Baron
Ampère, André Marie
Appert, Nicholas
Bramah, Joseph
Brunel, Isambard Kingdom
Buffon, Georges-Louis Leclerc,
  Comte de
Bunsen, Robert Wilhelm
Carrel, Alexis
Caxton, William
Cuvier, Georges
Dalton, John
Darwin, Charles Robert
Edison, Thomas Alva
Finsen, Niels Ryberg
Fokker, Anthony Herman Gerard
Fulton, Robert
Galton, Sir Francis
Gesner, Conrad

6

Halley, Edmund
Hubble, Edwin Powell
Hutton, James
Huxley, Thomas Henry
Kelvin, William Thomson, 1st
  Baron of Largs
Kepler, Johann
Mendel, Gregor Johann
Muller, Sir Ferdinand
Napier, John
Nernst, Walther Hermann
Newton, Sir Isaac
Pascal, Blaise
Penney, William George, Baron
Perkin, Sir William Henry
Perrin, Francis
Planck, Max
Ramsay, Sir William
Rennie, John
Sanger, Frederick
Singer, Isaac Merritt
Sloane, Sir Hans
Stokes, Sir George Gabriel
Talbot, William Henry Fox
Vauban, Sébastien le Prestre de
Wallis, Sir Barnes Neville
Wright, Orville
Yukawa, Hideki

7

Agassiz, Louis
Borlaug, Norman Ernest
Boyd-Orr, John, Baron
Braille, Louis
Compton, Arthur Holly
Crookes, Sir William
Daimler, Gottlieb
Faraday, Michael
Fleming, Sir Ambrose
Fourier, Jean Baptiste Joseph,
  Baron
Galileo (Galileo Galilei)

7

Galvani, Luigi
Gilbert, William
Gregory, James
Hodgkin, Alan Lloyd
Hodgkin, Dorothy Crowfoot
Hopkins, Sir Frederick Gowland
Huggins, Sir William
Huygens, Christiaan
Lalande, Joseph Jérome
 LeFrançois de
Lamarck, Jean Baptiste Pierre
 Antoine de Monet de
Laplace, Pierre Simon, Marquis de
Lesseps, Ferdinand, Vicomte de
Lysenko, Trofim
Macadam, John Loudon
Marconi, Guglielmo, Marchese
Maxwell, James Clerk
Meitner, Lise
Oersted, Hans Christian
Parsons, Sir Charles Algernon
Pasteur, Louis
Piccard, Auguste
Ptolemy (Claudius Ptolemaeus)
Réaumur, René-Antoine Ferchault de
Scheele, Carl Wilhelm
Siemens, Werner von
Telford, Thomas
Thomson, Sir Joseph John
Tyndall, John
Wallace, Alfred Russel
Whittle, Sir Frank

8

Ångström, Anders Jons
Avogadro, Amedeo
Bessemer, Sir Henry
Blackett, Patrick Maynard Stuart,
 Baron
Brewster, Sir David
Brindley, James

8

Chadwick, Sir James
Crompton, Samuel
Daguerre, Louis Jacques Mande
De Forest, Lee
Einstein, Albert
Ericsson, John
Herschel, Sir John
Herschel, Sir William
Jacquard, Joseph-Marie
Koroliov, Sergei
Lagrange, Joseph Louis, Comte
Linnaeus, Carolus
Mercator, Gerhardus
Millikan, Robert Andrews
Newcomen, Thomas
Rayleigh, John William Strutt,
 Baron
Sakharov, Andrei Dimitrievich
Weismann, August

9

Arkwright, Sir Richard
Arrhenius, Svante August
Berthelot, Marcellin Pierre
 Eugène
Berzelius, Jons Jakob
Cavendish, Henry
Eddington, Sir Arthur Stanley
Flamsteed, John
Gay-Lussac, Joseph Louis
Hopkinson, John
Kirchhoff, Gustav Robert
Lavoisier, Antoine Laurent
Leverrier, Urbain Jean Joseph
Michelson, Albert Abraham
Priestley, Joseph
Zuckerman, Solly, Baron

10

Cannizzaro, Stanislao
Cartwright, Edmund

10

Copernicus, Nicolas
Fraunhofer, Joseph von
Hargreaves, James
Heisenberg, Werner
Mendeleyev, Dimitri Ivanovich
Rutherford, Ernest, 1st Baron
Stephenson, George
Torricelli, Evangelista
Trevithick, Richard

10

Watson-Watt, Sir Robert
Wheatstone, Sir Charles

11

Al-Khwarizmi
Joliot-Curie, Jean Frédéric
Montgolfier, Jacques-Etienne
Montgolfier, Joseph Michel
Sherrington, Sir Charles Scott

Sculptors

4

Caro, Anthony
Doré, Gustave
Gabo, Naum

5

Degas, Edgar
Foley, John Henry
Moore, Henry
Myron
Rodin, Louis-François
Smith, David

6

Calder, Alexander
Canova, Antonio
Goujon, Jean
Houdon, Jean Antoine
Jochho
Pisano, Giovanni
Pisano, Nicola
Robbia, Luca della
Sluter, Claus

7

Bernini, Gianlorenzo
Cellini, Benvenuto
Epstein, Sir Jacob

7

Flaxman, John
Maillol, Aristide
Pevsner, Antoine
Phidias
Pigalle, Jean-Baptiste
Zadkine, Ossip

8

Brancusi, Constantin
Frampton, Sir George James
Ghiberti, Lorenzo
González, Julio
Hepworth, Dame Barbara
Lysippus
Nevelson, Louise
Paolozzi, Eduardo

9

Donatello
Mestrović, Ivan
Nollekens, Joseph
Oldenburg, Claes
Roubillac, Louis Francois

10

Archipenko, Alexander
Giacometti, Alberto

10
Polyclitus
Praxiteles

11
Callimachus
Thorvaldsen, Bertel

12
Michelangelo (Michelangelo
  Buonarroti)

14
Gaudier-Brzeska, Henri

Seven deadly sins

anger
covetousness
envy
gluttony

lust
pride
sloth

Seven dwarfs

Bashful
Doc
Dopey
Grumpy

Happy
Sleepy
Sneezy

Seven virtues

faith
fortitude
hope
justice

love (charity)
prudence
temperance

Seven wonders of the world

The Colossus of Rhodes
The Pharos of Alexandria
The Pyramids of Egypt
The Statue of Zeus at Olympia
The Temple of Artemis at Ephesus
The Tomb of Mausolus (Mausoleum) at Halicarnassus
The Walls and Hanging Gardens of Babylon

Shakespeare, William: plays and their characters

Titles of plays	Number of letters
(1) A Comedy of Errors	15
(2) A Midsummer Night's Dream	21
(3) All's Well That Ends Well	20
(4) Antony and Cleopatra	18
(5) As You like It	11
(6) Coriolanus	10
(7) Cymbeline	9
(8) Hamlet (Prince of Denmark)	6
(9) Julius Caesar	12
(10) King Henry IV (Part 1)	11
(11) King Henry IV (Part 2)	11
(12) King Henry V	10
(13) King Henry VI (Part 1)	11
(14) King Henry VI (Part 2)	11
(15) King Henry VI (Part 3)	11
(16) King Henry VIII	13
(17) King John	8
(18) King Lear	8
(19) King Richard II	13
(20) King Richard III	14
(21) Love's Labour's Lost	16
(22) Macbeth	7
(23) Measure for Measure	17
(24) Merry Wives of Windsor	19
(25) Much Ado About Nothing	19
(26) Othello (The Moor of Venice)	7
(27) Pericles (Prince of Tyre)	8
(28) Romeo and Juliet	14
(29) The Merchant of Venice	19
(30) The Taming of the Shrew	19
(31) The Tempest	10
(32) The Winter's Tale	14
(33) Timon of Athens	13
(34) Titus Andronicus	15
(35) Troilus and Cressida	18
(36) Twelfth Night (What You Will)	12
(37) Two Gentlemen of Verona	20

Characters (bracketed number = play reference)

3

Hal (10)
Nym (12/14)
Sly, Christopher (30)

4

Adam (5)
Ajax (35)
Cato (9)
Eros (4)
Ford, Mistress (24)
Grey (12)
Hero (25)
Iago (26)
Lear, King (18)
Page, Mistress (24)
Peto (11)
Puck (2)
Snug (2)

5

Aaron (34)
Ariel (31)
Belch, Sir Toby (36)
Blunt (10/11)
Caius, Doctor (24)
Celia (5)
Ceres (31)
Cleon (27)
Corin (5)
Diana (3/27)
Edgar (18)
Elbow (23)
Essex, Earl of (17)
Flute (2)
Froth (23)
Ghost (8)
Gobbo, Launcelot (29)
Julia (37)
Maria (21)

5

Paris (35)
Percy, Lady (9)
Phebe (5)
Pinch (1)
Poins (10/11)
Priam (35)
Regan (18)
Robin (24)
Romeo (28)
Snout (2)
Timon (33)
Viola (36)

6

Aegeon (1)
Albany, Duke of (18)
Alonso (31)
Angelo (23)
Antony (4)
Armado (21)
Audrey (5)
Banquo (22)
Bianca (30)
Blanch (17)
Bottom (2)
Brutus (6/9)
Caphis (33)
Cassio (26)
Chiron (34)
Cicero (9)
Dennis (5)
Dorcas (32)
Dromio (1)
Dumain (21)
Duncan, King (22)
Edmund (18)
Elinor (17)
Emilia (26)
Fabian (36)

6

Fenton (24)
Hamlet (8)
Hecate (22)
Hector (35)
Helena (2/3)
Hermia (2)
Imogen (7)
Juliet (23/28)
Lucius (34)
Marina (27)
Mutius (34)
Nestor (35)
Oberon (2)
Oliver (5)
Olivia (36)
Orsino (36)
Oswald (18)
Pistol (11/12/24)
Portia (29)
Quince (2)
Rumour (11)
Scroop, Lord (12)
Seyton (22)
Silius (4)
Silvia (37)
Tamora (34)
Thasia (27)
Thisbe (2)
Thurio (37)
Tybalt (28)
Venice, Duke of (26/29)
Verges (25)
Wolsey, Lord (16)

7

Adriana (1)
Aemilia (1)
Agrippa (4)
Alarbus (34)

7

Antonio (29/31)
Arragon, Prince of (29)
Bedford, Duke of (12/13)
Berkley, Earl (19)
Bertram (3)
Calchas (35)
Caliban (31)
Camillo (32)
Capulet, Lady (28)
Cassius (9)
Claudio (23/25)
Costard (21)
Cranmer,
  Archbishop of Canterbury (16)
Dauphin, The (13/17)
Douglas, Earl of (10)
Eleanor (14)
Escalus (23)
Flavius (33)
Fleance (22)
Goneril (18)
Gonzalo (31)
Helenus (34)
Horatio (8)
Hotspur (10/11)
Iachimo (7)
Jacques (5)
Jessica (29)
Laertes (8)
Lavinia (34)
Leontes (32)
Lorenzo (29)
Luciana (1)
Macbeth (22)
Macduff (22)
Malcolm (22)
Mariana (3/23)
Martius (34)
Miranda (31)
Nerissa (29)
Octavia (4)

7

Ophelia (8)
Orlando (5)
Othello (26)
Paulina (32)
Perdita (32)
Pisanio (7)
Proteus (37)
Quickly, Mistress (10/11/24)
Quintus (34)
Shallow, Justice (11/24)
Shylock (29)
Silence (11)
Silvius (5)
Slender (24)
Solinus (1)
Theseus (2)
Titania (2)
Troilus (35)
Ulysses (35)
William (5)

8

Achilles (35)
Aufidius (6)
Baptista (30)
Bardolph (10/11/12/24)
Bassanio (29)
Beatrice (25)
Belarius (7)
Benedick (25)
Benvolio (28)
Charmian (4)
Clarence, Duke of (11/20)
Claudius, King (8)
Colville (11)
Cominius (6)
Cordelia (18)
Cornwall, Duke of (18)
Cressida (35)
Diomedes (4/35)
Dogberry (25)

8

Don Pedro (25)
Falstaff (10/11/24)
Florizel (32)
Gertrude, Queen (8)
Gratiano (29)
Hermione (32)
Isabella (23)
Lucentio (30)
Lysander (2)
Malvolio (36)
Margaret, Queen (15)
Menelaus (35)
Menteith (22)
Mercutio (28)
Montague (28)
Mortimer, Lady (9)
Pandarus (35)
Parolles (3)
Pericles (27)
Polonius (8)
Prospero (31)
Roderigo (26)
Rosalind (5)
Rosaline (21)
Stephano (31)
Trinculo (31)
Violenta (3)
Volumnia (6)
Whitmore (14)

9

Antiochus (2)
Archibald (10/11)
Arviragus (7)
Bassianus (34)
Brabantio (26)
Cambridge, Earl of (12)
Cleopatra (4)
Constance (17)
Cymbeline (7)
Demetrius (2/4/34)
Desdemona (26)

9

Elizabeth (20)
Enobarbus (4)
Ferdinand (31)
Frederick (5)
Glendower, Owen (10)
Guiderius (7)
Helicanus (27)
Hippolyta (2)
Hortensio (30)
Katherina (30)
Katherine (21)
Mamillius (32)
Moonshine (2)
Nathaniel (21)
Patroclus (35)
Petruchio (30)
Polixenes (32)
Sebastian (31/36)
Tearsheet, Doll (11)
Valentine (37)
Vincentio (30)

10

Alcibiades (33)
Andronicus (34)
Antipholus (1)
Coriolanus (6)
Fortinbras (8)
Jaquenetta (21)
Longaville (21)
Lysimachus (27)
Saturninus (34)
Touchstone (5)
Winchester, Bishop of (16)

11

Peasblossom (2)
Rosencrantz (8)

12

Falconbridge (17)
Guildenstern (8)

Sheep

6	8	9	11
Merino	Cotswold	Southdown	Wensleydale
Romney	Herdwick	Swaledale	
	Portland	Teeswater	13
7	Shetland		Welsh Mountain
Caracul		10	Wiltshire Horn
Cheviot	9	Dorset Horn	
Gotland	Hebridean	Exmoor Horn	17
Karakul	Rough Fell	Poll Dorset	Scottish
Suffolk			Blackface

Sportsmen/women

3

Ali, Muhammad (boxing)
Coe, Sebastian (athletics)
Cox, Mark (tennis)
Fox, Uffa (yachting)
Law, Denis (football)
Lee, Bruce (kung fu)
May, Peter (cricket)

4

Amis, Dennis (cricket)
Ashe, Arthur (tennis)
Best, George (football)
Borg, Bjorn (tennis)
Bull, Steve (football)
Clay, Cassius (boxing)
Cram, Steve (athletics)
Duke, Geoffrey (motor cycling)
Graf, Steffi (tennis)
Hill, Graham (motor racing)
Hoad, Lewis (tennis)
Hunt, James (motor racing)
Hunt, Lord (mountaineering)
John, Barry (rugby union football)
King, Billie-Jean (tennis)
Kite, Tom (golf)
Mans, Perrie (snooker)

4

Moss, Stirling (motor racing)
Read, Phil (motor cycling)
Rush, Ian (football)
Wade, Virginia (tennis)
Webb, Capt. M. (swimming)

5

Banks, Gordon (football)
Bates, Jeremy (tennis)
Bruno, Frank (boxing)
Budge, Don (tennis)
Bueno, Maria (tennis)
Busby, Sir Matthew (association football)
Clark, Jim (motor racing)
Court, Margaret (tennis)
Curry, John (ice skating)
Davis, Joe (billiards)
Davis, Steve (snooker)
Evert, Christine (tennis)
Faldo, Nick (golf)
Grace, Dr William Gilbert (cricket)
Greig, Tony (cricket)
Hagen, Walter (golf)
Hobbs, Sir John (cricket)
Hogan, Ben (golf)

5

James, Steve (snooker)
Jones, Ann (tennis)
Jones, Steve (athletics)
Knott, Alan (cricket)
Kodes, Jan (tennis)
Lauda, Niki (motor racing)
Laver, Rod (tennis)
Lewis, Carl (athletics)
Lloyd, Clive (cricket)
Louis, Joe (boxing)
Meade, Richard (show jumping)
Meads, Colin (rugby union football)
Moore, Ann (show jumping)
Moore, Bobby (football)
Ovett, Steve (athletics)
Perry, Fred (tennis)
Pirie, Gordon (athletics)
Prost, Alain (motor racing)
Revie, Don (football)
Roche, Tony (tennis)
Senna, Ayrton (motor racing)
Short, Nigel (chess)
Smith, Harvey (show jumping)
Smith, Stan (tennis)
Spitz, Mark (swimming)
Virgo, John (snooker)
White, Jimmy (snooker)
Wills, Helen (tennis)

6

Barker, Sue (tennis)
Becker, Boris (tennis)
Border, Allan (cricket)
Botham, Ian (cricket)
Broome, David (show jumping)
Bugner, Joe (boxing)
Casals, Rosemary (tennis)
Cawley, Evonne (tennis)
Cooper, Henry (boxing)
Cruyff, Johann (football)
Dexter, Ted (cricket)

6

Drobny, Jaroslav (tennis)
Drurie, Jo (tennis)
Edberg, Stefan (tennis)
Edrich, John (cricket)
Foster, Brendan (athletics)
Gibson, Althea (tennis)
Hendry, Stephen (snooker)
Hughes, Mark (football)
Hutton, Sir Leonard (cricket)
Keegan, Kevin (football)
Korbut, Olga (gymnastics)
Lillee, Dennis (cricket)
Liston, Sonny (boxing)
Norman, Greg (golf)
Palmer, Arnold (golf)
Parrot, John (snooker)
Peters, Mary (athletics)
Piquet, Nelson (motor racing)
Player, Gary (golf)
Ramsay, Sir Alfred (football)
Rhodes, Wilfred (cricket)
Sheene, Barry (motor cycling)
Smythe, Pat (show jumping)
Sobers, Sir Gary (cricket)
Stolle, Fred (tennis)
Taylor, Dennis (snooker)
Taylor, Roger (tennis)
Thorne, Willie (snooker)
Titmus, Fred (cricket)
Turpin, Randolph (boxing)
Watson, Tom (golf)
Wilkie, David (swimming)

7

Boycott, Geoffrey (cricket)
Brabham, Jack (motor racing)
Bradman, Sir Donald (cricket)
Connors, Jimmy (tennis)
Cowdrey, Colin (cricket)
Dempsey, Jack (boxing)
Elliott, Herb (athletics)

7

Emerson, Roy (tennis)
Ferrari, Enzio (motor racing)
Fischer, Bobby (chess)
Foreman, George (boxing)
Frazier, Joe (boxing)
Greaves, Jimmy (football)
Hammond, Wally (cricket)
Higgins, Alex (snooker)
Hillary, Sir Edmund
 (mountaineering)
Jacklin, Tony (golf)
Johnson, Amy (aviation)
Johnson, Joe (snooker)
Lineker, Gary (football)
McEnroe, John (tennis)
McLaren, Bruce (motor racing)
Mansell, Nigel (motor racing)
Mottram, Buster (tennis)
Nastase, Ilie (tennis)
Nielsen, Gunnar (athletics)
Piggott, Lester (horse racing)
Reardon, Ray (snooker)
Spencer, John (snooker)
Stevens, Kirk (snooker)
Stewart, Jackie (motor racing)
Surtees, John (motor racing)
Trevino, Lee (golf)
Trueman, Fred (cricket)
Wattana, James (snooker)

8

Chappell, Greg (cricket)
Charlton, Bobby (football)
Charlton, Jack (football)
Chataway, Sir Christopher
 (athletics)
Connolly, Maureen (tennis)
Docherty, Tommy (football)
Graveney, Tom (cricket)
Hailwood, Mike (motor cycling)
Hawthorn, Mike (motor racing)

8

Ibbotson, Derek (athletics)
Kasparov, Gary (chess)
Marciano, Rocky (boxing)
Matthews, Sir Stanley (football)
Mortimer, Angela (tennis)
Mountjoy-Doug (snooker)
Newcombe, John (tennis)
Nicklaus, Jack (golf)
Phillips, Capt. Mark (show
 jumping)
Richards, Sir Gordon (horse riding)
Richards, Viv (cricket)
Robinson, Sugar Ray (boxing)
Rosewall, Ken (tennis)
Saunders, Dean (football)
Spedding, Charlie (athletics)
Thompson, Daley (athletics)
Thorburn, Cliff (snooker)
Williams, Rex (snooker)

9

Bannister, Dr Roger (athletics)
Beardsley, Peter (football)
Bonington, Chris (mountaineering)
D'Oliviera, Basil (cricket)
Gascoigne, Paul (football)
Griffiths, Terry (snooker)
Johannson, Ingomar (boxing)
Lindbergh, Charles (aviation)
Llewellyn, Harry (show jumping)
Patterson, Floyd (boxing)
Pattisson, Rodney (yachting)
Underwood, Derek (cricket)
Werbeniuk, Bill (snooker)

10

Barrington, Jonah (squash)
Chichester, Sir Francis (yachting)
Imran Khan (cricket)
Lonsbrough, Anita (swimming)

11
Ballesteros, Severiano (golf)
Constantine, Sir Leary (cricket)
Fitzsimmons, Bob (boxing)

11
Illingworth, Ray (cricket)
Kristiansen, Ingrid (athletics)
Weissmuller, Johnny (swimming)

Stadiums and venues

5
Ascot (horse racing)
Lord's (cricket)

7
Aintree (horse racing)
Nou Camp, Barcelona (football)
The Oval (cricket)

8
Moor Park, Rickmansworth (golf)

9
Croke Park, Dublin (Gaelic football/hurling)
Edgbaston (cricket)
Hickstead (show jumping)
Newmarket (horse racing)
The Belfry (golf)
White City (greyhound racing)
Wimbledon (tennis)

10
Brooklands (motor racing)
Epsom Downs (horse racing)
Headingley (cricket)
Meadowbank (athletics)
The Hexagon, Reading (snooker)
Twickenham (rugby union)

11
Belmont Park, Long Island (horse racing)
Brands Hatch (motor racing)

11
Eden Gardens, Calcutta (cricket)
Hampden Park, Glasgow (football)
Murrayfield (rugby union)
Old Trafford (cricket)
Silverstone (motor racing)
The Crucible, Sheffield (snooker)
Trent Bridge, Nottingham (cricket)
Windsor Park, Belfast (football)

12
Odsal Stadium, Bradford (rugby league)

13
Azteca Stadium, Mexico City (Olympics/football)
Caesars Palace, Las Vegas (boxing)
Crystal Palace (athletics)
Donington Park (motor cycling/motor racing)
Heysel Stadium, Brussels (football)

14
Landsdowne Road, Dublin (rugby union)
Wembley Stadium (football/rugby)

15
Bernabeu Stadium, Madrid (football)
Cardiff Arms Park (rugby union)
Maracana Stadium, Brazil (football)
Royal and Ancient (Golf Club of St Andrews) (golf)

20
Munich Olympic Stadium (athletics/football)

23
Wembley Conference Centre (darts)

Stage, screen, television and radio personalities

3	3	3
Day, Doris	Hay, Will	Loe, Judy
Day, Sir Robin	Lee, Christopher	Rix, Brian, Baron

4	5	5
Bass, Alfie	Blair, Lionel	Mills, Sir John
Bilk, Acker	Bloom, Claire	Moore, Dudley
Bird, John	Boyer, Charles	Mount, Peggy
Cole, George	Bryan, Dora	Negus, Arthur
Cole, Stephanie	Davis, Bette	Niven, David
Cook, Peter	Dench, Dame Judi	Paige, Elaine
Dean, James	Donat, Robert	Pasco, Richard
Dors, Diana	Evans, Dame Edith	Power, Tyrone
Eddy, Nelson	Faith, Adam	Quinn, Anthony
Gish, Lillian	Finch, Peter	Robey, Sir George
Gray, Dulcie	Flynn, Errol	Scott, Terry
Hall, Sir Peter	Fonda, Henry	Smith, Dame Maggie
Hope, Bob	Fonda, Jane	Swann, Donald
Kent, Jean	Frost, Sir David	Sykes, Eric
Kerr, Deborah	Gable, Clark	Terry, Dame Ellen
Lean, Sir David	Gabor, Zsa Zsa	Topol, Chaim
More, Kenneth	Garbo, Greta	Tracy, Spencer
Muir, Frank	Gould, Elliot	Tutin, Dame Dorothy
Peck, Gregory	Grade, Lord	Wayne, John
Rank, J. Arthur	Grant, Cary	Welch, Raquel
Reed, Sir Carol	Greco, Juliette	Wogan, Terry
Reid, Beryl	Green, Hughie	
Rigg, Diana	Haigh, Kenneth	6
Thaw, John	Handl, Dame Irene	Bacall, Lauren
Took, Barrie	Horne, Kenneth	Bardot, Brigitte
West, Mae	Horne, Lena	Bogart, Humphrey
Wise, Ernie	Irons, Jeremy	Brando, Marlon
Wise, Robert	James, Sid	Braden, Bernard
York, Michael	Jason, David	Briers, Richard
York, Susannah	Kelly, Barbara	Burton, Richard
	Kelly, Grace	Cagney, James
5	La Rue, Danny	Callow, Simon
Allen, Chesney	Leigh, Vivien	Canter, Eddie
Allen, Dave	Lloyd, Marie	Cleese, John
Allen, Woody	Loren, Sophia	Colman, Ronald
Arden, John	Magee, Patrick	Cooper, Gary
Aspel, Michael	Marks, Alfred	Coward, Sir Noel
Baker, Richard	Mason, James	Crosby, Bing
Baker, Sir Stanley	Melly, George	Curtis, Tony
Bates, Alan	Miles, Sir Bernard	Cushing, Peter
Benny, Jack	Mills, Bertram	De Sica, Vittorio

6	6	7
Disney, Walt	Robson, Dame Flora	Dotrice, Roy
Duncan, Isadora	Rooney, Mickey	Douglas, Michael
Fields, Dame Gracie	Savile, Sir Jimmy	Douglas, Kirk
Finlay, Frank	Sinden, Donald	Durante, Jimmy
Finney, Albert	Steele, Tommy	Edwards, Jimmy
Formby, George	Streep, Meryl	Elliott, Denholm
Garson, Greer	Suchet, David	Elphick, Michael
Harlow, Jean	Suzman, Janet	Feldman, Marty
Heston, Charlton	Tauber, Richard	Fonteyn, Dame Margot
Hiller, Dame Wendy	Taylor, Elizabeth	Garland, Judy
Howard, Frankie	Temple, Shirley	Garrick, David
Howard, Leslie	Tilley, Vesta	Gielgud, Sir John
Howard, Trevor	Waring, Eddie	Gingold, Hermione
Irving, Sir Henry	Welles, Orson	Goldwyn, Samuel
Jacobi, Derek	Wilder, Gene	Hancock, Sheila
Jacobs, David	Wolfit, Sir Donald	Hancock, Tony
Jolson, Al		Handley, Tommy
Keaton, Buster	7	Harding, Gilbert
Kendal, Felicity	Ackland, Joss	Hawkins, Jack
Lauder, Sir Harry	Andrews, Eamonn	Hawtrey, Sir Charles
Lemmon, Jack	Andrews, Julie	Hepburn, Audrey
Lennon, John	Astaire, Fred	Hepburn, Katherine
Lidell, Alvar	Barnett, (Lady) Isobel	Hickson, Joan
Lillie, Beatrice	Bennett, Alan	Hoffman, Dustin
Lipman, Maureen	Bennett, Hywel	Hopkins, Sir Antony
Martin, Mary	Bennett, Jill	Hordern, Sir Michael
Massey, Daniel	Bentine, Michael	Jackson, Glenda
Massey, Raymond	Bergman, Ingrid	Jacques, Hattie
McEwan, Geraldine	Blakely, Colin	Johnson, Dame Celia
McKern, Leo	Bogarde, Dirk	Karloff, Boris
Merman, Ethel	Branagh, Kenneth	Kendall, Kenneth
Monroe, Marilyn	Calvert, Phyllis	Kennedy, Ludovic
Morley, Robert	Celeste, Celine	Langtry, Lillie
Neagle, Dame Anna	Chaplin, Sir Charles	McQueen, Steve
Newman, Nanette	Chester, Charlie	Michell, Keith
Newman, Paul	Colbert, Claudette	Murdoch, Richard
Norden, Dennis	Connery, Sean	Novello, Ivor
Norman, Barry	Compton, Fay	Nureyev, Rudolf
O'Toole, Peter	Corbett, Harry	Olivier, Laurence, Lord
Parker, Eleanor	Denison, Michael	Pavlova, Anna
Porter, Eric	Dotrice, Michelle	Pickles, Wilfred
Quayle, Sir Anthony		

7

Plummer, Christopher
Portman, Eric
Quilley, Denis
Rantzen, Esther
Redford, Robert
Roberts, Rachel
Robeson, Paul
Rushton, William
Russell, Jane
Secombe, Sir Harry
Sellers, Peter
Shearer, Moira
Sherrin, Ned
Simmons, Jean
Stewart, James
Swanson, Gloria
Ustinov, Sir Peter
Vaughan, Frankie
Weldon, Sir Huw
Whicker, Alan
Withers, Googie

8

Anderson, Jean
Ashcroft, Dame Peggy
Baddeley, Hermione
Bancroft, Anne
Brambell, Wilfred
Buchanan, Jack
Bygraves, Max
Channing, Carol
Chisholm, George
Crawford, Joan
Crawford, Michael

8

De la Tour, Frances
Dietrich, Marlene
Dimbleby, David
Dimbleby, Richard
Eastwood, Clint
Flanagan, Bud
Flanders, Michael
Fletcher, Cyril
Grenfell, Joyce
Guinness, Sir Alec
Harrison, Sir Rex
Holloway, Stanley
Lansbury, Angela
Laughton, Charles
Lawrence, Gertrude
Liberace
Leighton, Margaret
Lockwood, Margaret
Matthews, Dame Jessie
Milligan, Spike
Pickford, Mary
Redgrave, Corin
Redgrave, Lynn
Redgrave, Sir Michael
Redgrave, Vanessa
Robinson, Edward G.
Robinson, Eric
Scofield, Paul
Whitelaw, Billie
Williams, Andy
Williams, Kenneth
Williams, Michael
Woodward, Edward
Ziegfeld, Florenz

9

Barkworth, Peter
Barrymore, Ethel
Barrymore, John
Barrymore, Lionel
Barrymore, Michael
Bernhardt, Sarah
Brannigan, Owen
Chevalier, Maurice
Courtenay, Tom
Dankworth, John
Engelmann, Franklin
Fairbanks, Douglas
Grisewood, Freddy
Hampshire, Susan
Hitchcock, Alfred
Humphries, Barry
Monkhouse, Bob
Morecambe, Eric
Nicholson, Jack
Pleasence, Donald
Plowright, Joan
Streisand, Barbra
Thorndike, Dame Sybil

10

D'Oyly Carte, Richard
Littlewood, Joan
Michelmore, Cliff
Muggeridge, Malcolm
Richardson, Sir Ralph

11

Hammerstein, Oscar

12

Attenborough, Sir David
Attenborough, Sir Richard
Marx Brothers

14

Warner Brothers

Theatrical terms

3	4	5	6
act	idol	debut	ballet
arc	joke	drama	barker
bow	lead	dry up	batten
box	line	enact	big top
cue	live	extra	boards
dub	mask	farce	busker
gag	mike	flies	camera
ham	mime	float	chorus
hit	mute	focus	cinema
pit	part	foyer	circle
rep	play	gauze	circus
run	prop	glory	comedy
set	role	halls	critic
wig	show	heavy	dancer
	skit	hoist	dimmer
4	slap	house	direct
bill	solo	inset	dubbed
book	spot	lines	effect
boom	star	lyric	encore
busk	tabs	mimer	finale
cast	take	mimic	lights
clap	team	on cue	make-up
clip	turn	opera	masque
crew	wing	oscar	motley
dais		props	on tour
diva	**5**	revue	one act
drag	above	scene	parody
drop	actor	slips	patron
duet	ad lib	sound	patter
emmy	agent	stage	player
epic	apron	stall	podium
exit	arena	stunt	poster
flat	aside	wings	prompt
flop	baton		puppet
foil	below	**6**	recite
gala	break	acting	repeat
gods	cloth	action	ring-up
grid	clown	appear	satire
hero	comic	backer	script

6	7	7	8
season	dancing	tableau	magician
singer	danseur	theatre	male lead
sitcom	deadpan	tragedy	off stage
sketch	dress up	trilogy	operatic
speech	dubbing	trouper	operetta
stalls	gallery	upstage	overture
stooge	heroine	variety	platform
studio	juggler		playbill
talent	leotard	8	playgoer
ticket	long run	applause	premiere
timing	manager	artistry	producer
tinsel	matinée	audience	prologue
troupe	mimicry	audition	prompter
walk-on	musical	backdrop	rehearse
warm-up	mystery	blackout	scenario
writer	on stage	chairman	set piece
	overact	clapping	side show
7	pageant	clowning	smash hit
acrobat	perform	comedian	stagebox
actress	pierrot	conjurer	star turn
amateur	players	conjuror	straight
balcony	playing	danseuse	stripper
benefit	pop star	designer	subtitle
bit-part	portray	dialogue	thespian
booking	present	director	third act
buffoon	produce	disguise	typecast
cabaret	quartet	dramatic	wigmaker
call boy	recital	duologue	
cartoon	re-enact	entrance	9
casting	resting	epilogue	acoustics
cat-call	revival	exit line	animation
catwalk	rostrum	fauteuil	announcer
charade	scenery	first act	arabesque
circuit	show biz	funny man	backcloth
close-up	showman	ham actor	backstage
company	sponsor	interval	ballerina
compere	stadium	juggling	bandstand
concert	staging	libretto	bit-player
console	stand-in	lighting	box office
costume	stardom	live show	burlesque
curtain	starlet	location	cameraman

9	9	10	10
character	programme	drag artist	theatrical
cinematic	projector	drama group	torch dance
cloakroom	provinces	first night	understudy
conjuring	publicity	floodlight	variety act
costumier	punch line	footlights	vaudeville
double act	quartette	get the bird	walk-on part
downstage	reflector	histrionic	
dramatics	rehearsal	impresario	11
dramatize	repertory	intermezzo	accompanist
dramatist	represent	in the wings	all-star cast
drop scene	royalties	junior lead	art director
entertain	second act	leading man	black comedy
first lead	slapstick	librettist	circus rider
flashback	soap opera	marionette	cliff-hanger
floorshow	soliloquy	masquerade	comedy drama
folk dance	soubrette	microphone	concert hall
footlight	spectacle	on location	credit title
full house	spotlight	opera house	curtain call
gala night	stage crew	performing	dance troupe
guest star	stage door	play acting	drama critic
hand props	stagehand	playwright	drama school
harlequin	stage left	prima donna	dramatic art
impromptu	stage name	production	dress circle
interlude	stage play	properties	electrician
limelight	stage prop	proscenium	entertainer
love scene	take a part	puppet show	fire curtain
major role	tap dancer	rave notice	folk dancing
melodrama	the boards	recitation	greasepaint
minor role	title role	repertoire	histrionics
monologue	tragedian	ringmaster	house lights
music hall		stage cloth	illusionist
noises off	10	stagecraft	impersonate
open stage	appearance	stage right	leading lady
orchestra	auditorium	star player	light comedy
pantomine	chorus girl	strip light	matinée idol
performer	comedienne	striptease	miracle play
photoplay	comic opera	substitute	opera singer
pirouette	commercial	sword dance	passion play
pit stalls	continuity	tap dancing	performance
playhouse	crowd scene	tear jerker	scene change
portrayal	denouement	theatre box	set designer

11
set the scene
showmanship
show stopper
sound effect
spectacular
stage design
stage effect
stage fright
stage-keeper
stage player
stage school
stage struck
star billing
star quality
star studded
strobe light
switchboard
talent scout
theatregoer
theatreland
theatricals
thespian art
tragedienne
tragicomedy
unrehearsed
upper circle

11
variety show
word perfect

12
Academy award
actor-manager
amphitheatre
ballet dancer
clapperboard
choreography
concert party
dressing room
exotic dancer
extravaganza
first nighter
front-of-house
impersonator
juvenile lead
light console
make-up artist
melodramatic
minstrel show
modern ballet
name in lights
natural break
opera glasses
orchestra pit
principal boy

12
Punch and Judy
puppet player
scene painter
scene shifter
scene stealer
screenwriter
scriptwriter
show business
song and dance
sound effects
stage manager
stage setting
stage whisper
starring role
steal the show
straight part
top of the bill

13
ballet dancing
burlesque show
contortionist
curtain raiser
emergency exit
entertainment
improvisation
musical comedy
platform stage

13
projectionist
Russian ballet
safety curtain
sleight of hand
sound engineer
stage director
stage lighting
studio manager
theatre school
ventriloquist
word rehearsal

14
ballet mistress
continuity girl
courtroom drama
dancing academy
domestic comedy
dramatic critic
dress rehearsal
prima ballerina
property master
proscenium arch
revolving stage
sound projector
stage direction
touring company
variety theatre

15
acrobatic troupe
classical ballet
incidental music
quick-change room
school of dancing
situation comedy
stage-door keeper
stage properties

15
strolling player
tightrope walker

16
dramatis personae
drawing-room drama
performing rights

16
touring companies
wardrobe mistress

18
female impersonator
technical rehearsal

21
assistant stage manager

Time

2	4	6	6
a.m.	year	autumn	ultimo
p.m.	yore	before	vesper
	yule	betime	weekly
3		decade	whilst
age	5	Easter	winter
ago	after	faster	yearly
B.S.T.	again	Friday	
day	April	future	7
eon	clock	heyday	almanac
era	cycle	hourly	already
G.M.T.	daily	Julian	ancient
May	dated	Lammas	bedtime
now	early	lately	betimes
oft	epoch	latest	by and by
	first	May Day	century
4	jiffy	memory	daytime
ages	later	midday	dog days
date	March	minute	earlier
dawn	month	modern	epochal
ever	never	moment	equinox
fast	night	Monday	eternal
hour	of old	morrow	evening
ides	often	o'clock	fast day
July	quick	off day	half-day
June	reign	pay day	harvest
last	spell	period	high day
late	teens	record	holiday
Lent	times	rhythm	holy day
morn	today	season	instant
noon	trice	second	interim
once	until	seldom	January
slow	watch	slower	jubilee
soon	while	slowly	Lady Day
span		spring	lay days
term	6	summer	mail day
tick	always	Sunday	mid Lent
time	annual	sunset	midweek
when	August	timely	monthly

7	8	8	9
morning	February	seed time	lean years
new moon	festival	slow time	Low Sunday
noonday	full moon	sometime	lunch-time
October	forenoon	speedily	market day
proximo	formerly	Stone Age	Martinmas
quarter	futurist	Thursday	midsummer
quicker	Georgian	timeless	midwinter
quickly	gloaming	tomorrow	nightfall
Ramadan	half-past	twilight	night time
rent day	half-term	untimely	overnight
sabbath	half-time	up-to-date	peacetime
sundial	half-year	vacation	postponed
sundown	high noon	whenever	premature
sunrise	high tide	Yuletide	presently
tea-time	hogmanay	zero hour	quarterly
tonight	holidays		right away
Tuesday	Holy Week	9	September
undated	interval	aforetime	sexennial
wartime	Jacobean	afternoon	sometimes
weekday	latterly	afterward	speech day
weekend	leap year	bimonthly	timepiece
workday	Lord's Day	Boxing Day	timetable
	mealtime	Candlemas	Victorian
8	midnight	centenary	Wednesday
annually	minutely	Christmas	yesterday
biennial	natal day	continual	
birthday	noontide	Easter Day	10
bi-weekly	noon time	Edwardian	aftertimes
calendar	November	Ember Days	afterwards
carnival	nowadays	Ember Week	beforehand
Caroline	oft times	eternally	before time
day by day	old style	feast days	behind time
daybreak	past time	fortnight	biennially
dead slow	periodic	Gregorian	centennial
December	postpone	Halloween	continuous
doomsday	punctual	hard times	days of yore
duration	quickest	hereafter	dinner-time
earliest	Ramadhan	honeymoon	Easter term
eternity	right now	hourglass	Ember weeks
eventide	Saturday	immediate	Good Friday
every day	seasonal	instantly	half-yearly

10	**10**	**11**	**12**
lunar cycle	Whit Sunday	jubilee year	bethrothal day
lunar month	wintertime	Judgment Day	bicentennial
Michaelmas	working day	leisure time	Christmas Day
Middle Ages		New Year's Day	Christmas Eve
occasional	**11**	New Year's Eve	continuously
olden times	All Fools' Day	Passion week	Easter Sunday
Palm Sunday	All Souls' Day	prehistoric	Judgement Day
quarter-day	anniversary	prematurely	luncheon-time
record time	bank holiday	present time	Midsummer Day
seasonable	behind times	punctuality	Midsummer Eve
septennial	bicentenary	quartz clock	occasionally
Sexagesima	Carolingian	ruby wedding	post meridiem
Shrovetide	closing time	synchronise	postponement
springtime	continually	synchronize	Quadragesima
summer term	Elizabethan	thenceforth	quinquennial
summertime	everlasting	Tudor period	red letter day
thereafter	fortnightly	ultramodern	Rogation Days
time enough	half-holiday	Whitsuntide	standard time
timekeeper	harvest home		synchronised
time signal	harvest time	**12**	synchronized
unpunctual	holiday time	afterthought	tricentenary
watch night	immediately	All Saints' Day	Twelfth Night
wedding day	interregnum	Ash Wednesday	

13	**13**	**14**
April Fools' Day	Michaelmas Day	Maundy Thursday
breakfast time	once upon a time	Michaelmas term
calendar month	Shrove Tuesday	
Christmastide	silver wedding	**15**
Christmastime	thenceforward	early closing day
Edwardian days	Trinity Sunday	prehistoric ages
everlastingly		St Valentine's Day
golden jubilee	**14**	synchronisation
golden wedding	behind the times	synchronization
Gregorian year	early Victorian	
holiday season		

Tools and machines

3	4	5	6
awl	plow	gauge	barrow
axe	rake	gavel	bender
bit	rasp	gouge	blower
die	rule	hoist	bodkin
fan	sock	incus	borcer
gad	spud	jacks	bow-saw
gin	tool	jemmy	brayer
hod	trug	jimmy	broach
hoe	vice	knife	burton
jig	whim	lathe	chaser
loy		level	chisel
saw	**5**	lever	colter
zax	anvil	mower	crevet
	auger	parer	cruset
4	beele	plane	dibber
adze	bench	plumb	dibble
bill	besom	preen	doffer
bore	betty	prise	dredge
brog	bevel	prong	driver
burr	blade	punch	fanner
cart	borer	quern	faucet
celt	brace	quoin	ferret
crab	burin	ratch	flange
file	chuck	razor	folder
fork	churn	sarse	gimlet
frow	clamp	screw	graver
gage	clams	spade	hackle
hink	clasp	spike	hammer
hook	cleat	spill	harrow
jack	cramp	swage	jagger
last	crane	temse	jigger
loom	croom	tommy	jig saw
mall	croze	tongs	ladder
maul	cupel	tromp	mallet
mule	dolly	trone	mortar
nail	drill	wedge	muller
pick	flail	winch	oliver
pike	forge		pallet

6	7	7	8
pencil	capstan	scalpel	dowel bit
pestle	catling	scauper	drill bow
pitsaw	cautery	scraper	edge tool
planer	chamfer	screwer	filatory
pliers	chip-axe	scriber	fire kiln
plough	chopper	seed lop	flame gun
pontee	cleaver	spaddle	flax comb
pooler	couloir	spanner	gavelock
rammer	coulter	spittle	gee cramp
rasper	crampon	sprayer	handloom
reaper	crisper	strocal	handmill
riddle	crowbar	tenoner	hand vice
ripsaw	cuvette	thimble	hay knife
rubber	derrick	trestle	horse hoe
sander	diamond	triblet	lapstone
saw-set	dog-belt	T-square	lead mill
screen	drudger	twibill	mitre box
scythe	fistuca	twister	molegrip
segger	forceps	whip-saw	muck rake
shears	fretsaw	whittle	nut screw
shovel	fruggin	woolder	oilstone
sickle	gradine		paint pad
sifter	grainer	8	panel saw
skewer	grapnel	bark mill	picklock
sledge	grub axe	bar shear	pinchers
slicer	hacksaw	beakiron	plumb bob
square	handsaw	bench peg	polisher
stiddy	hatchet	bill hook	power saw
stithy	hay fork	bistoury	prong-hoe
strike	jointer	bloomary	puncheon
tackle	mandrel	blowlamp	reap hook
tenter	mattock	blowpipe	saw wrest
trepan	nippers	boathook	scissors
trowel	nut hook	bowdrill	scuffler
tubber	pickaxe	bull nose	slate axe
turrel	piercer	butteris	stiletto
wimble	pincers	calipers	strickle
wrench	plummet	canthook	tenon saw
	pole axe	chopness	throstle
7	pounder	crow mill	tooth key
boaster	pricker	crucible	tweezers
brad-saw	salt pan	die stock	twist bit

8	9	10	11
watercan	lawnmower	mould board	monkey block
water ram	nail punch	nail drawer	paint roller
weed hook	nut wrench	paintbrush	ploughshare
windlass	pitch fork	perforator	pruning hook
windmill	plane iron	pipe wrench	rabbet plane
	planisher	safety lamp	reaping hook
9	plumbline	screw press	sawing stool
belt punch	plumbrule	sleek stone	screwdriver
bench hook	screwjack	snowplough	single-edged
bolt auger	scribe awl	steam press	skim coulter
boot crimp	shearlegs	stepladder	snatch block
callipers	sheep hook	tenterhook	spirit level
canker bit	steelyard	thumbscrew	squaring rod
can opener	sugar mill	thumbstall	steam hammer
centre bit	tin opener	tilt hammer	stone hammer
compasses	try square	trip hammer	straw cutter
corkscrew	turf spade	turf cutter	strike block
cotton gin	turn bench	turnbuckle	stubble rake
cramp iron	turnscrew	watercrane	sward cutter
curry comb	watermill	watergauge	swing-plough
cutter bar		waterlevel	tape-measure
dog clutch	10	wheel brace	turfing iron
draw knife	bush harrow		two-foot rule
draw plate	claspknife	11	warping hook
excavator	clawhammer	brace and bit	warping post
eyeleteer	cold chisel	breast drill	weeding fork
fillister	crane's bill	chaff cutter	weeding hook
fining pot	cultivator	chain blocks	weeding rhim
fork chuck	dray plough	chain wrench	wheelbarrow
gas pliers	drift bolts	cheese press	
hammer axe	drillpress	crazing mill	12
handbrace	drillstock	crisping pin	barking irons
handscrew	emery wheel	crosscut saw	belt adjuster
handspike	fire engine	drill barrow	branding iron
holing axe	firing iron	drill harrow	breast plough
hummeller	grindstone	drill plough	caulking tool
implement	instrument	fanning mill	counter gauge
jack-knife	masonry bit	grubbing hoe	cradle scythe
jack plane	masticator	helvehammer	cramping iron
jack screw	mitre block	jagging iron	crimping iron
lace frame	motor mower	machine tool	crisping iron

12	12	14
curling tongs	water bellows	blowing machine
drill grubber	weeding tongs	carding machine
driving shaft		draining engine
driving wheel	13	draining plough
emery grinder	butcher's broom	pneumatic drill
flour dresser	chopping block	reaping machine
glass furnace	chopping knife	smoothing plane
hydraulic ram	cylinder press	swingling knife
mandrel lathe	electric drill	three-metre rule
marline spike	grappling iron	thrusting screw
monkey wrench	hydraulic jack	weeding forceps
pruning knife	mowing machine	
pulley blocks	packing needle	15
running block	scribing block	carpenter's bench
scribing iron	sewing machine	crimping machine
sledge hammer	soldering bolt	dredging machine
sliding bevel	soldering iron	drilling machine
socket chisel	sowing machine	entrenching tool
stone breaker	spinning jenny	envelope machine
straight-edge	spinning wheel	pestle and mortar
swingle knife	stocking frame	pump screwdriver
touch needles	subsoil plough	weighing machine
trench plough	three-foot rule	
turfing spade	two-hole pliers	
turning lathe	weeding chisel	

Towns and cities

England

3	4	4	5
Ely	Clun	Looe	Acton
Eye	Deal	Lydd	Alton
Rye	Diss	Ross	Bacup
Wem	Eton	Ryde	Blyth
	Holt	Shap	Bourn
4	Hove	Ware	Calne
Bath	Hull	Wark	Chard
Bray	Hyde	Yarm	Cheam
Bude	Ince	York	Colne
Bury	Leek		Cowes

5	6	6	6
Crewe	Barnet	London	Thorne
Derby	Barrow	Ludlow	Totnes
Dover	Barton	Lynton	Walton
Egham	Batley	Lytham	Watton
Epsom	Battle	Maldon	Weston
Filey	Bawtry	Malton	Whitby
Fowey	Bedale	Marlow	Widnes
Frome	Belper	Masham	Wigton
Goole	Bodmin	Morley	Wilton
Hawes	Bognor	Naseby	Witham
Hedon	Bolton	Nelson	Witney
Hurst	Bootle	Neston	Wooler
Hythe	Boston	Newark	Yeovil
Leeds	Bruton	Newent	
Leigh	Bungay	Newlyn	7
Lewes	Burton	Newton	Alnwick
Louth	Buxton	Norham	Andover
Luton	Castor	Oakham	Appleby
March	Cobham	Oldham	Arundel
Olney	Cromer	Ormsby	Ashford
Otley	Darwen	Ossett	Aylsham
Poole	Dudley	Oundle	Bampton
Reeth	Durham	Oxford	Banbury
Ripon	Ealing	Penryn	Barking
Risca	Eccles	Pewsey	Beccles
Rugby	Epping	Putney	Bedford
Sarum	Exeter	Ramsey	Belford
Selby	Goring	Redcar	Berwick
Stoke	Hanley	Ripley	Bewdley
Stone	Harlow	Romney	Bexhill
Tebay	Harrow	Romsey	Bickley
Thame	Havant	St Ives	Bilston
Tring	Henley	Seaham	Bourton
Truro	Hexham	Seaton	Bowfell
Wells	Howden	Selsey	Brandon
Wigan	Ilford	Settle	Bristol
	Ilkley	Snaith	Brixham
6	Ilsley	Strood	Bromley
Alford	Jarrow	Stroud	Burnham
Alston	Kendal	Sutton	Burnley
Ashton	Leyton	Thirsk	Burslem

7	7	7	8
Caistor	Hornsey	Saltash	Abingdon
Catford	Horsham	Sandown	Alfreton
Cawston	Ipswich	Sazelby	Alnmouth
Charing	Ixworth	Seaford	Amesbury
Chatham	Keswick	Shifnal	Ampthill
Cheadle	Kington	Shipton	Axbridge
Cheddar	Lancing	Silloth	Aycliffe
Chesham	Langton	Skipton	Bakewell
Chester	Ledbury	Spilsby	Barnsley
Chorley	Leyburn	Staines	Berkeley
Clacton	Lincoln	Stilton	Beverley
Clifton	Malvern	Sudbury	Bicester
Crawley	Margate	Sunbury	Bideford
Croydon	Matlock	Swanage	Bolsover
Darsley	Molesey	Swindon	Brackley
Datchet	Moreton	Swinton	Bradford
Dawlish	Morpeth	Taunton	Brampton
Devizes	Mossley	Telford	Bridport
Dorking	Newbury	Tenbury	Brighton
Douglas	Newport	Tetbury	Bromyard
Dunster	Newquay	Thaxted	Broseley
Elstree	Norwich	Tilbury	Camborne
Enfield	Oldbury	Torquay	Carlisle
Everton	Overton	Twyford	Caterham
Evesham	Padstow	Ventnor	Chertsey
Exmouth	Penrith	Walsall	Clevedon
Fareham	Poulton	Waltham	Clovelly
Farnham	Prescot	Wantage	Coventry
Feltham	Preston	Wareham	Crediton
Glossop	Rainham	Warwick	Daventry
Gosport	Reading	Watchet	Debenham
Grimsby	Redhill	Watford	Dedworth
Halifax	Redruth	Weobley	Deptford
Hampton	Reigate	Wickwar	Dewsbury
Harwich	Retford	Windsor	Egremont
Haworth	Romford	Winslow	Eversley
Helston	Rossall	Winster	Fakenham
Heywood	Royston	Wisbech	Falmouth
Hitchin	Rugeley	Worksop	Foulness
Honiton	Runcorn		Grantham
Hornsea	St Neots		Grantown
	Salford		

8	8	9	9
Hadleigh	St Albans	Aldeburgh	Gateshead
Hailsham	St Helens	Aldershot	Godalming
Halstead	Saltburn	Allendale	Gravesend
Hastings	Sandgate	Alresford	Greenwich
Hatfield	Sandwich	Ambleside	Grinstead
Helmsley	Sedbergh	Ashbourne	Guildford
Hereford	Shanklin	Ashburton	Harrogate
Herne Bay	Shelford	Avonmouth	Haslemere
Hertford	Shipston	Aylesbury	Haverhill
Hinckley	Sidmouth	Blackburn	Hawkhurst
Holbeach	Skegness	Blackpool	Holmfirth
Hunmanby	Sleaford	Blandford	Ilchester
Ilkeston	Southend	Blisworth	Immingham
Keighley	Spalding	Bracknell	Kettering
Kingston	Stafford	Braintree	King's Lynn
Lavenham	Stamford	Brentford	Kingswear
Lechlade	Stanhope	Brentwood	Lambourne
Liskeard	Stanwell	Brighouse	Lancaster
Longtown	Stockton	Broughton	Leicester
Lynmouth	Stratton	Cambridge	Lichfield
Maryport	Surbiton	Carnforth	Liverpool
Midhurst	Swaffham	Castleton	Longridge
Minehead	Tamworth	Chesilton	Lowestoft
Nantwich	Thetford	Chingford	Lyme Regis
Newhaven	Thornaby	Clitheroe	Lymington
Nuneaton	Tiverton	Congleton	Maidstone
Ormskirk	Tunstall	Cranbrook	Mansfield
Oswestry	Uckfield	Crewkerne	Middleton
Penzance	Uxbridge	Cricklade	Newcastle
Pershore	Wallasey	Cuckfield	Newmarket
Peterlee	Wallsend	Dartmouth	New Romney
Petworth	Wanstead	Devonport	Northwich
Pevensey	Westbury	Doncaster	Otterburn
Plaistow	Wetheral	Donington	Pembridge
Plymouth	Wetherby	Droitwich	Penistone
Ramsgate	Weymouth	Dronfield	Penkridge
Redditch	Woodford	Dungeness	Penyghent
Richmond	Woolwich	Dunstable	Pickering
Ringwood	Worthing	Ellesmere	Rochester
Rochdale	Yarmouth	Faversham	Rotherham
Rothbury		Fleetwood	St Austell
			Salisbury

9	10	10	10
Saltfleet	Altrincham	Kenilworth	Warminster
Sevenoaks	Barnstaple	Kingsclere	Warrington
Sheerness	Beaminster	Kirkoswald	Washington
Sheffield	Bedlington	Launceston	Wednesbury
Sherborne	Bellingham	Leamington	Wellington
Smethwick	Billericay	Leominster	Westward Ho
Southgate	Birkenhead	Littleport	Whitchurch
Southport	Birmingham	Maidenhead	Whitehaven
Southwell	Bridgnorth	Malmesbury	Whitstable
Southwold	Bridgwater	Manchester	Whittlesey
Starcross	Bromsgrove	Mexborough	Willenhall
Stevenage	Broxbourne	Micheldean	Winchelsea
Stockport	Buckingham	Middlewich	Winchester
Stokesley	Canterbury	Mildenhall	Windermere
Stourport	Carshalton	Nailsworth	Windlesham
Stratford	Chelmsford	Nottingham	Wirksworth
Tarporley	Cheltenham	Okehampton	Withernsea
Tavistock	Chichester	Pangbourne	Woodbridge
Tenterden	Chippenham	Patrington	Workington
Todmorden	Chulmleigh	Peacehaven	
Tonbridge	Coggeshall	Pontefract	11
Towcester	Colchester	Portishead	Basingstoke
Tynemouth	Cullompton	Portsmouth	Berkhamsted
Ulverston	Darlington	Potter's Bar	Bognor Regis
Upminster	Dorchester	Ravenglass	Bournemouth
Uppingham	Dukinfield	Rockingham	Bridlington
Uttoxeter	Eastbourne	St Leonards	Buntingford
Wainfleet	Farningham	Saxmundham	Cleethorpes
Wakefield	Folkestone	Shepperton	Cockermouth
Warkworth	Freshwater	Sheringham	East Retford
Weybridge	Gillingham	Shrewsbury	Glastonbury
Whernside	Gloucester	Stalbridge	Great Marlow
Wimbledon	Halesworth	Stowmarket	Guisborough
Wincanton	Hartlepool	Sunderland	Haltwhistle
Wokingham	Haslingdon	Teddington	Hampton Wick
Woodstock	Heathfield	Teignmouth	Hatherleigh
Worcester	Horncastle	Tewkesbury	High Wycombe
Wymondham	Hornchurch	Thamesmead	Ingatestone
	Hungerford	Torrington	Leytonstone
10	Hunstanton	Trowbridge	Littlestone
Accrington	Huntingdon	Twickenham	Lostwithiel
Aldborough	Ilfracombe	Walsingham	Ludgershall

11
Lutterworth
Mablethorpe
Manningtree
Market Rasen
Marlborough
Much Wenlock
New Brighton
Newton Abbot
Northampton
Petersfield
Pocklington
Rawtenstall
St Margarets
Scarborough
Shaftesbury
Southampton
South Molten
Stalybridge
Stourbridge
Tattershall
Wallingford

14
Berwick-on-Tweed
Bishop Auckland
Bishop's Waltham
Chipping Barnet
Chipping Norton
Hemel Hempstead
Kirkby Lonsdale
Market Bosworth
Mortimer's Cross
Stockton-on-Tees

11
Walthamstow
Westminster
Whitechurch
Woodhall Spa

12
Attleborough
Bexhill-on-Sea
Castle Rising
Chesterfield
Christchurch
Gainsborough
Great Grimsby
Great Malvern
Huddersfield
Ingleborough
Long Stratton
Loughborough
Macclesfield

14
Stony Stratford
Sutton Courtney
Tunbridge Wells
Wellingborough
West Hartlepool

15
Ashton-under-Lyne
Barrow-in-Furness
Burnham-on-Crouch

12
Milton Keynes
Morecambe Bay
North Berwick
North Shields
North Walsham
Peterborough
Shoeburyness
Shottesbrook
South Shields
Stoke-on-Trent

13
Barnard Castle
Bishop's Castle
Boroughbridge
Brightlingsea
Burton-on-Trent
Bury St Edmunds
Chipping Ongar

13
Finchampstead
Godmanchester
Great Yarmouth
Higham Ferrers
Kidderminster
Kirkby Stephen
Knaresborough
Littlehampton
Lytham St Annes
Market Deeping
Market Drayton
Melcombe Regis
Melton Mowbray
Middlesbrough
Northallerton
Saffron Walden
Shepton Mallet
Wolverhampton
Wootton Basset

15
Castle Donington
Leighton Buzzard
Newcastle-on-Tyne
St Leonards-on-sea
Stratford-on-Avon
Sutton Coldfield
Weston-super-Mare

16
Bishop's Stortford
Welwyn Garden City

Republic of Ireland

4
Bray
Cobh
Cork

5
Balla
Boyle
Clare
Kells
Sligo

6
Arklow
Bantry
Carlow
Cashel
Dublin

6
Galway
Tralee

7
Athlone
Blarney

7	8	9	10
Clonmel	Clontarf	Connemara	Shillelagh
Dundalk	Drogheda	Killarney	
Kildare	Kilkenny	Roscommon	11
Shannon	Limerick	Tipperary	Ballymurphy
Wexford	Listowel	Waterford	
Wicklow	Maynouth		
Youghal	Rathdrum		

Northern Ireland

4	7	9	11
Muff	Clogher	Kircubbin	Carrickmore
	Dervock	Moneymore	Crossmaglen
5	Dundrum	Newcastle	Downpatrick
Derry	Dunmore	Portadown	Draperstown
Doagh	Fintona	Rasharkin	Enniskillen
Glynn	Gilford	Rostrevor	Letterkenny
Keady	Glenarm	Tovermore	Londonderry
Larne	Lifford		Magherafelt
Lough	Lisburn	10	Portglenone
Newry		Ballybofir	Randalstown
Omagh	8	Ballyclare	Rathfryland
Toome	Ahoghill	Ballyhaise	
	Ballybay	Ballymoney	12
6	Dungiven	Ballyroney	Castleblaney
Antrim	Hilltown	Castlederg	Castle Dawson
Augher	Portrush	Castlefinn	Castlewellen
Belcoo	Strabane	Cushenhall	Five Mile Town
Beragh	Trillick	Donaghadel	Hillsborough
Callan		Glengariff	Inishtrahull
Carney	9	Kilconnell	Slieve Donard
Comber	Ballintra	Markethill	Stewartstown
Lurgan	Ballymena	Portaferry	
Raphoe	Ballgmore	Saintfield	13
Shrule	Banbridge	Strangford	Brookeborough
	Belturbet	Stranorlar	Carrickfergus
7	Bushmills	Tangeragee	Derrygonnelly
Belfast	Coleraine		
Belleek	Cookstown	11	14
Caledon	Dungannon	Ballycastle	Newtown Stewart
Carrick	Glaslough	Ballygawley	
	Killybegs		

Scotland

3	5	6	7
Ayr	Govan	Forfar	Cargill
Uig	Insch	Forres	Carluke
	Islay	Girvan	Crathie
4	Keiss	Glamis	Culross
Alva	Keith	Hawick	Cumnock
Barr	Kelso	Huntly	Denholm
Duns	Lairg	Irvine	Douglas
Elie	Largo	Killin	Dunkeld
Kirn	Leith	Kilmun	Dunning
Luss	Nairn	Lanark	Evanton
Nigg	Perth	Lauder	Fairlie
Oban	Salen	Leslie	Falkirk
Reay	Troon	Linton	Galston
Rona		Lochee	Gifford
Stow	6	Meigle	Glasgow
Wick	Aboyne	Moffat	Glencoe
	Alford	Pladda	Golspie
5	Barvas	Reston	Gourock
Alloa	Beauly	Rhynie	Granton
Annan	Bervie	Rosyth	Guthrie
Appin	Biggar	Rothes	Halkirk
Avoch	Bo'ness	Shotts	Kenmore
Ayton	Buckie	Thurso	Kessock
Banff	Carron	Tongue	Kilmory
Beith	Cawdor	Wishaw	Kilmuir
Brora	Comrie	Yarrow	Kilsyth
Bunaw	Crieff		Kinross
Busby	Cullen	7	Kintore
Ceres	Culter	Airdrie	Lamlash
Clova	Dollar	Balfron	Larbert
Clune	Drymen	Balloch	Lybster
Crail	Dunbar	Banavie	Macduff
Cupar	Dundee	Bowmore	Maybole
Denny	Dunlop	Braemar	Meldrum
Downe	Dunnet	Brechin	Melrose
Elgin	Dunoon	Brodick	Melvich
Ellon	Dysart	Canobie	Methven
Errol	Edzell	Cantyre	Monikie
Fyvie	Findon	Carbost	Muthill

7	8	8	9
Newport	Dalkeith	Pooltiel	Lochnagar
Paisley	Dalmally	Quiraing	Lockerbie
Peebles	Dingwall	Rothesay	Logierait
Polmont	Dirleton	St Fergus	Mauchline
Poolewe	Dufftown	Stirling	Milngavie
Portree	Dumfries	Strichen	Peterhead
Portsoy	Dunbeath	Talisker	Pitlochry
Renfrew	Dunblane	Traquair	Port Ellen
Saddell	Dunscore	Ullapool	Prestwick
Sarclet	Earlston	Whithorn	Riccarton
Scourie	Eyemouth	Woodside	Ronaldsay
Selkirk	Findhorn		Rothiemay
Stanley	Fortrose	9	St Andrews
Strathy	Glenluce	Aberfeldy	St Fillans
Tarbert	Greenlaw	Aberfoyle	Saltcoats
Tarland	Greenock	Ardrossan	Shieldaig
Tayport	Hamilton	Berridale	Slamannan
Tranent	Inverary	Bettyhill	Stewarton
Tundrum	Inverury	Blacklarg	Stranraer
Turriff	Jeantown	Bracadale	Strathdon
Ullster	Jedburgh	Braeriach	Strontian
Yetholm	Kilbride	Broadford	Thornhill
	Kilniver	Broughton	Tobermory
8	Kilrenny	Buckhaven	Tomintoul
Aberdeen	Kinghorn	Cairntoul	
Aberlady	Kirkwall	Callander	10
Abington	Langholm	Carstairs	Abbotsford
Arbroath	Latheron	Dumbarton	Achnasheen
Armadale	Leuchars	Edinburgh	Anstruther
Arrochar	Loanhead	Ferintosh	Applecross
Auldearn	Markinch	Fochabers	Ardrishaig
Ballater	Marykirk	Inchkeith	Auchinleck
Banchory	Moniaive	Inveraray	Ballantrae
Barrhill	Montrose	Inverness	Blackadder
Beattock	Monymusk	Johnstone	Carnoustie
Blantyre	Muirkirk	Kildrummy	Carsphairn
Burghead	Neilston	Kingussie	Castletown
Canisbay	Newburgh	Kirkcaldy	Coatbridge
Carnwath	Newmilns	Leadhills	Coldingham
Creetown	Penicuik	Lochgelly	Coldstream
Cromarty	Pitsligo	Lochinvar	Dalbeattie

10	10	11	12
Drumlithie	Motherwell	Campbeltown	Auchterarder
East Linton	Pittenween	Charlestown	Ballachulish
Galashiels	Portobello	Cumbernauld	East Kilbride
Glenrothes	Rutherglen	Drummelzier	Garelochhead
Johnshaven	Stonehaven	Ecclefechan	Innerleithen
Kilcreggan	Stonehouse	Fettercairn	Lawrencekirk
Killenaule	Stoneykirk	Fort William	Portmahomack
Kilmainham	Strathaven	Fraserburgh	Strathpeffer
Kilmalcolm	Strathearn	Helensburgh	Tillicoultry
Kilwinning	Strathmore	Invergordon	
Kincardine	Tweedmouth	Kirmichael	13
Kirkmaiden	West Calder	Lossiemouth	Auchtermuchty
Kirkoswald	Wilsontown	Maxwelltown	Castle Douglas
Kirriemuir		Musselburgh	Cockburnspath
Lennoxtown	11	Port Glasgow	Dalmellington
Lesmahagow	Aberchirder	Port Patrick	Inverkeithing
Linlithgow	Balquhidder	Prestonpans	Inverkeithnie
Livingston	Bannockburn	Pultneytown	Kirkcudbright
Milnathort	Blairgowrie	Strathblane	Kirkintilloch
			Newton Stewart
			Rothiemurchus

Wales

3	6	7	8
Usk	Almwch	Swansea	Kidwelly
	Bangor	Wrexham	Knighton
4	Brecon		Lampeter
Bala	Builth	8	Llanelli
Holt	Conway	Aberavon	Llanrwst
Mold	Ruabon	Aberdare	Monmouth
Pyle	Ruthin	Abergele	Pembroke
Rhyl		Barmouth	Pwllheli
	7	Bridgend	Rhayader
5	Carbury	Caerleon	Skerries
Chirk	Cardiff	Cardigan	Skifness
Flint	Cwmbran	Chepstow	Talgarth
Neath	Denbigh	Dolgelly	Tredegar
Nevin	Maesteg	Ebbw Vale	Tregaron
Tenby	Newport	Hawarden	
Towyn	Newtown	Holyhead	9
	St Asaph	Holywell	Aberaeron
			Aberdovey

9	9	10	11
Aberffraw	Portmadoc	Llangollen	Braich-y-Pwll
Beaumaris	Welshpool	Llanidloes	Machynlleth
Carnarvon		Montgomery	Oystermouth
Criccieth	10	Plinlimmon	
Festiniog	Cader Idris	Pontypridd	12
Fishguard	Caernarfon	Port Nigel	Llandilofawr
Llanberis	Carmarthen	Port Talbot	Llantrissant
Llandudno	Crickhowel	Presteigne	
New Radnor	Ffestiniog		13
Pontypool	Llandovery	11	Haverfordwest
Porthcawl	Llanfyllin	Abergavenny	Merthyr Tydfil
		Aberystwyth	

USA

4	6	7	7
Gary	Boston	Atlanta	Spokane
Lima	Camden	Boulder	St Louis
Reno	Canton	Buffalo	Wichita
Troy	Dallas	Chicago	Yonkers
Waco	Dayton	Concord	
York	Denver	Detroit	8
	Duluth	Hampton	Berkeley
5	El Paso	Hoboken	Brooklyn
Akron	Eugene	Houston	Columbus
Boise	Fresno	Jackson	Dearborn
Bronx	Lowell	Key West	Green Bay
Butte	Mobile	Lincoln	Hannibal
Flint	Nassau	Madison	Hartford
Miami	Newark	Memphis	Honolulu
Omaha	Oxnard	Modesto	Lakeland
Ozark	Peoria	New York	Las Vegas
Salem	St Paul	Norfolk	New Haven
Selma	Tacoma	Oakland	Oak Ridge
Tulsa	Toledo	Orlando	Palo Alto
Utica	Topeka	Phoenix	Pasadena
	Tuscon	Raleigh	Portland
6	Urbana	Reading	Richmond
Albany		Roanoke	San Diego
Austin	7	Saginaw	Santa Ana
Bangor	Abilene	San Jose	Savannah
Biloxi	Anaheim	Seattle	Stamford

8	9	10	12
Stockton	Manhattan	Little Rock	Atlantic City
Syracuse	Milwaukee	Long Branch	Beverly Hills
Wheeling	Nashville	Los Angeles	Fayetteville
	New London	Louisville	Independence
9	Northeast	Miami Beach	Indianapolis
Anchorage	Princeton	Montgomery	Jacksonville
Annapolis	Riverside	New Bedford	New Brunswick
Arlington	Rochester	New Orleans	Niagara Falls
Baltimore	Waterbury	Pittsburgh	Oklahoma City
Bethlehem	Worcester	Providence	Philadelphia
Cambridge	Ypsilanti	Sacramento	Poughkeepsie
Champaign		San Antonio	St Petersburg
Charlotte	10	Washington	Salt Lake City
Cleveland	Atomic City	Youngstown	San Francisco
Des Moines	Baton Rouge		Santa Barbara
Fairbanks	Birmingham	11	
Fort Wayne	Charleston	Albuquerque	13
Fort Worth	Cincinatti	Cedar Rapids	Corpus Christi
Galveston	Evansville	Chattanooga	
Hollywood	Greensboro	Grand Rapids	14
Johnstown	Greenville	Minneapolis	Fort Lauderdale
Kalamazoo	Harrisburg	Newport News	
Lancaster	Huntsville	Palm Springs	15
Lexington	Jersey City	Schenectady	Colorado Springs
Long Beach	Kansas City	Springfield	

Rest of the world (*former name)

3	4	4	4
Aix (Fr)	Bâle (Switz)	Kano (Nig)	Lvov (Ukr)
Ava (Burma)	Bonn (Ger)	Kiel (Ger)	Lyon (Fr)
Fez (Moroc)	Brno (Czech)	Kiev (Ukr)	Metz (Fr)
Hue (Viet)	Caen (Fr)	Kobe (Japan)	Nice (Fr)
Pau (Fr)	Cali (Colomb)	Köln (Ger)	Omsk (Rus)
Ufa (Rus)	Gaza (Israel)	Lamu (Kenya)	Oran (Alg)
	Gera (Ger)	Laon (Fr)	Oslo (Nor)
4	Giza (Egypt)	Lima (Peru)	Pecs (Hun)
Agra (India)	Graz (Austria)	Linz (Austria)	Pisa (It)
Albi (Fr)	Homs (Libya)	Lodz (Pol)	Riga (Lat)
Baku (Azer)	Homs (Syria)	Luta (China)	Rome (It)

4	5	5	6
Sian (China)	Kotah (India)	Trier (Ger)	Darwin (Aust)
Suez (Egypt)	Kyoto (Japan)	Tulle (Fr)	Dieppe (Fr)
Suhl (Ger)	Lagos (Nig)	Turin (It)	Dinant (Belg)
Tyre (Leban)	Liège (Belg)	Varna (Bulg)	Dodoma (Tanz)
Vigo (Sp)	Lille (Fr)	*Vilna (Lith)	Durban (S.Af)
	Macon (Fr)	Worms (Ger)	Erfurt (Ger)
5	Mainz (Ger)	Wuhan (China)	Fushun (China)
Abuja (Nig)	Malmö (Swed)	Yalta (Ukr)	Gdańsk (Pol)
Ajmer (India)	Mecca (Saudi A)	Ypres (Belg)	Geneva (Switz)
Alwar (India)	Memel (Lith)		Harbin (China)
Arles (Fr)	Milan (It)	6	Hobart (Aust)
Arras (Fr)	Minsk (Bydo)	Aachen (Ger)	Howrah (India)
Aswan (Egypt)	Mosul (Iraq)	Abadan (Iran)	Ibadan (Nig)
Basel (Switz)	Namur (Belg)	Agadir (Moroc)	Imphal (India)
Basle (Switz)	Nancy (Fr)	Aleppo (Syria)	Indore (India)
Basra (Iraq)	Nîmes (Fr)	Amiens (Fr)	Jaipur (India)
Belem (Braz)	Osaka (Japan)	Ankara (Turk)	Jeddah (Saudi A)
Blida (Alg)	Ostia (It)	Anshan (China)	Jhansi (India)
Brest (Fr)	Padua (It)	Arnhem (Neth)	Juarez (Mex)
Cadiz (Sp)	Paris (Fr)	Athens (Gr)	Kanpur (India)
Cairo (Egypt)	Parma (Ir)	Bamako (Mali)	Kassel (Ger)
Cuzco (Peru)	Patna (India)	Baroda (India)	Kaunas (Lith)
Delhi (India)	Perth (Aust)	Bayeux (Fr)	Kohima (India)
Dhaka (Bangl)	Pinsk (Byelo)	Beirut (Leban)	Kraków (Pol)
Dijon (Fr)	Poona (India)	Berber (Sudan)	Lahore (Pak)
Enugu (Nig)	Posen (Pol)	Bergen (Nor)	Leiden (Neth)
Essen (Ger)	Pskov (Rus)	Berlin (Ger)	Le Mans (Fr)
Evian (Fr)	Rabat (Moroc)	Bhopal (India)	Leyden (Neth)
Galle (Sri L)	Reims (Fr)	Bilbao (Sp)	Lisbon (Port)
Genoa (It)	Rouen (Fr)	Bochum (Ger)	Lobito (Angola)
Ghent (Belg)	Seoul (Korea)	Bogotá (Colomb)	Luanda (Angola)
Gorky (Rus)	Sétif (Alg)	Bombay (India)	Lübeck (Ger)
Hague (Neth)	Sidon (Leban)	Bremen (Ger)	Lublin (Pol)
Haifa (Israel)	Siena (It)	Bruges (Belg)	Madras (India)
Halle (Ger)	Simla (India)	Calais (Fr)	Madrid (Sp)
Herat (Afghan)	Sofia (Bulg)	Cannes (Fr)	Málaga (Sp)
Izmir (Turk)	Split (Bos)	Canton (China)	Medina (Saudi A)
Jaffa (Israel)	Tanta (Egypt)	Cassel (Ger)	Meerut (India)
Kabul (Afghan)	Tokyo (Japan)	Cracow (Pol)	Meknes (Moroc)
Kandy (Sri L)	Tours (Fr)	Dairen (China)	Moscow (Rus)
Kazan (Rus)	Trent (It)	Danzig (Pol)	Mukden (China)

6	6	6	6
Munich (Ger)	Peking (China)	St Malo (Fr)	Tobruk (Libya)
Mysore (India)	Poznań (Pol)	Shiraz (Iran)	Toulon (Fr)
Nagoya (Japan)	Prague (Czech)	Skopje (Yugo)	*Trèves (Ger)
Nagpur (India)	Puebla (Mex)	Smyrna (Turk)	Tsinan (China)
Nantes (Fr)	Quebec (Can)	Soweto (S.Af)	Venice (It)
Napier (NZ)	Quetta (Pak)	Sparta (Gr)	Verdun (Fr)
Naples (It)	Rampur (India)	Sydney (Aust)	Verona (It)
Nelson (NZ)	Recife (Braz)	Tabriz (Iran)	Vienna (Austria)
Odessa (Ukr)	Reggio (It)	Tehran (Iran)	Warsaw (Pol)
Oporto (Port)	Regina (Can)	Thebes (Egypt)	Zagreb (Croat)
Ostend (Belg)	Rheims (Fr)	Thebes (Gr)	Zurich (Switz)
Ottawa (Can)	Riyadh (Saudi A)	Tiflis (Geo)	

7	7	7
Ajaccio (Fr)	Dunkirk (Fr)	Lucerne (Switz)
Alençon (Fr)	Erzerum (Turk)	Lucknow (India)
Algiers (Alg)	Fukuoka (Japan)	Malines (Belg)
Alma-Ata (Kazakh)	Geelong (Aust)	Mansura (Egypt)
Antwerp (Belg)	Granada (Sp)	Mashhad (Iran)
Avignon (Fr)	Gwalior (India)	Memphis (Egypt)
Badajoz (Sp)	Halifax (Can)	Mendoza (Arg)
Baghdad (Iraq)	Hamburg (Ger)	Messina (It)
Bandung (Indon)	Hanover (Ger)	Mombasa (Kenya)
Bayonne (Fr)	Homburg (Ger)	München (Ger)
Beijing (China)	Irkutsk (Rus)	Mycenae (Gr)
Benares (India)	Isfahan (Iran)	Nairobi (Kenya)
Bologna (It)	Jakarta (Indon)	Nanking (China)
Breslau (Pol)	Jodhpur (India)	Orléans (Fr)
Calgary (Can)	Kalinin (Rus)	Palermo (It)
Caracas (Venez)	Karachi (Pak)	Palmyra (Syria)
Coblenz (Ger)	Karbala (Iraq)	Piraeus (Gr)
Cologne (Ger)	Kharkov (Ukr)	Pompeii (It)
Colombo (Sri L)	Koblenz (Ger)	Potsdam (Ger)
Córdoba (Arg)	Kunming (China)	Rangoon (Burma)
Córdoba (Sp)	Lanchow (China)	Ravenna (It)
Corinth (Gr)	La Plata (Arg)	Rosario (Arg)
Cottbus (Ger)	Le Havre (Fr)	Rostock (Ger)
Donetsk (Ukr)	Leipzig (Ger)	St Johns (Can)
Dongola (Sudan)	*Lemberg (Ukr)	Salerno (It)
Dresden (Ger)	Limoges (Fr)	San Remo (It)
Dunedin (NZ)	Lourdes (Fr)	Sapporo (Japan)

7

Seville (Sp)
Skoplje (Mac)
Spandau (Ger)
Taiyuan (China)
Tallinn (Est)
Tangier (Moroc)
Tbilisi (Geo)
Tel Aviv (Israel)
Toronto (Can)
Trieste (It)
Tripoli (Leban)
Tucumán (Arg)
Uppsala (Swed)
Utrecht (Neth)
Vatican (It)
Vilnius (Lith)
Vitoria (Sp)
Yakutsk (Rus)
Yerevan (Arm)
Zagazig (Egypt)

8

Acapulco (Mex)
Adelaide (Aust)
Agartala (India)
Alicante (Sp)
Amritsar (India)
Auckland (NZ)
Augsburg (Ger)
Belgrade (Yugo)
Benguela (Angola)
Besançon (Fr)
Biarritz (Fr)
Bordeaux (Fr)
Boulogne (Fr)
Brasilia (Braz)
Brisbane (Aust)
Brussels (Belg)
Budapest (Hun)
Calcutta (India)
Canberra (Aust)
Cape Town (S.Af)

8

Cawnpore (India)
Chartres (Fr)
Chemnitz (Ger)
Damascus (Syria)
Dortmund (Ger)
Edmonton (Can)
Florence (It)
Göteborg (Swed)
Grenoble (Fr)
Hamilton (Can)
Hannover (Ger)
Ismailia (Egypt)
Istanbul (Turk)
Jabalpur (India)
Kandahar (Afghan)
Khartoum (Sudan)
Kingston (Can)
Kingston (Jam)
Kinshasa (Zaïre)
Lausanne (Switz)
Mafeking (S.Af)
Mandalay (Burma)
Mannheim (Ger)
Montreal (Can)
Nagasaki (Japan)
Novgorod (Rus)
Nürnberg (Ger)
Omdurman (Sudan)
Pamplona (Sp)
Peshawar (Pak)
Port Said (Egypt)
Pretoria (S.Af)
Przemyśl (Pol)
St Tropez (Fr)
Salonika (Gr)
Salzburg (Austria)
Santiago (Chile)
São Paulo (Braz)
Sarajevo (Bos)
Schwerin (Ger)
Shanghai (China)
Shenyang (China)

8

Shillong (India)
Smolensk (Rus)
Soissons (Fr)
Srinagar (India)
Surabaja (Indon)
Syracuse (It)
Tangiers (Moroc)
Tashkent (Uzbek)
The Hague (Neth)
Tientsin (China)
Timbuktu (Mali)
Toulouse (Fr)
Valencia (Sp)
Varanasi (India)
Veracruz (Mex)
Victoria (Can)
Winnipeg (Can)
Yokohama (Japan)
Zanzibar (Tanz)
Zaragoza (Sp)

9

Abbeville (Fr)
Agrigento (It)
Ahmedabad (India)
Allahabad (India)
Amsterdam (Neth)
Astrakhan (Rus)
Bangalore (India)
Barcelona (Sp)
Beersheba (Israel)
Brunswick (Ger)
*Byzantium (Turk)
Cartagena (Colomb)
Cartagena (Sp)
Changchun (China)
Cherbourg (Fr)
Cherkessk (Rus)
Chungking (China)
Darmstadt (Ger)
Dordrecht (Neth)

9

Dunkerque (Fr)
Eindhoven (Neth)
Frankfurt (Ger)
Gold Coast (Aust)
Hiroshima (Japan)
Hyderabad (India)
Hyderabad (Pak)
Innsbruck (Austria)
Jalalabad (Afghan)
Jerusalem (Israel)
Karaganda (Kaz)
Karlsruhe (Ger)
Kimberley (S. Af)
Krivoi Rog (Ukr)
Kuibyshev (Rus)
Ladysmith (S.Af)
Las Palmas (Sp)
*Leningrad (Rus)
Ljubljana (Sloven)
Magdeburg (Ger)
Maracaibo (Venez)
Marrakech (Moroc)
Marrakesh (Moroc)
Marseille (Fr)
Melbourne (Aust)
Montauban (Fr)
Monterrey (Mex)
Newcastle (Aust)
Nuremberg (Ger)
Palembang (Indon)
Panmunjon (Korea)
Perpignan (Fr)
Rotterdam (Neth)
St Etienne (Fr)
Samarkand (Uzbek)
Santander (Sp)
Saragossa (Sp)
Saskatoon (Can)
Stockholm (Swed)
Stuttgart (Ger)

9

Trondheim (Nor)
Vancouver (Can)
Volgograd (Rus)
Wiesbaden (Ger)
Wuppertal (Ger)

10

Alexandria (Egypt)
Baden-Baden (Ger)
Bad Homburg (Ger)
Bratislava (Slovak)
Casablanca (Moroc)
Chandigarh (India)
Chittagong (Bangl)
Darjeeling (India)
Düsseldorf (Ger)
Gothenburg (Swed)
Heidelberg (Ger)
Jamshedpur (India)
Kitakyushu (Japan)
*Königsberg (Rus)
Lubumbashi (Zaïre)
Marseilles (Fr)
Montelimar (Fr)
Nova Lisboa (Angola)
Port Arthur (China)
Rawalpindi (Pak)
Sevastopol (Ukr)
Simonstown (S. Af)
*Stalingrad (Rus)
Strasbourg (Fr)
*Sverdlovsk (Rus)
Thunderbay (Can)
Townsville (Aust)
Trivandrum (India)
Valparaiso (Chile)
Versailles (Fr)
Wellington (NZ)
Wollongong (Aust)

11

Armentières (Fr)
Bahia Blanca (Arg)
Bhubaneswar (India)
Brandenburg (Ger)
Buenos Aires (Arg)
Constantine (Alg)
Fredericton (Can)
Grahamstown (S.Af)
Guadalajara (Mex)
Helsingborg (Swed)
Kaliningrad (Rus)
Mar del Plata (Arg)
Montpellier (Fr)
Novosibirsk (Rus)
Porto Alegre (Braz)
Saarbrücken (Ger)
Sharpeville (S.Af)
Trincomalee (Sri L)
Vladivostok (Rus)

12

Alice Springs (Aust)
Barranquilla (Colomb)
Bloemfontein (S. Af)
Christchurch (NZ)
Johannesburg (S. Af)
Mazar-I-Sharif (Afghan)
Niagara Falls (Can)
Rio de Janeiro (Braz)
St Petersburg (Rus)
San Sebastián (Sp)
Sidi-bel-Abbés (Alg)

13

Aix-la-Chapelle (Ger)
Belo Horizonte (Braz)
Charlottetown (Can)
*Karl-Marx-Stadt (Ger)
Port Elizabeth (S. Af)

14
*Constantinople (Turk)
Dnepropetrovsk (Ukr)

15
Clermont-Ferrand (Fr)

18
San Miguel de Tucumán (Arg)

Trees and shrubs

3	4	5	6
ash	twig	osier	mimosa
bay	vine	papaw	myrtle
box		peach	orange
elm	5	pecan	pawpaw
fig	alder	plane	pepper
fir	apple	rowan	poplar
gum	aspen	trunk	privet
haw	balsa		quince
hip	beech	6	red gum
ivy	birch	acacia	rubber
may	broom	almond	sallow
oak	cacao	azalea	sappan
tea	caper	balsam	spruce
yew	cedar	bamboo	walnut
	copse	banana	willow
4	dwarf	banyan	
aloe	ebony	bog oak	7
arum	elder	bonsai	amboyna
bark	fruit	bo tree	aniseed
bole	furze	branch	arbutus
cork	gorse	Brazil	avocado
date	grove	cashew	blossom
deal	hazel	catkin	blue gum
jaca	heath	cherry	boxwood
lime	holly	citron	coconut
palm	karri	coffee	conifer
pear	larch	deodar	cork oak
pine	lemon	ginkgo	cypress
plum	lilac	jujube	dogwood
rose	mango	laurel	foliage
sloe	maple	linden	fuchsia
teak	olive	locust	heather

7
hemlock
hickory
holm oak
jasmine
juniper
oil palm
orchard
redwood
rosebay
sapling
sequoia
soursop

8
bass wood
bayberry
beechnut
box elder
calabash
camellia
chestnut
cinchona
corkwood
date palm
date plum
gardenia
hawthorn
hornbeam
ironwood
japonica
laburnum
lavender
magnolia
mahogany
mulberry
oleander
pine cone
red cedar
red maple
rosewood

8
royal oak
sago palm
Scots elm
Scots fir
scrub oak
seedling
silky oak
sweet bay
sweet gum
sycamore
tamarind
tamarisk
white ash
white fir
white gum
white oak
wistaria
wisteria
witch elm
woodbine

9
alpine fir
araucaria
blackwood
buckthorn
crab apple
deciduous
evergreen
forest oak
forsythia
grapevine
ground ash
ground oak
jacaranda
Judas tree
mistletoe
poison ivy
sassafras
satinwood
Scotch elm

9
Scotch fir
Scots pine
screw pine
silver fir
stone pine
tulip tree
whitebeam

10
blackthorn
blue spruce
brazilwood
coniferous
cottonwood
Douglas fir
eucalyptus
frangipani
golden rain
greenheart
Joshua tree
mangosteen
pine needle
poinsettia
prickly ash
sandalwood
Scotch pine
strawberry
sugar maple
white cedar
wild cherry
witch hazel
yellowwood

11
bottlebrush
coconut palm
copper beech
cypress pine
golden chain
honey locust

11
mountain ash
pomegranate
silver birch
stephanotis
white poplar
white spruce
white willow

12
betel nut palm
cucumber tree
custard apple
horse chestnut
monkey puzzle
Norway spruce
silver wattle
tree of heaven
umbrella pine
white cypress
winter cherry

13
Christmas tree
horse chestnut
Japanese cedar
Japanese maple
weeping willow

14
bougainvillaea
cedar of Lebanon

15
trembling poplar
Virginia creeper

16
flowering currant

Trophies, events and awards

Admiral's Cup (sailing)
All-Ireland Championship (Gaelic football)
All-Ireland Championships (hurling)
Alpine Championships (skiing)
America's Cup (yachting)
Ashes (cricket)
Badminton Three-day Event (equestrian)
B.B.C. Sports Personality of the Year
Benson & Hedges Cup (cricket)
Boat Race (rowing)
British Open Championship (golf)
Camanachd Association Challenge Cup (shinty)
Cheltenham Gold Cup (horse racing)
Classics (horse racing)
Commonwealth Games (athletics)
Cornhill Test (cricket)
David Cup (tennis)
Decathlon (athletics)
Derby (greyhound racing/horse racing)
Embassy World Indoor Bowls Crown
Embassy World Professional Snooker Championship
English Greyhound Derby (greyhound racing)
European Champions Cup (basketball)
European Championships (football)
European Cup Winners' Cup (football)
European Footballer of the Year
European Super Cup (football)
Federation Cup (tennis)
Football Association Challenge Cup
Football Association Charity Shield
Football League Championship
Football League Cup
Gillette Cup (cricket)
Grand National Steeplechase (horse racing)
Grand Prix (motor racing)
Harmsworth Trophy (power boat racing)
Henley Regatta (rowing)
Highland Games
International Championship (bowls)

International Cross-country Championship (athletics)
Isle of Man TT Races (motor cycle racing)
John Player Cup (rugby league)
John Player League (cricket)
King George V Gold Cup (equestrian)
Lancaster Park, NZ (cricket)
Le Mans 24 hours (motor racing)
Littlewoods Challenge Cup (football)
Lombard Rally (motor racing)
Lonsdale Belt (boxing)
Marathon (athletics)
Milk Cup (football)
Milk Race (cycling)
Monte Carlo Rally (motor racing)
National Hunt Jockey Championship (horse racing)
National Westminster Bank Trophy (cricket)
Nations' Cup (football)
Nordic Championships (skiing)
Oaks (horse racing)
Olympic Games
One Thousand Guineas (horse racing)
Premiership Trophy (rugby league)
Queen Elizabeth II Cup (equestrian)
Ranji Trophy (cricket)
Red Stripe Cup (cricket)
Refuge Assurance Trophy (cricket)
Rugby League Challenge Cup
Ryder Cup (golf)
St Leger (horse racing)
Scottish Football Association Cup
Sheffield Shield (cricket)
Shell Trophy (cricket)
Stanley Cup (ice hockey)
Swaythling cup (table tennis)
Thomas Cup (badminton)
Tour de France (cycling)
Triple Crown (rugby union; horse racing)
Two Thousand Guineas (horse racing)
Uber Cup (badminton)
U.E.F.A. Cup (football)
U.S. Open Championship (golf)
U.S. Masters Championship (golf)

U.S. Professional Golfers Association
Wightman Cup (sailing)
Wimbledon (tennis)
Women's World Cup (cricket)
World Masters Championships (darts)
World Series (baseball)
Yellow Jersey (cycling)

Typefaces

4	6	7	8
Bell	Corona	Johnson	Palatino
Gill	Fenice	Madison	Perpetua
	Futura	Memphis	
5	Glypha	Plantin	9
Aster	Gothic	Raleigh	Americana
Bembo	Italia	Spartan	Athenaeum
Block	Janson	Stempel	Barcelona
Doric	Lucian	Tiffany	Britannic
Folio	Modern	Univers	Caledonia
Goudy	Oliver	Wexford	Clarendon
Ionic	Ondine	Windsor	Clearface
Kabel			Criterion
Lotus	7	8	Dominante
Mitra	Antique	Berkeley	Excelsior
Times	Basilia	Breughel	Fairfield
	Bernard	Cloister	Grotesque
6	Bookman	Concorde	Helvetica
Aachen	Bramley	Egyptian	Worcester
Adroit	Candida	Ehrhardt	
Auriga	Century	Fournier	10
Becket	Coronet	Franklin	Avant Garde
Bodoni	Cushing	Frutiger	Cheltenham
Bulmer	Electra	Galliard	Leamington
Caslon	Floreal	Garamond	11
Cochin	Imprint	Olympian	Baskerville
Cooper	Iridium	Rockwell	Copperplate

Universities in the United Kingdom

4	6	8	10
Bath	Napier	Stirling	East Anglia
City	Oxford	Teesside	East London
Hull	Surrey		Heriot-Watt
Kent	Sussex	**9**	Humberside
Open	Ulster	Cambridge	John Moores
York		Cranfield	Manchester
	7	Edinburgh	Nottingham
5	Belfast	Glamorgan	Portsmouth
Aston	Bristol	Greenwich	Sunderland
Derby	Brookes	Guildhall	
Essex	Glasgow	Lancaster	**11**
Keele	Paisley	Leicester	Bournemouth
Leeds	Reading	Liverpool	North London
Trent	Salford	Middlesex	Northumbria
Wales	Warwick	Sheffield	Southampton
		South Bank	Strathclyde
6	**8**	St Andrews	Westminster
Brunel	Aberdeen		
Dundee	Bradford	**10**	**12**
Durham	Brighton	Birmingham	Huddersfield
Exeter	Coventry	Buckingham	Loughborough
Hallam	Kingston	Caledonian	Robert Gordon
London	Plymouth	De Montfort	Thames Valley

13	14	17
Hertfordshire	Central England	Leeds Metropolitan
Staffordshire		Newcastle upon Tyne
West of England	**17**	
Wolverhampton	Anglia Polytechnic	**22**
	Central Lancashire	Manchester Metropolitan

Cambridge colleges

5	6	7	7
Clare	Darwin	Christ's	St John's
Jesus	Girton	Downing	Trinity
King's	Queens'	New Hall	Wolfson
	Selwyn	Newnham	

8	9	11	13
Emmanuel	Magdalene	Fitzwilliam	Corpus Christi
Homerton	St Edmund's	Trinity Hall	Lucy Cavendish
Pembroke			
Robinson	10	12	16
	Hughes Hall	St Catherine's	Gonville and
9	Peterhouse	Sidney Sussex	Caius
Churchill			
Clare Hall			

Oxford colleges

5	7	8	11
Green	St Anne's	St Hilda's	Campion Hall
Jesus	St Cross	St Peter's	Regent's Park
Keble	St Hugh's		Rewley House
Oriel	St John's	9	
	Trinity	Brasenose	12
6	Wolfson	Mansfield	Christ Church
Exeter		St Antony's	St Benet's Hall
Merton	8	Templeton	St Catherine's
Queen's	All Souls	Worcester	St Edmund Hall
Wadham	Hertford		
	Magdalen	10	13
7	Nuffield	Greyfriars	Corpus Christi
Balliol	Pembroke	New College	
Linacre		Somerville	16
Lincoln		University	Lady Margaret
			Hall

Vehicles

3	4	4	5
BMX	cart	tram	crate
bus	dray	trap	cycle
cab	jeep	tube	float
car	loco		lorry
gig	mini	5	metro
van	pram	bogie	moped
	skis	brake	motor
4	sled	buggy	sedan
auto	tank	coach	sulky
bike	taxi	coupé	tonga

5	7	8	9
train	caboose	carriage	dining car
truck	caravan	carriole	dodgem car
wagon	chariot	clarence	dormobile
	coaster	curricle	estate car
6	dog cart	dustcart	guard's van
banger	droshky	four door	hansom cab
barrow	flivver	goods van	horse cart
berlin	fourgon	handcart	landaulet
calash	growler	horse box	Land Rover
chaise	hackney	milk cart	limousine
diesel	hard top	motorbus	mail coach
engine	mail car	motor car	mail train
fiacre	mail van	motor van	milk float
go-cart	minibus	pony cart	milk train
hansom	minicab	push bike	monocycle
hearse	minicar	pushcart	motor bike
hot-rod	omnibus	quadriga	motorcade
jalopy	open car	rickshaw	muletrain
jitney	phaeton	roadster	palankeen
landau	Pullman	runabout	palanquin
litter	railbus	sociable	prison van
oxcart	railcar	staff car	racing car
rocket	scooter	stanhope	saloon car
saloon	shunter	toboggan	sports car
sledge	side car	tricycle	street car
sleigh	taxi cab	unicycle	tarantass
surrey	tilbury	victoria	tin lizzie
tandem	tractor		two seater
tanker	trailer	**9**	wagonette
tender	tramcar	ambulance	water cart
tourer	trolley	amphibian	
tricar	tumbrel	applecart	**10**
troika	tumbril	bandwagon	automobile
whisky	two door	bathchair	black maria
		boat train	boneshaker
7	**8**	bobsleigh	conveyance
autobus	barouche	bubblecar	donkey cart
autocar	brake-van	bulldozer	fire engine
bicycle	britzska	cabriolet	four in hand
bob sled	brougham	charabanc	glass coach
britzka	cable car	diligence	goods train

10	10	11	12
hackney cab	tramway car	sleeping car	single decker
invalid car	trolley bus	state landau	station wagon
local train	trolley car	steam engine	three-wheeler
locomotive	two wheeler		
motor coach	velocipede	12	13
motor cycle	waggonette	baby carriage	electric train
motor lorry	war chariot	coach-and-four	horse carriage
night train		coach-and-pair	pennyfarthing
Pullman car	11	double decker	shooting brake
post chaise	armoured car	express train	state carriage
Range Rover	bone breaker	freight train	
rattletrap	brewer's dray	furniture van	14
sedan chair	Caterpillar	hackney coach	passenger train
shandrydan	convertible	horse and cart	traction engine
Sinclair C5	delivery van	invalid chair	
snowplough	diesel train	luggage train	15
stage coach	four wheeler	motor scooter	hackney-carriage
stage wagon	gun carriage	perambulator	invalid carriage
state coach	landaulette	Puffing Billy	railway carriage
touring car	sit-up-and-beg	railway train	

Waterfalls

6
Foyers (Scot)
Guaira (Braz)
Ribbon (USA)

7
Glomach (Scot)
Niagara (Can)
Roraima (Guyana)
Stanley (Zaïre)

8
Gavarnie (Fr)
Gullfoss (Ice)
Hamilton (Can)
Kaleteur (Guyana)

8
Krimmler (Austria)
Victoria (Zambia)

9
Churchill (Can)
Debbifoss (Ice)
Giessbach (Switz)
Multnomah (USA)
Vettisfos (Nor)

10
Salto Angel (Venez)
Sete Quedas (Braz)
Sutherland (NZ)

11
Trümmelbach (Switz)

12	13
Eas-Coul-Aulin (Scot)	Upper Yosemite (USA)
Pistyll-y-Llyn (Wales)	

Weapons and armour

3	4	5	6
arm	pike	salvo	dagger
axe	shot	shaft	dragon
bow	tank	shell	dualin
dag	tock	skean	feltre
gun	whip	skene	glaive
jet		sling	gorget
ram	**5**	spear	hanger
wad	A-bomb	staff	helmet
	aegis	stake	homing
4	armet	stick	jezail
ammo	arrow	sword	lariat
arms	bacyn	tasse	lorica
ball	baton	tawse	mailed
bill	bilbo	visor	mauser
bolt	birch	vizor	morion
bomb	clean	waddy	mortar
butt	crest		musket
cane	estoc	**6**	muzzle
club	fusée	ack-ack	napalm
colt	fusil	air-gun	petard
dart	grape	anlace	pistol
dirk	H-bomb	armlet	pom-pom
epée	hobit	armour	popgun
flak	knife	barrel	powder
foil	knout	basnet	primer
gaff	lance	bodkin	quarry
goad	lasso	Bofors	quiver
helm	lathi	bonnet	ramrod
ICBM	Maxim	buffer	rapier
jack	poker	bullet	recoil
kris	pouch	cannon	rocket
mace	rifle	casque	scythe
mail	royal	cudgel	Semtex
mine	sabre	cuisse	shield

6	7	8	8
sickle	gasmask	arquebus	jazerant
stylet	greaves	atom bomb	langrage
swivel	grenade	attaghan	Lewis gun
tabard	gunshot	ballista	magazine
tonite	halbert	bascinet	mangonel
tulwar	handgun	basilisk	mantelet
umbril	harpoon	birdbolt	Maxim gun
weapon	hatchet	blowpipe	munition
Webley	hauberk	bludgeon	naval gun
zipgun	holster	broad axe	Oerlikon
	javelin	Browning	ordnance
7	langrel	burgonet	paravane
anelace	longbow	carabine	paterero
assagai	long tom	case-shot	pectoral
assegai	lyddite	catapult	pederero
ataghan	machete	chanfron	petronel
balista	megaton	chausses	pistolet
bar-shot	missile	claymore	plastron
basinet	murrion	corselet	port-fire
baslard	musquet	crossbow	pryoxyle
bayonet	nuclear	culettes	repeater
bazooka	oil-bomb	culverin	revolver
brasset	panoply	damaskin	ricochet
Bren gun	Polaris	dynamite	ringmail
buckler	pole-axe	eel-spear	scabbard
calibre	quarrel	elf-arrow	scimitar
chopper	rabinet	falchion	Scorpion
cordite	roundel	falconet	shrapnel
couteau	shotgun	field-gun	siege-gun
cuirass	side-arm	firearms	spadroon
cuisses	Skybolt	fire-ball	spontoon
cutlass	Sten gun	firelock	springal
djerrid	tear gas	fireship	steam gun
dualine	torpedo	gadlings	stiletto
dudgeon	trident	gauntlet	stinkpot
ejector	twibill	gavelock	stonebow
elf-bolt	vamplet	gunsight	tomahawk
espadon	ventail	half-pike	Tommy-gun
firearm	warhead	hand-pike	umbriere
fire-pot	wind-gun	haquebut	vambrace
gantlet		howitzer	vamplate

8	9	10	11
whin-yard	habergeon	broadsword	bow and arrow
yataghan	half-track	burrel-shot	breastplate
	half-staff	cannonball	breast strap
9	headpiece	cannon shot	contact mine
ack-ack gun	heavy tank	cataphract	cruiser tank
angel shot	heelpiece	coat armour	Dahlgren gun
arquebuse	light tank	coat of mail	depth-charge
arrowhead	matchlock	cross arrow	grande-garde
artillery	Mills bomb	demi-cannon	gun carriage
aventaile	munitions	field-piece	gun-howitzer
backpiece	musketoon	fire-barrel	hand grenade
ballistic	needle-gun	flick knife	harping iron
battleaxe	poison gas	Gatling gun	Jacob's staff
Big Bertha	quaker-gun	grainstaff	morning star
Blue Water	shillalah	harquebuse	mountain gun
Boar-spear	slow-match	knobkerrie	neutron bomb
Bofors gun	slung-shot	Lee-Enfield	plate armour
bomb-chest	smallarms	letter bomb	powder chest
bombshell	smallbore	machine-gun	powder flask
boomerang	spring-gun	medium tank	safety catch
Brown Bess	starshell	Minié rifle	scale armour
brownbill	stinkbomb	mustard-gas	Snider rifle
carronade	sword cane	paixhan gun	stern chaser
cartouche	teeth arms	pea shooter	Thompson gun
cartridge	troopship	powder horn	
chain-mail	truncheon	projectile	12
chain-shot	turret gun	pyroxyline	Armstrong gun
defoliant	ward staff	recoilless	battering ram
demi-lance	welsh-hook	safety fuse	boarding pike
derringer	xyloidine	shillelagh	bombing plane
deterrent	zumbooruk	six shooter	breech loader
detonator		small sword	cartridge-box
doodle-bug	10	sticky bomb	conventional
epaulette	ammunition	sword stick	demi culverin
face-guard	arcubalist	touchpaper	double charge
fish-spear	banderolle		flame-thrower
garde-bras	battery gun	11	fowling piece
gelignite	blind shell	antitank gun	hydrogen bomb
grapeshot	Blue Streak	armoured car	Lancaster gun
gun cotton	Bowie-knife	basket sword	landing craft
gunpowder	brigandine	blunderbuss	Mills grenade

12	13	13	14
mitrailleuse	ball cartridge	submachine-gun	powder magazine
muzzle loader	brass knuckles	submarine mine	sawn-off shotgun
quarterstaff	cartridge case	thermonuclear	small-bore rifle
rocket mortar	cat o'nine tails	two-edged sword	
spigot mortar	Damocles sword		15
stokes mortar	duelling sword	14	anti-aircraft gun
sword bayonet	guided missile	armour-piercing	lachrymatory gas
tracer bullet	high explosive	blank cartridge	
trench mortar	knuckleduster	Brennan torpedo	16
wheel-lock dag	life preserver	duelling pistol	ballistic missile
	percussion cap	incendiary bomb	
13	poisoned arrow	miniature rifle	22
aerial torpedo	scalping knife	nitroglycerine	double-barrelled
arming-doublet	shrapnel shell	nuclear weapons	shotgun

Weather

3	4	6	7
dry	smog	Arctic	blowing
fog	snow	bright	climate
hot	warm	chilly	clouded
icy	wind	clouds	cold day
wet		cloudy	coldish
	5	colder	cyclone
4	cloud	deluge	drizzle
calm	dusty	floods	drought
cold	flood	freeze	fogbank
cool	foggy	frosty	freshen
damp	frost	hot day	fresher
dark	gusty	mizzle	hailing
dull	misty	mizzly	icy cold
gale	muggy	shower	mistral
gust	rainy	squall	monsoon
hail	sleet	starry	muggish
haze	snowy	stormy	rainbow
hazy	still	sultry	raining
heat	storm	torrid	set fair
mild	sunny	warmer	showery
mist	windy	wet day	snowing
rain		winter	squally
		wintry	

7

summery
sunspot
tempest
thunder
tornado
typhoon
warm day
warmish
wintery

8

autumnal
black ice
blizzard
cold snap
dead calm
downpour
east wind
freezing
heatwave
hot night
overcast
rainfall
snowfall
sunlight
thundery
tropical
west wind
wet night

9

cold night
drift wind
drizzling
dry season
hailstorm
hard frost
hoarfrost
hurricane
lightning
moonlight
north wind
rain cloud
sea breeze
snow storm
south wind
sou'wester
starlight
trade wind
unsettled
warm night
whirlwind

10

arctic cold
changeable
depression
frostbound
hot climate
hot weather
March winds
Scotch mist

10

storm cloud
wet weather

11

anticyclone
cats and dogs
cold climate
cold weather
dull weather
foul weather
hard weather
lowering sky
meteorology
rain or shine
rainy season
stiff breeze
storm signal
temperature
tempestuous
thunderbolt
thunderclap
warm weather
wind veering

12

April showers
atmospherics
easterly wind
freezing rain
shooting star
storm brewing

12

thundercloud
thunderstorm
tropical heat
tropical rain
weather glass
westerly wind
windy weather

13

autumn weather
frosty weather
north-east wind
northerly wind
north-west wind
south-east wind
southerly wind
south-west wind
wintry weather

14

meteorological
moonlight night
sheet lightning
starlight night
torrential rain

15

forked lightning
prevailing winds
summer lightning
tropical climate

Beaufort scale

Force no.	Descriptive term
0	calm
1	light air
2	light breeze
3	gentle breeze
4	moderate breeze
5	fresh breeze
6	strong breeze

Force no.	Descriptive term
7	near gale
8	gale
9	strong gale
10	storm
11	violent storm
12	hurricane

Wedding anniversaries

1st	cotton/paper	14th	ivory
2nd	paper/cotton	15th	crystal
3rd	leather	20th	china
4th	fruit/flowers	25th	silver
5th	wood	30th	pearl
6th	sugar	35th	coral
7th	wool/copper	40th	ruby
8th	bronze/pottery	45th	sapphire
9th	pottery/willow	50th	golden
10th	tin	55th	emerald
11th	steel	60th	diamond
12th	silk/linen	70th	platinum
13th	lace		

Weights and measures

2	3	3	4
A3	amp	tun	feet
A4	are	vat	foot
A5	cwt		gill
cm	dwt	4	gram
ft	ell	acre	half
gr	erg	bale	hand
in	keg	bolt	hank
kg	mho	cask	hide
km	mil	cran	hour
lb	ohm	demy	inch
mm	rod	dram	kilo
yd	ton	drum	knot
	tot	dyne	link

4	5	7	9
load	month	acreage	foot pound
mile	ounce	calorie	hectogram
nail	perch	centner	kilocycle
pail	point	century	kilohertz
peck	pound	coulomb	kilometre
pint	quart	decibel	light year
pipe	quire	emperor	megacycle
pole	royal	furlong	megahertz
post	sheet	hectare	metric ton
ream	skein	maximum	microwatt
reel	stere	measure	milligram
rood	stone	megaton	net weight
sack	therm	minimum	yardstick
span	toise	outsize	
torr	tonne	quarter	10
troy		quintal	barleycorn
unit	6	scruple	centigrade
volt	ampere	tonnage	centilitre
watt	barrel		centimetre
week	bundle	8	cubic metre
yard	bushel	angstrom	decagramme
year	casing	elephant	decigramme
	cental	foolscap	dekagramme
5	degree	hogshead	double demi
brief	denier	imperial	double post
cable	drachm	kilogram	dry measure
carat	fathom	kilowatt	fluid ounce
chain	firkin	megawatt	grand eagle
crown	gallon		hectolitre
cubic	gramme	9	hectometre
cubit	league	centigram	horsepower
cycle	megohm	cubic foot	kilogramme
gauge	metric	cubic yard	millimetre
grain	micron	decalitre	square foot
gross	minute	decametre	square inch
hertz	noggin	decilitre	square mile
litre	octave	decimeter	square yard
meter	quarto	dekametre	super royal
metre	second	dimension	troy weight
minim			

11	11	11	13
avoirdupois	double crown	pennyweight	hundredweight
baker's dozen	double royal	thermal unit	linear measure
centigramme	imperial cap		

Writers

3

Fry, Christopher
Gay, John

4

Amis, Kingsley
Amis, Martin
Bolt, Robert Oxton
Buck, Pearl S.
Cary, (Arthur) Joyce (Lunel)
Dahl, Roald
Ford, Ford Madox
Foxe, John
Gide, André
Gray, Thomas
Gunn, Victor
Hogg, James
Hood, Thomas
Hope, Anthony
Hugo, Victor
Hunt, James Henry
Hunt, Leigh
Lamb, Charles
Lear, Edward
Mann, Thomas
Mill, John Stuart
More, Sir Thomas
Muir, Edwin
Nash, Ogden
Ovid (Publius Ovidius Naso)
Owen, Wilfred
Penn, John
Pope, Alexander
Read, Charles

4

Read, Sir Herbert
Read, Miss
Sadi, Muslih Addin
Sand, George
Shaw, George Bernard
Snow, Charles Percy
Wood, Mrs Henry
York, Margaret
Zola, Emile Edouard

5

Aesop
Albee, Edward
Auden, Wystan Hugh
Bacon, Francis
Bates, H.E.
Blake, William
Bowen, Elizabeth
Broch, Hermann
Burke, Edmund
Burns, Robert
Byatt, Antonia Susan
Byron, George Gordon, Lord
Camus, Albert
Clare, John
Defoe, Daniel
Donne, John
Doyle, Sir Arthur Conan
Dumas, Alexandre
Eliot, George
Eliot, Thomas Stearns
Frost, Robert
Gogol, Nikolai

5

Gosse, Sir Edmund
Gower, John
Hafiz, Shams al-Din Muhammad
Hardy, Thomas
Heine, Heinrich
Homer
Ibsen, Henrik Johan
James, Henry
Joyce, James
Kafka, Franz
Keats, John
Lewis, Clive Staples
Lewis, (Percy) Wyndham
Lewis, Sinclair
Locke, John
Lowry, Malcolm
Marsh, Dame Ngaio
Milne, Alan Alexander
Moore, George
Moore, Thomas
Otway, Thomas
Ouida (Marie Louise de la Ramée)
Paine, Thomas
Pepys, Samuel
Pound, Ezra Loomis
Powys, John Cowper
Powys, Theodore Francis
Reade, Charles
Rilke, Rainer Maria
Sachs, Hans
Scott, Sir Walter
Seton, Ernest Thompson
Shute, Nevil
Smith, Adam
Smith, Rev. Sydney
Spark, Muriel
Stowe, Harriet Beecher
Swift, Jonathan
Synge, John Millington
Tasso, Torquato
Twain, Mark
Verne, Jules

5

Waugh, Evelyn
Wells, Herbert George
Wilde, Oscar
Woolf, Virginia
Yeats, William Butler

6

Alcott, Louisa May
Ambler, Eric
Arnold, Matthew
Atwood, Margaret
Austen, Jane
Balzac, Honoré de
Barham, Richard Harris
Barrie, Sir James Matthew
Belloc, (Joseph) Hilaire (Pierre)
Bellow, Saul
Besant, Sir Walter
Binyon, Laurence
Blyton, Enid
Borges, Jorge Luis
Borrow, George Henry
Brecht, Bertold
Bridie, James
Brontë, Anne
Brontë, Charlotte
Brontë, Emily
Brooke, Rupert
Browne, Sir Thomas
Buchan, John
Bunyan, John
Burney, Fanny
Burton, Robert
Butler, Samuel
Conrad, Joseph
Cowper, William
Cronin, A.J.
Darwin, Charles
Dryden, John
Dunbar, William
Evelyn, John
Fowles, John

6

Gibbon, Edward
Goethe, Johann Wolfgang von
Graves, Robert Ranke
Greene, Graham
Hamsun, Knut
Heller, Joseph
Hobbes, Thomas
Hudson, William Henry
Hughes, Richard
Hughes, Ted
Huxley, Aldous
Irving, Washington
Jonson, Ben
Keynes, John Maynard
Larkin, Philip
London, Jack
Lowell, Robert
Mailer, Norman
Malory, Sir Thomas
Miller, Arthur
Milton, John
Morris, William
Murray, George
Neruda, Pablo
Nesbit, Edith
Newman, John Henry
Newton, Sir Isaac
O'Casey, Sean
O'Neill, Eugene
Orwell, George
Pinero, Sir Arthur Wing
Pinter, Harold
Potter, Beatrix
Powell, Anthony
Proust, Marcel
Racine, Jean
Ruskin, John
Savage, Richard
Sayers, Dorothy Leigh
Sidney, Sir Philip
Silone, Ignazio

6

Smiles, Samuel
Spring, Howard
Sterne, Laurence
Stoker, Bram
Tagore, Rabindranath
Thomas, Dylan
Thomas, Edward
Walton, Izaak
Wesker, Arnold
Wilson, Sir Angus

7

Addison, Joseph
Alarcón, Pedro Antonio de
Alfieri, Vittorio, Count
Ariosto, Ludovico
Bagehot, Walter
Baldwin, James
Beckett, Samuel
Bennett, (Enoch) Arnold
Blunden, Edmund Charles
Boswell, James
Bridges, Robert Seymour
Bromige, Iris
Burgess, Anthony
Burnett, Frances Eliza Hodgson
Calvino, Italo
Carlyle, Thomas
Carroll, Lewis
Chaucer, Geoffrey
Chekhov, Anton Pavlovich
Cobbett, William
Colette, Sidonie Gabrielle
Collins, (William) Wilkie
Cookson, Catherine
Dickens, Charles
Douglas, Norman
Drabble, Margaret
Durrell, Lawrence
Flecker, James Elroy
Fleming, Ian

7

Forster, Edward Morgan
Gaskell, Elizabeth
Gilbert, Sir William Schwenck
Gissing, George Robert
Golding, William
Grahame, Kenneth
Haggard, Sir (Henry) Rider
Hartley, Leonard Poles
Hazlitt, William
Herbert, Sir Alan Patrick
Herrick, Robert
Hopkins, Gerard Manley
Housman, Alfred Edward
Johnson, Dr Samuel
Kipling, (Joseph) Rudyard
Le Carré, John
Lessing, Doris
Marlowe, Christopher
Marryat, Frederick
Maugham, William Somerset
Moravia, Alberto
Murdoch, Dame Iris
Nabokov, Vladimir
Osborne, John
Patmore, Coventry
Peacock, Thomas Love
Pushkin, Aleksandr
Ransome, Arthur
Rimbaud, Arthur
Rushdie, Salman
Sassoon, Siegfried
Shelley, Mary Wollstonecraft
Shelley, Percy Bysshe
Simenon, Georges
Sitwell, Dame Edith
Southey, Robert
Spenser, Edmund
Surtees, Robert Smith
Thoreau, Henry David
Tolkien, John Ronald Reuel
Tolstoy, Leo, Count

7

Toynbee, Arnold Joseph
Travers, Ben
Wallace, Edgar
Walpole, Sir Hugh Seymour
Whitman, Walt

8

Andersen, Hans Christian
Beaumont, Francis
Beerbohm, Sir Max
Betjeman, Sir John
Browning, Elizabeth Barrett
Browning, Robert
Cartland, Dame Barbara
Chandler, Raymond
Christie, Dame Agatha
Congreve, William
Crompton, Richmal
Day-Lewis, Cecil
De La Mare, Walter
Disraeli, Benjamin
Faulkner, William
Fielding, Henry
Flaubert, Gustave
Kingsley, Charles
Langland, William
Lawrence, David Herbert
Lawrence, Thomas Edward
Macaulay, Thomas Babington
Macneice, Louis
Melville, Herman
Meredith, George
Mitchell, Margaret
Petrarch (Francesco Petrarca)
Rabelais, François
Rattigan, Sir Terence
Rossetti, Dante Gabriel
Schiller, Friedrich
Sheridan, Richard Brinsley
Sillitoe, Alan
Smollett, Tobias George

8

Spillane, Mickey
Stendhal (Marie Henri Beyle)
Stoppard, Tom
Tennyson, Alfred, Lord
Thompson, Francis
Townsend, Sue
Trollope, Anthony
Turgenev, Ivan
Voltaire (François Marie Arouet)
Williams, Tennessee

9

Allingham, Margery
Ayckbourn, Alan
Blackmore, R.D.
Cervantes Saavedra, Miguel de
Charteris, Leslie
Clarendon, Edward Hyde, Earl of
Coleridge, Samuel Taylor
Corneille, Pierre
D'Annunzio, Gabriele
De La Roche, Mazo
De Quincey, Thomas
Du Maurier, Daphne
Du Maurier, George
Eckermann, Johann Peter
Goldsmith, Oliver
Hawthorne, Nathaniel
Hemingway, Ernest
Highsmith, Patricia
Isherwood, Christopher
Jefferies, Richard
Lampedusa, Giuseppe Tomasi di
Llewellyn, Richard
Mackenzie, Sir Compton
Mansfield, Katherine
Masefield, John
Pasternak, Boris

9

Priestley, John Boynton
Rosenberg, Isaac
Steinbeck, John
Stevenson, Robert Louis
Swinburne, Algernon Charles
Thackeray, William Makepeace
Trevelyan, George Macaulay
Wentworth, Patricia
Wodehouse, Sir Pelham Grenville

10

Baudelaire, Charles Pierre
Carmichael, Harry
Chesterton, Gilbert Keith
Drinkwater, John
Fitzgerald, Edward
Fitzgerald, F. Scott
Galsworthy, John
Longfellow, Henry Wadsworth
Maupassant, Guy de
Pirandello, Luigi
Richardson, Samuel
Strindberg, August
Wordsworth, William

11

Dostoyevsky, Fyodor
Machiavelli, Niccolò
Maeterlinck, Maurice
Shakespeare, William

12

Solzhenitsyn, Aleksandr
Quiller-Couch, Sir Arthur Thomas

14

Compton-Burnett, Dame Ivy

Zodiacs

Signs of the Zodiac

Aries (Ram) 20 March–20 April
Taurus (Bull) 21 April–21 May
Gemini (Twins) 22 May–21 June
Cancer (Crab) 22 June–22 July
Leo (Lion) 23 July–23 August
Virgo (Virgin) 24 August–23 September
Libra (Scales) 24 September–23 October
Scorpio (Scorpion) 24 October–22 November
Sagittarius (Archer) 23 November–21 December
Capricorn (Goat) 22 December–20 January
Aquarius (Water-carrier) 21 January–18 February
Pisces (Fish) 19 February–19 March

Chinese Zodiac

Rat	Hare	Horse	Rooster
Ox	Dragon	Sheep	Dog
Tiger	Snake	Monkey	Pig

GENERAL INDEX

Abbreviations 1
Administrative centres 134
Admirals 251
Adventurers 163
African peoples 28
Agriculture 29
Air Force ranks 32
Aircraft 59
Alloys 33
Alphabets 33
American Indian nations
  and peoples 34
American States 35
Americanisms 37
Amphibians 361
Animals 41
Animals and their
  gender 44
Animals and their
  young 45
Anniversaries 425
Apocrypha 88
Applied arts people 46
Archbishops of
  Canterbury 48
Architects 49
Architecture 95
Armour 420
Army ranks and
  appellations 51
Art terms 52
Arthurian legend 55
Artists 295
Astronomers Royal 56
Astronomy 56
Australian States and
  Territories 58
Authors 427
Aviation 59

Ballet terms 62
Battles 63

Beaufort Scale 424
Biblical characters 70
Biology 71
Birds 74
Birthstones 78
Boats 78
Bones in the human
  body 251
Book titles 80
Books of the Bible 88
Botany 71
Boys' names 89
Boys' schools and colleges 95
Building 95
Business 101
Butterflies 216

Calendars 109
Cambridge colleges 416
Capital cities 140
Car Registration Letters 218
Cartoonists 46
Cats 110
Cattle 110
Cereals 111
Characters in literature 165
Cheeses 111
Chemical elements 112
Chemistry 113
Chinese calendar 109
Chinese Zodiac 432
Christian names 89, 203
Cities
  England 395
  Northern Ireland 401
  Republic of Ireland 400
  Rest of the world 406
  Scotland 402
  U.S.A. 405
  Wales 404
Classical singers 294
Clergy 115

Clothes 115
Clouds 122
Coins 122
Collective names 125
Colleges 95, 416
Colours 126
Comets 56
Commerce 101
Composers 128
Computer language 132
Conductors 133
Constellations 56
Cookery terms 133
Counties
  England 134
  Northern Ireland 136
  Republic of Ireland 137
  Scotland 137
  Wales 139
Countries 140
County towns: Northern
  Ireland 136
Crafts 190
Currency 122

Dances 146
Decorations 147
Deserts 148
Dickens, Charles,
  books and characters 148
Dogs 153
Domestic fittings 186
Dramatists 427
Drinks 155
Dyes 126

Educational terms 157
Egyptian mythology 274
Elementary particles 159
Elements 112
Engineering 159
Explorers 163

Fashion designers 46
Ferns 164
Fictional characters 149, 165, 201, 374
Field Marshals 251
Film stars 381
Film titles 171
Fish 173
Five senses 175
Flowers 312
Food 175
Football grounds 179
Football teams 179
Foreign numbers 290
Fossils 182
French phrases 183
French Revolutionary Calendar 109
Fruit 184
Fungi 185
Furniture 186

Games 190
Gems 224
Generals 251
Geographical terms 196
Geological time divisions 199
Geometrical figures and curves 200
Gilbert and Sullivan 201
Girls' names 203
Grammar 317
Greek alphabet 33
Greek mythology 274
Gregorian Calendar 109
Group terms 125
Groups, pop 328

Hebrew alphabet 34
Hebrew calendar 109
Heraldic terms 211
Herbs 213
Hills 263
Hindu deities 275
Hobbies 190
Horses 214

Insects 214
Instruments 217
International Car Registration Letters 218
Inventors 368
Islamic calendar 109
Islands 222

Jewellery 224
Journalism 225

Kings of England and Great Britain 228
Kitchen utensils 229

Labours of Hercules 276
Lakes 231
Languages 232
Latin phrases 235
Law sittings 238
Legal terms 238
Legislatures 241
Literary terms 242
Lochs 231

Machines 392
Marine growths 243
Materials 115
Mathematics 244
Measures 425
Medals 147
Medical terms 245
Metallurgy 113
Metals 33
Meteor showers 56
Military leaders 251
Military ranks 51
Military terms 253
Minerals 364
Molluscs 259
Money 122
Motoring terms 259
Mountains 263
Muses 276
Music 266
Musical instruments 269
Musical terms 266
Musicals 270

Musicians 272
Mythology 274

Names 89, 203
Nationalities 233
Native Americans 34
Nautical terms 276
Naval ranks 280
New Testament 88
Nine Muses, the 276
Nobel Prize winners 281
Nobility 300
Norse mythology 276
Numbers 290

Occupations 341
Oceans 290
Officials 291
Old Testament 88
Operas 293
Operatic singers 294
Ores 364
Oxford colleges 417

Painters 295
Paints 126
Parliamentary terms 320
Pastimes 190
Patron Saints 367
Peerage 300
People words 300
Personal effects 186
Phobias 309
Physics 310
Pigs 312
Pioneers 163
Planets 56
Plants 312
Play titles 315
Playwrights 427
Poetry 317
Poets 427
Poets Laureate 319
Poisons 320
Political terms 320
Politicians 322
Ponies 214
Popes 327

Popular musicians 328
Ports 333
Poultry 337
Precious stones 224
Prehistoric animals 338
Presidents of the USA 338
Prime Ministers of
 Great Britain 339
Printing 225
Professions 241
Prose 317
Provinces: Republic of
 Ireland 137
Pseudonyms 353
Publishing 225

Queens of England and
 Great Britain 228

Races 232
Radio personalities 381
Regions: Scotland 137
Religious buildings 354
Religious movements 355
Religious orders 355
Religious terms 356
Reptiles 361
Rivers 362
Rocks 364
Roman mythology 274
Roman numerals 290
Rulers of England and
 Great Britain 228

Saints 366
Satellites 56

Schools, boys' 95
Sciences 367
Scientists 368
Screen personalities 381
Sculptors 371
Seas 290
Seven deadly sins 372
Seven dwarfs 372
Seven virtues 372
Seven wonders of the
 world 372
Shakespeare, William,
 characters 374
 plays 373
Sheep 377
Shells 182
Ships 78
Shrubs 411
Sieges 63
Signs of the Zodiac 432
Space travel 59
Spices 213
Sports 190
Sportsmen/women 377
Stadiums and venues 380
Stage personalities 381
Stars 56
Statesmen 322

Tableware 229
Television personalities 381
Theatrical terms 385
Time 389
Titles 300
Tonic sol-fa 269
Tools 392

Towns
 England 395
 Northern Ireland 401
 Republic of Ireland 400
 Rest of the World 406
 Scotland 402
 USA 405
 Wales 404
Trade 101
Trades 341
Trees 411
Trophies, events and
 awards 413
Twelve labours of
 Hercules 276
Typefaces 415

Universities 416
Utensils 229

Vegetables 184
Vehicles 417
Volcanoes 263

Waterfalls 419
Weapons 420
Weather 423
Wedding anniversaries 425
Weights and measures 425
World leaders 322
Writers 427

Zodiacs 432
Zoology 71

THEMATIC INDEX

Armed forces

Air Force ranks 32
Army ranks and
    appellations 51
Battles and sieges 63
Decorations and medals 147
Military terms 253
Naval ranks 280
Weapons and armour 420

The arts

Applied arts people 46
Ballet terms 62
Building and
    architecture 95
Composers 128
Conductors 133
Film titles 171
Gilbert and Sullivan 201
Music and musical
    terms 266
Musical instruments 269
Musicals 270
Musicians 272
Operas 293
Operatic and classical
    singers 294
Painters 295
Popular musicians and
    groups 328
Sculptors 371
Stage screen, television and
    radio personalities 381
Theatrical terms 385

Business and professions

Business, trade and
    commerce 101
Journalism, printing and
    publishing 225
Professions, trades and
    occupations 341

Domestic

Cheeses 111
Clothes and materials 115
Coins and currency 122
Cookery terms 133
Dances 146
Drinks 155
Food 175
Football teams and
    grounds 179
Furniture, fittings and
    personal effects 186
Games, sports, hobbies and
    pastimes 190
Herbs and spices 213
Jewellery, gems, etc. 224
Kitchen utensils 229
Stadiums and venues 380
Trophies, events and
    awards 413

Education

Boys' schools and
    colleges 95
Educational terms 157
Universities in the UK 416

Geography

American States 35
Australian States and
    Territories 58
Capital cities of the
    world 140
Counties
England 134
Northern Ireland 136
Republic of Ireland 137
Scotland 137
Wales 139
Countries of the world 140
County towns — Northern
    Ireland 136

Deserts 148
Geographical terms 196
Islands 222
Lakes, lochs, etc. 231
Oceans and seas 290
Ports 333
Rivers 362
Towns and cities
England 395
Northern Ireland 401
Republic of Ireland 400
Rest of the world 406
Scotland 402
USA 405
Wales 404
Waterfalls 419

Law and government

Legal terms 238
Legislatures 241
Political terms 320

Literature

Book titles 80
Dickens, Charles: books
    and characters 148
Fictional characters 165
Literary terms 242
Play titles 315
Poetry, prose and
    grammar 317
Poets Laureate 319
Pseudonyms 353
Shakespeare, William: plays
    and characters 373
Writers 427

Miscellaneous

Abbreviations 1
Alphabets 33
Americanisms 37
Birthstones 78

Boys' names 89
Calendars 109
Collective names/group terms 125
Five senses 175
French phrases 183
Girls' names 203
Heraldic terms 211
International Car Registration Letters 218
Latin phrases 235
Law sittings 238
Numbers 290
Peerage 300
Phobias 309
Seven deadly sins 372
Seven dwarfs 372
Seven virtues 372
Seven wonders of the world 372
Time 389
Typefaces 415
Weather 423
Wedding Anniversaries 425
Zodiacs 432

The natural kingdom

Animals 41
Animals and their gender 44
Animals and their young 45
Birds 74
Butterflies 216
Cats 110
Cattle 110
Cereals 111
Dogs 153
Ferns 164
Fish 173
Fossils 182
Fruit and vegetables 184
Fungi 185
Horses 214
Insects 214
Marine growths 243
Molluscs 259
Pigs 312
Plants and flowers 312

Poultry 337
Prehistoric animals 338
Reptiles and amphibians 361
Rocks, minerals and ores 364
Sheep 377
Trees and shrubs 411

People

African peoples 28
American Indian nations 34
Applied arts people 46
Architects 49
Artists and Painters 295
Astronomers Royal 56
Composers 128
Conductors 133
Explorers, pioneers and adventurers 163
Kings and Queens of England and Great Britain 228
Languages, nationalities and races 232
Military leaders 251
Musicians 278
Nobel Prize winners 281
Officials 291
Operatic and classical singers 294
Painters 295
People words 300
Poets Laureate 319
Politicians and statesmen 322
Popular musicians and groups 328
Presidents of the USA 338
Prime Ministers of Great Britain 339
Scientists and inventors 368
Sculptors 371
Sportsmen/women 377
Stage, screen, television and radio personalities 381

Religion and mythology

Archbishops of Canterbury 48

Arthurian legend 55
Biblical characters 40
Books of the Bible 88
Clergy 115
Mythology 274
Popes 327
Religious buildings 354
Religious movements 355
Religious orders 355
Religious terms 356
Saints 366

Science and technology

Agriculture 29
Alloys 33
Astronomy 56
Biology, botany and zoology 71
Chemical elements 112
Chemistry and metallurgy 113
Clouds 122
Colours, dyes and paints 126
Computer language 132
Elementary particles 159
Engineering 159
Geological time divisions 199
Geometrical figures and curves 200
Instruments 217
Mathematics 244
Medical terms 245
Physics 310
Poisons 320
Sciences 367
Tools and machines 392
Weights and measures 425

Transport

Aviation and space travel 59
Boats and ships 78
Motoring terms 259
Nautical terms 276
Vehicles 417